ECONOMICS AND UTOPIA

For many, the collapse of the Eastern Bloc after 1989 signalled the obsolescence of all forms of utopian thinking. It was said that history had reached its end-state in the form of Western, individualistic capitalism. *Economics and Utopia* challenges this argument and opens up space for novel, pluralist and flexible discourses concerning possible futures.

Both the past utopias of traditional socialism and market individualism are shown to be inadequate, and especially inappropriate for a complex economy driven by innovation and rapid human learning. The idea of the 'end of history' is challenged partly on the grounds that it ignores the immense and persistent variety of institutions and cultures within capitalism itself. In the final part of the book, possible yet hitherto unfamiliar futures beyond capitalism are explored, using a developed theoretical framework and modern techniques of scenario planning.

More than a consideration of alternative economic systems, *Economics and Utopia* shows that visions of a possible future require a new and reconstructed economic theory that gives full consideration to the processes of learning and innovation, and to their cultural and institutional integument. Accordingly, in order to understand the processes of transformation in modern economies and to consider future possibilities, changes at the core of economic theory are necessary.

Geoffrey M. Hodgson is a Reader in Economics in the Judge Institute of Management Studies, University of Cambridge. He is the author of, among many other works, *Economics and Evolution* (1993), *Economics and Institutions* (1988) and *The Democratic Economy* (1984). A recent survey of opinion carried out by the *Diamond* business weekly in Japan ranked him as one of the twenty-three most important economists of all time.

ECONOMICS AS SOCIAL THEORY
Series edited by Tony Lawson
University of Cambridge

Social theory is experiencing something of a revival within economics. Critical analyses of the particular nature of the subject matter of social studies and of the types of method, categories and modes of explanation that can legitimately be endorsed for the scientific study of social objects, are re-emerging. Economists are again addressing such issues as the relationship between agency and structure, between the economy and the rest of society, and between enquirer and the object of enquiry. There is renewed interest in elaborating basic categories such as causation, competition, culture, discrimination, evolution, money, need, order, organisation, power, probability, process, rationality, technology, time, truth, uncertainty and value, etc.

The objective of this series is to facilitate this revival further. In contemporary economics the label 'theory' has been appropriated by a group that confines itself to largely asocial, ahistorical, mathematical 'modelling'. *Economics as Social Theory* thus reclaims the 'theory' label, offering a platform for alternative, rigorous, but broader and more critical conceptions of theorising.

Other titles in this series include:

ECONOMICS AND LANGUAGE
Edited by Willie Henderson

RATIONALITY, INSTITUTIONS AND ECONOMIC METHODOLOGY
Edited by Uskali Mäki, Bo Gustafsson and Christian Knudson

NEW DIRECTIONS IN ECONOMIC METHODOLOGY
Edited by Roger Backhouse

WHO PAYS FOR THE KIDS?
Nancy Folbre

RULES AND CHOICES IN ECONOMICS
Viktor Vanberg

BEYOND RHETORIC AND REALISM IN ECONOMICS
Thomas A. Boylan and Paschal F. O'Gorman

FEMINISM, OBJECTIVITY AND ECONOMICS
Julie A. Nelson

ECONOMIC EVOLUTION
Jack J. Vromen

THE MARKET
John O'Neil

Forthcoming:

CRITICAL REALISM IN ECONOMICS
Edited by Steve Fleetwood

THE NEW ECONOMIC CRITICISM
Edited by Martha Woodmansee and Mark Osteen

ECONOMICS AND UTOPIA

Why the learning economy is not the
end of history

Geoffrey M. Hodgson

London and New York

First published 1999
by Routledge
11 New Fetter Lane, London EC4P 4EE

Simultaneously published in the USA and Canada
by Routledge
29 West 35th Street, New York, NY 1001

© 1999 Geoffrey M. Hodgson

The right of Geoffrey M. Hodgson to be identified as the Author of this Work
has been asserted by him in accordance with the Copyright, Designs and
Patents Act 1988

Typeset in Palatino by Routledge
Printed and bound in Great Britain by
Clays Ltd, St Ives PLC

British Library Cataloguing in Publication Data
A catalogue record for this book is available from the British Library

Library of Congress Cataloging in Publication Data
Hodgson, Geoffrey Martin
Economics and Utopia: why the learning economy is not the end of history/
Geoffrey M. Hodgson.
p. cm. – (Economics as social theory)
Includes bibliographical references and index.
1. Liberalism. 2. Economics. 3. Utopian socialism. 4. Marxian economics.
I. Title. II. Series.
HB95.H63   1999   98–18791
330–dc21   CIP

ISBN 0–415–07506–8 (hbk)
ISBN 0–415–19685–X (pbk)

Anyone who fears that we face a future of ever more strident market individualism can take comfort from this eloquent counterblast. It is not just that Hodgson's economic philosophy rests on broader, more congenial, more human values. He also offers hope that ever more knowledge-intensive economies will have to adapt to such broader values to survive.

Professor Ronald Dore,
Centre for Economic Performance,
London School of Economics, UK

Institutions, evolution – and now utopia. Geoff Hodgson's confident and creative reworking of critical perspectives in economics continues. Economic theories that ignore alternative ways the world could be are not only morally empty but inefficient. Yet the necessity of variety requires not a static utopia but an adaptable 'evotopia'. These are ideas for all social scientists, not just economists.

Professor Ian Gough,
Department of Social and Policy Sciences,
University of Bath, UK

This book makes all of us think again about what should be (and regrettably are not) the main topics of economics. It shows how economics can still be useful to understand the possible directions that our society may take and it helps us in the choice of policies that may favour one of them. It is very well written and engages the reader in a challenging dialogue with the author and, at the same time, with the most important economists who have shaped the history of economic analysis. It deserves to be a great success and I am confident that it will be one.

Professor Ugo Pagano,
Department of Economics,
University of Sienna, Italy

This is a brilliant, very ambitious and sensible work. It is more a work of diagnosis and critique than of prescription and prognosis, but it does focus on key elements of any future economy: diversity, innovation, learning, the structure and culture of governance and the forms of participatory democracy, and so on. The work further enhances the reputation of Hodgson as the leading institutionalist theorist of the present day; more important, it should stimulate much further work by others.

Professor Warren Samuels,
Department of Economics,
Michigan State University, USA

This book is exceedingly pertinent to current economic discourse. It is a most creative and persuasive contribution, adding important and new insights both in particular and in general, and exhibiting a superior level of professional scholarship, awareness and capacity.

Professor Marc Tool,
California State University (Emeritus),
Sacramento, USA

By the same author

Socialism and Parliamentary Democracy (1977)
Labour at the Crossroads (1981)
Capitalism, Value and Exploitation (1982)
The Democratic Economy (1984)
Economics and Institutions (1988)
After Marx and Sraffa (1991)
Economics and Evolution (1993)
Evolution and Institutions (in press)

To those with whom I have climbed mountains
– and to the memory of Nikos, who was one of them.

CONTENTS

CONTENTS

Part II The blindness of existing theory

Part III Back to the future

CONTENTS

ILLUSTRATIONS

FIGURES

PREFACE

Lord, give me the strength to change what can be changed. Lord, give me the endurance to bear what cannot be changed. And Lord, grant me the wisdom to know the difference.

Old Russian prayer

On 9 November 1989 the Berlin Wall fell. A few weeks later, Germany was reunified. Eastern Europe turned away from its former 'socialist' ideology and returned to conventional capitalism.[1] By the end of 1991, the Soviet Union had disintegrated and its newly independent republics had set course for the restoration of capitalism and the inauguration of democracy. Although they were originally conceived as models of human emancipation and scientific rationalism, only a few mourned the passing of these totalitarian, Eastern Bloc regimes, and the present author was not one of them.

Much more worrying were the attempts to claim that the events of 1989–91 amounted to the unalloyed victory of some vaguely defined variety of liberal–democratic capitalism, thereby not only to proclaim 'the death of socialism' but also to draw a final line under all forms of 'utopian' discourse concerning a better and different future. It seemed to many that not only had Soviet 'communism' passed away, but so also had all alternative futures or utopias. Wolf Lepenies (1991, p. 8) was one of many who captured the mood when he wrote: 'two years of unbelievable political change in Europe have been sufficient to proscribe the use of the word "utopia" … no one talks about utopia any more'. Seemingly, the only possible future had materialised in the present. All speculation concerning any alternative society was proclaimed futile. History had come to a stop. It was in reaction against such pronouncements that the idea for the present book was conceived.

Indeed, from a different perspective the proclamations of the 'end of history' seem strange and incongruous. The last two decades of the twentieth century have witnessed momentous economic and technological

xv

changes. Computer technology is revolutionising the methods of production and itself developing at breakneck pace. Between the 1950s and the 1990s, computers have become over a million times faster. The components of electronic memory are less than a thousandth of their 1950s' price, in real terms. Not simply because of technological changes, the world economy has undergone spectacular and unprecedented transformations. From 1955 to 1990 the real value of the global production of goods and services more than tripled. Although the 'Golden Age' from 1945 to 1973 has long passed, subsequent years have also seen sensational economic developments. A group of fast-growing economies in the East, including India, China, and about half of the world's population, has acquired the capability to produce numerous technologically advanced manufactured goods at low cost. Generally, national production systems have become increasingly specialised. The flows of goods, services, finance and information have intensified enormously on a global scale. More than a quarter of global output is now traded across national boundaries. China, containing about one quarter of humanity, has grown at such a rate that, if its pace of expansion continued, it could quickly rival the two largest economies of the late twentieth century: the United States and Japan. Yet China's institutions are far from the Western liberal and capitalist norm. The world is changing at such a rate that proclamations of 'the end of history' seem naïve, to say the least. The 1997–8 financial crisis in East Asia, and any subsequent downturn in the world economy, are no basis to assume that all countries are about to converge on a single and existing institutional model. Even if we recognise the strength and resilience of liberal–democratic capitalist institutions, it would be unwise to suggest that they are going to remain unaltered by this technological and economic climacteric of historic proportions.

This is much more a book of economic and social theory than a political tract. It is concerned first and foremost with the third plea in the above prayer: the need to attain 'the wisdom to know the difference'. But no author is free of ideological dispositions. This work is written in the conviction that a modernised variant of social-democracy is most appropriate to deal with the technological and socio-economic developments of the twenty-first century. Such a version of social-democracy retains a prominent place for industrial and participatory democracy, worker cooperatives, government intervention, egalitarian values and social solidarity. In addition, this book shares some common ground with the American pragmatic liberalism of John Dewey, and with that important tradition of British social liberalism, which stretches from John Stuart Mill through Thomas H. Green to John A. Hobson, John Maynard Keynes and William Beveridge.

In writing this book, I had an additional motive. I am of the firm opinion that the conceptual apparatus of much of mainstream economic theory is ill-suited to the task of both understanding our present condition and of envisioning a viable future. In particular, mainstream economics has become increasingly narrow and formalistic, unable even to grasp the institutional and cultural essentials of the market system that many of its exponents propound.

These limitations become even more acute in any analytical discourse concerning any feasible future alternative to the existing socio-economic system. In pursuing a highly abstract analysis based on supposedly universal presuppositions, mainstream economics neglects institutional specificities and cultural variations, even in the existing range of economies. With its focus on equilibrium outcomes, it neglects structural transformation and ongoing dynamic change. Yet without adequate analytical tools to understand and distinguish socio-economic systems, we cannot hope to achieve anything more than the most superficial consideration of future opportunities.

In order to understand the present and outline the possibilities for the future, we must look beyond the narrow formalisms and equilibrium-oriented theorising of mainstream economics. Our search must involve economic heretics as diverse as Karl Marx, Thorstein Veblen, John Maynard Keynes, Joseph Schumpeter and Friedrich Hayek, all of whom have made major and enduring contributions to our understanding of the structure and dynamics of real economies. Marx enhanced our understanding of socio-economic systems, Veblen addressed economic evolution and institutional change, Keynes diagnosed the pathologies of money and employment, Schumpeter broke the bonds of equilibrium in mainstream theory and highlighted innovation and entrepreneurship, and Hayek analysed the nature and role of knowledge in market economies. Yet the works of such authors do not receive the prominence they deserve. The direct and detailed study of their writings is widely neglected even in the most prestigious university departments of economics. This book attempts to show the value of their ideas for both the dissection of the present and the prognostication of the future.

Consider just one of the aforementioned heretics. The events of 1989 brought the particular risk that, despite its many theoretical and political defects, Marx's brilliant and penetrating analysis of the workings of the capitalist system was at risk of consignment to the dustbin with the other detritus of the collapse in the East. As the old statues were pulled down, Marx's analysis would be junked, despite the fact that Marx's incisive writings are mainly about capitalism, and have little to say on the nature and future of any form of socialism. To a large degree this has happened. Today, Marxian economics is rarely taught in the universities of the West, and many university professors of Marxian economics in the former Eastern Bloc have been relieved of their academic positions.[2]

Marx's analysis has many serious flaws – and the present work is better described as institutionalist rather than Marxist – but, in my view, *Capital* remains one of the greatest achievements in economic theory since Adam Smith. Although little read by economists today, Marx's works have deeply influenced other prominent members of that profession, from Joseph Schumpeter to Joan Robinson. There has always been much to learn from an in-depth understanding of both the strengths and the weaknesses of the Marxian analytical system. The events of 1989–91 provided no reason why this view should be abandoned. The spectre of Marx still haunts modern capitalism. While Marx's economics has many limitations, these should not allow some of its important insights to remain ignored. As long as a theorist such as Marx is regarded at best as an irrelevance and at worst as a demon, then there is no hope of progress in economic science. It is necessary that Marx be discussed and understood before, it is hoped, he is transcended. Marx's analytical ideas pervade the present book: as testimony to their historical influence, their penetrative power and – lastly but significantly – their instructive failings.[3]

Despite the author's fears, shortly after the collapse in the East there was a unprecedented flowering of discussion of socio-economic and policy futures.[4] Nevertheless, much of this discourse followed different trails and the impetus behind the author's original project remained, albeit frequently interrupted by other commitments. Furthermore, intellectual attempts to come to grips with the transforming former Eastern Bloc economies led to a rich theoretical and policy discourse addressing the realities and possibilities in those countries attempting to build a market-based economy. Despite the flowering of 'post-socialist' discussion in the West, visits to parts of Eastern Europe confirmed that there was a general disillusionment with any hint of utopianism, new or old, in the nations that had endured the 'socialist' experiment for so many decades. Dissatisfaction with this state of affairs gave the author a further reason to complete this project.

The author is very grateful to, among many others, Ash Amin, Jacob Biernan, John Davis, Simon Deakin, Ronald Dore, Nicolai Foss, Chris Freeman, Ian Gough, Charles Hampden-Turner, Jeromy Ho, Chris Hope, Hella Hoppe, Stavros Ioannides, Makoto Itoh, Björn Johnson, Derek Jones, Matthew Jones, Janet Knoedler, Tony Lawson, Paul Lewis, Gianpaolo Mariutti, Jonathan Michie, Masashi Morioka, Klaus Nielsen, Ugo Pagano, Luigi Pasinetti, Hugo Radice, Warren Samuels, Herman Schmid, Heinz-Jürgen Schwering, Ernesto Screpanti, Colin Shaper, Giles Slinger, David Stark, Ian Steedman, Rick Tilman, Marc Tool, Andrew Tylecote, Lazlo Vajda and several anonymous referees, for discussions or critical comments on various sections of this work. Parts of the book were written during a two-month stay in Japan in 1997. The author is also indebted to the Japan Society for the Promotion of Science for financial support, and to Kansai University for hosting his stay in that country.

Having completed much of the first draft of the book in Japan, a lone ascent of Ben Cruachan in Scotland was the scene where the system of measurement outlined in Chapter 10 was developed in the author's mind. For the remaining chapters, I am very grateful to my family – Vinny, Sarah and Jamie – for their stimulation and support in writing this book.

This book makes some use of some material previously published in *Economy and Society*, the *Journal of Economic Issues*, the *Review of Social Economy* and the *Review of International Political Economy*. The author is grateful to the publishers, and to the Association for Evolutionary Economics, for permission to use these passages. In addition, some ideas are taken up from my earlier works, such as *The Democratic Economy* (1984), *Economics and Institutions* (1988), *After Marx and Sraffa* (1991) and *Economics and Evolution* (1993), and are developed further in the present volume.[5]

Finally, the author would like to thank A. P. Watt Ltd, on behalf of Graham Swift, for permission to reproduce an extract from *Waterland* (1983).

1

INTRODUCTION

History is that impossible thing: the attempt to give an account, with incomplete knowledge, of actions themselves undertaken with incomplete knowledge. So that it teaches us no short-cuts to Salvation, no recipe for a New World, only the dogged and patient art of making do. ... Yes, yes, the past gets in the way; it trips us up, bogs us down; it complicates, makes difficult. But to ignore this is folly, because, above all, what history teaches us is to avoid illusion and make believe, to lay aside dreams, moonshine, cure-alls, wonder-workings, pie-in-the-sky – to be realistic.

Graham Swift, *Waterland* (1983)

The road to utopia is devious. I set out equipped with political philosophy and a liking for literary utopias, and arrived with the conviction that utopianism is a distinctive form of social science.

Barbara Goodwin, *Social Science and Utopia* (1978)

The ideological polarisation between socialism and communism, on the one hand, and capitalism, on the other, has dominated the twentieth century. Today, however, the People's Republic of China remains the only major power still claiming attachment to a communist ideology, and even there private property and markets are now extensive and well established. The world is no longer so starkly polarised as it was from 1917 to 1989. Ideas of wholesale central planning and public ownership have become widely unpopular. Despite the fact that the Eastern Bloc may have been remote from the socialist ideal, the events of 1989 and after have been associated with a further decline in faith in a socialist future. All forms of socialism and social-democracy have suffered, despite the numerous socialist critics of Joseph Stalin or Mao Zedong, and the many who have long proposed more liberal, moderate or democratic versions of socialism. Their voices have hardly survived the disintegration of the Eastern Bloc.

Nowhere is this more clearly illustrated than in Sweden, where the Social-Democrats suffered a collapse of will and belief once the ideological guy-rope of the Soviet Union gave way. This is despite their long tradition of proclaiming a third road – one divergent from both individualistic capitalism and Soviet-style 'socialism'. Since 1945, Sweden had been widely proclaimed as the pioneer of a humane and radical version of social-democracy. But by 1989 even the advocates of a relatively egalitarian and democratic variety of capitalism were enduring a crisis of vision and purpose. As Ralf Dahrendorf (1990, p. 71) has remarked: 'communism has collapsed: social democracy is exhausted'.

Nevertheless, the loss of confidence within social-democracy began earlier than the collapse in the East. In much of Europe and elsewhere, social-democracy has been in retreat since before 1989. The leaderships of many social democratic parties have abandoned many of their traditional goals. The British Labour government of 1974–79 rejected its own radical economic programme as early as 1975 and embraced monetarism by 1976. In 1981 the Socialist Party was elected to govern France, committed to Keynesian, reflationary, macroeconomic policies and an agenda of social and economic reform. Within a short time, these policies were largely abandoned, and the French government inaugurated a programme of privatisation of publicly owned corporations. All major socialist and social democratic parties have long lost their faith in their former core idea of public ownership. Proponents of capitalism have long set the terms of debate. The dramatic events of 1989 consolidated and reinforced a trend which was already well under way in several major European countries.

Strikingly, what has emerged out of the recent developments is the view that this is 'the end of history'. Francis Fukuyama (1992, p. xiii) argued that liberal democracy marks the 'end point of mankind's ideological evolution' and the 'final form of human government'. Liberal democracy 'remains the only coherent political aspiration that spans different regions and cultures around the globe'. Even before Fukuyama's fashionable treatise, it was widely held that liberal–democratic capitalism is the normal or ideal state of affairs: once established and refined, it cannot be surpassed. What Fukuyama and his followers neglected, however, was that 'liberal democracy' is not a singular prospect. Itself it contains infinite possibilities and potential transformations. The 'end of history' phrase denies this.

It has also been proclaimed that there is no alternative to liberal democratic *capitalism*: something close to the politico-economic system in the United States is seen to be the ideal. As *The Economist* announced on 26 December 1992: 'The collapse of communism brought universal agreement that there was no serious alternative to free-market capitalism as the way to organise economic life.' This suggests an even more restricted set of options.

According to all these pronouncements, the protracted convolutions and sufferings of the years from 1917 to 1989 in the countries of the East amounted to little else but a long detour from the ideal or normal condition. It has thus been argued that neither the Eastern Bloc, nor the socialist movement as a whole, were ever on the road to a superior or even durable alternative future.

In such terms the 'communist experiment' in the East could be viewed in retrospect as an historical oddity. Consider an example of a much earlier deviation from the perceived mainstream of history. Established against the odds by the dedication of an army of crusaders, the Kingdom of Jerusalem survived as a substantial Christian state against hostile Saracens for nine decades (1099–1189). This almost forgotten Kingdom is now regarded as an atypical deviation from an otherwise unbroken millennium of Islamic power in the Middle East.

Similarly, a group of dedicated Bolsheviks secured power in Russia in 1917. They and their successors held out in their Communist enclave against the repeated and varied military and economic incursions of capitalism for 74 years. Just as the Kingdom of Jerusalem appears in retrospect as an awkward deviation from the course of history, so too the Soviet Union has begun to be treated as an unnatural aberration. The bifurcated, bipolar world of much of the twentieth century was displaced in the 1990s by a singular vision of capitalist ascendancy. Along the lines of a science fiction novel,[1] it was as if history had previously made an extraordinary leap to an alternative universe at the time of the First World War, only to return again to the 'normalcy' of Western capitalism in the last decade of the century.

History itself seemed to oblige with dramatic endorsements of this view. Soon after the collapse in the East, civil war erupted in the former Yugoslavia, with vicious ethnic hatred that was tragically redolent of the earlier Balkan War of 1912–13. Furthermore, Europe as a whole experienced outbreaks of anti-Semitism and ethnic nationalism, again reminiscent of an earlier era. In the early 1990s Europe seemingly returned to the 'normalcy' of the years prior to 1917.

It was likewise with the balances of international power. Germany, the rising European nation of the 1871–1914 years, was repeatedly defeated and humiliated from 1918 to 1945. The country was divided from 1945 to 1989, but Western Germany gained relative and absolute economic strength. With reunification in 1989, Germany seemed to announce that it had fully rejoined with its own destiny, exhibited by the rising overall tendency of its political power. The earlier – seemingly aberrant – failures and losses had been overcome.

It is thus tempting to see the present world as a natural, inevitable and even permanent outcome, to which all past deviations have at last returned. From this point of view the end of both history and of utopia is declared. Tempting as it is, this perspective is untenable. It is fallacious

3

not simply because it ignores the pace and consequences of technological and economic change. It also fails to recognise the manifest diversity of existing capitalist development, and the way in which each socio-economic formation is moulded unavoidably by its own history. This book elaborates these critiques.

SOME REMARKS ON UTOPIA

However, at least in conventional terms, no utopian scheme or blueprint is outlined in this work. The aim in this area is more modest: to review utopian thinking by way of a few key exponents and to raise the possibility of a more developed utopian discourse. This does not mean that the author is indifferent between varied proposals for an improved society. On the contrary, it is insisted here that critical engagement with, and evaluation of, such proposals are both desirable and ultimately unavoidable. Furthermore, this work attempts to identify some of the intellectual tools required for such an engagement.

Humankind has been inspired by the idea of a perfect society since ancient times, and especially since the sixteenth-century *Utopia* of Thomas More.[2] Often such utopias have been socialistic or communistic in character, involving collectivist ideals and shared property. However, as Cosimo Quarta (1996, p. 154) rightly insists: 'it must be understood that utopia is a much older and complex phenomenon than socialism'. Even today, as noted below, there are other, quite different, utopian proposals. Recognising that we are not confined to one set of possible scenarios, there is much to be said for an ongoing dialogue on such 'idealistic' and 'utopian' themes, removing many of the negative and pejorative associations of these words. But we must also learn from the errors and horrors of utopianism in the past.

As Zigmunt Bauman (1976, p. 10) has remarked, there is an essential ambiguity in the word 'utopia'. One relates to its Graeco-Latin origin, as contrived by More: 'a place which does not exist'. The other common-place meaning is 'a place to be desired'. These two meanings are not mutually exclusive. In this book we are concerned with the intersection of the two. 'Utopia' is here taken to mean a socio-economic reality that is both non-existent and alleged by some to be desirable.

A third connotation of the word 'utopian' is one of implausibility or unattainability. If adopted, this meaning would exclude any feasible alternative future, and is thus too restrictive. A useful distinction can be made between possible and impossible utopias, and there is no good reason to assume that the former category is empty. It is important not to confuse possibility with actuality. Contrary to those who are cynical about the possibility of change, or who have an excessive faith in the efficiency or virtues of the present, actual circumstances are a small subset of all possible circumstances. Non-existence is a question of fact, but such facts do not imply that non-existing and alternative systems are unfeasible. The pejorative use of the word 'utopian', as implausible or impossible, is rejected here.

The word 'utopia' fosters a likelihood of change, and points to an unfulfilled future that differs from the present. In general, a utopia is a description of a desired world to come: whether or not such prognostications are feasible and whether or not such a desire is shared by others.

Karl Marx and Frederick Engels were highly critical of what they called 'utopian socialism'. Marx (1976a, p. 99) wrote disdainfully of those 'writing recipes ... for the cook-shops of the future'. Although sympathetic to the goals of the utopian socialists, these radicals were criticised by Marx and Engels for failing to root their ideal in an analysis of the real forces in capitalist society that could lead to their realisation. The term 'utopian socialist' was used by Marx and Engels to deprecate and dismiss proposals for a socialist future that were not based on a 'scientific' identification and analysis of the economic forces and political movements that could lead to their own realisation (Schumpeter, 1954, p. 206).

However, Marx and Engels took many presuppositions of the utopian socialists for granted, including the rational transparency and feasibility of socialism itself. As a result, 'Marx and Engels thus left an ambiguous legacy in which vigorous attacks on utopianism accompanied utopian speculation' (Geoghegan, 1987, p. 34). Even Marx's analysis of capitalism is entwined with presuppositions concerning the nature of economic processes that pointed to a utopian future. Overall, the analysis is capped by the thesis that capitalism engenders its own negation and itself prepares the preconditions for the transition to communism. Marxism, in the words of Bernard Chavance (1985, p. 255), is a 'utopia which is presented under the guise of an anti-utopia'.

Utopian thinking is typically associated with socialism and communism. However, the contrasting politico-economic schemes of pro-market libertarians can equally be described as utopian. Karl Polanyi (1944, p. 3) referred to the free-market ideal of many in the nineteenth century as 'a stark utopia'. Robert Boguslaw (1965, p. 136–42) cited similarly 'the utopia of laissez faire'. The utopia of the free market has had prominent exponents in both the nineteenth and twentieth centuries. For example, Krishan Kumar (1987, p. 49) noted that 'the utopian element in "free trade" was especially clear in the writings and pronouncements of John Bright and Richard Cobden'. Vincent Geoghegan (1987, p. 3) pointed out that 'Thatcherite conservatism is a glaring example of right-wing utopianism, with its summoning up of the supposed glories of Victorian Britain.'

Friedrich Hayek, the Nobel Laureate and intellectual champion of free-market individualism, was candid about his own utopian agenda.

He also wrote: 'it is probably no exaggeration to say that economics developed mainly as the outcome of the investigation and refutation of successive Utopian proposals' (Hayek, 1933, p. 123). This same forceful idea reappears many years later:

> Utopia, like ideology, is a bad word today; and it is true that most utopias aim at radically redesigning society and suffer from internal contradictions which make their realization impossible. But an ideal picture of a society which may not be wholly achievable, or a guiding conception of the overall order to be aimed at, is never-theless not only the indispensable precondition of any rational policy, but also the chief contribution that science can make to the solution of the problems of practical policy.
>
> (Hayek, 1982, vol. 1, p. 65)

Indeed, Hayek's own utopian vision pervades his writings and it is much more considered and detailed than that of Marx. Unlike Marx, Hayek (1960) devoted a whole book to an exposition of his own utopian thinking. Whatever their virtues or failings, free market utopias have to be considered alongside socialism or communism. Subsequent chapters of the present work scrutinise utopias of both the socialist and free-market variety.

To some, market ultra-liberalism is 'realistic', while collectivism is the unreal scheme of dreamers. This is often a manifestation of ideological bias, based on the presumption that pure free-market economies are more feasible than those based purely on collective property. It is argued in subsequent chapters and elsewhere (Hodgson, 1984, 1988) that neither 'pure' extreme is feasible and that all economies necessarily involve a plurality of forms of property and systemic regulation.

Furthermore, 'the market' itself is not a pure and unambiguous entity. This fact is typically ignored by both critics and supporters of market systems. All markets are institutions and many types of market institu-tion are possible. Be it of either distaste or admiration, 'the market' is not a singular object. Unless this is properly understood, that widely-used term 'the market' is potentially misleading. The singular term 'the market' has always to be used with qualification and caution.[3]

Likewise, the deceptive worldly rhetoric of 'market forces' invokes a physical metaphor, wrongly suggesting that all markets are subject to the same universal – as if mechanical – laws. On the contrary, not only do markets vary from time to time and place to place, but each market is set in a particular, and potentially variable, cultural context. This creates a wide variety of possible, internal market rules, routines and outcomes.

Furthermore, the notion of a singular and unfettered market system is mistaken. All markets involve rules and norms and are never fully 'free'. Likewise, no market is entirely 'chaotic' or 'anarchic'; all markets involve institutional structures. Both advocates and opponents of markets have to specify *which* type of market they advocate or oppose. The market is not a singular extreme, unambiguously representing one end of a utopian spectrum.

Leaving aside the precise features of any desired utopia – and without confining the notion of utopia to the socialist and communist proposals – the abandonment of any debate about socio-economic goals is both undesirable and impossible. The lack of such an ongoing dialogue creates a void in higher values and aspirations. In the modern, commercial epoch, such a vacuum is likely to be filled instead by a base individualistic ethic of monetary and material gain. The attempt to abandon all utopian thinking unwittingly opens the door to the hedonistic utopia of the selfish, disregarding, enjoyment of material wealth. Arguably, such materialism and individualism are more symptoms of social and moral decay than engines of economic growth.

The events of 1989–91 should not mark the end of utopian discourse. The absence of utopia is not a state to be desired. As Oscar Wilde argued a century ago in his essay 'The Soul of Man Under Socialism':

> A map of the world that does not include Utopia is not worth even glancing at, for it leaves out the one country at which Humanity is always landing. And when Humanity lands there, it looks out, and, seeing a better country, sets sail. Progress is the realisation of Utopias.
>
> (Wilde, 1963, p. 924)

Accordingly, as Bauman (1976, p. 13) noted: 'Utopias revitalise the present. ... The presence of a utopia, the ability to think of alternative solutions to the festering problems of the present, may be seen therefore as a necessary condition of historical change.'

To repeat: utopian thinking in some form is both desirable and unavoidable. But an important caveat is necessary. Utopianism itself has a deserved bad name because millions have died and suffered as the direct consequence of ruthless political movements led by idealists who were convinced that extreme measures were necessary to bring humanity to their version of the promised land. Wilde himself became a victim of an embittered 'utopian' pursuing the goal of an exclusively heterosexual society. As a result, four years after Wilde had published the above words he was in gaol. He died shortly afterwards.

Simply consider those describing themselves as followers of Marxism–Leninism. Their actions may not have been in accord with the word or spirit of Marx or of Lenin, but that is beyond the immediate point. The fact is that the *name and alleged inspiration* of Marxism–Leninism carry an appalling legacy. Perhaps as many as 100 million people have died since 1917 in assassinations, purges and

7

famines, *carried out in the name of that ideology*: Stalin, Mao, Pol Pot. Stalin himself is now believed to be directly or indirectly responsible for the deaths of about 30 million people.[4] Mao does not escape significant culpability: it is estimated that in the famines following Mao's 'Great Leap Forward' in 1958–60 there were also around 30 million deaths.[5] A significant proportion of humankind in the twentieth century has been sacrificed on the altars of utopia.

This negative legacy cannot be ignored. Utopian discussion is desirable, but only if the horrendous mistakes of the past can be avoided. A new and more cautious way of thinking about utopia is required. What is suggested here is the beginnings of what could be described as 'meta-utopian' discourse: the comparative theoretical examination of utopias and anti-utopias, rather than another detailed prescription of a Utopian blueprint. We may be able to articulate some general ideas and principles to guide and evaluate utopian thinking, unconfined to the values and constraints of a single utopia.[6]

In contrast, some have argued that all forms of utopianism should be entirely rejected: the discourse on and about utopias should be ended. It is suggested here, however, that such a stance typically admits utopianism through the back door while keeping all eyes to the front. Prominent anti-utopian discourses have often inadvertently presumed, or ended up suggesting, a utopia of their own. This point has been recognised by David Steele (1992, p. 375), himself an advocate of 'free' markets: 'The attempt to abstain from utopianism merely leads to unexamined utopias.' The validity and importance of this proposition should be acknowledged, whatever our political philosophy.

Marx railed against utopians of all varieties but simply assumed that his version of socialism or communism was both possible and desirable. For him, the possibility of an economy organised as a single unit, and without money or markets, was so 'rational' and obvious that it did not need detailed exposition. His own hidden utopianism relied on the belief that such matters could be readily dealt with, once the vested interests of the capitalist order were swept aside. His attempt to abstain from utopianism led unfortunately to an unexamined and undeveloped utopia.

There is some ambiguity in the writings of Hayek on this question. On the one hand, he warned us endlessly against 'constructivism' and the drawing of blueprints for the future. Nevertheless, in some passages, he openly accepted utopian agendas. Indeed, he had a utopian and 'constructivist' vision of his own, that drove and permeated his work from beginning to end, and was consummated in political blueprints such as in *The Constitution of Liberty* (1960). Ironically, Hayek's utopian project was an appeal to reason to limit the scope of rationalist thought. It involved, as Michael Oakeshott (1962, p. 21) wittily remarked, 'a plan to resist all planning'.

8

In general, social science and politico-economic policy – however pragmatic – can never be entirely free of goals and ends, of visions, and of fragments of utopian thinking. Even if we regard the existing order as perfect or near-perfect, such a standpoint still requires an outline picture in our imagination. It is wrong to see socio-economic systems as blindly working out their own logic, simply according to their own in-built tendencies and mechanisms, as if no imagination or creativity were relevant or possible. The past and its legacy bear down upon the living, but history has no single, inexorable logic, and real change and choice are possible to a degree. Economies are not machines. Economic systems are made up of reflexive human actors, each pursuing their own goals and visions of an acceptable or improved life. Humankind depends upon, and cannot avoid, an imagined future.

The theorists of 'the end of ideology' and 'the end of history' forget all this. For them, we have reached the point in time where no ideology is relevant and no utopia is pertinent. We have reached the final equilibrium of capitalist liberal democracy, and no learning or discovery are possible.

Yet, on reflection, the history of our own time suggests that the visions of the future held by leaders (whether appropriate or inappropriate, feasible or otherwise) have a great deal of impact on events. How else can we explain the rise of Margaret Thatcher, Ronald Reagan and the New Right in the 1970s, and the neo-liberal regimes in the former Soviet Bloc in the 1990s, without referring to the place of their own utopian goal of a 'free market' society? Conversely, no account of the disintegration of the Soviet Bloc in 1989–91 would be complete without an account of the corrosive cynicism that destroyed the faith in state collectivism well before the collapse of the Berlin Wall. Similarly, to understand the crisis in the Swedish Social Democratic Party in the late 1980s and early 1990s, some reference must be made to the loss of faith in the social-democratic ideal. Ideology and utopia are always with us. Those that forget this are destined to become the unwitting architects or accomplices of utopia themselves. It is better to know where one is going, rather than to arrive somewhere blind.

THE THEME OF THIS BOOK

This book touches on a number of issues. Nevertheless, its main argument can be summarised in just five paragraphs:

1 The desired utopias of both the traditional left and of the neo-liberal right are unfeasible, and *partly for similar reasons*. Just as complete central planning has failed, so too will any attempt to apply consistently and completely the individualistic and market-oriented

principles of neo-liberalism. A major and common reason why they both are unfeasible is that both blueprints – albeit in different ways – misunderstand the nature of learning and knowledge in a modern economy. In addition, both place insufficient stress on the functional importance of structural variety in a complex socio-economic system.

2 History has no pre-ordained path or goal of any kind. It has no *necessary* movement towards a refined liberal–democratic capitalism, nor towards a socialism or communism of any variety. Historical development is not teleological. The fact that the present-day capitalist system can evolve in a number of quite different but sustainable ways is shown by the huge existing variety of very different national capitalist economies.

3 This book explores a scenario along which capitalism could feasibly evolve, not into socialism but into a different type of socio-economic system. Emphatically, it is not being suggested that such an evolution is predestined. An aim is to suggest in outline the possibility of another system, which differs substantially from the prominent twentieth-century utopias of both state socialism and individualistic capitalism. This alternative future is driven by the growth of knowledge-intensive production. The claim to feasibility of such as system derives from its ability to deal more adequately with the acquisition and use of knowledge and dynamic processes of learning.

4 The aforementioned developments within capitalism do not necessarily lead to a post-capitalist society. The contractarian relations within capitalism are stretched to the limit by the growth of information and the multiplication of specialist knowledge. There is thus also the possibility of a reaction within capitalism: an attempt to contain these developments and defend the integrity of the contractarian core. Prefigured in some respects by the New Right governments in America and Britain in the 1980s, such a development, it is argued, would lead to social dislocation and economic stagnation. Accordingly, the final chapter of this book considers the normative issues involved in the choice of alternative futures, and briefly addresses some broad policy measures.

5 Contemporary mainstream economics has a limited capacity to deal with the issues involved in the above propositions. With regard to 1, mainstream economics has a very inadequate conceptualisation of knowledge and learning. With regard to 2, the analytical apparatuses of mainstream, Marxian and Austrian[7] economics are largely blind to the institutional and cultural variety within actually existing capitalism, because of weaknesses at the core of their theory. With regard to 3, the alternative future system is not fully imaginable or assessable with the analytical tools of mainstream, or even Marxian or Austrian economic analysis. Accordingly, the argument in this volume is not

10

only an exploration of some future scenarios but also an appeal for a different kind of economic theory. It is argued that the tradition of the 'old' institutional or evolutionary economics, founded by Thorstein Veblen in the 1890s, is a good place to search for materials to build a theoretical foundation, combined with important insights from other thinkers such as Joseph Schumpeter and John Maynard Keynes. The book is not simply about future socio-economic systems – that is, different types of social structure involving the production of wealth – it is also a contribution to the construction of a future economic theory. With such an economic theory a utopia can first be imagined, and perhaps eventually be realised.

UTOPIAN ECONOMICS AND THE ECONOMICS OF NOWHERE

Accordingly, this work is as much about economic theory and method, as it is about utopia. Normative issues are visited fully only in the very last chapter. The remainder of the book is much concerned with matters of economic analysis. Some readers may see this as a strange imbalance for a book of this title. But it is nevertheless necessary to use economic theory, both to explain why the 'end of history' thesis is unsustainable and to envision feasible possibilities for the future.

A key element in all human progress is the growth of knowledge. Yet it is precisely on this issue that the polar utopias of socialism and market individualism have foundered. Socialism has neglected the enormous problems of gathering together all relevant knowledge in the service of an overall plan. Market individualism has neglected learning and the growth of knowledge by assuming that the individual somehow always knows *now* what is in his or her best interest in the future. It is assumed that the individual acquires knowledge but is somehow unchanged in the process.

The phenomenon of learning is an unavoidable issue for utopian thought. In general, utopianism involves the creation of the new, but in part by gaining knowledge of the ways and limitations of the old. In particular, it is argued in this book that the transformative phenomenon of learning is ultimately corrosive of the contractarian and utilitarian manifestations of Enlightenment thought. The common, Enlightenment preconceptions of both market individualism and collectivist socialism are thus undermined.

Yet the concepts of knowledge and learning are treated inadequately in economic theory. Rarely is there any distinction between sense data and knowledge. Information is treated as unambiguous 'bits' signalled to the agent like data being sent to a computer down a telephone line. Analytically, the central issues of learning and knowledge themselves contain enough high explosive to destroy the conceptual foundations of standard economic theory. For this and other reasons, it is argued throughout this work that mainstream economics really is the economics of *nowhere*. We have to supersede it with a genuine economics: *beyond utopia*.

As well as questions of theoretical analysis, one part of the process of theoretical development is to supplement the limited normative dichotomies of 'planning versus markets' and public versus private ownership with a much rich discourse concerning the choices and issues of the twenty-first century. Consider an earlier venture by the author into utopian thinking, entitled *The Democratic Economy* (1984). That book retained much of the conventional – analytical and normative – emphasis on the importance of forms of ownership and on the existence or non-existence of a degree of central planning. These issues are consequential, but other underlying matters of social culture, social values and relations of power were given too little weight. Within the framework of the impurity principle – retained and developed here – planning was previously focused on as the main element of 'impurity' in a capitalist market system. Other elements, such as loyalty and trust, were understressed as necessary and sustaining 'impurities' within the system. To a greater degree the present work stresses culture, values and power, rather than forms of ownership and organisation alone. It shows, furthermore, how the growth of a knowledge-intensive economy challenges, and partially displaces, the established formalities of ownership and contract.

Nevertheless, these formalities should not be ignored. Typically, the relevant legal formulations have to change to give economic developments full expression. Socio-economic reality has both legal form and economic content. That reality cannot be understood adequately unless both levels are encompassed. Both legal and economic relations are real, and expressed in behavioural regularities, routines and habits of thought. The claim that one is more fundamental does not give grounds to ignore the other. What is required is a theoretical approach that can embrace and give due weight to both.

Above all, this book focuses on individual and group learning and knowledge. It emphasises that an understanding of the nature and importance of learning in modern socio-economic systems undermines both the individualistic, free market utopia of the right and the collectively planned utopia of the left. The reasons for this are outlined in the next two chapters.

Part I

VISIONS AND ILLUSIONS

2

SOCIALISM AND THE LIMITS TO INNOVATION

It will be better next time.

Slogan painted in 1989 on a statue of Karl Marx
and Frederick Engels in East Berlin

The fact that 'socialist planning', in the original sense of a rational economy which replaced market relationships by direct calculation and direct product exchange, has nowhere been established, reflects not the malevolence of this or that social group, not the backwardness of the countries concerned, but the theoretical inadequacy of the traditional conception.

Michael Ellman, *Socialist Planning* (1989)

By the second half of the twentieth century, the word 'socialism' had become associated with a huge variety of doctrines. The word has been claimed by devotees of the Soviet order, Trotskyists, Maoists, anarchists, communitarians, revolutionaries, Fabians, social-democrats and even lukewarm advocates of a more humane capitalism. To some it has connoted positive and radical values such as compassion, sharing, freedom from poverty, and equality of opportunity. To others it has meant totalitarianism and suffering. It has stretched to the point where it has become almost evacuated of meaning.

It would be tedious and unnecessary to explore all these varied meanings, at least in the present work. The concerns here are different. First, it is to show that the origins of the term 'socialism' betray shared misconceptions and common problems that span its 'utopian', Marxian and Fabian wings. Second, in this broad tradition there has been a common difficulty in dealing with novelty and accommodating politico-economic diversity. Third, there has been a general rejection of markets and private property and a failure to understand that some elements of private commodity exchange are necessary to sustain the institutional frameworks of innovation and diversity. Fourth, these original conceptions of socialism have, to the present day, inspired repeated proposals for various forms of collectively planned economy, based on common ownership of the means of production, within which the market plays at most a marginal role. Fifth, these conceptions lack both theoretical coherence and practical viability.

It is not our concern here to analyse the historical experience of the former 'socialist' economies. Neither, to repeat, is it necessary for our purposes to insist that they be described as 'socialist'. Instead the focus here will be on the *theoretical* arguments of socialists from the 1830s to the 1990s in favour of an economy in which most or all production is collectively planned. It will be maintained that these theoretical arguments are deeply flawed. The reason for concentrating on the theoretical issues is straightforward: the historical failures are now widely recognised, but the theoretical failures are not.

The aim in this chapter is to show the theoretical limitations of the core socialist project, as conceived by Robert Owen, Karl Marx, Fabians and others in the nineteenth century, and as subsequently refined and elaborated by other thinkers. That core socialist project is the ideal of a collectively planned economy based on common ownership of the means of production.

It is in this sense that the term 'socialism' is used here. It will be argued below that the general idea of collective planning based on common ownership, combined with a hostility to markets and private property, has been thematic to socialism from the beginning. These notions were shared by very different socialist traditions, from Marxism to Fabianism. Socialism, from its inception, has been collectivist and anti-market.

Some may wish to preserve a different and perhaps more pluralistic connotation for the term 'socialism'. On reading an earlier draft of this book, a socialist friend advised that phrases such a 'central planning' should be used instead to describe the theoretical ideas that are placed under critical scrutiny in this chapter. This was seemingly a plea to disassociate the term 'socialism' from all past errors of theory or practice, and thereby to retain the purity and chastity of the word. I rejected this advice for the following reasons. First, it ignores and evades the persistent historical association of 'socialism' with collective planning and common ownership and the persistent blanket hostility of 'socialism' to markets and private property. Second, it leaves the nature and structure of this supposedly virtuous 'socialism' extremely vague. With very few exceptions, socialist writings have been notoriously obscure about the structure and workings of a 'socialist' economy. Without a fundamentally different, and detailed alternative proposal, we have no sound basis to give 'socialism' a meaning that is different from that which it has acquired and largely retained since its exception.

The subject of this chapter is 'socialism' in its historic and mainstream sense in the literature. An important aim is to show that no complex

16

socio-economic system can survive and develop without structural economic variety and genuine markets. Accordingly, *if* socialism is to be rescued from its theoretical and practical failures, then it *has to be* both a mixed economy and 'market socialism' in some genuine sense. Without these crucial and major qualifications, 'socialism' is definitely on the road to oblivion. To reinforce this point I have turned down the request to substitute the s-word by 'central planning'. It is argued below that as long as socialists resist (and misunderstand) the market, mainstream and unqualified 'socialism' does not have a viable future.

THE EMERGENCE AND MEANING OF THE TERM 'SOCIALISM'

The idea of common ownership, of holding property in common, stretches back to the origins of Western civilisation itself. It is found, for instance, in the writings of the Ancient Greeks, in the Bible, in the doctrines of several medieval Christian reformers, and in the *Utopia* of Thomas More (Kumar, 1987; Manuel and Manuel, 1979). However, in all its diverse meanings, the modern concept of socialism is very much a product of the eighteenth-century Enlightenment. Socialism has made strong appeals to the Enlightenment ideals of equality and co-operation. It has also emulated the rationalistic ethos of that age. Socialism has also frequently called upon the power of reason, both to justify itself as an allegedly superior form of society, and – in calls for the 'rational' reconstruction of the socio-economic system – to provide the guiding operational principles for the future social and economic order.

The word 'socialism' is quite recent in origin and dates from the nineteenth century. Apart from *socialismo* in Italian, which had a quite different meaning, the terms individualism, socialism and communism did not exist in Europe prior to the 1820s. In France, one Pierre Leroux claimed to have originally coined the word 'socialism' sometime before 1834 (Gide and Rist, 1915, p. 263 n.). In 1827 the word 'socialist' appeared in English for the first time, in the *Co-operative Magazine*, published in London by followers of Robert Owen. It appeared again in the *Poor Man's Guardian* in 1833, and moved into wider usage from thereafter (Bestor, 1948). From the 1830s, Owen and his followers associated socialism with the 'abolition of private property' and used this frequently as their slogan.

It is interesting to note that the word 'individualism' was coined at almost exactly the same time and in the same general context. It appeared first in its French form in 1820 (Lukes, 1973, p. 4) and in English in 1840 (Bestor, 1948, p. 282). 'Socialism' and 'individualism' were then widely adopted as antonyms of each other. In particular, in the 1820s, the influential followers of Saint-Simon – the French radical utopian –

17

systematically adopted the term *'individualisme'* as a description of the competitive and fractured society that they opposed, and eventually used the term 'socialism' to describe the egalitarian and harmonious system that they favoured. Not only did Leroux claim to be the origi-nator of the term 'socialism' but also he used it explicitly 'as an antithesis to "individualism"'. In this spirit he published an article entitled 'De l'in-dividualisme et du socialisme' in the *Revue encyclopédique* in 1834 (Gide and Rist, 1915, p. 263 n.).

A secondary and minor connotation acquired by the term 'socialism' was a matter more of theory than of policy. This was the idea that the individual was socially formed. As early as 1814 Owen (1991, p. 43) had stressed: *'that the character of man is, without a single exception, always formed for him ... by his predecessors; who give him ... his ideas and habits, which are the powers that govern and direct his conduct'*. This thesis was a persistent and prominent feature of Owen's thought. From about 1830 it was linked with the term 'socialism'. While 'individualism' pointed to the individual as the primary and elemental unit in society, 'socialism' signified the contrasting view that individuals were largely formed by their social and economic context. Although the normative and policy aspects of the term 'socialism' were always dominant, for a while it had this additional, analytical ramification. *Socialism was thus in part a doctrine that individuals are moulded by society*. It pointed both to the social character of individuality and to the mutual interdependence of society and the individual.

But that was not the totality of Owen's message. It was also a crusade for harmony and equality, and against markets and competition. Owen devel-oped a number of ingenious administrative schemes for his socialist utopia, including the payment of wages in the form of 'labour notes' denominated in terms of the number of hours worked. It should be emphasised that in no meaningful sense did this involve the introduction of exchange, competi-tion or markets. Owen was for both the abolition of private property and the complete suppression of all competition and profit.

Although they found his political strategy to be naïve, Marx and Engels admired Owen's utopian ideas. In a similar manner they also drew some inspiration from the schemes of Claude Henri de Saint-Simon, Charles Fourier, Louis Blanc and other Continental utopian socialists.[1] Marx and Engels often used the term 'communism' instead of 'socialism'. However, this was primarily to distance themselves from the analytic, strategic and tactical ideas of contemporary socialists rather than to postulate a radically different goal. For them, 'communism' was more a label for their movement, rather then their goal. Thus, in the mid-1840s, they wrote: 'We call communism the real movement which abolishes the present state of things' (Marx, 1977, p. 171).

In so far as they were formulated explicitly, the objectives of Marx and

Engels for a post-capitalist society were, in essential terms, very similar to many other socialists of their time. While they attacked the strategic naïveté of the 'utopian' socialists, they were much less critical of utopian socialist goals. In the *Communist Manifesto* Marx and Engels reproduced the rhetoric of many socialists when they welcomed efforts 'to centralize all instruments of production in the hands of the state'. They looked forward to a time when 'all production has been concentrated in the hands of a vast association of the whole nation' (Marx, 1973a, pp. 86–7).

This statist vision of socialism persisted throughout their lives. It appeared, for example, in the second volume of *Capital* where Marx (1978, p. 434) wrote of the planned system of 'social production' where 'society distributes labour-power and means of production between the various branches of industry'. Likewise, in one of his very last manuscripts, completed in 1880, Marx (1976b, p. 207) remarked that in the society of the future 'the "social-state" will draw up production from the very beginning ... The scope of production ... is subject in such a state to rational regulation.'[2]

Like Owen, Marx and Engels (Marx, 1973a, pp. 80–1) applauded unreservedly the 'abolition of private property'. They were not inclined to defend or reinstate even 'the property of the petty and of the small peasant' on the spurious ethical grounds that 'to a great extent' it was 'already destroyed'. They wished for an economic order in which 'capital is converted into common property, into the property of all members of society'. They advocated the abolition of 'bourgeois freedom' including the 'free selling and buying' of commodities.

At the time, in contrast to the idea of nationalised property and national planning proposed by Marx and Engels, the alternative idea began to emerge of a system of legally autonomous communes, explicitly linked and coordinated by contracts and market exchanges. Philippe Buchez, a follower of Saint-Simon, was one of the early proponents of this idea. He had proposed the formation of worker co-operative associations as early as 1831, and his ideas became prominent during the French Revolution of 1848 (Gide and Rist, 1915, p. 258; Reibel, 1975). Originally, like Marx and others, Buchez argued that the individual co-operatives should gradually merge into a single 'universal association'. Gradually, however, and contrary to most contemporary socialists and communists, Buchez and his followers recognised the need for multiple, smaller, autonomous worker co-operatives, linked by contracts and markets (Reibel, 1975, pp. 44–5). In response, writing in 1875, Marx (1974, pp. 353–4) described Buchez's developed ideas as 'reactionary', 'sectarian', opposed to the workers' 'class movement', and contrary to the true revolutionary aim of 'cooperative production ... on a national scale'.

A similar accommodation of markets was suggested by Pierre Joseph Proudhon. It is notable that in all of Marx's writings, Proudhon is one of the thinkers most frequently criticised, both for his socio-economic theory and for his proposed utopia. Among these statements can again be found clear evidence of the hostility of Marx to any retention of commodity exchange and markets in a future society. Proudhon described himself as an anarchist, not a socialist. In some respects, his political position resembles that of many radical, pro-market libertarians of the late twentieth century. Alternatively, in the terminology of today, it could be described as an early form of 'market socialism'. But it is important to emphasise that from the 1830s to the 1940s – or even later – such a term was almost universally regarded as a contradiction in terms, as socialism meant the *exclusion* of competition and markets. By contrast, Proudhon proposed a permanent system of 'mutualist associations' involving groups of workers who would pool their labour and their property, holding and using these resources in common. Proudhon realised that without a decentralisation of contractual powers, meaningful economic decentralisation could not flourish. Thus he proposed that each co-operative association would be able to enter into contractual relations with others. These contracts were assumed to be mutually defining and self-policing, thus dispensing with the need for a legal system, a government and a state. Proudhon's anarchism was thus sustained by contracts between politically and economically autonomous associations. As Proudhon (1969, p. 98) proposed: 'The notion of government is succeeded by that of contract.'

In contrast, Marx and Engels emphatically rejected the notion that contracts and competition should survive after the proletarian revolution. In accord with most socialists and communists of his time, Marx and Engels proposed that all the means of production should be owned by society as a whole, not by small, autonomous communes or associations. Engels (1962, p. 388) thus wrote in the 1870s: 'With the seizing of the means of production by society, production of commodities is done away with ... Anarchy in social production is replaced by a plan-conforming, conscious organization.' In a detailed study of Marx's works, Stanley Moore (1980) has shown that he repeatedly and emphatically rejected the idea of any form of market coordination in a future socialist society, even if all the means of production were owned and managed as worker co-operatives.[3]

Marx saw that, within capitalism, worker co-operatives would have an ideological and demonstrative value and he supported them for that reason. Such co-operatives showed that the workers were capable of managing production without capitalists. Marx's attitude to worker co-operatives is clear from the 'Inaugural Address of the International Working Men's Association' drafted by him in 1864. This address praised the established producer co-operatives, but did not see their future alongside other forms of collective productive organisation under a future socialism. Instead, it saw their eventual salvation in their urgent development 'to national dimensions … fostered by national means' (Marx, 1974, p. 80). Marx and his followers in the First International thus proposed that worker co-operatives would have to grow to, or become part of, nationalised industries. For them, any form of common ownership of less than national scope would have to be subsumed into the unitary national 'association', which would be owned and controlled at the national level.

Throughout their lives, Marx and Engels refrained from giving any more than the barest hints of the form of organisation of their proposed future society. It is thus all the more significant and remarkable that the singular notion of 'a vast association of the whole nation' involving collective production 'fostered by national means' reappears several times, without amendment or qualification, in their writings over the decades. *It would be a particularly blinkered Marxist who would read the words of Marx and Engels on their proposed socialist future, and see no threat to a plurality of forms of common ownership and see no antagonism to the market nor any type of mixed economy.* There is no evidence in any of their works that they saw any value in institutional and structural diversity, under capitalism or socialism. In their stated proposal 'to centralize all instruments of production in the hands of the state' they favoured a single, all-encompassing arrangement, subject to rational principles of accounting and control.

Despite the merits of Marx's incisive analysis of the workings of capitalism, his picture of a socialist future was both complacent and obscure. He and his followers rejected detailed analysis of future socialist and communist possibilities as 'idealist' and 'utopian'. Nevertheless, they themselves adopted a utopian scheme in outline, with large-scale public ownership and central or collective planning, and they rested somewhat on the former authority of the 'utopian socialists' in taking its feasibility for granted. The assumption of collective, rational planning in Marxism was redolent of the Owenite faith in the triumph of reason. More fundamentally, these common, rationalist ideas are a reflection of the European intellectual culture of the nineteenth century. The feasibility and rationality of the socialist utopia were largely taken as demonstrated.

The Marxian criticism of the 'utopian socialists' had little to do with their blueprint for a future society, and much more with their assumption that rational persuasion rather than class struggle were the *route* to utopia. For Marx and Engels, the key problem was not the detailed design of the collective utopia, for its workability on a national scale was taken for granted. The primary goal was the victory of the proletariat in the struggle against the capitalist class and the removal of all vested interests in the allegedly irrational, existing system. Of course, this victory was a necessary – but not a sufficient – condition for socialism itself. Nevertheless, for Marx and Engels, it took precedence over the detailed explication of the organising principles of the socialist system. The reason for this emphasis was the faith in the power of a singular, rational socialist vision, once the working masses were elevated to political power. After the revolution, the guidance of a future and complex society could be entrusted to the emancipated powers of human reason.

Marx and his followers thus made two crucial errors. First, they downgraded the task of detailed exposition of the structure and workings of a future socialist society. This task was given a much lower priority than the analysis of the capitalist mode of production and of the politics of the epoch in which they lived. The failure of Marx and his followers to produce an adequate outline of a planned economy was little short of disastrous when Vladimir Ilich Lenin and the Bolsheviks came to power in 1917. Second, in their sparse words on the economic organisation of socialism, they betrayed an overwhelming adherence to the national ownership and organisation of the means of production, without any space or favour for economic pluralism and a mixed economy. In both these errors, Marx showed an excessive faith in the power and scope of human reason, implicative of the Enlightenment intellectual milieu into which he was born.

By the 1860s, 'socialism' had become a broad term, not confined to the co-operative movement, with 'communism' used often but not universally to refer to more extreme or revolutionary political strategies. Both terms were typically associated with a policy for the abolition of private property, and for the common ownership of the means of production in some form or another. On this general question, 'socialists' and 'communists' were largely united. The ideas of earlier thinkers as Owen and Marx dominated the socialist movement, and Marxism rose to even greater prominence after the Paris Commune of 1871. Disputes among socialists concerning the future society concerned matters such as the degree of decentralisation of administration. The speed at which private property had to be abolished was also a matter of controversy, although there was much more agreement on the question of its ultimate abolition. Other major differences concerned strategy and tactics, such as the use of parliamentary versus revolutionary means.

Accordingly, a definition of socialism in terms of a policy of common ownership rapidly became predominant in the last three decades of the nineteenth century. These years saw the development of mass socialist parties and trade unions in Western Europe. It was taken for granted by socialists that the social individual could only be served properly by an economy guided by some form of common ownership. This central motif pervaded the writings of socialists as diverse as the Continental revolutionary communists, German 'state socialists' and British Fabians. By the time that socialist ideas had established a significant influence in the last

quarter of the nineteenth century, the word socialism was almost universally defined in terms of common ownership of the means of production
(Beer, 1940; Landauer, 1959). Degrees of scepticism or hostility towards
both markets and private property were thematic for socialism as a whole.

For most socialists, markets had no role in the desired socialist society
of the future. For example, the influential socialist utopia of Edward
Bellamy (1888) in *Looking Backward* foresaw centralised control of production and the absence of markets and money. His views were typical.
As Noel Thompson (1988, p. 281) put it: 'The market was anathematised
by almost all nineteenth century socialist writers.' Among the few exceptions were John Ruskin and some of the Christian socialists, who 'sought
to tame the [market] beast rather than to shoot it' (p. 284). Even Fabian socialists had an 'ultimate vision of a fully planned and consciously controlled
socialist economy' where markets were gradually marginalised to insignificance. Thompson (p. 285) concluded:

> For the most part, however, their critique of the functioning of the
> market led nineteenth century socialist writers to throw the market
> baby out with the bath water. … the consequences of this determi-
> nation to abandon the market were little short of disastrous for the
> subsequent evolution of socialist economic thinking.

The basis of this rejection was a deeply rooted judgement that the market
fostered competition, encouraged greed, and led to inequality and
exploitation. Socialists typically believed that markets could be abolished
by replacing them with collective planning. The word 'socialism' entered
and endured for much of the twentieth century with this meaning it was
associated with the goal of collective planning, common ownership, and
the complete or virtual abolition of the market. Although there were
many varieties of socialist policy, the idea of wholesale social ownership
was thematic and prominent. This was true of socialists who favoured
decentralisation, as it was for 'state socialists'.

The case of George D. H. Cole, the prominent Fabian dissident and
pioneer of – allegedly decentralised – 'guild socialism', is symptomatic.
Despite favouring 'decentralisation', he supported the wholesale nationalisation of industry. His distinctive concern was not to oppose national
ownership but national management and control. His proposal for 'guild
socialism' meant, in short, devolved worker control of a nationalised
economy (Cole, 1917). However, it was not clear how worker 'self-
government in industry' could function and be meaningful without the
powers of devolved ownership, including the power to set product
prices. Cole (1932, p. 589) recognised that under guild socialism 'no
industry could be left to run itself absolutely, and that such matters as
the pricing of the product and the remuneration of the workers must
be decided by some authority wider than that of the industry itself'.

Consistent with this, Cole (1932, p. 616) advocated 'national economic planning' which would involve 'strongly organised control over almost every aspect of the economic life and above all over production, over the distribution of purchasing power in all its forms, and over the fixing of prices'. The fact that such views were maintained by a leading theorist of an allegedly more decentralised and participatory form of socialism is all the more illustrative of the attitude of the socialist movement as a whole.

When, in 1918, Clause IV made its way into the constitution of the Labour Party in Britain, it advocated, and referred broadly to, 'common ownership' of the means of production. No explicit reference was made to markets or a private sector, enabling the prominent interpretation that 'common ownership' as a policy referred to *all* means of production. The term 'common ownership' rather than 'national', 'social' or 'co-operative' ownership was chosen after some dispute. The Labour Party united around a single phrase, each interpretation of which offered the possibility of a complete and uniform system of economic organisation in a future socialist society. At least until the 1950s, there was little explicit support in the Labour Party for the idea of economic pluralism, nor recognition of the functional importance of economic diversity. The wording of Clause IV proved remarkably durable, showing the dominance of ideas of all-encompassing 'common ownership' in a mass 'socialist' party. They were reaffirmed by future Labour Prime Minister Clement Attlee (1937, p. 153) when he declared that: 'All major industries will be owned and controlled by the community'. Although Attlee accepted that many smaller private enterprises would 'exist for a long time', he implied that even small private enterprise would eventually come under collective ownership. Significantly, the Labour Party resisted the attempts in the late 1950s of its leader Hugh Gaitskell to acknowledge the more pluralistic goal of a mixed economy. The indelible wording of Clause IV, part IV remained displayed on the party card of every member. This situation lasted without alteration until 1995, with the radical amendment of Clause IV after the initiative of future Labour Prime Minister Tony Blair. Explicitly, if not in the actual practice of Labour governments, the all-embracing goal of 'common ownership' has dominated the rhetoric of the Labour Party for most of the twentieth century.

THE VERY LATE INCEPTION OF SOCIALIST ECONOMIC PLURALISM

Despite the many differences between the gradualist and the revolutionary wings of the socialist movement, they had very similar views concerning the desirability of 'common ownership'. Bolsheviks were little different from Fabians in this respect. Both made compromises, but held out for a similar ultimate goal of ubiquitous communism. After the inauguration of the 'New Economic Policy' in 1921, the Soviet leaders accepted a role for the market, but this was generally perceived as a transitional phase, to be ended and surpassed by planning as the system moved towards full socialism. From 1921, Lenin accepted the market as an immediate practical necessity in Russia, but he had no enthusiasm for it.[4] On this question, the position of Leon Trotsky and his followers was no different. Although Trotsky accepted a role for markets under the transitional regime, no permanent place was claimed for them under socialism. Nikolai Bukharin accepted a role for markets and independent worker co-operatives in the Soviet system. However, although he went further down this road than Trotsky, he too never achieved a clear and unambiguous revision of the socialist goal that involved a place for substantial markets. Outside Russia, Antonio Gramsci was later hailed as a forerunner of a more tolerant and pluralistic Marxism. Yet he too maintained an adherence to overall common ownership and a hostility to all market institutions. Democratically-minded socialists, believing in substantial decentralisation and local autonomy, have not been rare in the history of the socialist movement. But, until very recently, most of these have thought that a democratic and decentralised socialism was possible without the use of markets, and without equivalently decentralised property rights.

It was not until the 1950s that the notion of using markets alongside planning, in a more decentralised economy with mixed forms of ownership, began to emerge in Eastern Europe, and later in Russia and China. The lateness of such developments must be emphasised. From the 1830s to the 1950s, the word 'socialism' has been linked to the idea of overall common ownership, emanating from writers such as Owen or Marx. In the long history of the socialist movement, only two significantly distinct alternative forms of proposed 'socialist' economic organisation have emerged, but until the 1950s they were marginalised to the extreme.

The first alternative is often today described as 'market socialism'. It has not been popular among socialists because it involves the use of the market as an overall mechanism of coordination and regulation. In this respect it is a definite break from the mainstream socialist tradition. The idea of a socio-economic system made up of autonomous worker co-operatives, each selling its products on the open market, was never popular in the socialist movement, from its inception. As noted above, the idea emerged in France in the middle of the nineteenth century, in the writings of Buchez and Proudhon. Subsequently, it survived only on the fringes of socialism: in the small Christian socialist movement, in Proudhonist and other forms of anarchism, and in the economic doctrines of radical Catholics. Notably, the British economist John Stuart Mill (1871, vol. 2, p. 352) became a convert to this vision.

Apparently, the term *Marktsozialismus* was first coined by Eduard

Heimann (1922).[5] The term 'market socialism' gained currency in the Anglophone world in the 1930s, after the work of Frederick Taylor, Henry Dickenson, Abba Lerner, Evan Durbin, Oskar Lange and others. However, it will be shown below that the models proposed by Lange and others are both unworkable and do not involve genuine markets at their core: they are not *market* socialism' proper. The idea of promoting the market coordination of worker co-operatives as a permanent socialist alternative to central planning was not properly formulated and widely discussed until after Josip Tito's 1948 break with Joseph Stalin and the beginnings of the Yugoslav experiment in self-management in the 1950s. Although, the Yugoslav system retained nominal associations with 'socialism' and Marxism, it was closer, in reality, to the associationist ideas of anarchists such as Pierre Joseph Proudhon, than it was to the anti-market, centralist socialism of Marx.

An economic model of a worker co-operatives in a market context, using neoclassical theoretical tools, was first devised by the Benjamin Ward (1958). Ward – an American economist – described his model as 'market syndicalism'. It was not until after these events that a tiny minority of socialists, desiring a genuine decentralisation of economic and political power, began to realise that the only way to safeguard this participatory goal was to employ the market mechanism, and hence allow a substantial number of production units to make their own decisions concerning output and prices. Proudhon had come to a similar conclusion more than a century earlier.

The second alternative is the adoption of socialists of the idea of a particular type of 'mixed economy', in which markets remain but redistributive taxation and social welfare are intended to bring greater equality of income and wealth. Although several socialist thinkers began to accept, in the early decades of the twentieth century, the idea that different forms of common ownership could coexist, sometimes even alongside a limited number of small private firms, this mixture generally excluded any single and substantial capitalist enterprise. The idea of a mixed economy, involving a substantial presence for both privately and publicly owned enterprises, did not become conspicuous in the mainstream socialist movement until after the Second World War. Previously, it was the credo of Anglo-American liberals such as William Beveridge and John Maynard Keynes in Britain, and President Franklin D. Roosevelt in America. The moderate Conservative politician Harold Macmillan published *The Middle Way* in 1938. The idea of a mixed economy was not widely adopted by socialists until the 1950s. It came to prominence in this movement with the publication of *The Future of Socialism* by C. Anthony Crosland in 1956, and the decision of the (West) German Social Democratic Party to abandon the goal of widespread nationalisation at its Bad Godesburg conference in 1959.[6]

Clearly, because they retain a place for genuine markets, the 'mixed economy' and 'market socialism' are not necessarily mutually exclusive. They both can represent examples of forms of economic pluralism, by tolerating a number of different and relatively autonomous economic structures and institutions. However, some proposals for 'market socialism' have been less pluralistic, in that they have proposed the ubiquity of a singular structural form, with all production to take place within worker co-operatives. Other proposals have envisaged co-operatives existing alongside other forms of public or private enterprise. Partly because they are not representative of the broad socialist tradition up to 1950s, neither market socialism nor the social democratic mixed economy is discussed in this chapter. They are addressed later in the present work.

Although the experience of the first Soviet state led to a debate after 1920 about the use of quasi-markets under socialism, rapid Russian industrialisation in the 1930s actually reinforced the confidence of social-ists in the West in a planned economy, especially as the world capitalist system was in a deep depression. What subsequent factors led to the development – and accommodation by the socialist movement – of both genuine 'market socialism' and the social democratic 'mixed economy'? These developments were not only the products of the relative success of capitalism in the long, post-war boom from the 1950s to the 1970s. They were also a result of the 1948–89 Cold War between East and West. The first hammer blow to the confidence of the orthodox socialist movement came with the inception of the Cold War, leading to the rise of formerly heretical ideas such as the 'mixed economy' in Western Europe, and the Yugoslav 'third way' of 'market socialism'. The events of the late 1980s and early 1990s led to further revisionism and fragmentation. Each impact moved mainstream 'socialism' further from its traditional ideo-logical legacy of planning and common ownership. The first impact undermined belief in their universality, the second in their general supe-riority.

These post-1948 developments should not obscure the fact that, since its adoption in the 1830s, the word 'socialism' has been almost univer-sally associated with wholesale common ownership within some form of planned economy. Since the 1940s, socialism has been on a long retreat from this original conception, to the degree that many are unaware of its former ubiquity. Socialists have differed on matters of political strategy and on their view of the administrative structure of the social goal. However, almost without exception, until recently there has been widespread hostility to anything more than a minimal private sector and the minimal use of market mechanisms. To repeat, it is in this traditional sense that the unqualified term 'socialism' is used here. The resistance and endurance of this traditional socialist vision, outlasting even the

hammer blows of Cold War, are shown be the emergence of two extensive and relatively detailed proposals for versions of collective planning,
as late as 1988 and 1993. These two proposals – both being consistent
with the traditional socialist conception – are discussed in detail below.

THE PROBLEM OF SOCIALISM AND DIVERSITY

Having established the classical meaning of 'socialism', we now begin to
examine its limitations. These have been present from the outset, and
precede Marxism. Owen, for instance, rejected economic and social
diversity, desiring that all society be organised together into one uniform
and harmonious unit. Owen's concerns in this respect were by no means
confined to questions of property and ownership. He addressed all the
alleged evils of the 'competitive system', viewed 'not merely as a class-
based economic order, but as an arena of multiple divisions and
antagonisms, each of them living in the hearts and minds of women and
men, as well as in their material circumstances' (Taylor, 1983, p. 21).

Owen believed that any plurality and variety of structures, institutions or arrangements would foster the vested interests of minorities and
encourage disruptive dissent. This went much further than a hostility to
nationalism or to class divisions. Owen even opposed institutionalised
professions, including medicine. In his New Society, *everyone* would
supposedly be educated in such specialist skills. From 1830, Owen
attacked marriage, private property and religion as the unholy trinity of
malign influences upon humankind. Marriage was opposed, in part
because it created separate family units; it allegedly raised the vested
interests of a family above those of society as a whole. Owen even
opposed parliamentary democracy and the 1832 Reform Bill. Political
parties, he argued, were little more than organised dissent and discord.

In the socialist literature, there has been much criticism of Owen's
political strategy. Owen believed that the new order would come
through the triumph of education and the guidance of enlightened
reason. He did not adequately explain how education and reason would
overcome the power and vested interests of the rich elite and the
entrenched state machine. Owen and his followers ignored the fallibility
of the educators, the limits of human knowledge and the boundaries of
reason.

There has been much less criticism of the Owenite utopia itself. In
terms of its final goal, one of the most serious weaknesses in the Owenite
programme was that it overlooked the economic and social value of
institutional, individual and domestic autonomy. All members of the
Owenite society would have to conform to its all-embracing principles.
Political and economic experiments by a minority would be disallowed.
Such a lack of pluralism and variety is both an impediment to creativity

28

and a threat to freedom. In general, a key problem for socialism since its inception has been the incorporation of economic and other forms of diversity.

An important anomaly should be noted. If private property is an unmitigated evil, then it is also necessary to end the private ownership by the individual of his or her own person. If *all* property has to be held in common then that would also have to be true of corporeal property (including individual limbs and organs) and of labour power itself. This, if enacted, would be a severe threat to individual autonomy. The collective ownership of all labour power would be virtually a form of collective enslavement. This difficulty could be overcome by retaining inalienable private ownership of individual bodies and capacities, but opposing private ownership of other forms of wealth and productive capability. However, it would then have to be assumed that private ownership in some spheres was not objectionable after all. By what criterion could we establish such a demarcating rule? If there is a place for *some* private property, particularly to protect individual autonomy, then socialism might be placed on a slippery slope towards the acceptance of the (limited) value and importance of private ownership of some resources.

Although they were critical of Owenite and other forms of 'utopian socialism', Marx and Engels made a similar mistake in neglecting the importance of economic variety and pluralism. In their repeated calls for efforts 'to centralize all instruments of production in the hands of the state' they denied the enduring value of decentralisation, markets and a mixed economy. In this manner, the enduring mould of 'socialism' was cast. Following Owen and Marx, socialists of all types have typically prescribed a single – allegedly ideal – set of structures for the future society. The goal of social harmony has been seen as compatible only with a large degree of uniformity of economic institutions. Private ownership has often been seen as the root of exploitation. Accordingly, socialists have often taken the view that all forms of private enterprise, even at the level of the self-employed unit or the family firm, are immoral and thus have to be abolished. Proclamations in favour of variety and autonomy have not typically been supported by the promotion of variety and autonomy in forms of ownership. Despite all sincere proclamations in favour of liberty of expression, the promotion of socialism and harmony has often led to a suspicion of diversity and an intolerance of dissent.

A prominent element in much socialist thinking is the Enlightenment-inspired belief that it is possible for people under the right conditions to act in harmony and rational agreement to design and construct a better society in its entirety. Once minority vested interests were removed, all rational people would accept the logic of a socialist plan grounded in objective conditions and addressing human needs. Such ideas are found in both nineteenth- and twentieth-century socialist writings, including Owenites, Bolsheviks and Fabians. They have spanned both 'moderate' and 'revolutionary' wings of the socialist movement. For example, leading Fabians, such as Sidney and Beatrice Webb, argued 'that there is an ultimate and objective social goal to which all rational men would submit if they understood both the true nature of man and society and the imperatives of long-term social survival' (Crowley, 1987, p. 2).

Such stances display the naïveté that Friedrich Hayek has usefully described as 'constructivism'. Socialism is just one class of possible 'constructivist' ideals. The assumption is that society can be ordered according to reason, without any cognisance of the limits and potential fallibility of all rational discourse. Such views incorporate no checks or balances, implemented in the light of experience and practice; they have insufficient means of dealing with error or unforeseen circumstances. That is their fatal flaw.

Nevertheless, it is important to emphasise that socialists have often paid lip-service to diversity and variety. It is not the absence of words and sentiments that is a problem here, but their insufficient grounding in practical policies and real social structures. William Morris, for instance, favoured administrative decentralisation, and wrote in 1889 of the importance of 'variety of life' (Thompson, 1955, p. 688). Yet he was simultaneously bold and obscure about the society of the future. He wrote, for example, in 1887 that: 'Private property of course will not exist as a right' and described no permanent place for exchange or markets in his desired socialist utopia (Morris, 1973, p. 195). Throughout the socialist movement, almost all discussions of a future socialist system were extremely vague about the permissible economic forms of such variety, and about the mode of overall co-ordination of multiple, decentralised, decision-making bodies. Karl Kautsky (1902, p. 166) was exceptional in that he went further, and insisted that under socialism, 'the greatest diversity and possibility of change will rule. ... The manifold forms of property in the means of production – national, municipal, cooperatives of consumption and production, and private – can exist beside each other in a socialist society.'

In the same work he even wrote that under socialism 'money will be found indispensable until something better is discovered' (p. 129). But despite this, he saw prices as being set by a central administration. Kautsky was also unclear on the role of markets in that future society, and failed to explain how otherwise such a diversity of interdependent, productive organisations could be co-ordinated in a coherent manner.[7]

Without some explanation of how the system as a whole is to operate, all this well-meaning talk of diversity and variety under socialism amounts to little more than pious wishes. The nettle that relatively few socialists have grasped is this: to reconcile and co-ordinate diversity within developed economies, including any laying claim to be 'socialist', there is no alternative to the use of commodity exchange and markets. No convincing scheme for durable economic decentralisation has been proposed, without the equivalent decentralisation of the powers to make contracts, set prices, and exchange products and property rights, through markets or other forms of property exchange. This does not mean that markets are regarded as optimal or ideal, nor that the entire economy is made subject to 'market forces'. It does mean, however, that markets and exchange are necessary to sustain genuine economic pluralism and diversity.

Nevertheless, many socialists have failed to accept a significant role for the market. Generations of socialist thinkers have been unable to dislodge the anti-market influence of the nineteenth-century founding fathers. The tenacity with which the blanket 'anti-market mentality' still clings to the modern socialist movement is illustrated below when we come to discuss two relatively sophisticated proposals for a planned economy that have emerged in the 1980s and 1990s. Throughout its existence, and in most of its variants, socialism has been associated with an excessive optimism in the possibility of an ordered and rational society, according to an overall, conscious plan.

Furthermore, the danger of intolerance lurking in the idea of achieving social harmony through the construction of a uniform set of socio-economic arrangements has beset socialism since the beginning. What socialists have generally failed to recognise is that an irreducible plurality within both economy and society is not a barrier to but, on the contrary, is essential for enduring political and economic order. A society that does not challenge its prevailing values and arrangements by nurturing within it some values and arrangements of a different type is extraordinarily brittle and vulnerable. It has insufficient internal variety to innovate or deal with the unforeseen. It runs the risk of complacency and political atrophy. In a uniform universe we are no longer habituated to deal with the unusual. We must treat it as alien, and dispel it from our midst. Our minds become closed. We no longer refresh our knowledge by wonder: we fail to learn anew.

The central issue in the long debate between socialism and capitalism is often characterised as one of planning versus markets. But this can be misleading. Planning in some form exists in all socio-economic systems. Both individuals and organisations can have plans. A central problem in any socio-economic system is how the inevitably diverse plans of many varied individuals or organisations can be reconciled, without conflict or disorder. Human beings differ by both nature and nurture, and to some degree will always do so. Institutions differ in their histories and in their paths of development. If we accept the inevitability of this diversity, then this problem has to be faced. How can the varied plans of multiple agents be reconciled?

31

One solution is to crush dissent. The plan of the party or the dictator becomes the plan of the whole society and other plans are disregarded. All by law must conform to the single, central plan. This solution is not attractive to many socialists. A popular alternative is often described as 'democratic socialism'. This involves democratic debate between the exponents of various plans, reaching some decision by a system of voting. In this case the minority plans may still be blocked, but by democratic vote rather than dictatorship. The possibility of such a democratic system will be discussed in more detail below.

A third method is to use the market and the price mechanism. One person plans to produce a new commodity. In a market system it is not generally necessary to impose a dictatorship or persuade a majority on some committee before the new commodity is produced. Principally, it is required to obtain enough buyers to keep production viable. This is not to suggest that the market always encourages creativity or enterprise. As a system it has many flaws. However, its capacity to reconcile conflicting plans and maintain a degree of diversity should not be overlooked. By contrast, collective planning, whether democratic or dictatorial, has a crucial disadvantage. As Hayek (1944, p. 46) pointed out:

> That [collective] planning creates a situation in which it is necessary for us to agree on a much larger number of topics than we have been used to, and that in a planned system we cannot confine collective action to the tasks on which we can agree, but are forced to produce agreement on everything in order that any action can be taken at all, is one of the features which contribute more than most to determining the character of a planned system.

In contrast, in a market system we are not 'forced to produce agreement on everything in order that any action can be taken at all'. Separate, diverse plans can be reconciled by multiple, bilateral deals of negotiated exchange. Whatever its manifest limitations, this crucial advantage of the market should not be disregarded.

Consider also the possible economic arrangements by which some degree of diversity may be fostered. Can diversity be manufactured and maintained merely as an act of political will? It would be dangerous to rely on political structures alone. Political systems are vulnerable to bureaucratisation and manipulation. The compelling conclusion is that one of the best means of helping to maintain institutional diversity is through the appropriate use of private property, exchange and market relations. It is a fact of history that neither genuine political pluralism nor political democracy have survived or emerged in any centrally planned economy, from China to Cuba. Of course, the fact that the two have never endured together does not prove that such a coexistence is impossible. But the historical facts should undermine any complacency and lead to probing analysis. Private property and commodity exchange may be necessary – but not sufficient – conditions for both genuine political democracy and adequate economic diversity. We ignore this proposition at our peril.

Traditionally, socialists have failed to recognise the force of these arguments. The fact that the market itself is no guarantor of democracy and pluralism is itself important, but irrelevant to the central issue here. The key question is whether attempts to abolish or marginalise the market throughout the economy are conducive to democracy and socio-economic diversity. Both theoretical analysis and the historical record suggest otherwise. In a modern society, democracy and pluralism cannot prosper without markets, although markets alone cannot provide them. Accordingly, the traditional socialist attempt to attain social harmony would require the imposition of severe constraints on economic autonomy, variety and pluralism.

It has been shown above that socialists have traditionally rejected the market because it led to competition, greed, inequality and exploitation. Socialists have believed that markets could be abolished by replacing them with all-embracing, rational institutions of evaluation, planning, and control. Two crucial and connected theoretical issues are exposed here. One concerns the analysis and evaluation of the market itself. This issue will be addressed later, and especially in subsequent chapters. The other issue concerns the feasibility or otherwise of socialism without markets. It was precisely the question of the possibility or otherwise of replacing a genuine market with a simulated market mechanism – within the framework of central planning – that the famous 'socialist calculation' debate addressed from about 1920 to 1945. It is to this debate that we now turn.

THE SOCIALIST CALCULATION DEBATE

In 1920 Ludwig von Mises published in German a path-breaking article. In it he made the claim that comprehensive, rational, central planning in a socialist economy was bound to fail (Mises, 1935). This was not an argument about the desirability or otherwise of socialism, but primarily about its workability. It was necessary for the socialists either to counter its arguments, or to face up to the possibility that their ideal society would not function effectively, if at all.

On this basis the 'socialist calculation debate' emerged. It is one of the most illuminating and significant debates in economic theory in the twentieth century. But, for reasons concerning the embarrassment of the mainstream position, it is rarely dissected in the economics textbooks. Regrettably, it is impossible here to go into all the twists and turns of this important controversy. Fortunately, a number of instructive analytical reviews of the arguments exist.[8]

Some features of this debate are well known. In response to von Mises, a number of socialist economists in Britain and the United States developed the notion that it was possible for the planners to substitute for the market and its functions, within a framework where the means of production were owned and managed by the state. A model of socialism was outlined in the following terms. The planners would somehow observe whether each good or service was in short, or excess, supply. If there was an excess supply, the price would be lowered; if an excess demand, it would be raised. Through such incremental adjustments, supply and demand would eventually be matched, and equilibrium prices would be formed.

The most famous formalisation of this approach was the model of so-called 'market socialism' developed by Lange and Taylor (1938). Lange and Taylor showed how such a notional process of price adjustment could be fitted into the general equilibrium theory developed in the 1870s by the neoclassical economist Léon Walras (1954). Although the Walrasian model was purportedly a model of a market economy, it used the fiction of a single auctioneer to formalise the process by which prices are formed. The auctioneer would adjust prices up or down until an equilibrium of supply and demand was reached. Lange and Taylor simply substituted the central planning authority for the auctioneer, and without any violation of the core precepts of the Walrasian model.

In the absence of private ownership of the means of production, how would efficient production be maintained? Lange and Taylor added the rule that the central planning authority would instruct the managers of firms to expand production until marginal costs were equal to the established price of the product. Thereby, productive surpluses would be maximised. With rules governing price formation and managerial behaviour, it was seemingly possible for the means of production to be publicly rather than privately owned. Without much apparent difficulty, the Walrasian model of capitalism was transformed into a planned, socialist system, with public ownership of the means of production. Other socialist economists – such as Dickenson (1933, 1939), Durbin (1936) and Lerner (1934, 1944) – developed the approach or produced similar models.[9]

It is worth dwelling for a while on some of the theoretical implications of this 'socialist' application of the Walrasian model. An upshot of the economic arguments of Lange, Taylor and others was that neoclassical economics could equally apply to both capitalism and socialism. Consequently, it was admitted implicitly there was nothing in neoclassical core theory that encapsulated prominent institutional features – such as private property and genuine markets – that were vital to capitalism but absent within socialism. As far as neoclassical core theory is concerned, neither the form of ownership nor the existence of real markets, actually matters. Neoclassical economics, despite often having additional ideological overtones, at root is near-neutral in this respect. Although often used today by pro-marketeers, in fact neoclassical theory does not provide us with a sufficient understanding of markets or private property. It thus has no adequate explanation of the workings of the *capitalist* system.[10]

This conclusion should have led the socialist side of the debate to question the value of, and their adherence, to the neoclassical paradigm. Unfortunately – with rare exceptions such as Maurice Dobb (1937) – the penny did not drop. Neoclassical economics was then, and has remained since, the prestigious doctrine of the mainstream. Leading socialist economists attempted to use this conventional theory to demonstrate the viability of socialist central planning. It was their opponents, namely von Mises and Hayek, who – and largely as a result of this very debate (Kirzner, 1991, Ch. 2; Caldwell, 1988) – realised increasingly the limitations of neoclassical economic theory. The so-called 'Austrian school' of economists, originally inspired by Carl Menger in the 1870s, thus acquired, due to von Mises and Hayek, an even more distinctive identity, and separated themselves even further from the neoclassical mainstream.

Lange and others based their arguments on the allegedly universal precepts of neoclassical economics. They were aware of this fact and even tried to turn it against their Austrian school opponents. Lange noted that 'Mises argues that private ownership of the means of production is indispensable for rational allocation of resources' (Lange and Taylor, 1938, p. 61). Lange also noted that von Mises and other members of the Austrian school 'did so much to emphasize the universal validity of the fundamental principles of economic theory' (p. 62). Lange saw this as an inconsistency, and endorsed the second stance but not the first. He wrote that it was 'most surprising' to find von Mises claiming that 'the economic principles of choice between different alternatives are applicable only to a special institutional set-up ... to a society which recognizes private ownership of the means of production' (p. 62).

Because von Mises was perceived to have undermined his own precept of the universality of economic principles, he was thus tarred by Lange with the brush of the institutionalists and the German historical school. Lange accused von Mises of adopting 'the institutionalist view ... that all economic laws have only historico-relative validity. ... The implications of the denial of rational choice in a socialist economy are plainly institutionalist' (p. 62). Unfortunately, von Mises would not have taken this 'institutionalist' charge as a compliment. For him too, the institutionalists were an anathema.[11]

In fact, nowhere does von Mises deny that rational *choice* is possible in a socialist society. What von Mises did deny was the possibility of rational *calculation* in a completely planned economy. Assuming that there are such things as universal economic principles, Lange seemed to suggest that their existence implies that *any* conjectured form of socio-economic organisation is feasible. However, the existence of universal economic principles neither confirms nor denies a universal need for markets or private property. Lange's argument is illogical and absurd. It is also insensitive to the historical importance of property relations and institutions. Lange's extraordinarily illogical argument was even more extraordinary, coming from an alleged Marxist and a persistent advocate of mathematical economics and theoretical rigour.

A further confusion exists because Lange and others used the term 'market socialism' to refer to their models of an economy in which the workings of the market were merely simulated, rather than any true market itself being accommodated. In fact, the models developed by Lange and his collaborators involved a high degree of centralised co-ordination and knowledge that excluded any real-world market. It is notable that no attempt has ever been made to implement a Lange-type model in reality. Lange himself made no effort to persuade the post-1945 'socialist' government in his native Poland of the value of the idea. At best, the proposal was an attempt to mimic the market through central controls. For this reason, the use of the term 'market socialism' in this context is highly misleading. Lange's proposal certainly did not involve a true market at its core, and many would declare that it was not socialist. Given this legacy of confusion, it would be better that in these debates the term was not used, at least to refer to Lange-type models.

This reproach applies not only to the followers of the Lange-type model but also to some of its critics. Joseph Stiglitz (1994) discussed the Lange-type approach at length, and raised some powerful criticisms. However, he retained the confusing term 'market socialism' to describe these *models*. He added further to the mess when he also described his book as a critique of 'market socialism', as if it were a critique of market socialism *in reality*. In fact, Stiglitz failed completely to examine the real-world socialist attempts – from Mondragon to Yugoslavia – to use genuine markets with worker co-operatives instead of capitalist firms. Stiglitz's book addressed neither real markets nor socialism. It cited a small and unrepresentative fraction of the literature on the economics of socialism. It was much less a critique of market socialism than an attack on Walrasian theoretical presuppositions associated with the Lange-type approach.

Stiglitz criticised the theoretical basis of the attempts, by Lange and his followers, to demonstrate that specific mechanisms, in models bearing a very remote resemblance to actual markets, can accomplish the assumed goals within a theoretical model of central planning. Hence, in one respect, despite being a critic of Lange, Stiglitz followed him to the letter. He took the same view that real-world problems can be solved entirely in the idealised world of theoretical models, thus mistaking the model for reality itself. Stiglitz claimed superiority for his own models on the basis that they involved assumptions (particularly concerning imperfect information) ignored by Lange and others in their models. The question of whether a model gives a true depiction of actual structures and causal mechanisms in the real world was downplayed by both Lange and Stiglitz. It seems that, despite taking different stances in a long debate, both Lange and Stiglitz have preferred to inhabit their own models rather than the real world.

As one of the rising generation of mathematical economists of the 1930s and 1940s, Lange helped to develop the now reigning convention among mainstream economists. Stiglitz has adopted the same methodology: Because the world is messy and complicated, it is first necessary to develop a simplified model of it. Assume such a model. Then discuss that instead, without any further reference to the real world. After all, it is easier to demonstrate mathematical prowess on the basis of assumptions of your own choosing. You can thus gain a reputation as an economist without too much involvement with the disorder of reality. An outcome of this methodology was to make much of the debate over 'market socialism' irrelevant to any real-world attempt at practical policy. It is thus not surprising that Lange had little inclination to persuade politicians to implement his model. Mainstream economics truly is the economics of nowhere.[12]

In the real world, all practical implementations of 'market socialism' have taken a very different form from that devised by Lange and his co-thinkers. A system involving worker co-operatives and real markets was pioneered in the ill-fated Yugoslav Socialist Federal Republic. A cluster of market co-ordinated, worker co-operatives has endured for decades in the Mondragon district in Spain. In general, instead of Lange-type models, the term 'market socialism' is more appropriately used to refer to such systems. Market socialism, in this more appropriate and meaningful sense, involves producer co-operatives that are owned by the workers within them. Such co-operatives sell their products on markets, with genuine exchanges of property rights. Such markets are real, not merely simulated. Genuine market socialism is addressed later in this book. In this chapter we evaluate proposals for all-pervasive collective planning, including models of the type proposed by Lange.[13]

Despite the manifest limitations of their approach, the overwhelming verdict by about 1945 was that Lange and others had 'won' the socialist calculation debate with sound economic arguments. It was widely believed, even by leading and erudite economists, that the argument of von Mises concerning the unfeasibility of socialism had been answered and refuted by Lange, Dickenson and others.

Thus Joseph Schumpeter (1976, p. 167) asked in a volume originally published in 1943: 'Can socialism work?'. Although he personally did not favour such a system, he echoed contemporary and widespread opinion with his immediate answer: 'Of course it can'. He further insisted that: 'There is nothing wrong with the pure theory of socialism' (p. 172). Like others, Schumpeter (p. 173) clearly accepted the Lange–Taylor model as a convincing demonstration of the feasibility of a socialist system. For him, von Mises and Hayek were 'definitely wrong' (Schumpeter, 1954, p. 989 n.).

Similar opinions were reached in a crucial and influential survey article, published in the United States and written by Abram Bergson (1948). Bergson also gave Lange a clear victory in the controversy over the possibility of socialist calculation. He remarked that 'there can hardly be any room for debate; of course socialism can work. On this, Lange certainly was convincing' (Bergson, 1948, p. 447). A similar assessment of the outcome of the debate was widely popularised in Paul Samuelson's (1948) seminal and best-selling neoclassical textbook.

It was not until the 1980s that the tide of opinion began to turn. The swell was increased by the growing political influence of the New Right and by the rising academic stature of Friedrich Hayek and other Austrian economists. In this context, some careful and scholarly re-evaluations of the socialist calculation debate appeared in the 1980s, notably by Karen Vaughn (1980), Peter Murrell (1983) and Donald Lavoie (1985a). The overwhelming and persuasive conclusions of these studies were that:

1 Lange and his followers had failed to answer adequately the criticisms and responses of von Mises and Hayek in the debate.
2 Lange and his followers had failed to provide a satisfactory outline of a workable and dynamic socialist system.
3 Lange and his followers had failed to recognise the inadequacies of the Walrasian theoretical approach to the analysis of real-world capitalism and markets.

Also in the 1980s, some works appeared by authors more sympathetic to socialism, but who also argued that some use of market mechanisms in a socialist economy was unavoidable (Nove, 1983; Hodgson, 1984; Aganbegyan, 1988; Brus and Laski, 1989; Le Grand and Estrin, 1989; D. Miller, 1989).

Despite other limitations, at least von Mises and Hayek had attempted to uncover the real mechanisms of a market economy, and had tried to show that they could not be replaced by central planning. Instead of facing these real mechanisms, the methodology of the neoclassical socialist economists was instead focused on the internal consistency of a chosen model. Fortunately, the theoretical limitations of the Lange approach have gradually become more widely appreciated. For example, long-standing scholars of real-world socialist systems, Wlodzimierz Brus and Kazimierz Laski (1989, p. 57) have argued:

> Formally there are entrepreneurs in the Walrasian model, but they behave like robots, minimizing costs or maximizing profits with the data given. Their behaviour is that of pure optimizers operating in the framework of exclusively passive competition, reduced to reactive adjustment of positions to an exogenous change.

Going further, Mark Blaug (1993, p. 1571) wrote with appropriate derision:

> The Lange idea of managers following marginal cost-pricing rules because they are instructed to do so, while the central planning board continually alters the prices of both producer and consumer goods so as to reduce their excess demands to zero, is so administratively naive as to be positively laughable. Only those drunk on perfectly competitive, static equilibrium theory could have swallowed such nonsense. ... in all the recent calls for reform of Soviet bloc economies, no one has ever suggested that Lange was of any relevance whatsoever. And still more ironically, Lange's 'market socialism' is, on its own grounds, socialism without anything that can be called market transactions.

However, there are still many economists who continue to believe that Lange and his followers had won the earlier debate with their theoretical arguments.[14] The lack of informed summaries of this important debate in the economics textbooks does not help.

In retrospect, it is clear that Hayek had responded in the 1940s with a powerful reply to the ideas of Lange, Taylor and Dickenson. As an illustrative example, consider the crucial problem of incentives. How are managers to be encouraged to take some risks, but not to be too reckless? Dickenson (1939) had proposed a system of managerial bonuses to reward the competent entrepreneur. However, Hayek (1948, p. 199) rightly pointed out that 'managers will be afraid of taking risks if, when the venture does not come off, it will be somebody else who will afterward decide whether they have been justified in embarking on it'. It is an observed characteristic of bureaucratic behaviour to eschew risk-taking, minimise personal exposure to responsibility, and stick to established routine. Hayek (1948, p. 194) also had noted that Lange, Taylor and Dickenson were 'deplorably vague' about key issues, including how competent managers were to be selected.

Hayek showed that these authors had a limited and naïve view of the nature of knowledge in socio-economic systems. These writers had assumed that all relevant technical and economic information would be readily available to the decision makers. As Dickenson (1939, p. 9) wrote: 'All organs of the socialist economy will work, so to speak, within glass walls.' As a result, the central planning authority would be the 'omnipresent, omniscient organ of the collective economy' (p. 191). Likewise, in 1942, Lange (1987, p. 23) argued that under socialism all relevant information concerning production would be available to all, so that 'everything done in one productive establishment would and should also be done by the managers of each productive establishment'.

In taking this limited view of information and knowledge, Lange, Taylor and Dickenson reflected the weaknesses of the neoclassical theory they had embraced. Addressing the prevailing neoclassical approach, Hayek (1948, p. 46) concluded that by depicting 'economic man' as 'a quasi-omniscient individual', economics has hitherto neglected the problem that should be its major concern, that is 'how knowledge is acquired and communicated' (ibid., p. 33).

The models proposed by Lange and others did not deal adequately with the central problem of 'how knowledge is acquired and communicated'. Tacit knowledge held by workers and managers was entirely ignored. Different cognitive interpretations of identical information were not considered. The assimilation of new scientific concepts or interpretations was assumed unproblematic. Contrary to Lange, Taylor and Dickenson, it would not be possible for managers to calculate accurately marginal costs, nor for central planners to make fully 'rational' investment decisions on this basis. In any case, in a dynamic and uncertain world, investment depends on entrepreneurial expectations and hunches, not merely explicit costs. These failures are crucial to matters of learning, innovation and economic growth.

Nevertheless, a stagnant and bureaucratic version of the Lange–Taylor–Dickenson system might be possible in practice, if patched up by illegal but genuine markets and spurred on by ideological exhortations. After all, the former Soviet Union incorporated a routinised and bureaucratic system of central planning, without even attempting a general replication of the market forces of supply and demand. Although bureaucratic and ultimately sluggish, the system worked for several decades. What had been shown by von Mises and Hayek was that such systems, according to acceptable criteria, could be neither rational, dynamic nor efficient.

Accordingly, the greater force of Hayek's economic criticisms of the pseudo-market models of Lange, Taylor and Dickenson does not centre on the question of their feasibility, but on their capacity or otherwise for innovation and economic growth. It is on the germane questions of knowledge and learning that Hayek produced his strongest arguments. The proper appreciation of these dynamic issues involves a fundamental challenge to the equilibrium framework of neoclassical theory.

Consider the questions of price formation and competition. Although prices were formed in the Lange-type models, they did not perform a competitive function, as in a genuine market economy. As Hayek (1948, p. 196) argued:

> The force which in a competitive society brings about the reduction of price to the lowest cost at which the quantity saleable at that cost can be produced is the opportunity for anybody who knows a cheaper method to come in at his own risk and to attract customers by underbidding the other producers. But, if prices are fixed by the authority, this method is excluded.

Also at issue was the nature of costs and prices themselves. To a large degree the problem disappears if prices are conceptualised within the general equilibrium framework of neoclassical economics or within an input–output framework of the type developed by Piero Sraffa (1960). In both these cases we are essentially dealing with a stationary state in which the future resembles the past. In contrast, in a dynamic context, we are obliged to deal with an uncertain future. Such uncertainty rules out the possibility of any calculation of probabilities or expected returns.[15] Instead, we have to rely on intuition and judgement. As a result, prices depend as much upon subjective expectations as upon objective costs. Hayek (1948, p. 198) argued this point clearly:

> In no sense can costs during any period be said to depend solely on prices during that period. They depend as much on whether these prices have been correctly foreseen as on the views that are held about future prices. Even in the very short run costs will depend on the effects which current decisions will have on future productivity. … almost every decision on how to produce … now depends at least in part on the views held about the future.

Notably, the problems of uncertainty in addressing the future, and of decision-making in a dynamic context, are neglected in Marxian, Sraffian and neoclassical economics.

Lange, Taylor and Dickenson assumed that, in addition to the managers in charge of each productive plant, there would be planners in charge of each industry as whole. These planners would make investment decisions concerning the expansion or contraction of the industry, and the number of productive plants within it. These industry managers would be charged with the problem of making estimates of the future productivity and viability of their industry. As a result, both the plant and the industry managers would be responsible for crucial investment decisions. In such circumstances, as Hayek (1935, p. 237) pointed out, it would be very difficult to assess and assign responsibility for mistakes:

> To assume that it is possible to create conditions of full competition without making those who are responsible for the decisions pay for

their mistakes seems to be pure illusion. It will at best be a system of quasi-competition where the person really responsible will not be the entrepreneur but the official who approves his decisions and where in consequence all the difficulties will arise in connection with freedom of initiative and the assessment of responsibility which are usually associated with bureaucracy.

The above argument was formulated by Hayek before the publication of Lange and Taylor's (1938) book. It applies to all forms of collective planning and control of investment decisions. As argued below, problems of dynamic inefficiency and bureaucratic sclerosis are ubiquitous in all socialist proposals to eliminate or marginalise the market. It is to some recent proposals along these lines that we now turn.

A PROPOSAL FOR 'DEMOCRATIC PLANNING'

The idea of 'democratic planning' has long been posed as an alleged antidote to the problems of bureaucracy in non-market organisations. An important recent proposal along these lines has been advanced by Pat Devine and his student Fikret Adaman (Devine, 1988; Adaman and Devine, 1994, 1996a, 1996b, 1997). Alongside a second recent proposal discussed below, the ideas of Adaman and Devine are important and illustrative, and deserving of detailed discussion. Together they represent two of the more detailed blueprints in the entire history of socialism. They are both representative of the enduring opposition of traditional socialists to the extensive use of markets and private ownership.

The particular proposal of Adaman and Devine is also important because it has attracted the support of some leading 1990s' socialists, and because it illustrates, with notable poignancy, some crucial theoretical errors concerning the market mechanisms and tacit knowledge. Adaman and Devine opposed all versions of 'market socialism' and proposed that large portions of the economy should be directed and co-ordinated, not through markets or bureaucratic planning, but through a 'third way' involving 'democratic planning based on negotiated coordination' (Devine, 1988, p. 3).[16]

In their proposal, Devine and Adaman accepted that labour markets, and markets for consumer goods, should remain. However, decisions concerning 'the pattern of investment, in the structure of productive capacity, in the relative size of different industries, in the geographical distribution of economic activity, in the size and even the existence of individual production units' should not be the 'result of atomized decisions' under the sway of 'market forces' (Devine, 1988, p. 23).[17]

This may suggest to some readers that markets are to be abolished in industries producing machines, raw materials and all other goods not part of final consumption. But no: it is 'market forces', not markets, that are to be abolished. Their model 'retains market exchange, but replaces market forces by the process of negotiated coordination' (Adaman and Devine, 1996b, p. 534). In all sectors, enterprises still 'compete', prices are still set, money still exists, and goods and services are bought and sold (Devine, 1988, pp. 208 ff.).

There is very much an element of having it both ways here. Devine's (1988, p. 6) book opened with a lament over the degree to which 'the doctrine of market socialism has achieved near hegemony' among non-dogmatic socialists. 'The crisis of the traditional socialist vision has enabled the new right's market-orientated project to gain the ascendancy.' Yet, when it came to the crunch – the economic detail of the system – Devine himself was impelled to advocate some version of the market mechanism. Yet this pill was sweetened with layers and layers of sweet-sounding proposals concerning 'negotiated coordination' and 'democratic planning'. In all, the layers are so thick that it is difficult to find the bitter pill itself. Devine thus simultaneously opposed what he called 'market socialism' and proposed a version of 'socialism' – with 'market exchange'. It is not thus a 'third way', as he suggested, but a radical variant of a system of market exchange.

Nevertheless, the proposals for negotiated co-ordination are of interest and importance. Similar in some respects to ideas for a 'stakeholder capitalism' (Hutton, 1995), they involve the idea that new integrative structures and social relationships can limit the damaging effects of sectional and individual greed. Such interlocking social institutions can make both producers and consumers more aware of the interests of others, of society as a whole, and of the environment. By suggesting that such institutions could be integrated with the market, the vista is opened up of transforming the market itself.

What is highly problematic, however, is the extent to which such bodies can 'replace market forces'. Devine's proposal to replace 'market forces' but to retain 'market exchange' depends upon a clear distinction between the two. Unfortunately, as shown below, the basis of such a differentiation is unclear.

Devine (1988, p. 236) noted that with 'the operation of market forces … production and investment decisions are made atomistically and coordinated *ex post*'. However, it would be a mistake to regard the market as purely a mechanism of *ex post* co-ordination. All costs in markets involve calculations by social agents concerning the future. In addition, futures markets are specialist institutions concerned largely with *ex ante* adjustments: that is purchases and sales of titles to commodities that may not yet exist. It is thus quite wrong to see planning as largely or exclusively future-oriented and markets, in contrast, as largely or exclusively concerned with the reconciliation of past decisions. All future-oriented economic activity has to use and assess resources bequeathed from the past. Markets are not simply mechanisms for price and resource reconciliation, they are also means by which new products, involving ideas and expectations concerning the future, can be launched.

Both markets and planning are simultaneously involved with both *ex post* adjustment and *ex ante* expectations. Both markets and planning are processes, looking forward into the future with the knowledge and judgement of the past. The difference between the two does not lie primarily in the direction of their temporal orientation but elsewhere. Market-orientated systems involve multiple, potentially conflicting, plans of many production units, whereas collectivised planning involves just one overall plan. Notably, and despite the masking rhetoric, Devine's model is explicitly an example of the former rather than the latter.

The conceptual separation of 'market exchange' from 'market forces' is difficult, to say the least. Like all structured interactions between individuals, the market is a process, involving a degree of creativity and discovery. People, and the relations between them, are changed by such interactions. In whatever form, 'market exchange' must involve a measure of human learning and development. It is thus difficult to separate any 'market exchange' from the dynamic effects that Devine placed under the separate heading of 'market forces'.

In practice, any attempt to permit the operation of 'market exchange' without the pressure of 'market forces' would be highly problematic. How would such a distinction be managed and policed? Devine's criterion seems to be the following:

> In the model of negotiated coordination a distinction is drawn between the use of existing capacity, which is decided by production units in response to current demand, and changes in capacity, which are decided by negotiated coordination bodies covering all production units in a particular branch of production. Changes in productive capacity affect those who work in the production units concerned, and in interdependent production units, those who live in the communities where these units are located, customers, and usually also the concerns of some interest and cause groups. All would participate in the decision-making.
>
> (Devine, 1988, pp. 190–1)

Seemingly, as long as the resources and processes of production and consumption do not change, then 'market exchange' can operate without the need for 'negotiated coordination'. The latter would come into play when a new product is proposed, or new technologies emerge, or new processes of production are developed, or consumer tastes alter, or people move their location, or incomes change, or people get older, or new diseases arise or are discovered. All such changes involve investment. As a result, according to Adaman and Devine, decisions concerning them must be consigned not to the market but to the 'negotiated coordination bodies'.

However, no real world socio-economic system is static. All socio-economic systems, past and present, involve a degree of innovation and learning. Consumer tastes change incrementally through experience, and repeated application may enhance productive skills. Accordingly, it would be difficult to avoid the conclusion that *every* decision should be referred to some 'negotiated coordination body' because to some extent it involved something new. As Heraclitus pointed out, we never step in the same river twice. Taken literally, Devine's (1988, p. 23) list of substantial issues requiring negotiated co-ordination ('the pattern of investment ... the structure of productive capacity ... the relative size of different industries ... the geographical distribution of economic activity ... the size and even the existence of individual production units') could be taken to refer to almost every economic decision, throughout the economy.

With the possibility that every economic decision would have to be referred to a network of deliberative bodies, for negotiations in which 'all would participate', the system faces the danger that it will grind to a halt. Every citizen would be faced with an endless succession of meetings and discussions. There would be no time left for work, leisure or consumption. For such a system to be remotely workable, some boundaries have to be drawn to the jurisdiction of the committees and some limits have to be put to the potentially endless processes of discussion and negotiation. Over this very real problem of limits and boundaries, Devine and Adaman were, to say the least, very vague.[18]

At root, the most severe set of problems with Devine's proposal concern the implementation, scale and boundaries of 'negotiated coordination' itself. Long ago, Oscar Wilde was reported as being responsible for the quip that socialism was impossible because it would take 'too many meetings'. Faced with this direct criticism of their 'overloaded' scheme of negotiated co-ordination by Robin Blackburn (1991, p. 48), Adaman and Devine (1996b, p. 534) made the riposte that this criticism is 'based on a fundamental misunderstanding of the model being proposed' and does not apply 'with the same force' because 'market exchange' is retained in their proposal, and 'all transactions' are not to be the subject of 'negotiated exchange'.

The problem here was not the misunderstanding of critics, however. It lay with the proposal of Adaman and Devine, and their failure to see that their own criteria cannot prevent almost every significant economic decision being paralysed by potentially endless discussion in a network of committees. Taken literally, their own criteria suggested that the role of the market would be confined merely to static and routinised activity, bereft of any innovation and change. As argued above, this hardly leaves any scope for the market at all.

45

Once again, Adaman and Devine wanted it both ways. When convenient, they deprecated 'market socialism'. On the other hand, when their 'alternative' proposal was closely scrutinised, and its workability is questioned, then they retreated and freely admitted a significant role for 'market exchange' in their system. Yet when their criteria for the admission of 'market exchange' are placed under the light of examination, they evaporate to insignificance. They switched from a fanfare of anti-market rhetoric, to an admission of markets in principle, and back to criteria that would largely rule them out in practice. As long as their proposal is merely a matter of published words, and not constructive deeds, then it is easier to shift the stress from one to the other, and back again. When faced with the real-world practicalities of implementation, however, much clearer and less elastic formulations would be required.

A crucial and widespread problem with all proposals – whether bureaucratic or democratic – for all-embracing socialist planning, concerns the scope for novelty, innovation, learning and change. These issues emerged at the centre of the Austrian contribution to the socialist calculation debate.

For Adaman and Devine (1994, 1996b), the Austrian argument against centralised planning hinged on the role of tacit knowledge. In response, Adaman and Devine 'contest the view that the discovery of tacit knowledge is possible only through entrepreneurial activity in the market process and argue that participatory planning would promote the discovery and social mobilisation of dispersed tacit knowledge more efficiently' (1996b, p. 524). This formulation of the problem is symptomatic, especially with regard to its notion that tacit knowledge is something to be 'discovered'. The issue became clearer in another passage, where they argued that through 'democratic participatory planning ... tacit knowledge is discovered and articulated and, on the basis of that knowledge, economic decisions are consciously planned and coordinated' (ibid., pp. 531–2).[19] Accordingly, for Adaman and Devine, tacit knowledge is something that we can eventually 'discover', 'articulate' and thereby use for conscious planning.

We shall quickly pass over the faulty epistemological suggestion that knowledge in general is something – out there – to be 'discovered'. Note that this empiricist conception of knowledge is also ubiquitous among mainstream economists. It is flawed because all knowledge depends on preconceptions and prior cognitive frameworks that in principle are not there to be 'discovered' and cannot be established simply through reason or fact. Our minds may receive sense data, but sense data are not the same as information or knowledge. Information is data to which some meaning has been attributed. Knowledge is the product of information use. Many of the cognitive processes that we use to obtain and use information are tacit and inaccessible. Rooted in an untenable, empiricist

46

epistemology is the idea that any knowledge – including tacit knowledge – can be 'discovered'.

Some knowledge can be codified, but to what extent can tacit knowledge be 'articulated'? To answer this we must examine the meaning of tacit knowledge. Tacit knowledge means *knowing how* rather than a *knowing that*. It is in principle both prior to, and beyond the reach of, explicit articulation. In his classic text on the topic, Michael Polanyi[20] (1967) wrote: *'we can know more than we can tell'* (p. 4). We can recognise a familiar face in a crowd of thousands but be unable tell how, and incapable of drawing or describing it in detail. We use many gestures, body language and interpersonal skills with limited awareness and self-reflection.

Tacit knowledge is a necessary foundation to all knowledge. Just as logically we cannot adequately define every single word in the dictionary in terms of the other words, generally and ultimately we must rely on intuitions or tacit meanings. Although the boundary between the tacit and the explicit may shift, especially as our scientific understanding improves, it cannot be all brought up to a visible level where everything is rendered explicit. Organisational learning, for example, may involve transforming some tacit knowledge into codified knowledge, so that it can be communicated to others. But it is important to realise that, in principle, not all tacit knowledge can be rendered explicit. Indeed, as Polanyi put it: 'an unbridled lucidity can destroy our understanding of complex matters. Scrutinize closely the particulars of a comprehensive entity and their meaning is effaced, our conception of the entity is destroyed' (ibid., p. 18).

Polanyi argued convincingly that the foundation of all knowledge must remain inexplicit, because all codifiable knowledge is necessarily an emergent property of underlying and tacit rudiments. Accordingly, 'the ideal of eliminating all personal elements of knowledge would, in effect, aim at the destruction of all knowledge. ... the process of formalizing all knowledge to the exclusion of any tacit knowledge is self-defeating' (ibid., p. 19). It is thus a serious misunderstanding of the concept of tacit knowledge to see it as being something that generally and readily can be discovered, articulated or communicated.

Polanyi forcibly maintained that tacit knowledge is essential for all human activity, including science, but it cannot generally be made explicit or codified. Some tacit knowledge may become explicit, but a thick layer of irredeemably tacit knowledge is essential to all acts of interpretation and communication. Indeed, for Polanyi, to attempt to dispense with tacitness, and to attempt to subject *all* human affairs to open reason and discussion, would be a dangerous and destructive enterprise. There is much of importance in human activity and interaction that cannot be the matter of rational deliberation and discussion. Much has to be taken for granted. We are forced to rely on tacit knowledge which is necessarily beyond our full scrutiny.

Tacit knowledge forms the indissoluble core of all skills. All skilful human activity involves the use of rules and principles which are not known openly to the person involved. For example, we may be unable to articulate the rules of grammar, but in our use of language we largely conform to them. We may be able to ride a bicycle or fly an aeroplane but we shall be unable to communicate anything but the barest principles of these activities in codifiable form. Indeed, all productive human activity has these features: we use rules but we are unable to make many of them explicit. The tacit realm is irreducible. As Richard Nelson and Sidney Winter (1982, pp. 81–2) argued:

> much operational knowledge remains tacit because it cannot be articulated fast enough, because it is impossible to articulate all that is necessary to a successful performance, and because language cannot simultaneously serve to describe relationships and characterize the things related.

In a major article on technological innovation, Giovanni Dosi (1988b, p. 1131) developed a related point: 'In each technology there elements of *tacit and specific* knowledge that are not and *cannot* be written down in a "blueprint" form, and cannot, therefore, be entirely diffused either in the form of public or proprietary information'. It is this type of resolutely tacit knowledge that is problematic for any planning process, participatory or otherwise. The insurmountable barrier is the vast amount of vital knowledge that cannot be the subject of rational deliberation. As Anthony Giddens (1994, p. 29) pointed out:

> In politics as elsewhere, rationalism presumes the superiority of 'universal' solutions to the problems over answers coming from tradition or embedded practice. ... All forms of knowledge, no matter how general they appear to be, are saturated by practice, by what cannot be put into words because it is the condition of linguistic communication.

As Hayek and others have argued, the widespread existence and indispensable qualities of tacit knowledge make completely centralised planning, 'as if in a single head', impossible. Adaman and Devine did not propose completely centralised planning, but an interlocking network of negotiation committees to formulate the plans. The proposal is different but the same central problem remains. How can these committees discuss and deliberate on matters which individuals (or groups) may 'know but cannot say'? Adaman and Devine avoided this problem by wrongly assuming that all tacit knowledge can be articulated. Having made this untenable assumption, they then argued that all relevant knowledge can be made explicit and subject to discussion and reason. The same erroneous argument underlay former proposals for centralised planning that have been found wanting, both in their theoretical formulation and their practical application. Such proposals for 'centralised' and 'democratic' planning are both founded on a similar misapprehension of the nature of knowledge, and a corresponding overestimation of the power and scope of human reason.

Hilary Wainwright (1994) has given some support to Devine's (1988) ideas. At the same time she has provided a more in-depth treatment of the issue of tacit knowledge. Her key argument against the individualistic ideas of Hayek was that tacit knowledge is largely social, and often held by groups of workers rather than simply by individual entrepreneurs. This is an important and valid point and it shall be elaborated in more detail in later chapters. However, the team-based character of tacit knowledge does not save the Adaman–Devine proposal from fatal criticism. Tacit knowledge is tacit. Whether tacit knowledge is held by an individual or by a team, it cannot, in principle, be widely dispersed and fully appreciated throughout the economy. Although knowledge is social in character, this does not mean that it is transparent, nor readily accessible to any member of society. Wainwright's argument pointed to the limits of an individualistic understanding of productive knowledge and organisation. It did not demonstrate, however, the possibility of an all-embracing collective plan. If knowledge resides in productive teams of workers, then the question remains as to how the economic organisations encompassing those teams are to be co-ordinated. Further hand-waving in the direction of 'social knowledge' does not solve this crucial problem. The need to rely to some significant degree on markets and the price mechanism remains. True to their traditional socialist roots, Wainwright and others are reluctant to admit this.

Knowledge is both social and contextual; it is rooted in practice (Neisser, 1983). For it to be accessible, conceptions and practices have to be shared. But there are limits to the amount of shared or widely accessible knowledge. Learning depends on ingrained familiarity, obtained through repeated routine. For this reason – and contrary to both Owen and Marx – in any complex society, people have no alternative but to be specialists. There are limits to the amount of knowledge that can be understood by any individual or group. The failure of leading members of the socialist tradition to recognise the true character of knowledge has led to a gross underestimate of the importance of specialised learning, and of the inevitability of a division of labour based on differentiated skills.[21]

As Polanyi explained, all scientific advances and technological innovations are bound up with tacit knowledge. They rely on accumulated skills and habits, implanted in individuals and institutions. The creative spark is often a result of the striking of intuition upon the flintstone of tacit skills, rather than by logical deduction or rational deliberation.[22]

Yet novelty, by its nature, challenges established belief. Inventions often require much development and pragmatic refinement before they are deemed plausible. Accordingly, a socio-economic system that fosters innovation must enable the eccentric inventor or entrepreneur to develop an idea that may seem, at first sight, to be implausible or far-fetched. To some degree, a system with markets and private property may allow this, as long as other important cultural and institutional conditions are met. Some critics of socialism wrongly suggest that markets and private property are alone sufficient for entrepreneurship and creativity. The experiences of varied capitalist systems show that innovation also depends on specific cultural and institutional supports.[23] But that does not mean that we should underestimate the importance of property rights and market incentives. A benefit of systems based on private property and exchange is that they allow some entrepreneurs to test the demand for new innovations by bringing them to the market. Such a system has its limitations. But it is an open question whether an alternative set of arrangements could exist.

Any alternative proposal must take account of tacit knowledge. A system that compelled every innovation to the deliberations of multiple committees, however democratic and well meaning, would stifle the creative impulse. The tacit knowledge of the innovators cannot readily become the general knowledge of the committee. In principle, the creative idea cannot be given full, open consideration. It cannot be the subject of full, rational deliberation. The Adaman and Devine model of 'negotiated coordination' thwarts innovation, and is thus a recipe for economic stagnation.

Furthermore, in proposing 'negotiated coordination' in almost every area of economic life, Adaman and Devine ignored the problem of severe information overload in modern socio-economic systems. Modern economies product millions of types of product. If every attribute of every new or modified produce is potentially the subject of 'negotiated coordination' then each committee faces an agenda that will take it to eternity. The Adaman–Devine proposal was motivated by the fine and admirable sentiments of democracy and co-operation, but it simply ignored the key issues upon which the appraisal of its feasibility must depend.

Basically, planning operates either through direction or through agreement. In the former case, orders are given by those in authority. In the latter case, agreement is reached through some democratic procedure. In a modern, complex economy, vast numbers of decisions are involved. Through command or through agreement, all these decisions must be made. The more 'democratic' the decision-making process, the more decisions each individual has to make. An attempt to gain agreement on an extensive scale on many issues is likely to lead to frustration. Like it or not, there would be pressure to delegate decision-making powers to experts and permanent officials, unless planning itself were to be abandoned. Adaman and Devine failed to address and answer this argument, made by Hayek (1944, pp. 45–50) long ago. There can be little confidence that their proposal, if it managed to function at all, would not develop along the same bureaucratic and elitist lines.

After all, in a highly complex world it is difficult for everyone to gain the requisite specialist knowledge to be involved in many aspects of decision-making. Only to a limited degree can a democratic committee understand and analyse the complexities of every scientific, technological and economic issue that comes under its jurisdiction. There are limits to what can be discussed and negotiated, requiring deputised powers to expert subgroups. Yet all this goes against Devine's principle that 'all would participate in the decision-making'. This principle simply ignores the degree of complexity and the amount of information pertaining to decisions in modern economies. These issues were raised by the Austrian critics of socialism long ago. Yet they were ignored by Adaman and Devine.

Whatever the limitations of the market system, it has the supreme advantage that it does not require everyone to agree on everything, before a decision can be made. And it can do this without creating authoritarian concentrations of bureaucratic power. To an important extent, markets create zones of partial autonomy within an interrelated socio-economic system; agents attempt to enact their decisions through negotiated contracts with others. It is possible for technological or institutional innovations to be pioneered without the prior agreement of committees or bureaucrats.

We may imagine a system of 'democratic planning' where 'all would participate' and ignore the vast amount of decision-making involved. In such a dream we may dismiss the market, or confine it – in the manner of Adaman and Devine – to a static and repetitive sphere where the decisions are already made. But in any real and genuine attempt to extend economic democracy, we would face the problem of confining decision-making to manageable proportions. We ignore this problem at the cost of democracy itself: a system overburdened with decisions would create the impetus for bureaucratic power. The market has many deficiencies, but no-one has shown how its use can be avoided without creating the alternative of a bureaucratic and authoritarian juggernaut. Seen in this light, the market can be the protector of viable economic democracy, rather than its enemy.

Surprisingly, despite the frequent occurrence in the socialist literature of the notion of 'democratic planning', there are too few attempts to explain how such an idea would work in practice. Despite its limitations, the proposal by Adaman and Devine is one of the few examples of such an attempt. However, their endeavour to marginalise both the market and private opportunity is likely to be deleterious to technological innovation, human learning and economic growth. While markets do not themselves guarantee economic dynamism, they are likely to remain indispensable to any innovative and advancing economy. Within practical limits, some measures of economic democracy and negotiated planning are worthy, positive and attainable. But, in addition, in any dynamic economy there seems to be little alternative to the significant use of markets and private opportunity, to facilitate innovation and to help stimulate creativity. Contrary to Adaman and Devine, the market cannot be confined to the mere allocation of resources.

These arguments are further reinforced after critical examination of another recent proposal for a system of socialist planning. In this proposal extensive use is made of indices of value, calculated by computers. Seemingly, such calculations would make it possible to reduce the amount of negotiated decision-making, on the basis that these indices of value were usable as representations of social worth. Markets use prices as (imperfect) representations of the interrelated decisions of many agents. Is it possible to abolish the market, but use the computer to calculate some usable, social indices of value? In this manner, can the number of decisions in a modern economy be reduced? It is to this proposal that we now turn.

COMPUTERS TO THE RESCUE?

Since the Second World War and the development of the modern computer, the idea has repeatedly been put forward that these machines can resolve key problems with central planning. Notably, in 1967 Lange revisited his proposal of thirty years before, still claiming that in it he had 'refuted' the arguments of Hayek and others. He then asked himself:

> Were I to rewrite my essay today my task would be much simpler. My answer ... would be: so what's the trouble? Let us put the simultaneous equations on an electronic computer and we shall obtain the solution in less than a second. The market process with its cumbersome *tâtonnements* appears old-fashioned. Indeed, it may be considered as a computing device of the pre-electronic age.
>
> (Lange, 1967, p. 158)

This was written perhaps at a high point of post-war, technocratic optimism. Lange's electronic solution had, at least for committed socialists, some persuasive appeal. Since then, the idea of a computer solution to socialism's planning problems has been repeated many times.[24]

However, considerations of the practical implementation of computer algorithms to price calculations, and to other planning problems in a socialist system, revealed unforeseen impediments. In an important article by a knowledgeable expert on the Soviet economy, Alexander Nove (1980, p. 4) quoted a Soviet estimate that there were 12 million types of commodity being produced in the USSR in 1977. In my book *The Democratic Economy* I used this as a ball-park minimum figure to estimate the amount of time it would take to calculate, using standard computers and input–output techniques, the prices of all the commodities in a modern economy. Such a calculation would involve the inversion of a matrix with 12 million rows and 12 million columns. My estimate was that such a set of computer calculations would take more than 18 years (Hodgson, 1984, p. 170).[25] Central planning in such a time scale would be totally impractical. Lange's 1967 statement that such calculations would take 'less than a second' was evidently wrong, and the idea of rescuing central planning by use of the computer seemed doomed.

What was overlooked in my 1984 book was the reckless pace of development of computer technology. Compared with 1967, or even 1980, computers are now much more powerful and are produced at a much lower cost. Recognising this, W. Paul Cockshott and Allin Cottrell have attempted to revive the idea of wholesale central planning (Cockshott and Cottrell, 1993). They have also suggested that modern computer technology has rebutted the view of the Austrian school that rational, socialist planning is unworkable (Cottrell and Cockshott, 1993). Building on the fast and relatively cheap computer technology of the 1980s and 1990s, the works of Cockshott and Cottrell are important markers in the long socialist calculation debate.

For some time, strong arguments have been put forward that no form of socialism can function adequately without markets. Many on the socialist left have met these arguments with mere rebuttals, and have not even attempted to show in detail how socialism could function without a market. The market has been rejected for moral rather than practical reasons. The work of Cockshott and Cottrell (1993) is an exception. Instead of ritual displays of anti-market angst and moral indignation, Cockshott and Cottrell attempted to give a detailed explanation of how a centrally planned socialist system could work. The fact that this argument is ultimately unconvincing does not detract from either its rarity or its importance.

Cockshott is a computer expert and he has outlined the calculations needed and the technology available. Using appropriate numerical methods, and supercomputers that were just available in 1985, a 10 million square, 'sparse'[26] matrix could be inverted in less than 20 minutes (Cockshott and Cottrell, 1993, pp. 57–60; Cottrell and Cockshott, 1993, pp. 101–3). Moreover, much faster computers became available in the 1990s. On this basis they concluded, quite reasonably, that such calculations are well within the scope of modern computer technology.

However, it is still an open question whether modern computers can tackle the actual amount of information involved in the modern context. Today it is likely that the number of different types of commodity in any advanced economy would vastly exceed 10 million. Many of these individual commodities have variations and varied specifications. Stiglitz (1994, p. 84) noted that the specification of the characteristics of a particular, but standard, white t-shirt filled up thirty small-print pages. If this amount of information applied to each one of millions of commodities, would even the fastest of modern computers be able to cope? And then there are the variations of delivery time and location for each good. As Hayek (1948, p. 193) remarked long ago, once we try to replace the market there is the limitation that 'the price-fixing process will be confined to establishing uniform prices for classes of goods and that therefore distinctions based on the special circumstances of time, place, and quality will find no expression in prices'. It is still not clear whether modern computers can handle all the relevant, detailed information in modern economies. Nevertheless, given the spectacular advances in computer technology in the 1980s and 1990s, and the possibilities for further advances in the technology, a decisive criticism of centralised planning cannot be based on this point.

More than half a century after the publication of the 1920 article by von Mises, Cockshott and Cottrell would have it that the problem of socialist calculation had been finally solved by the development of computing technology. Ironically, these developments came to fruition at the very time of the collapse of the Soviet Bloc itself. Seemingly, just as the computer technology was developed to make comprehensive planning possible, the economies that had cherished that socialist ideal imploded, and turned to capitalism instead.

Cockshott and Cottrell were aware of these ironic setbacks, but stood firm in their belief in the possibility of centralised planning. They devised ingenious methods to communicate and update, throughout the economy, the information required for central planning. Their ideas here include the employment of standard bar-code readers and the use of televisions with teletext. All this is now familiar and readily available technology.

With such technological instruments, Cockshott and Cottrell (1993, pp. 29, 57–9) revived some of the fundamentalist socialist ideas of Owen and others. Prices should generally reflect the amount of socially necessary labour time embodied in each commodity. Workers should be paid not with money but in non-transferable tokens, in proportion to the number of hours of performed work, by which they could purchase consumer goods. Allegedly, with modern computers, the amount of socially necessary labour time embodied in each good or service can be readily determined. This calculation is a matter of constructing the technological input and output matrices for the economy, and performing a matrix inversion. The wheel has turned full circle. By the aid of the modern computer we are now able to revisit the ideological debates of the 1840s, now seemingly unencumbered by the intervening objections of the Austrian school.

However, there is more to the running and functioning of an economy than the inputting of data and the solving of equations. In their book, Cockshott and Cottrell addressed a number of possible problems with, and objections to, their scheme. There is the problem of varying levels of skill. The two authors proposed a system of calculating the amount of labour expended, by teaching and in teaching materials, on raising the skill level of the worker (Cockshott and Cottrell, 1993, pp. 40–7). It is thus possible, with a number of *ad hoc* assumptions, to calculate a 'skilled labour multiplier' by which skilled labour is augmented in the embodied labour calculations. However, it is not proposed that the skilled worker is *paid* at a greater rate per hour, because the cost of his or her education has been financed by society as a whole. The skilled labour multipliers are calculated solely for the purpose of determining the prices of commodities.

Another problem is the lack of a time dimension in production involved in the use of prices based on embodied labour. With a growing economy their use is suboptimal, by standard criteria (Baisch, 1979). Their use is equivalent to the assumption of a zero interest rate, and a zero rate of time preference. This means that two projects involving equal remuneration and equal investments of overall labour time, but expenditures or remunerations occurring at different times, are treated as equivalent. As a result, embodied labour time prices may bias the system excessively towards future investments. Cockshott and Cottrell (1993, pp. 76–7) proposed that this bias is alleviated by the use, by the central planners, of a discount rate equal to the projected rate of future productivity growth.

Yet another problem is how the system is to respond to changes in consumer tastes or demand. Cockshott and Cottrell (1993, pp. 118–26) envisaged a market for consumer goods, in which 'prices' are adjusted, in Lange-type fashion, in response to excess demand or excess supply. The idea introduced by Cockshott and Cottrell would be to use – instead of the firm's profit level – the ratio between calculated labour embodied and market-clearing, labour token price as an indicator for planning purposes. The ratio of market-clearing price to labour content is calculated for each consumer product, and production increased or decreased by the planners, depending on the outcome.

Another vital problem is how to encourage production plants to improve their productivity. By the mechanism outlined above, firms producing consumer goods will be pressured to maintain product quality and market demand for their product, and to save as much as possible on the use of direct and indirect labour time. They proposed that the principle may be extended indirectly, by imputation, to those goods and services which enter the production of consumer goods.

At first sight, Cockshott and Cottrell seemed to have responded to a number of key problems and constructed a feasible model of a centrally planned socialist economy. On closer inspection, however, some deeper problems remain. Notably, to some extent, these were problems already raised by von Mises and Hayek. Yet Cottrell and Cockshott (1993) claimed to have answered these Austrian critics of central planning. This claim turns out to be false. There was no adequate discussion in the works of Cottrell and Cockshott of the nature of learning and of the importance of tacit knowledge.

Symptomatically, addressing the Austrian argument that the Lange-type model failed to deal properly with dynamics, innovation and economic development, Cottrell and Cockshott (1993) skipped quickly over the issue, and belittled its importance. In their attempt to reply to the Austrian arguments, they alleged that problems such as 'the speed of adjustment following parametric changes' were 'more substantial' than the question of dynamic development (ibid., p. 89). Yet the issues of dynamics, learning, discovery and creativity are indeed central. They pose severe problems for any model of collective socialist planning.

It has been noted above, in relation to the model of Adaman and Devine, that a key problem with central planning is the impossibility of accessing all the tacit knowledge dispersed throughout an economy. Although they eventually assumed the problem away, at least Adaman and Devine addressed this issue. In contrast, Cockshott and Cottrell failed to give it any significant attention. Essentially, they had a techno-cratic and empiricist conception of information, and were most incautious concerning the limits of artificial intelligence and computing technology. The importance of tacit knowledge has been discussed above, so it is unnecessary to repeat the arguments here. Nevertheless, they apply to Cockshott and Cottrell's work as well.

How did these authors propose that the planners deal with innovation in their proposed system? Cockshott and Cottrell (1993, p. 131) wrote:

> Suppose we have a system by which production engineers *register* possible technologies with the planning computers. They would give details of the inputs required and the predicted output. On the basis of a central evaluation of the different production technolo-gies, the planning system would choose the intensity with which each technology was to be used.

A crucial problem with this rather bureaucratic proposal is that the managers have little incentive to take risks. Cottrell and Cockshott (1993, p. 90) proposed an 'innovation budget' in which firms would apply for funds to develop innovations. Potential innovators would have to convince the planning board *ex ante* of their ideas, prior to their practical realisation. It would be a cumbersome and bureaucratic process, acting on balance to stifle rather than encourage initiative. Standard criticisms voiced by Austrian school economists concerning the potential stagnation of a centrally planned economy still apply.

From their proposals it is clear that Cockshott and Cottrell had a conception of technology and innovation as transparent, allowing them to be adequately summarised in explicit and codifiable information, such as in the technical coefficients of an input-output table. They assumed that investment planning is possible, but only on the assumption of complete knowledge at the centre concerning all production functions. This involved a complete misapprehension of the nature of technical knowledge and of the foci of economic innovation. It was based on a false epistemological assumption that knowledge is directly attainable from codified data.

The tacit and idiosyncratic nature of much technical knowledge makes any 'central evaluation of different production technologies' ineffective and unviable. Often a new technology does not emerge as a given package, with known 'details of the inputs required and the predicted output'. Typically, the development of a new technique or product is a matter of repeated experiment, over a long period of time. A decision to invest in a technology involves hunch and conjecture, not simply given, objective data.

Furthermore, much innovation in modern economies is not product innovation but process innovation (Davenport, 1993; Rothwell, 1992). It involves changes in the way of producing things, rather than the product itself. In this context, organisational innovation is often as important as technical innovation. Process information typically entails a great deal of tacit knowledge, held by workers close to the production process.

It is also important to note that many products are not standardised and are designed for specific users. Especially in these cases, much innovation involves extended interaction and dialogue between users and producers. A focus on the registration of specified inputs ignores the ongoing process of negotiation between producer and user which is directed towards the use of alternative components or materials. Central registration itself would be time-consuming. The central registration bureau would be overwhelmed with countless piecemeal innovations, or its use as an administrative focus would deter innovation itself.

Technical knowledge is highly contextual. It is often difficult to understand the nature or value of an innovation without intimate knowledge of the situation to which it relates. It is often difficult or impossible for one unit to convey to another what precisely is required. Unless there are shared ideas and patterns of experience then agents are unlikely to understand the raw data in the same terms. Because of the lack of these common conceptions, they may not, in effect, speak the same language.

The key difficulty in a system dominated by central or collective planning is one of the communication of appropriate knowledge. If we reduce knowledge to data, then the problem appears to be overcome. But knowledge is not, and cannot be reduced to, data. To make sense of data we require concepts and cognitive frames, involving tacit meanings and ideas. For knowledge to be communicated, the sender and receiver must hold the appropriate concepts in common. Any large economy is unlikely to have or achieve the degree of conceptual uniformity and integration required to enable the ready transfer of most relevant knowledge.

This issue of organisation and cultural integration is of vital importance and relates to the critique of both market-dominated systems and proposals for central or collective planning. We shall return to it in the next chapter. But a measure of irony can be noted here. By treating technological innovation as transparent, Cockshott and Cottrell made a similar epistemological error to those that believe that the price system can adequately communicate all the important economic information. Problems concerning the lack of common cognitive frameworks are ignored in both cases.

Furthermore, despite their hatred of the market, some aspects of their proposal are strangely and resolutely contractarian in nature. Like the advocates of free markets, Cockshott and Cottrell seem to assume that changes in the form of property and ownership are sufficient to transform individual incentives and social culture. As in the case of many free market economists, there is little discussion of the role of institutions and culture in transforming perceptions and goals.

At the same time, unlike the advocates of free markets, they ignore the bureaucratic and totalitarian dangers of such enormous concentrations of economic and administrative power. Yet it would be more consistent with a Marxian approach to propose that a centralised economic 'basis' would lead to an equally centralised and monolithic political 'superstructure'. As Hayek (1944) argued, a state which played a central role in important matters, that could not be codified in explicit rules, would lack constraints on the arbitrary exercise of power and seriously threaten liberty and the overall rule of law. The political dangers in concentrating so many crucially decisions in the hands of the state and its central planners remain very real.

Cockshott and Cottrell (1993, p. 206) proposed that the employee 'signs a contract with the employment agency stating that she will work for so many hours a week on a particular project'. This is an explicitly contractarian focus, with a notion of contracted work, delimited by time. In the third part of this book it will be argued that this notion is becoming increasingly obsolete in the context of modern economic and technological complexity. As work becomes more varied and skills more specific, then measures of work in terms of time are increasingly problematic.

Clearly this would have major implications for any proposal to use labour hours as a major unit of economic accounting. A further irony emerges. In fact, just as the computer technology emerged in the 1980s to make its extensive use in central planning possible, the transformation of work, partly under the impetus of the new technology, made discussion of 'labour hours' increasingly obsolete. In the 1980s computers proved capable of handling and rapidly processing huge amounts of data relating to large numbers of mass-produced products. At the same time, however, these and other related economic and technological developments opened up huge possibilities for more complex, flexible and specialised methods of production. These developments undermined both traditional employment contracts and the meaningfulness or applicability of labour time as a measure of economic value.

Furthermore, they undermined the viability of central or collective planning. Stiglitz (1994, p. 205) noted that in the technological evolution of the world economy, there may have been only 'a short window of time, the period of heavy industry associated with steel, autos, coal, and so on, in which some variant of socialism may have been able to work'. In this period, the degree of quality variation and complexity was not too great to pose insurmountable problems in the meaningful formulation and use of aggregative measures of output, and output per hour. But beyond this time, the level of complexity has increased to the point that the economy can no longer be placed under the deliberative control of any group or planning agency (Luhmann, 1982).

CAN SOCIALISM LEARN?

There is a strong argument that the greatest weakness of all attempts to dispense with the market in centrally planned systems has been the loss of dynamic, rather than static, efficiency. This argument has empirical support in studies of the former Soviet bloc. Peter Murrell (1991) argued from empirical data that the former 'Communist' countries were apparently no less efficient in allocating resources than capitalist societies. Where they lagged was in terms of dynamic efficiency: the ability to innovate. Dynamic efficiency concerns not the allocation of existing resources but the potential for dynamic and transformative growth.

Despite the criticisms of the former Soviet system by Adaman, Cockshott, Cottrell, Devine and others, their proposals suffer from the same defect. There is an insufficient appreciation of both the role of tacit knowledge and the need for shared experiences and cognitive frameworks in order to communicate technological and other information.

Their proposals rely exclusively on explicit, readily codifiable and communicable, knowledge. Ironically, if economic and technological knowledge really was of this character, then there would be stronger arguments for the exclusive use of contracts and markets, as well as a seemingly greater possibility of completely centralised planning. If knowledge was readily communicable, then contracts and markets would be less problematic, just a collective planning would be more feasible. Despite their intentions, Lange and others in fact demonstrated that empiricist notions of knowledge do not support socialist planning but a massive and unacceptable indifference concerning the institutional structure and cultural content of the socio-economic system.

The proposals to subject a large number of decisions to the open deliberations of committees (Adaman and Devine), or to the calculations of computers (Cockshott and Cottrell), both ignore a key feature of socio-economic reality and misunderstand the nature of knowledge. Socio-economic systems are essentially and unavoidably built up of historically layered and densely entangled institutions and routines. The more advanced the society, then the more complex the institutions and the more dense the entanglement. These institutions store and support both tacit and explicit knowledge. In customs and traditions, the knowledge of the past is accreted. The idea that this knowledge can be readily extracted from its institutional carriers, and freely codified and processed by a committee or by a computer, perpetuates a fatal error of Enlightenment thought: that such matters can largely be made subject to reason and deliberation; and that the mind may soar free of all the habits, preconceptions and institutions – of which in fact it is unavoidably obliged to make extensive use.[27]

Like many others, Adaman, Cockshott, Cottrell and Devine were clearly motivated by a strong moral opposition to the market system. Strangely, however, they were all forced to admit a place for genuine markets in their proposals for an ideal society. Adaman and Devine admitted a role for markets in the vaguely defined and non-dynamic zone of economic allocation. Cockshott and Cottrell (1993, p. 214) 'make no apology for advocating a market in many items of personal consumption'. Yet, while admitting the market, they too did not refrain from a generalised deployment of anti-market rhetoric. There are the warnings against 'the recent tide of right-wing pro-market opinion ... market socialism reflects not a bold new conception on the part of socialist theorists, but a damaging accommodation to the dominance of the right' (ibid., p. 216). In their work, markets in general, rather than capitalist markets in particular, were seen as the source of inequality and exploitation. Yet if markets, in general, are the problem, then why not press for their total abolition? Such inconsistencies are typical. Indeed, from its inception, socialism has failed to resolve the conundrum of the market.

In the socialist literature as a whole there is little recognition that vastly different types of market may exist, often with very different consequences in terms of the distribution of income and wealth and the tenor of the prevailing social culture. A very similar error is committed by the zealous advocates of the market system. It is to the possibility or otherwise of an individualistic and market-dominated utopia that we turn in the next chapter.

Before we move on, there is an important additional question: to what degree do the failures of the former Eastern Bloc constitute, or illustrate, the failures of 'socialism' *per se*? Some socialists avoid this question completely, by simply declaring that the Soviet or Chinese Communist systems have nothing to do with socialism in its true or original meaning.[28] Of course, leaders such as Christ, or Mohammed, or Marx cannot be blamed for all the actions carried out in their name. Furthermore, an ideology such as Marxism cannot be condemned for all the crimes committed by the regime of a Stalin or of a Pol Pot.

But that is not the end of the matter. The fact is that the Russian, Chinese, Cambodian and other revolutions were inspired by a vision of an economy based on common ownership of all means of production and subject to an all-embracing plan. This vision is traceable to founding socialist thinkers such as Owen and Marx. Accordingly, these revolutions were eventually followed by attempts to build a version of such a planned economy. As this economic project was based on misunderstandings concerning the role of key economic mechanisms or institutions, then these revolutionary movements, despite their noble intentions, were always heading unwittingly towards some form of impasse. Such an impasse would precipitate a severe political crisis. A revolutionary government would attempt to consolidate its power. It may make moves to crush dissent. One possible outcome would be totalitarianism and terror. Although the original socialist doctrine cannot be blamed for all the excesses and atrocities carried out in its name, and this chain of events is subject to no iron law of inevitability, it did help to create the attendant circumstances. The original misconception and practical economic failure created the circumstances and the opportunity.[29]

To repeat: we cannot condemn the original socialist project simply on the basis of the excesses of the totalitarian regimes of the twentieth century. But the Soviet and Chinese experiments do tell us a great deal about the general problems within this design, particularly concerning central planning, and the role of property and markets in sustaining politico-economic diversity. To understand that experience we do need to understand the limitations of the original socialist project. If socialism is to survive at all it must overcome its congenital *agoraphobia* – which means, literally, 'fear of markets'. It has to learn to inhabit open systems and open spaces.

61

3

THE ABSOLUTISM OF
MARKET INDIVIDUALISM

Never, on this Earth, was the relation of man to man long carried
on by Cash-payment alone. If, at any time, a philosophy of
Laissez-faire, Competition and Supply-and-demand, start up as
the exponent of human relations, expect that it will end soon.

Thomas Carlyle, *Past and Present* (1847)

The New Right accepts the economism of classical liberal thought.
It thereby ignores, or cannot cope with, that 'non-contractual
element in contract' which Durkheim, drawing in fact on conservative ideas, long ago identified. Market institutions, as an
Oakeshottian conservative would also argue, cannot prosper in an
autonomous way. They imply norms and mechanisms of trust,
which can be protected by law but only to a limited degree by
legal formulations.

Anthony Giddens, *Beyond Left and Right* (1994)

Many people believe that a 'free market' system is more 'natural' than
any form of socialism. Socialism is often said to be dangerously interventionist, whereas leaving things to the undirected sway of markets is to
leave them to their allegedly 'natural' course. Even if it were persuasive,
this view is of strikingly recent origin. The idea of maximising individual
liberty, within a system of private property that is co-ordinated by the
market, is much more recent that the ancient idea of holding property in
common. Admittedly, the basic idea of individual liberty can be traced
back to Antiquity. But liberty was not always tied in with private property and markets.

When were the notions tied together? The first stage was the development, as outlined by Crawford B. Macpherson, of a theory of 'possessive
individualism' in England in the seventeenth century. According to this
novel idea – originally promulgated by Thomas Hobbes, James
Harrington and John Locke – there was 'a conception of the individual as
essentially the proprietor of his own person or capacities, owing nothing
to society for them' (Macpherson, 1962, p. 3). But 'possessive individu-

alism' did not itself bestow the notion that individual rights and liberties must be sustained and protected by maximising the use of the market and minimising state power. Although they favoured the use of markets, Hobbes, Harrington and Locke accepted a substantial political and economic role for the state. The idea of transferring overall economic regulation to the market, and minimising the role of the state, emerged later. The notion that the market could be so pervasive, and could play such a crucial regulatory role in society, first appeared in the eighteenth century. The idea of holding property in common, and regulating society according to some kind of plan, is more than two thousand years older.

In 1714 it was a blast of heresy – for which its author suffered virulent attack and legal censure – for Bernard Mandeville to argue in *The Fable of the Bees* that private vices can lead to public virtues. Following this, a 'decisive contribution' to market-based individualism appeared in 1776; *The Wealth of Nations* by Adam Smith was an early 'account of a self-generating order which formed itself spontaneously if the individuals were restrained by appropriate rules of law' (Hayek, 1978, pp. 124–5). Like socialism, free-market individualism has its roots in the eighteenth-century Enlightenment. It picked up from the Enlightenment the threads of individual liberty, absolute property rights and equality under the law, and wove them together into its visionary fabric of a market system.

As noted in the preceding chapter, the word 'individualism' was coined in 1820s, in the same decade that 'socialism' appeared in English. The idea of individualism has fed off its adversary ever since. Existing together in a symbiotic relationship, and sharing similar Enlightenment roots, the two terms have often shared fundamentally the same common and sometimes questionable presumptions. For instance, as the one has stressed common property, the other has typically emphasised the importance of ownership by individuals. Despite this obvious difference, they both in these guises have shared the common presumptions that the absolute *ownership* of all key economic and other assets is both possible, and that the form of ownership – whether individual or collective – is crucially important. Although seemingly diametrically opposed, they have existed in many respects on the same conceptual plane. Other examples of the uncannily common underlying assumptions of much 'socialist' and 'individualist' thought are elaborated further below. It will also be shown that some of the reasons why socialism and market individualism are defective are common to them both.

This chapter does not address all varieties of 'individualist' philosophy.[1] It is confined to the modern tradition of 'market individualism' which, from Mandeville and Smith to Nobel Laureates Friedrich Hayek and Milton Friedman, has seen the widespread use of 'the market' as the solution to fundamental political and economic problems. This is an individualistic utopia, in which private property is ubiquitous and competitive markets mediate most or all economic activity. This utopia of 'market individualism' is criticised here, and on the grounds of its unfeasibility as well as its undesirability.

In many mainstream economics textbooks there are discussions of the limits of free-market solutions to economic problems. Typically, this textbook critique of universal reliance on the market is based largely on the idea of 'externalities'. We are invited to consider the social and environmental cost imposed by a car driver who pollutes the air and adds to road congestion. The car driver does not individually suffer most of that environmental cost: it is imposed on others. The market does not impose a penalty on the driver that is commensurate with the social cost. The decision to drive the car will be taken with regard to the costs and benefits for the individual driver, not for society as a whole. This is an example of what is termed an 'externality'.

Among mainstream economists there are broadly two types of policy response to this problem. The first, based on alleged 'market failures', follows the work of neoclassical economist Arthur Pigou (1920) and others. In this approach, ways in which the market system fails to take into account social or environmental costs and benefits are identified. The market failures approach aims to identify such externalities and to use measures such as road taxes, fuel taxes, and so on to attempt to alleviate the problem. In general, this approach relies on the use of government legislation, the tax system, and informed experts to estimate the economic costs and benefits involved.

A second approach emerged in the 1960s and is generally associated with the 'Chicago school' of economists (Coase, 1960; Demsetz, 1967). It takes earlier inspiration from some members of the Austrian school, particularly Ludwig von Mises (1949). Here the policy focus is on the creation and distribution of clearly defined 'property rights'. Proponents of the 'property rights' approach argue that pollution, congestion and resource depletion can be dealt with by creating property rights in such resources, and in the environment itself, and by allowing the market – and if necessary the courts – to deal with the problem. Hence the Pigovian externality problem is seen as arising primarily because of the absence of clearly defined and enforceable property rights. It is remedied in practice 'by rescinding the institutional barriers preventing the full operation of private ownership' (von Mises, 1949, p. 658). Over-grazing of common land and over-fishing of the sea, for example, are regarded as results of a lack of clear and meaningful ownership of such resources. With well-defined property rights, the owners of the rivers or open spaces that suffer pollution would have recourse to the courts to obtain compensation. The idea, therefore, is to internalise the externalities, by defining the rights of private property over all resources and amenities.

Severe information and enforcement problems are involved in each of these two approaches. Pigovian solutions required detailed expert information concerning externalities that is often very difficult to obtain. The property rights 'solution' relies on specific knowledge of violations, and extended means of enforcement, that are highly difficult to obtain and troublesome in practice.

There is a parallel here with the information problems that are involved with collective planning. Both socialism and market individualism face problems of information, incentives and enforcement. Just as some advocates of socialism have proposed hi-tech solutions to information, incentive and enforcement problems, so too have some advocates of free markets. Walter Block (1989), for instance, proposes the 'fencing off' of the atmosphere with laser beams to establish and enforce property rights, just as the American range was fenced by barbed wire in the nineteenth century. Here there is the same implausible reliance on a technological 'fix' just as with some advocates of complete, centralised planning. In both cases technology can be useful, but it is unlikely to resolve all the problems of information involved.

An enormous and often controversial literature exists on these issues and it is not feasible to attempt even a rudimentary survey.[2] However, it is possible to sidestep much of this literature because it is concerned with narrow conceptions and measures of economic efficiency. What concerns us here is the possibility of a market individualist utopia in which contracts and private property dominate much, if not all, of economic and social life. Questions of efficiency are important and should not be disregarded. However, several proponents of an individualistic utopia *define* efficiency in terms of the maximisation of individual liberty, which markets and property alone are alleged to provide. Furthermore, much of the mainstream discussion of economic efficiency invokes this term in a static sense, ignoring the issue of dynamic efficiency which is arguably more important.

THE LIMITS TO CONTRACTS AND MARKETS

A fundamental question that is relevant to the evaluation of a market-based economy is the limits to its co-ordinating system of contract and exchange.[3] One of the most important criticisms of market individualism in this regard was provided by the French sociologist Emile Durkheim. In his book *The Division of Labour in Society*, originally published in French in 1893, Durkheim saw the limitations of a contract-based system as lying within the contract itself. Durkheim argued that every contract itself depends on factors other than full, rational calculation: 'For in a contract not everything is contractual' (Durkheim, 1984, p. 158). He explained that whenever a contract exists there are factors, not reducible to the intentions or agreements of individuals, which have regulatory and binding functions for the contract itself. These factors consist of rules and norms that are not necessarily codified in law. In a complex world no complete and fully specified contract can be written. The parties to the agreement are forced to rely on institutional rules and standard patterns of behaviour, which cannot for practical reasons be established or confirmed by detailed negotiation. Typically, each person takes for granted a set of rules and norms and assumes that the other party does the same.

Note that Durkheim's argument hinges on the question of information. The relevant information pertaining to the typical contract is too extensive, too complex or too inaccessible for anything more than a small part of it to be all subject to rational deliberation and contractual stipulation. The more complex the decision situation, the greater amount of information involved, or the more tacit and dispersed the information itself, the more relevant Durkheim's argument becomes.

Even the most simple economic activities rely on a taken-for-granted network of institutional supports. Ludwig Wittgenstein used the example of signing a cheque. Such an act depends upon the prior existence of many institutions, routines and conventions – banks, credit, law – that are the practical antecedents and frameworks of socio-economic actions and interaction. Without such institutions the activity would be hopeless. Similar remarks apply to other everyday activities, such as posting a letter or waiting for a bus. In every case, we habitually and unthinkingly depend upon a dense network of established institutions and routines. All socio-economic activity enters 'complex entanglements of systems of interaction' (Boudon, 1981, p. 86).

It is widely argued that in such circumstances we rely to some degree on trust. By definition, if we trust another party that means we engage voluntarily in a course of action, the outcome of which is contingent on choices made by that other party. Such an outcome is typically beyond our own control. Study after study has shown that trust is vital for the world of business and trade.

Take, for example, the work of Stewart Macaulay (1963) on non-contractual relations between firms. It might be expected that in the world of business, relations-based trust and fellowship would be driven out by hard cash. Yet Macaulay found that capitalist firms rely on values such as 'common honesty and decency' when making deals. Even when high risks were involved, business people do not necessarily respond by insisting on a formal contract that covers every possibility. Macaulay's survey showed that a clear majority of orders did not involve formal contracts, and relied on word of mouth or established relationships between the persons involved.

Consideration of the uncertainty governing the employee–employer relationship in the capitalist firm led Alan Fox (1974) to argue convincingly that an element of supra-contractual trust is essential to industrial relations, and that a purely contractual system is not feasible.[4] To some degree the firm sets up a 'trust dynamic'. Likewise, Herbert Frankel (1977) examined the extent to which money itself is based on trust.

The functional role of morality and trust in a capitalist system has been stressed by a number of authors. Arthur Denzau and (Nobel Laureate) Douglass North (1994, p. 20) wrote:

> a market economy is based on the existence of a set of shared values such that trust can exist. The morality of a business person is a crucial intangible asset of a market economy, and its nonexistence substantially raises transaction costs.

Will Hutton (1995, p. 20) has elaborated a similar theme: 'The degree to which an economy's institutions succeed in underpinning trust and continuity is the extent to which longterm competitive strength can be sustained.' Institutional and cultural bonds have an essential function, even in an individualistic and capitalist economy.

Yet the whole point about co-operation based on trust, and trust itself, is that they are undermined by the over-use of contractual negotiation and of the cost calculus. As another Nobel Laureate, Kenneth Arrow (1974, p. 23), candidly remarked: 'Trust is an important lubricant of the social system. ... If you have to buy it, you already have some doubts about what you've bought.'

Neoclassical economists see such phenomena as trust and culture as resulting from utility maximising, individual agents. However, trust is not best explained as a phenomenon resulting simply from the rational calculation of costs and benefits by given individuals: something else is involved. It is not adequate to model 'trust', 'co-operation' or 'altruism' on the basis of the assumption that individuals are acting solely as the result of the maximisation of their individual utility. In this view, if an individual increases his or own utility by trusting, helping or co-operating with others then he or she is still self-serving, rather than being genuinely altruistic in a wider and more adequate sense.

Accordingly, as Fox (1974), Elias Khalil (1994) and others have argued, trust cannot be modelled exclusively within the universal contractarian framework of utility-maximisation and exchange upon which neoclassical economics is based. Such an approach misses the specific cultural features and social relations involved in the generation and protection of trust. It is thus unable to understand some essential and specific features of any capitalist system. Again, as in the case of the discussion of socialism in the previous chapter, we come up against the limitations of standard economic theory: its failure to find an adequate conceptual framework to understand key features of prominent economic systems.[5]

There is now a widespread opinion, supported by a substantial literature, that business depends for its own prosperity on a degree of trust and moral obligation. This means that an exclusive search for profit, without regard to trust and obligation, would be self-defeating. Furthermore, exclusively pecuniary evaluations are corrosive even for a capitalist society. Writing in 1962, François Perroux observed that:

> For any capitalist society to function smoothly, there must be certain social factors which are free of the profit motive, or at least of the quest for maximum profits. When monetary gain becomes uppermost in the minds of civil servants, soldiers, judges, priests, artists or scientists, the result is social dislocation and a real threat to any form of economic organisation. The highest values, the noblest human assets – honour, joy, affection, mutual respect – must not be given a price tag; to do so is to undermine the foundations of the social grouping. There is always a more or less durable framework of pre-existing moral values within which a capitalist economy operates, values which may be quite alien to capitalism itself.
>
> (Quoted in Albert, 1993, p. 104)

Much earlier, Joseph Schumpeter (1909) argued that even an atomistically competitive economy depends on irreducibly social values. Similarly, writing in the 1940s, Schumpeter (1976, pp. 423–4) argued shrewdly that 'no social system can work which is based exclusively upon a network of free contracts between (legally) equal contracting parties and in which everyone is supposed to be guided by nothing except his own (short-run) utilitarian ends'. More recently, Joseph Stiglitz (1994, p. 271) has warned: 'Capitalism, as it promotes self-interested behavior, may create an environment less conducive to efficiency.' For its very survival, capitalism depends upon a moral dimension, apart from cash payment and naked self-interest (Etzioni, 1988).

Especially as it hinges on the existence of a legally voluntary contract, the exercise of employer authority depends in part on the assumption of legitimacy by those involved. However, as Hannah Arendt (1958) has pointed out, the legitimacy of a form of authority can only be 'proven', in the eyes of those involved, by invoking a source beyond the authorities themselves. Hence capitalism throughout its history has relied to some degree – and in a manner depending on its specific local or national culture – on non-contractarian norms of obligation, whether of religious or secular origin. The legitimacy of the contractual system cannot itself be established by an appeal to the force or veracity of contract. This has important implications for the productivity and durability of the system.

Capitalism has survived because it has combined, in different ways and with different degrees of success, the fluidity and incentives of property exchange with sufficient social cohesion and moral obligation to keep the contract system going in a complex environment. In some ways – as Schumpeter, Karl Polanyi and others have noted – this is a precarious combination. The system depends on cash incentives and individual acquisitiveness. Yet if a social culture of greed and self-interest becomes overwhelming it threatens the bonds of duty and loyalty which are also necessary for the market system to function. If social cohesion and trust are undermined too far, then the system becomes incapable of sustaining the enduring social ties that are required for organisational cohesion and longevity, in the sphere of production and elsewhere.

This point is of vital significance for the understanding of the nature of the capitalist system. It is important to appreciate the different ways in which specific capitalist systems combine pecuniary motives with a sufficient culture of moral and social order. It is essential to understand the possibilities and limits of a creative tension between these two elements of the system. These issues are developed later in this book.

The key argument here, however, is to show that an overly individualistic market system is not feasible, and that if a self-orientated individualism goes too far then it undermines the very system that it typically extols. When Friedman (1962, pp. 1–2) argued that 'the country is the collection of individuals who compose it, not something over and above them', he revealed his conceptual blindness to emergent properties of the system that transcend individuals. These properties, furthermore, are necessary for the very survival of the capitalist system that he advocated.

THE INDIVIDUAL AS BEING THE BEST JUDGE OF HER NEEDS

Typically, market individualists frame both their analysis and their policies in individualistic terms. Accordingly, at the root of their utopia is the idea that the individual is generally the best judge of his or her own welfare. For example, Hayek (1944, p. 44) wrote:

This is the fundamental fact on which the whole philosophy of individualism is based. It does not assume, as is often asserted, that man is egoistic or selfish, or ought to be. It merely starts from the indisputable fact that the limits of our powers of imagination make it impossible to include in our scale of values more than a sector of the needs of the whole society, and that, since, strictly speaking, scales of value can exist only in individual minds, nothing but partial scales of values exist, scales which are inevitably different and often inconsistent with each other. From this the individualist concludes that the individuals should be allowed, within defined limits, to follow their own values and preferences rather than somebody else's, that within these spheres the individual's system of ends should be supreme and not subject to any dictation by others. It is this recognition of the individual as the ultimate judge of his ends, the belief that as far as possible his own views ought to govern his actions, that forms the essence of the individualist position.[6]

The important germ of truth in this argument should not be overlooked. Personal knowledge, perceptions and values are to an important degree dissimilar, from individual to individual. The individual has intimate knowledge and evaluations of her circumstances which are not shared – and cannot be shared fully – by others. For this reason there is a case for a degree of individual autonomy, and a strong argument against the universal claims of a paternalistic ruler or state. To some degree, individual autonomy should be reinforced by limited rights to hold and trade private property. Although these limits are a matter of controversy, the general case for *some* individual property is today denied by very few. The fact that individuals have intimate knowledge of their situation, and that circumstances vary from individual to individual, has major implications for any utopian project, especially concerning the preservation of liberty and the regeneration of diversity. We shall return to this theme at a later stage.

What concerns us here is the view that the individual, and their capacity to make judgements concerning their needs over a wide and virtually unlimited range of issues, can be taken as given and for granted. Within a wide and vaguely defined zone, and throughout adult life, it is assumed that the individual has unchallengeable knowledge of what is best: he is 'the ultimate judge of his ends'. It is assumed that his preferences are entirely 'his own' and without rival 'ought to govern his actions'.

The answer to these individualist tenets has existed as long as the word 'individualism' itself. It is the response associated with Robert Owen, Karl Marx and other socialists: the idea that the individual is not an isolated innocent but socially formed. The individual is not an atom, but an organic part of society: necessarily gaining interpretations, meanings and values through social interaction with others. This point is important even if we eschew socialism. The contracting individuals that are central to market individualism have to acquire in society the capacity to seek wealth and make trades. The very autonomy that we cherish becomes possible and viable only through social interaction with other human beings. As John Dewey (1935, p. 39) observed:

> The underlying philosophy and psychology of earlier liberalism led to the conception of individuality as something ready-made, already possessed, and needing only the removal of certain legal restrictions to come into full play. It was not conceived as a moving thing, something that is attained only by continuous growth.

In order to participate in society as an individual, we have to go through an extensive period of learning and socialisation. Socialisation is more than mere incorporation into society. It means the acquisition of categories and habits of thought and action, by which we make sense of the world and constitute our own individuality. From the moment we are born we experience the world through others. We mimic. We acquire a language. We begin to assimilate a shared symbolic order. Our sense of identity and being depends upon social interaction.

Crucially, individual knowledge of available choices is also generated through social interaction. For the individual to make use of any information, it is necessary for them to use conceptual frameworks and categories, to invest it with meaning. These concepts are part of the heritage of our culture and language, and are acquired through learning and socialisation. We perceive much of the world through language and symbols that are acquired through social interaction. The values and purposes which give meaning to our desires and intended actions are necessarily formulated in such a social language. This is much more than an argument that individual choices and preferences are affected by powerful institutions or mass media advertising. Our choices and preferences reflect the social character of individuality itself.

We are moulded by our social culture, with all its quirks and limitations. For example, a culture in which the belief prevails that women are inferior to men will not invest adult women with sufficient self-confidence and authority to aspire for their emancipation. A society that preaches that everyone has a pre-ordained place in the social order is unlikely to encourage those of lower station to pursue their own self-development beyond traditional boundaries. The social character of individuality means that individual choices are not merely constrained, but are partially formed by, factors outside the individual. In these circumstances, the policy that the individual is generally the best judge of his or her ends may fail even to challenge, let alone undermine, such taken-for-granted phenomena as sexism or elitism. If we assume that the individual is generally the best judge of their needs then we take for granted not only the individual, but also their cultural circumstances.

The fact that we are immersed and socialised through a common social culture does not deny space for individuality and diversity. Our particular life-experiences and perceptions are unique. Nevertheless, we understand and perceive these unique experiences through socially acquired cognitive filters. This commonality on the basis of diversity allows communication and social interaction between distinct individuals.

Note also that these arguments do not necessarily lead us into a version of cultural, institutional and structural determinism. Some critics have reacted against individualism by proposing such a determinist view. However, it is a serious and widespread mistake to presume that any opposition to individualism necessarily leads to determinism. Some significant zone for individual discretion and choice can be retained. It is not being argued here that individual aspirations and choices are *entirely* formed by circumstances, but that they are *partially* constituted and guided by culture and institutions.

Some sophisticated market individualists may accept the above argument, as long as it retains this significant zone for individual discretion and choice. They would then go on to argue that, given this real zone of discretion, there is always a subjective agent, filtering and evaluating social influences, thus making the individual truly creative rather than merely reactive. The present author would find no disagreement with such a reaction.

The disagreement with the market individualist starts elsewhere, with some of the further conclusions that may be drawn. The notion that the individual is 'the ultimate judge of his ends' is compatible with the position argued in the previous two pages *only if* those judgements are recognised as socially conditioned, and not 'ultimate' in the sense of necessarily being final or unchallengeable. This severely qualifies any normative conclusions that may be drawn, by noting that individual choices result *in part* from past conditioning and (perhaps unchosen) circumstances. As a result, the views and preferences of any individual are never entirely 'his own', because the individual is not their sole author.[7]

The individual may always be the ultimate judge, but that does not mean that such judgements should never be overridden. In many *specific* cases it can be agreed that the individual's views and preferences 'ought to govern his actions'. But there is no basis for deducing such a *universal* principle from the preceding observations.

Furthermore, the argument concerning human subjectivity and discretion is neither necessary nor sufficient to establish the importance of markets. It is possible to accept the notion of 'free will' without accepting the utopia of the market individualists. After all, many socialists accept the reality of human choice, but believe (albeit wrongly) that markets can be largely or entirely replaced by 'democratic planning'. As we have seen in the preceding chapter, the key argument against such 'democratic planning' does not centre on human discretion and subjectivity but on *the nature of knowledge*. Hence the stress on human subjectivity is not sufficient to defend markets.

Neither is it necessary. Even if knowledge can be said to be 'social' rather than subjective, then the problem of the coordination, development and application of this knowledge remains, and the solution must involve markets rather than exclusive reliance on a collective plan. Even if human discretion or free will were illusory, then there would be a case for markets. Today there is a strong 'compatibilist' current of opinion among philosophers who argue that free will and determinism are compatible, for the reason that although our choices *are* in fact determined they *appear* to us to be free. Assume that, some time in the future, the combined work of neurophysiologists, psychologists, anthropologists and sociologists were to show that we have much less discretion over our choices than we believe: that many apparently 'free' choices could be explained by physiological or cultural mechanisms. Would this diminish a robust case for retaining markets in modern socio-economic systems? No. Furthermore, the economics profession today is full of pro-market determinists. Indeed, the 'economic man' of the neoclassical economics textbooks is little more than a taste-satisfying machine. Generally, a robust argument that markets are important and unavoidable in complex socio-economic systems is quite independent of the outcome of the philosophical debate between determinism and free will. The political battle between socialism and individualism has little to do with this debate or its outcome.

As argued in the preceding chapter, some markets are essential for a modern, dynamic economy. Where many market individualists go wrong is in seeing an atomistic subjectivism as a necessary theoretical foundation of any argument for markets. In basing their case on such allegedly universal behavioural or philosophical assumptions, they then attempt to jump to the universal conclusion that the market is the solution to all pressing economic problems. As well as the assumptions being questionable, the conclusion does not follow. The economic case for the market, or any other institution, does not spring from the general and enduring features of the human mind. Such an argument neglects the historical specificity and efficacy of institutions. Indeed, the theoretical defence of the need for some markets in modern socio-economic systems is too important to be left to the market individualists.

Neoclassical and Austrian proponents of market individualism are divided on several key philosophical issues. What unites them is their broad answer to the normative question of who should make choices. It is asserted that most choices should remain with the individual, without government constraint or interference. This stance is questioned by the fact that all choices are socially conditioned and circumscribed. If choices are left entirely to the individual, then existing social circumstances, as well as the individual, have to be taken for granted as well. The counter-argument is that, while individuals have genuine discretion, we cannot be indifferent to all the processes by which perceptions and preferences are formed, and the pressures of conformism and socialisation which frame and constrain their choices.

It is also crucial to note that, even by emphasising human discretion and subjectivity, market individualists do not get rid of the problem of deciding when the individual becomes an adequate judge of their own interests. Sensibly, the doctrine that the individual is the best judge of their own interests has to draw a line above infancy and adolescence, and proclaim that individuals below a particular age do not have this capacity. The same problem arises with the allocation of the right to vote in a democracy, and with the attribution of legal responsibility for one's actions. Infants are not allowed to trade, even if they evidently understand and say 'yes' to the proposed transaction. In each case an arbitrary line must be drawn, denying some rights or capacities to a subset of the population, and assuming that all the others are equally entitled to these rights and take full responsibility for their own actions. There are good reasons for drawing such arbitrary lines. But nevertheless they are arbitrary, and market individualists are forced to draw them with the rest of us, challenging their seemingly universal assumption that the individual is always the best judge of their interests.

LEARNING A CHALLENGE TO MARKET INDIVIDUALISM

The process of socialisation during childhood was emphasised in the previous section. But some form of socialisation continues during our adult life. Especially in a rapidly developing socio-economic system, individuals face changing institutions, rules and technologies. We are obliged to adapt to the evolving reality: we are required to learn.

The phenomenon of learning is another challenge to the doctrine that the individual is always the best judge of their interests. The key point here can be stated simply: how can individuals always be capable of such complete and superior judgements, concerning their interests at any given moment, when they are in the process of learning? The very act of learning means that not all information is possessed and that a fully informed judgement is ruled out. Furthermore, learning is much more than the acquisition of information; it is the development of the modes and means of calculation and assessment. This exacerbates the problem. Learning means that not only that we lack all relevant information but also the means by which we assess any information and reach a judgement can be improved at a later date. Assume that at Time B an individual changes their former perception of their wants or needs at Time A. Judgements concerning interests or wants at Time A may thus be revoked by the same individual at Time B. In short, the phenomenon of learning is antagonistic to the doctrine that the individual always knows best. Strikingly, it is the inadequate treatment of learning that is also one of the crucial problems with the socialist proposals for complete central or collective planning. Both socialism and market individualism share this common defect.

The issue of learning and 'the learning economy' is one of the major themes of this book. Learning is treated inadequately in the neoclassical economics. Basing itself on the idea of 'rational economic man', neoclassical economics has thereby to assume that the individual is capable of appraising all the known choice possibilities. Furthermore, each choice is appraised on the basis of a fixed 'preference function' which is mysteriously bestowed upon the individual at the beginning of their (adult?) life. Typically, neoclassical economics treats learning as the cumulative discovery of pre-existing 'blueprint' information, as stimulus and response, or as the Bayesian updating of subjective probability estimates in the light of incoming data. With the 'input' of this new information we are supposed to determine mechanically our choices on the basis of our unchanging preference function.

In some versions of this story, such as those advanced by Nobel Laureate Gary Becker (1996), the function is already 'there', ready to deal with unpredictable and unknowable circumstances. For instance, it already 'knows' how to react to the technology and inventions of the next century. Miraculously, its parameter space already includes variables representing the ideas and commodities of the future. Mysteriously, it has already learned how to recognise them. The question is posed as to what is meant by learning in such circumstances when we already know essentially what is to be learned. Such a conception of learning must be sorely inadequate.[8]

Instead of the mere input of 'facts', learning is a developmental and reconstitutive process. Learning is much more than a process of blueprint discovery, stimulus-response, input enhancement or statistical correction. Learning is a process of problem-formulation and problem-solving, rather than the acquisition and accumulation of given 'bits' of information 'out there'. Learning is not the cumulative addition of knowledge upon a *tabula rasa*: it entails getting rid of old ideas as well as acquiring new ones. Developing the capacity to unlearn, and learn anew, is itself a part of the learning process. This process involves conjecture and error, in which mistakes become opportunities to learn rather than mere random perturbations. Neoclassical economics has fundamental problems with learning because the very notion of 'rational learning' is problematic. Learning involves adaptation to changing circumstances, in contrast to the neoclassical emphasis on equilibrium.[9]

The treatment of learning by Hayek and other Austrian school economists is a significant improvement on the neoclassical approach. Instead of an empiricist treatment of information, in which information flows readily into the memory banks of the individual, Hayek in particular insisted that information is always perceived through a cognitive framework. This framework may be unique to the individual and different people may interpret the data in different ways. At least in this respect, Hayek made break from empiricist conceptions of knowledge. Furthermore, Hayek recognised that learning is not simply the progressive acquisition of codifiable knowledge. Especially in his later years, he was influenced by the work on tacit knowledge by Michael Polanyi (1958, 1967).

Nevertheless, the Austrian improvement on the neoclassical approach is inadequate. Essentially, Hayek treated knowledge as a scarce and dispersed resource. For instance, for Hayek (1948, pp. 77–8) the 'economic problem of society ... it is a problem of the utilization of knowledge which is not given to anyone in its totality'. Notice that, for Hayek, it was a problem of the 'utilization' of knowledge, not its creation or construction. For Hayek the focus was on the discovery and use of existing knowledge, particularly that represented by price information. It is significant that – even in his mature work – Hayek treated learning largely as a 'discovery procedure'. The metaphor of discovery, significantly repeated at length by Hayek and other Austrians, suggests that the facts are 'out there' and independently given, just as an explorer discovers new topographical features of the earth. When Hayek (1978, pp. 181–8) argued that 'economic competition ... is a method of discovering particular facts' or 'a process of exploration', he was using formulations entirely compatible with empiricism. He assumed that the facts, like mountains and new species, were out there simply to be discovered. Hayek thus re-admitted an empiricist notion of learning, rather than seeing it as an interactive, adaptive and creative process resulting from both objective circumstances and subjective cognition.[10]

It is ironic that Hayek has replicated the same empiricist mistake committed by some socialists, who, in their arguments for planning, also underestimate the processes and problems involved in the attribution of meaning to data, and in the development and communication of knowledge. We noted in the preceding chapter that Fikret Adaman and Pat Devine (1994, 1996b) used the very same metaphor of 'discovery' in reference to knowledge in their arguments for 'democratic planning'.[11]

Nobel Laureate James Buchanan and Viktor Vanberg (1991) have criticised Hayek on this point, arguing that the market is a 'creative process' as well as a 'discovery procedure'. What Buchanan and Vanberg failed to recognise, however, was that socio-economic systems do not simply create new products and perceptions. *They also create and re-create individuals.* In a learning economy, the individual not only changes their purposes and preferences, but also revises their skills and their perceptions of their needs. Both in terms of capacities and beliefs, the individual is changed in the process.

Much follows from this important point. Learning is more than the discovery or reception of information: it is the reconstitution of individual capacities and preferences, tantamount to a change in individual personality. Today, we may not like opera, but after exposure to it we may acquire a taste for the art form. Learning *reconstitutes* the individual. Douglas Vickers (1995, p. 115) rightly identified this as a key 'difficulty that economic analysis has been reluctant to confront'. He stressed that with changing knowledge and learning 'the individual is himself, economically as well as epistemologically, a different individual'. A similar proposition is underlined in an important study of innovation and knowledge in the Japanese firm by Ikujiro Nonaka and Hirotaka Takeuchi (1995, p. 10):

> Once the importance of tacit knowledge is realized, then one begins to think about innovation in a whole new way. It is not just about putting together diverse bits of data and information. It is a highly individual process of personal and organizational self-renewal. ... In this respect, the creation of new knowledge is as much about ideals as it is about ideas. ... The essence of innovation is to re-create the world according to a particular ideal or vision. To create new knowledge means quite literally to re-create the company and everyone in it in an ongoing process of personal and organizational self-renewal.

To repeat, learning changes preferences, goals, capacities, skills and values. All this undermines the view that the individual can be taken as given and is always the best judge of their own interests. It weakens all approaches to welfare economics that are based upon such presuppositions. The standard welfare-theoretic basis of much economic policy is thus called into question (Gintis, 1972, 1974; Steedman, 1980).

Mainstream and Austrian economists have readily addressed the phenomenon of socio-economic development: the evolution of human society from its primitive to more complex forms. What they have been reluctant to do, however, is to admit the possibility of the reconstitutive development – through learning – of each human individual: the possibility that individual goals, preferences and personalities may change.

There is another sense in which learning is a challenge to market individualism. In a capitalist economy there can be no futures markets for labour. The existence of such markets would tie the worker to an employer in a future period. Such bonding would be illegal and if extended could slip into a form of voluntary slavery. The absence of futures markets for labour is an important safeguard of the freedom of the employee. However, it constitutes a 'missing market' and a potential inefficiency, by standard criteria, of the market system. Under capitalism there is no futures market for human skills. The danger, therefore, is that the system will underinvest in human learning and education. As Alfred Marshall (1949, p. 470) pointed out in his *Principles* (first published in 1890):

we meet the difficulty that whoever may incur the expense of investing capital in developing the abilities of the workman, these abilities will be the property of the workman himself: and thus the virtue of those who have aided him must remain for the greater part its own reward.

If skills are to be adequate, then their development under capitalism must unrealistically depend, as Marshall put it, 'in great measure on the unselfishness of the employer'. If markets are a cure for this problem, as the market individualist might suggest, then these futures markets for labour can only be established at the cost of human liberty.[12]

Another limitation of the treatment of learning in both Austrian and mainstream economics is the lack of recognition of its social character. Hayek rightly stressed that each individual is unique, and that individual knowledge is framed by cognitions that are acquired in a unique life history and in particular environment. The mistake is then to go on to conclude that knowledge is merely individual or subjective. While unique, each individual interacts with others, acquires a social language and acquires concepts, values and norms that are common to a particular social culture. Furthermore, it is not possible to learn most of these ideas except through social interaction.

This fact is widely recognised in modern anthropology and cognitive psychology. Prominent in the cognitive literature is a social, cultural and institutional dimension that is difficult to avoid. Cognitive theorists emphasise that while living and acting in the world we are continuously in receipt of a vast amount of sense data. The attribution of meaning to this apparently chaotic mass of data requires the use of acquired concepts, symbols, rules and signs. Perception is an act of categorisation, and in general such categories are learned.

Whilst cognitive theorists differ in their interpretation of cognitive phenomena, and in the significance they attribute to the social dimension in the acquisition of concepts, it is rarely excluded. They are generally agreed that much of our conceptual apparatus is acquired through social interaction with others. There is a widespread acceptance, for example, that our education and socialisation in early years help us to develop our innate perceptual equipment and form a conceptual basis to understand and act in a complex and changing world.

Just as our knowledge of the world does not spring out alive from the sensory data as they reach the brain, only through the acquisition of a complex and culturally specific conceptual framework can sense data be understood. The acquisition of knowledge about the world is not simply an individual but a social act. As cognitive psychologists Jack McLeod and Steven Chaffee (1972, pp. 50–1) wrote:

Each of us likes to think of himself as being rational and autonomous.

> Our ideas seem to be peculiarly our own. It is hard for us to realize how little of our information comes from direct experience with the physical environment and, how much comes only indirectly, from other people. ... One's prior beliefs, attitudes, and values form a frame of reference – a kind of cognitive map for interpreting reality that precedes and controls the exchange of information and influence.

Developments in philosophy have pointed in a similar direction. For example, in his later writings, Ludwig Wittgenstein (1972) argued against the notion of private language games. This pointed towards the social character of language and meaning, and consequently of our knowledge of the world. Such arguments undermined the idea that knowledge is a matter for the individual alone, and that perception and understanding are simply an issue for the individual facing the world. Learning is not the absorption of sense data by individual atoms.

Among others, Chris Argyris and Donald Schön (1978) have pointed out that learning is not simply information absorption. Learning begins when individuals discover that their mental models, which indicate the expected consequences of particular actions under a variety of assumed conditions, are in error. Because of discrepancies between actual and expected outcomes, people may revise their models: that is, they learn. New models have to be acquired. This is often done through intensive interaction with others, within the common culture of an organisation or society.

Market individualists have warned against such arguments, seeing them as promoting a paternalistic state which 'knows better' than the individual. However, such reactions involve a misinterpretation. To argue that the individual does not always know what is in their best interest does not imply that the state necessarily knows any better. Furthermore, the argument that knowledge is social should not be taken to imply that it can be readily held and deliberately manipulated by society. Knowledge has both individual and social dimensions, reinforced by the social character of individuality itself.

Neither the individual nor the state can be omniscient. What is remarkable about both socialism (in the traditional sense) and market individualism is that they both presume a high degree of capability and enlightenment on behalf of one or the other. In socialism the planning committees are assumed to be capable of knowing what is best. In market individualism the individual alone is ascribed with this capability. It is necessary to escape from this false dichotomy.

All knowledge is partial and provisional. Society, and the individuals within it, are involved in an interactive and mutually interdependent process where all are learning on the basis of conjecture, error, experience and experiment. It is suggested here that this open-ended and experimental process cannot be encapsulated adequately in these two systems.

Neither a universal system of planning (democratic or otherwise), nor a set of atomistic individuals acting solely through markets and contracts, can give full reign to experimentation and learning. They require a set of varied and pluralistic economic structures, frowned upon by centralist socialists and market individualists alike.

MARKET INDIVIDUALISM AND THE IRON CAGE OF LIBERTY

A problem for both market individualism and centralist socialism is that of prescribing their own limits. If common ownership and planning are morally and economically superior, then, without undermining these tenets, on what basis can any exceptions be admitted? Likewise, the unqualified statements that individuals are always the best judges of their own welfare, and that markets and contracts the best way of organising an economy, admit no exceptions. Market individualism extols the virtues of voluntary exchange and concedes little ground to any alternative system. Economists of the Austrian school, for example, have typically argued that no form of mixed economy is possible. As von Mises (1949, p. 259) put it:

> The market economy or capitalism, as it is usually called, and the socialist economy preclude one another. There is no mixture of the two systems possible or thinkable; there is no such thing as a mixed economy, a system that would be in part capitalist and in part socialist.

Hayek (1944, p. 31) similarly argued that:

> Both competition and central direction become poor and inefficient tools if they are incomplete; they are alternative principles used to solve the same problem, and a mixture of the two means that neither will really work and that the result will be worse than if either system had been consistently relied upon.

It was assumed by these authors that the extension of commercial contracts and individual property rights is both possible and desirable, and even necessary if civilisation is to survive.[13] Furthermore, any move towards socialism and central direction would undermine liberty and propel modern society down the slippery slope towards totalitarianism.

The problem is, however, that there is not a hermetic division between 'competition' and 'central direction'. As Thomas Robert Malthus noted long ago in his *Principles of Political Economy*, 'the line' between interference and non-intervention in economic matters is difficult to draw in practice. He thus remarked that 'it is impossible for a government strictly to let things take their natural course' (Malthus, 1836, p. 16). Crucially, the generation or extension of markets requires an activist government, creating and regulating new institutions and routines. The experience of governments that have aimed to extend 'free markets' and to 'roll back the state' confirms this. The Italian Marxist, Antonio Gramsci (1971, p. 160) wrote in his *Prison Notebooks* of 1929–35:

> it must be made clear that *laissez-faire* too is a form of State 'regulation', introduced and maintained by legislative and coercive means. It is deliberate policy, conscious of its own ends, and not the spontaneous, automatic expression of economic facts.

The early development of the modern market system itself required substantial state and legal intervention. Writing at the end of the nineteenth century, John Commons (1965, pp. 77–8) accepted that:

> slavery and serfdom disappeared, not because of state prohibition, but primarily through the economic fact of the wastefulness of coerced labor in competition with voluntary labor. ... But while this may cause the disappearance of slavery and serfdom, it is not enough to bring about the positive rights of freedom. ... It required the positive interference of the state in the creation of legal rights, such as free industry, free movement, free employment, free ownership of property, to enable individuals from the serf caste ... to be free from direct coercion.

The neoclassical economist Léon Walras (1936, p. 476) also saw the state as playing an essential role in the inauguration and maintenance of competition: 'Instituting and maintaining free economic competition in society is a work of legislation, and of very complex legislation, which the state must undertake.'

A related and more extensive argument was developed by Karl Polanyi (1944). In his classic study of the British Industrial Revolution and the rise of capitalism, he argued that the initial expansion of the market was very much an act of the state. The extension of markets during the ascendancy of capitalism in the nineteenth century did not mean the diminution of the powers of the state, but instead led to increasing intrusion, meddling and regulation by central government. Strong pressure grew up from all quarters to restrict markets through legislation: to limit the working day, ensure public health, institute social insurance and regulate trade. Not only to provide social cohesion but also to ensure the smooth working of the market itself, the state had to protect, regulate, subsidise, standardise and intervene.

Accordingly, even in Victorian Britain, the introduction of free markets, far from doing away with the need for control, regulation and intervention, enormously increased their range. This was true *a fortiori* in France and Germany, where markets were often imposed from above and generally more closely regulated. Even in the supposed model 'free market' economy of the United States, there was systematic state intervention in the nineteenth as well as the twentieth century (Kozul-Wright, 1995).

As well as an active state, a 'free' market system requires substantial cultural preconditions. It requires the rational, calculative mentality of a market system, the 'habit of mind begotten by the use of money' (Mitchell, 1937, p. 306). It requires, further, ingrained cultural norms protecting the sanctity of property and contract. The preservation and reinforcement of this pecuniary and property culture require action by both the state and individual. Consequently, as Leszek Kolakowski (1993, p. 12) has argued:

> The radically liberal state is a utopia whose principles finally turn against themselves. The liberal state cannot survive by the mere inertia of a nonintervening, neutral policy; it demands – as it has been affirmed many times over – the vigilant attention of its citizens, of all who feel responsible to the common cause, *res publica*. And the civic virtues on which the viability of the liberal state depends are not simply born spontaneously; they demand a type of 'indoctrination'. A perfectly neutral liberal state is unviable.

It is thus no accident that governments committed to market individualist ideas have often taken an authoritarian tone, such as in Britain in the 1980s under the premiership of Margaret Thatcher. This government, dedicated to the alleged virtues of the 'free' and 'spontaneous' market, itself orchestrated a sustained ideological and cultural campaign, and effected a substantial extension and centralisation of institutionalised government authority (Hutton, 1995).

All this confirms the earlier insights of Malthus, Gramsci and Polanyi. The creation and maintenance of private property rights and functioning market institutions require the sustained intervention of the state to constrain or eject economic forms and institutions that are antagonistic to private ownership and the market system. 'Free' markets have to be preserved by an activist and effective state. This explains the apparent paradox that 'free market' policies can lead to a substantial centralisation of economic and political power. Market individualist policies in practice actually threaten both economic and political pluralism and must grant extended powers to the central state machine. Even when it is silent, the threat of totalitarianism lies within a zealous and unrestricted individualism. Authoritarianism may be necessary to impose a liberal order: This is the 'iron cage of liberty' (Gamble, 1996).

It does not end there. The widespread implementation of 'free market' ideas creates a system with a relative degree of structural uniformity, dominated by pecuniary relations of contract and trade. Of particular relevance here is the experience of American capitalism. This has been discussed by Louis Hartz (1955) and by Albert Hirschman (1982), who saw a problem of potential or actual stagnation, of both a moral and an economic kind, in the type of developed market individualism that is most advanced in the United States of America: 'Having been "born equal," without any sustained struggle against ... the feudal past, America is deprived of what Europe has in abundance: social and ideological diversity. *But such diversity is one of the prime constituents of genuine liberty'* (Hirschman, 1982, p. 1479).

Liberalism driven to extremes may become its opposite. A fervent market individualism drives social forms and ideologies, other than free-market individualism and private property, to the margins. The variety of structures and institutions is threatened. The diversity proclaimed by devotees of the competitive and individualistic golden age is thus a fake. A monolithic order arises, embracing an uniformity of both ideology and structure, the tyranny of the like-thinking majority and a 'colossal liberal absolutism' (Hartz, 1955, p. 285).

Not only may a policy of 'free markets' threaten personal freedom: the rhetoric of 'free markets' often obscures the difference between personal freedom and freedom of contract. As Frank Knight (1921, p. 351) observed, with a few possible exceptions,

> it is doubtful if there is a more abused word than 'freedom'; and surely there is no more egregious confusion in the whole muddled science of politics than the confusion between 'freedom' and 'freedom of contract.' Freedom refers or should refer to the range of choices open to a person, and in its broad sense it is nearly synonymous with 'power.' Freedom of contract, on the other hand, means simply absence of formal restraint in disposal of *'one's own.'* ... The actual content of freedom of contract depends entirely on what one *owns.*

The confusion of personal freedom, on the one hand, with 'freedom of contract' and 'free markets', on the other, has led to a policy focus on enlarging the licence of the property owners, rather than the general enhancement of true personal freedom, autonomy and power. Genuine freedom of choice is constrained for all if there is a limited set of institutional alternatives, and for many if they are consigned to a relatively powerless state of poverty, unemployment or social exclusion.

It should again be emphasised that the unqualified goal of the 'free' market ignores the fact that trade and markets rely on other antiquated and often rigid institutions and other traditional features of social culture. Despite their policy differences, both Marx and Hayek ignored the necessary 'impurities' in a market system. In contrast, Schumpeter (1976, p. 139) argued persuasively that such older institutions provide an essential symbiosis with capitalism, and are thus 'an essential element of the capitalist schema'. Schumpeter's insight was to show that capitalism depends on norms of loyalty and trust which are in part descended from a former epoch. The institutions of contract and trade are not enough.

There are many examples of essential, but non-commercial, spheres of activity within capitalism. One such example is the family, but this topic was awkwardly side-stepped by Hayek and other thinkers of the Austrian school. Not only is the family rarely analysed in any detail, but also some challenging normative issues are typically ignored. As Jim Tomlinson (1990, p. 131) pointed out, families 'are extremely problematic in their implications for liberty in Hayek's sense'. Hayek ignores the question of what kind of liberty is provided for children within this institution, as well as the implications for liberalism of a lifelong marriage contract between partners.

Generally, if contract and trade are always the best way of organising matters, then many functions that are traditionally organised in a different manner should become commercialised. This implies the widespread use of prostitution to obtain sexual gratification. It also suggests the production and sale, for commercial gain, of babies and children. Yet in modern democracies the sale of persons is regarded as slavery and is illegal.[14] Furthermore, prostitution is typically frowned upon, and is often legally restricted. Likewise, there are often legal limits to the commercialisation of such activities as surrogate parenting. Yet absolute individual liberty and freedom of trade must admit the possibility of prostitution, of the selling of babies, and even of voluntary enslavement. Assaulting our 'individual liberty' and 'freedom of contract', the central legislatures of most countries typically place bounds or prohibitions upon such activities.

Especially on these grounds, market individualism is not a conservative or traditionalist doctrine. Pushed to the limit, market individualism implies the commercialisation of sex and the abolition of the family. A consistent market individualist cannot be a devotee of 'family values'. There is thus an internal contradiction in the thinking of prominent proponents of market individualism such as Thatcher and Hayek. Their support for the family as an institution, and their wider devotion to tradition, is incompatible with their market individualism.[15]

The proponents of market individualism cannot have it both ways. To be consistent with their own arguments, all arrangements must succumb to property, markets and trade. They cannot in one breath argue that the market is the best way of ordering all socio-economic activities, and then deny it in another. If they cherish family values then they have to recognise the practical and moral limits of market imperatives and pecuniary exchange. Extreme market individualists rarely recognise such boundaries. Even those, such as Hayek and Friedman, who would cautiously confine, here and there, the power and scope of the market, refrain from attempting any general statement of the limitations of market arrangements. For them, the market is an unalloyed good; just as for many socialists it is an unalloyed evil. The truth lies elsewhere.

THE ALLEGED UBIQUITY OF THE MARKET

The firm, likewise, presents a severe analytical problem for market individualists. Marx noted in *Capital* that the division of labour was present both in society at large and within the capitalist firm. In the former, the division of labour sustains market exchange. In the latter, 'labour is systematically divided in every factory, but the workers do not bring about this division by exchanging their individual products' (Marx, 1976a, p. 132). This foreshadows the similar remark by Nobel Laureate Ronald Coase (1937, p. 388): 'Within a firm, these market transactions are eliminated and in place of the complicated market structure with exchange transactions is substituted the entrepreneur-co-ordinator, who directs production.' Although from quite different theoretical perspectives, both Marx and Coase emphasised that commodity exchange and the price mechanism are absent within the firm.

However, many market individualists have neglected this fact, as if they were embarrassed by the ubiquitous limitation of the market mechanism within the very citadels of capitalism. Indeed, it is typical of market individualists to ignore the interior of the firm and the factory floor. According to them, what matters is the knowledge and imagination of entrepreneurs: ignoring the knowledge and imagination of workers. What matters to them is the liberty of the entrepreneur to trade on the market with minimum hindrance: ignoring the fact that the capitalist firm itself exists by virtue of the *exclusion* of genuine markets from within its boundaries.

The foundations of entrepreneurship are too important to be left to the market individualists. By their own logic, market individualists are forced to disregard the organisational structure of the firm, or to falsely imagine that markets exist inside it. To do otherwise would be to admit that a system as dynamic as capitalism depends upon a mode of organisation from which markets are excluded. As Marx and Coase both pointed out, the essence of the capitalist firm is that within it commodity exchange and the price mechanism are replaced by an employment contract between the workers and the corporation.[16]

There is widespread confusion over this issue, with many writers suggesting that the boundaries between the firm and the market are being eroded. This confusion allows market individualists to ignore the reality of non-market organisation in the private sector and bring everything there under the umbrella of market analysis. They can thus ignore

the reality of control and authority within the private capitalist corporation but remain critical of public sector bureaucracy and state planning.
Such misconceptions are aided by the lack of clear and adequate definitions of 'firm' or 'market' in social science.

Consider some frequently cited but misleading examples. Some firms
may use price indicators for internal accounting, and products may be
'exchanged' by one internal department with another. It may be
concluded that these are evidence of an 'internal market'. But typically
these exchanges do not involve the exchange of property rights. The
objects of 'exchange' remain the property of the firm. What are involved
are accounting transfers, rather than genuine commodity exchanges.
Even if a subdivision of the firm is delegated the power to enter into
contracts with outside bodies, legally it is the firm as a whole that is
party to the contract. The subdivision is merely exercising delegated
powers: it acts 'in the name' of the corporation, and the corporation as a
whole is legally responsible for its liabilities under the agreed contract.

Pursuing a typical line of argument, Ken-ichi Imai and Hiroyuki Itami
(1984) discuss the alleged 'interpenetration of organization and market'
in Japan. However, they define both market and organization without
any reference to property rights or contracts, referring instead to factors
such as the durability of the relationship and the use or otherwise of
price as a major information signal. By this flawed methodology it is not
difficult to find elements of so-called 'organisation' in the highly structured and regulated 'markets' of Japan, and to find elements of an
alleged 'market' inside many firms. These conclusions follow, however,
from the inadequate definitions of 'market' and 'organisation' in the first
place. In contrast, superior definitions of these terms would lead to the
conclusion that markets – in Japan and elsewhere – are often organised
to a greater or lesser degree, but that any market is a quite different type
of organisation from the property-owning and contracting legal entity of
the firm.

There is also a widespread supposition that 'internal labour markets'
exist inside the firm. However, even the pioneers of the concept, Peter
Doeringer and Michael Piore (1971, pp. 1–2) admitted that 'internal labor
markets' are not governed primarily by the price mechanism but by 'a
set of administrative rules and procedures'. David Marsden (1986, p. 162)
went further: 'internal labour markets offer quite different transaction
arrangements, and there is some doubt as to whether they fulfil the role
of markets'. Much of the loose talk about 'internal markets' within firms
derives from a sloppy use of the term 'market' which, unfortunately,
pervades mainstream economics today. In terms of genuine, regular and
organised exchanges of goods or services, 'markets' are rarely, if ever,
found *within* the firm.

To repeat: confusion over the nature of markets and exchange allows market individualists to ignore the reality of non-market organisation in capitalist firms and to understand everything in 'market' terms. In addition, it allows others, often from a different ideological perspective, to ignore legal and contracting realities and to focus exclusively on questions of control. 'Market' and 'organisation' become again confused. The universal conceptual focus becomes one of co-ordination and control rather than legal contract or price. Just as market individualists stress price and contract to the neglect of other relations, the obverse position neglects them in favour of the ideas of control and co-ordination. Both viewpoints are inadequate.

As an example of the obverse position, Keith Cowling and Roger Sugden (1993, p. 68) defined the firm as 'the means of co-ordinating production from one centre of strategic decision-making'. This definition entirely neglects the legal aspect of the firm and focuses exclusively on the matter of strategic control. As an illustration, consider the case of a large corporation which has a number of smaller subcontractors and suppliers – such as Benetton, or Marks and Spencer. According to Cowling and Sugden's definition, the large corporation, plus all the subcontracted suppliers, are together regarded as a single firm. However, this is simply – and confusingly – shifting the definition of 'the firm' from one type of phenomenon to another. Clearly, we require two words, one to describe productive organisations constituted as legal entities, and another to describe the entire clustered complex of a dominant organisation above a network of subordinate subcontractors which are to some degree under its control. It is simply confusing to shift the word 'firm' from the former – with which it is normally associated – to the latter. One mistaken reason for doing so, is to notice, following George Richardson (1972) and others, that the relationship between large corporation and the subordinate contractors is more durable and intensive than a typical market relationship. This valid and important observation does not change the argument, however. An enduring relationship between a dominant firm and a subordinate subcontractor is not an open market relationship, *but it is still one of commodity exchange, involving the legal transfer of property rights*. It remains a relationship of commodity exchange between two distinct firms. It is *not* evidence of commodity exchange or a 'market' *within* a single firm.

In modern economies there are many cases of complex forms of interaction between productive agencies (Ménard, 1996). However, on inspection most of these 'hybrid' cases turn out to be interlocking relations or networks between multiple and distinct legal entities, rather than a single, encompassing, organisation or firm. Part of the problem here is the failure to recognise that markets are a special case of commodity exchange (Hodgson, 1988). If we adhere to the false dichotomy between firms and markets then truly we have some difficulty in classifying non-market contractual relations between firms. The real-world ensemble of such interactive relations is neither a firm nor a market so – according to the logic of this false dichotomy – it must assume the 'strange' form of a 'hybrid'. The first error here lies in the assumption of a dichotomy, ignoring the third (Richardsonian) possibility of non-market contractual exchange. The second error is to have an inadequately precise definition of the firm, even to the extent that the difference between 'firm' and 'industry' may potentially dissolve.

Recognition of the exclusion of markets and commodity exchange from within the firm is important for several reasons. In particular, it is an important illustration of how non-market and market modes of co-ordination are *combined* within all real-world capitalist systems. However, the notion that they are combined is quite different from the assumption that they have become a strange hybrid, with the merged qualities of both. The firm exists as a distinct legal entity: it is technically a 'legal person'. It owns its products and sells or hires them to others. It enters into contracts with its workforce and its customers. Accordingly, its external relations are dominated by commodity exchanges or markets. Internally, however, the firm is not ruled primarily by prices, markets or commodity exchange. It is primarily a sphere of administration, organisation and managerial direction.

ORGANISATIONS AND THE CONDITIONS FOR INNOVATION AND LEARNING

The capitalist firm has been so successful and dynamic for the last two centuries precisely because it combines these two attributes: externally, the price-oriented exchange of products, and internally, the organisational mobilisation and development of labour power. *The spectacular historic success of this symbiotic combination of dissimilars places both the market individualists, and the socialist opponents of the market, in theoretical difficulties.* Against the prescriptions of market individualists, the capitalist firm internally is neither a market, nor simply a collection of trading individuals. Yet, contra the anti-market socialists, the firm depends on markets and commodity exchange for much of its autonomy and competitive stimulation.

We have to consider why the exclusion of market and exchange contracts from within the firm is conducive to its dynamism. Markets play an important and flexible signalling and co-ordinating role in modern economies. An organisation does not merely co-ordinate. It has a number of often ill-defined but nevertheless explicit objectives. In pursuit of these goals, the management of the organisation divides up its problems and tasks into different sub-tasks and delegates them to its subdivisions (Kay, 1997). In any complex, uncertain and dynamic context this must involve novelty and learning, to cope with the new and the unexplained. Within the firm, as Massimo Egidi (1992, p. 167) has argued:

> the execution of plans requires the ability to interpret and adapt these general ideas or to reject them, and to solve the new problems arising from attempts to put plans into practice; a continuous process of transmission of information and knowledge among subjects is thus required and their coordination is possible only if a learning process takes place ... coordination involves essentially a process of organized learning.

A number of case studies and other analyses lead to the conclusion that a major reason for the existence of the firm rather than the market is that because it provides a relatively protected cultural enclave in which wider group and individual learning can take place. In contrast, a market relationship would undermine inter-personal communication and both individual and group learning. As David Teece and Gary Pisano (1994, p. 539) put it:

> The essence of the firm ... is that it displaces market organization. It does so in the main because inside the firms one can organize certain types of economic activity in ways one cannot using markets. This is not only because of transaction costs ... but also because there are many types of arrangements where injecting high powered (market-like) incentives might well be destructive of the cooperative activity and learning.

This is an important argument. It suggests that much learning depends on co-operative and enduring relationships that may need protection from the potentially corrosive power of markets.

This argument is consistent with our understanding of joint ventures, strategic alliances and other close, enduring, contracts between firms. This 'relational contracting' is a form of commodity exchange, but it is not market exchange (Dore, 1983; Goldberg, 1980b; Richardson, 1972). The fact that these relational contracts are of benefit to the firm is consistent with the view that, by contrast, market exchange would place co-operation and learning on a much more precarious foundation. Relational contracting can provide greater flexibility than is found within the firm, but it preserves a degree of enduring co-operation that could be undermined by open markets.

Relationships between firms can also be based on informal and non-contractual co-operation. Much innovation is based on informal dialogue and ongoing negotiation. There is much informal exchange of technical know-how. Word of mouth, informal networks and imitation are thus very important in modern economies (Czepiel, 1975; von Hippel, 1987,

1988; Martilla, 1971). Much of this dialogue is not bound by formal contract nor primarily motivated by price signals (Stiglitz, 1994, p. 85). In a learning economy, the culture of co-operation within the firm spills over and affects relationships between firms as well.

It is vitally important to understand that technical knowledge is highly contextual. It is often impossible to understand the nature or value of an innovation unless one has intimate or direct knowledge of the situation to which it relates. This places limits on *both* central planning and the market system as mechanisms to stimulate innovation. It is often difficult or impossible for one unit to convey to another what precisely is required. Unless there are shared ideas and patterns of experience, there may be unmanageable dissonances between the cognitive frameworks used by the two sets of agents. Because of the lack of these common habits and conceptions, they may not, in effect, speak the same language.

As a result, in a market system, vertical integration between firms may occur. Vertical integration means pushing back the boundaries of the market and commodity exchange, and enlarging the organised, non-commodified zone of activity. By combining producer and user in the same organisation, closer bonds and deeper communication can develop in this shared organisational culture (Foss, 1993; Hodgson, 1998b, 1998c; Sah, 1991).

The need for innovation places some limits on the use of the market mechanism and its price signals. Nevertheless, it is necessary to explain why markets retain a role, and why not all mergers between firms are advantageous. The market can nurture a competitive stimulus for invention. Without market competition, firms can be featherbedded and deprived of the impetus for innovation and change. On the other hand, innovation and detailed product development typically require the sustained social bonding and common organisational culture of an integrated team. With a significant degree of success, the capitalist firm embraces both these imperatives. But in doing so it denies the universal precepts of market individualism.

If this argument is correct, then market individualism is defective in the area of learning and innovation, and in precisely the same domain as centralist socialism. Both systems, albeit for different reasons, would stultify learning and technological development. Both systems, to overcome this defect, must impose limits to the zone of application of their core principles, and admit a substantial degree of internal, structural diversity. This issue is explored in regard to market individualism in the next section.

MARKET INDIVIDUALISM AND THE INTOLERANCE OF STRUCTURAL DIVERSITY

In practice, all socio-economic systems contain a diversity of regulating principles. Even capitalist systems that are dominated by a libertarian and free-market ideology prohibit the buying and selling of political votes, frown upon prostitution and pornography, and limit the sale of dangerous drugs. Slavery, and lifetime employment contracts without possible exit, are illegal, even if both parties consent to the deal. Such voluntary transactions are prohibited, despite the fact that mainstream economics teaches us that such transactions generally increase the utility and so-called 'welfare' of the sellers as well as the buyers.

As noted above, market individualists such as von Mises and Hayek reject any dilution of the market-based system that they advocate. If the prerogatives of property and the market are undermined, they argue, then the system is in danger of a runaway development towards state domination and totalitarianism. However, in failing to place limitations on its own ethic, market individualism once again offers a mirror image of the centralist socialism that it is so keen to undermine. Both philosophies search for pure and extreme solutions. In each case the practicality of the chosen utopia is thereby nullified. John Maynard Keynes made a related criticism of Hayek's market individualism. In response to the appearance of Hayek's book *The Road to Serfdom*, Keynes wrote to Hayek on 28 June 1944:

> you greatly under-estimate the practicality of the middle course. But as soon as you admit that the extreme is not possible, and that a line has to be drawn, you are, on your own argument, done for, since you are trying to persuade us that as soon as one moves an inch in the planned direction you are necessarily launched on the slippery path which will lead you in due course over the precipice.
>
> (Keynes, 1980, pp. 386–7)

A pure socio-economic system, of whatever kind, is not feasible. Advocates of the capitalism have to admit a place for non-market institutions such as the family or the firm. In practice, all economies are mixed economies. Market individualists have often claimed that they are devotees of diversity, variety and experimentation in economic life. However, the diversity they proclaim is a constrained diversity of individuals, working within a single, common and overwhelming pecuniary culture. Any structural diversity of different forms of economic arrangement – self-employed enterprises and capitalist firms alongside worker co-operatives and public corporations, for example – is denied. Yet such structural diversity could sustain a much greater degree of cultural and behavioural variety than the system advocated by market individualists. The ideology of market individualism has been stubbornly resistant to a genuine economic pluralism.[17]

A major achievement of von Mises, Hayek and other Austrian school economists has been to explain the essential co-ordinating function of the market in the modern economy. On this basis, they have shown that a system dependent entirely on centralised planning would not work, at least rationally or efficiently. Yet they fail to consider the limitations of the opposite extreme, and the dependence of the market itself on its institutional and cultural context.

Hayek and von Mises were wrong to presume that *no* central planning was useful or viable. They showed that knowledge is tacit and dispersed, and cannot be all gathered together and processed at the centre. True. But not all knowledge is of this kind. For instance, particular types of knowledge are usefully and functionally centralised or organised in a network, so that they are obtainable by all. Why else do we have telephone directories, or the Internet, for example? Not all knowledge is irrevocably dispersed and there is at least an indicative or co-ordinative role for central authority, even in a market system. The arguments of Hayek and von Mises against a mixed economy are unconvincing. And contrary to many Austrian school economists, acceptance of much of the economic calculation argument against centralist socialism is compatible with a belief in the viability of a mixed economy.[18]

Market individualists argue that the successes of modern capitalist economies are due to the driving forces of market competition and the harnessing of individual initiative. However, any modern economy is much more than, and owes its dynamism to considerably more than, entrepreneurial individuals and market transactions. As Nobel Laureate Herbert Simon (1991) has argued with great eloquence, the texture of modern capitalism is dominated much more by non-market organisations and their internal relations, than by markets and their contractual haggling. And a forceful and extensive work, William Lazonick (1991, p. 335) points to 'the growing importance of collective organization for successful capitalist development'. Likewise, in a penetrating study of leading industrial nations, Lane Kenworthy (1995) attributed capitalist success not to unrestrained free markets but to institutions combining competition with co-operation. As Wolfgang Streeck (1989, 1992) has elaborated, highly productive economies are both flexible and 'institutionally rich'. A capitalist economy is much more than individualistic atoms and their interactions. Market individualists downplay the institutional and cultural embeddedness of human cognition and action (including the activity of trade itself). In neglecting this embeddedness of knowledge and skill, they make the same mistake as the advocates of central planning.

Admittedly, the market continues to play an indispensable role in the modern era, but it is deceptive to suggest that it is the primary arena of social interaction for most agents. In contemporary economies much more daily activity is internal to organisations and outside markets. True, the growth of capitalism is characterised by the development and extension of markets on a global scale. Yet, in comparison to all earlier socio-economic systems, the growth in organisational diversity, complexity and size is also a vital feature of the capitalist order. Along with many other modern economists, market individualists obscure this fact with their individualistic and contractarian bias.

EVALUATING DIFFERENT TYPES OF MARKET INSTITUTION

As shown in the preceding chapter, socialists have traditionally believed that it was possible to remove the market from the centre of economic life, to relegate it to the periphery or to banish it entirely. It was believed that competition, greed, inequality and exploitation were the inevitable consequences of the market system. From a diametrically opposite position, advocates of market individualism suggest that almost every social problem can be resolved by instituting markets and property rights. Each position is the mirror image of the other. What is contested here is the possibility of a sweeping evaluation of all market-based systems, reaching a single set of universal conclusions, whether negative or positive. Both absolutist positions are rejected.

Instead, it is important to consider each market system in its historical and cultural context. The experiences in Britain and America contrast not only with each other but also with, for example, Germany, Japan and much of the remainder of the world. Capitalism emerged in Britain in a fractured and class-divided society, where an individualist ideology had been long established. The United States of America adopted many of the political ideas of English individualist thinkers such as Thomas Hobbes and John Locke. An even stronger individualism could be realised on the wide-open plains, lacking any indigenous remnants of a feudal past. With loosely structured communities and highly mobile individuals, America fostered a particularly individualistic form of capitalism, where money – rather than God, nation or duty – was the pre-eminent criterion of personal success.

The dominance, for more than a century, of Anglo-American individualism, has led to the assumption that such an individualistic culture is a necessary concomitant of capitalism itself. We must ask, however, the extent to which the characteristics of greed and competitive individualism were specific to the prevailing capitalist cultures of the time, rather than to capitalism as a socio-economic system *per se*. Clearly, markets and capitalism do encourage pecuniary values and specific forms of behaviour over others. However, the scope for cultural and behavioural variation within these social structures has been widely underestimated, by social theorists of all varieties and political hues. The rectification of this error is a major theme of this book.

It is important to emphasise that the market itself is a social institution. Different types of market institution are possible, involving different routines, pricing procedures, and so on. Furthermore, each particular market is entwined with other institutions and a particular social culture. Accordingly, there is not just one type or set of markets – perhaps differentiated merely by the type and degree of market structure and competition according to textbook typology – but many different markets, each depending on its cultural and institutional context. Among others, Werner Sombart, the German historical school economist, recognised this vital point. He argued that the concept of exchange depended for its meaning on the social and historical context in which the exchange takes place:

> 'Exchange' in the primitive economy (silent barter), 'exchange' in the handicraft economy, and 'exchange' in the capitalist economy are things enormously different from one another. ... Price and price are completely different things from market to market. Price formation in the fair at Vera Cruz in the seventeenth century and in the wheat market on the Chicago Exchange in the year 1930 are two altogether incomparable occurrences.
>
> (Sombart, 1930, pp. 211, 305)[19]

Although Sombart may have here overemphasised the degree of historical specificity, and neglected the common generic features of all markets, his statement is an important corrective to the notion of a pure and undifferentiated market that is promoted by both its critics and its supporters.[20]

Similar points were made by American institutionalists such as Sumner Slichter, an influential labour economist who became president of the American Economic Association in 1941. Slichter (1924, pp. 304–5) complained of neoclassical theory in the following terms: 'The influence of market organization and institutions upon value is ignored. No distinction, for example, is made between forms of market organization' such as 'the stock exchange or the wheat market' or 'the labour market'. Similarly, he lamented: 'Interest theories are constructed without reference to the credit system, to corporate or to governmental saving'. On these points and others, institutionalists had very similar views to their historical school forebears.

In at least one respect, this rejection of the concept of the undifferentiated market goes against the view of Karl Polanyi (1944) who seemed to regard the market as an alien imposition on traditional society, and 'disembedded' in social relations. Bernard Barber (1977, p. 27) rightly criticised Polanyi in the following terms:

> Polanyi describes the market as disembedded [but] ... this is a somewhat misleading image. While the modern market economy

could be viewed as somewhat more structurally differentiated, somewhat more concretely separate, from the other institutional subsystems of society, this image diverts attention from the basic sociological fact that all types of exchange institutions are interdependent with their environing value patterns and other institutional subsystems.

Rectification of the misleading image of the disembedded market does not negate the overall importance and stature of Polanyi's contribution. Polanyi also argued that the development of the market was not a spontaneous matter, and it required deliberate intervention and legislation. This important point is not undermined by Barber's criticism. Indeed, Polanyi's central message could be reinforced by a recognition of the cultural and context-dependence of the market system. In discussions of Polanyi's work, Mark Granovetter (1985, 1993) argued that *both* specific institutional structures *and* the general forces of supply and demand – common to all markets – affect market outcomes.

Accepting the existence of some general market principles, it must be emphasised that the nature of the market always depends to some degree on its cultural and institutional substance and context. This argument goes against typical views of both pro-market libertarians and anti-market socialists. Marxian and Austrian economists, for example, despite their diametrically opposed political evaluations of the market, both treat markets as a straightforward, uniform, context-independent, entities. Both groups fail to differentiate markets on the basis of their varied institutional arrangements and prevailing cultures.[21]

In the real world, and even in a single country, we may come across many different examples of the market, and we rarely treat them uniformly. We encounter fish and vegetable markets, organised and regulated by the local council, or car boot markets (or tag sales) with some goods of dubious origin. The use of designated tokens to purchase baby-sitting services within an organised baby-sitting collective is an example of a market. There are also markets for the sexual services of prostitutes. Such examples of markets are clearly quite different in substance and connotation. We should thus refrain from judging them with identical moral yardsticks.

Consider two stylised cases. The first concerns a society with an individualistic culture and a high degree of geographic mobility. Acts of purchase and sale involving the same pairs of participants are of limited frequency. Accordingly, in participating in market exchanges, we are less disposed to be concerned about the personal welfare and personal feelings of the person with which we are engaging in trade. It is less likely that we shall meet that person again, and we are disposed to focus almost exclusively on the price and characteristics of the good being traded. In contrast, in a less mobile system, with a less individualistic culture, there may be a propensity for two persons engaged in trade to develop a closer personal relationship. In such circumstances we may develop a degree of general concern for the other person that is independent of wants or desires relating to the trade itself. The other person becomes *more* than simply a means to an end.[22]

Instead of recognising the important role of different possible cultures and trading customs, opponents and advocates of the market have focused exclusively on its general features. Thus, for instance, Marxists have deduced that the mere existence of private property and markets will itself encourage acquisitive individual behaviour, with no further reference to the role of ideas and culture in helping to form the aspirations of social actors. This de-cultured viewpoint has difficulty explaining, for example, the high degree of acquisitiveness and commodity fetishism that prevailed in the allegedly 'socialist' Eastern Bloc, with decades of official propaganda extolling co-operation and shunning greed, long before the collapse in 1989. It has difficulty, furthermore, in recognising the often limited and contrasting versions of consumerism that prevail in different capitalist societies. To some degree, both Marxists and market individualists underestimate the degree to which all market economies are unavoidably made up of densely layered social institutions.[23]

Although it is reasonable to consider and evaluate the generic features of the market, such an analysis only gets us so far. A full evaluation of each market, and each market system, requires consideration of its own institutional and cultural features and contexts. This task is traditionally neglected both by socialists and by the opposing advocates of the 'free' market. Socialists denigrate markets and 'market forces', without realising that different market institutions can work in quite different ways. The general and the specific levels of analysis are conflated. When it comes to questions of evaluation and the formulation of policy, this confusion of the general with the specific is nothing short of disastrous.

Similar and related arguments concerning the general importance of context and culture in socio-economic systems are pursued later in this book. An important immediate objective here has been to begin to open the door to the possibility of some variant of what some may describe as 'market socialism'. Such a possibility is explored in more detail in Chapter 9.

Diane Elson (1988) is one of the few socialist writers who has explored the possibility of reconstituting markets, rather than marginalising or abolishing them. She endorses the proposal for a basic income, paid unconditionally out of taxation by the state to all adults, partly on the grounds that it civilises the ethos and changes the balance of power in the labour market.[24] An extensive regulatory system, involving wide public participation, would enforce environmental and social standards in the market process. The proposal is to transform and 'socialise' the market, rather than to claim that it can, and should, be cast out of the socialist utopia. In contrast to prevailing notions found on both the right and left of the political spectrum, Elson recognised the fact that the market can take a wide variety of forms, and some of these are much more objectionable than others.

There is some justice in the accusation that market-based socio-economic systems can lead to increasing inequality of income and wealth. As Gunnar Myrdal (1957), Nicholas Kaldor (1967, 1972, 1978, 1985) and others have argued, cumulative processes of divergence are typical within market economies. However, the degrees and rates of divergence vary enormously. Accordingly, the degree of inequality of earnings, income or wealth can differ greatly from economy to economy. For example, a survey (OECD, 1993) of the distribution of earnings in several countries found that in 1989–91 there were substantial differences in the distribution of wage and salary incomes between different industrial countries, with the United States being the most unequal. In those years, the ratio between the lowest wage or salary rate in the first decile, and the lowest wage or salary rate in the ninth decile was about 5.6 in the United States, 4.4 in Canada, 3.2 in the United Kingdom, 3.0 in France, 2.8 in Japan, 2.4 in Germany, 2.1 in Italy and 2.1 in Sweden.[25] Hence, by this measure, the United States is a much more unequal capitalist economy than Japan, Germany, Italy and Sweden. This same survey showed that wage inequality had increased substantially in the 1980s in the United States and the United Kingdom, but not nearly to the same degree in other countries. Germany, in particular, showed no increase of inequality in the 1980s (Nickell and Bell, 1996). Capitalist economies exhibit substantial variations in inequality, and changes in inequality, of both income and wealth.[26]

Markets cannot be given an adequate moral evaluation independently of their peculiarities, or of their specific context. It is striking that both the extreme supporters and the extreme critics of market systems, like Hayek on the one hand and Marx on the other, pay little attention to the analysis of varieties of capitalism. Both are thinkers of great analytical depth, but when it comes to an evaluation of the more immediate problems and practicalities – such as the appropriate policy outlook for the existing national governments – they both lose us in grand and useless platitudes such as pure markets, on the one hand, and socialist revolution, on the other. Both fail to understand that the market is a good servant but a bad master. There is no recognition of the variety of forms and consequent policy discretion within capitalism itself. It is to this issue that we now turn.

Part II

THE BLINDNESS OF EXISTING THEORY

4

THE UNIVERSALITY OF MAINSTREAM ECONOMICS

Political economy is not a body of natural laws in the true sense, or of universal and immutable truths, but an assemblage of speculations and doctrines which are the result of particular history.

Thomas E. Cliffe Leslie, *Essays in Political Economy* (1888)

We have paid a big price for the uncritical acceptance of neoclassical theory.

Douglass North, *Institutions, Institutional Change and Economic Performance* (1990)

Part II of this book further challenges the view that we have reached 'the end of history'. But this is not done by arguing for the feasibility or superiority of any alternative to capitalism. Instead it is argued that the pronouncements of the 'end of history' ignore the tremendous variety of forms of capitalism itself. In addition, a theoretical blindness to the immense variety within the modern system is curiously engendered by influential economic theorists from both the right and the left. In particular, although both Karl Marx and Friedrich Hayek have contributed an enormous amount to our understanding of how capitalist systems function, they both sustain a view of a singular and purified capitalism. They both ignore the fact that variable systemic impurities are essential to the functioning and development of the system. Overall, there is a gaping hole in even the most inspired theoretical analyses of capitalist systems.

Furthermore, there is no unique or optimal combination of subsystems and institutions within capitalism that will necessarily triumph over other combinations. Although not all capitalisms are equal in performance, the advantages or efficiencies of one type of capitalism over another are typically dependent on their historical path and context and thereby none can be said to be ultimately superior to all the others.

It is not intended here to survey the variety of forms that capitalism presents today, or has passed through over the last two hundred years. This work is not a comparative study of institutions, structures and

101

cultures. Instead, this part is an examination of different theoretical approaches to the analysis of capitalism, involving an explanation why some are essentially blind to that variety, and why others offer some means to perceive and understand the differences that exist in the real world.

In these three chapters we search for theoretical and conceptual lenses to perceive and understand the actually existing variety of different forms of capitalism. This chapter considers the limitations of neoclassical and Austrian economics in this area. Neoclassical economics is defined as an approach which assumes rational, maximising behaviour by agents with given and stable preference functions, focuses on attained, or movements towards, equilibrium states, and excludes chronic information problems.[1]

The economics of Marx will be addressed in the following chapter. Chapter 6 considers institutional economics in the Veblenian tradition. The conclusion will be reached that the 'evolutionary' views of the American institutional economist Thorstein Veblen and subsequent institutionalists provide an important counter to the differing analytical approaches of Marx, Hayek and others. The institutionalist approach of Veblen and others is found to have a potentially superior, albeit underdeveloped, stance on the three points.

Each chapter addresses three issues in turn: first, the extent to which each theoretical system relies on universal or specific theoretical assumptions; second, the place of non-market and non-commercial relations within the theoretical analysis; and third, the general conception of the link between human actors and social structures in the theory.

Although they are quite different in many respects, it is possible to address both Austrian and neoclassical economics together in this chapter. It is important to acknowledge that Austrian and neoclassical economics differ on issues as fundamental as the purpose and nature of economic theory. However, it is striking that they share similar universalist claims concerning their core assumptions. They both place the purposeful and (in some sense) 'rational' individual at the foundation of the analysis of all economic phenomena. Furthermore, in the crucial *Methodenstreit* (clash of methods) of the 1880s, the Austrian economist Carl Menger attacked the denial, by members of the German historical school, of universal assumptions and laws in economics. In turn, Menger's attack reinforced the belief of many neoclassical economists – including Alfred Marshall and Lionel Robbins – in an universalist view on the nature and scope of economic theory.

Other leading neoclassical theorists include Léon Walras, William Stanley Jevons, Philip Wicksteed and Vilfredo Pareto. As the most sophisticated exemplar of the Austrian approach, Hayek's views on these issues are discussed in more detail than other Austrian theorists such as

Carl Menger and Ludwig von Mises. It is to the question of universality versus specificity in economic theory that we now turn.

THE UNIVERSALIST CLAIMS OF MAINSTREAM ECONOMICS

Since its inception in the end of the eighteenth century, and despite its theoretical development, mainstream economics has always had a serious limitation. Classical economists such as Adam Smith and David Ricardo, neoclassical theorists such as Walras, Jevons and Marshall, and Austrian school economists such as Menger, von Mises and Hayek, all saw the economy as a kind of interrelated system. However, despite this, they gave inadequate theoretical recognition of the possibility or implications of different types of system through history. In their analyses the starting point was universal rather than particular. It was the general idea of human nature and 'moral sentiments' (Adam Smith), or an ahistorical conception of the individual with exogenously determined 'tastes and preferences' (neoclassical theory) or with similarly given 'purposes and individual knowledge' (the Austrian school). Analysis was founded upon these universals in the pursuit of general and ahistorical truths.

After neoclassical economics was established by Walras, Jevons and others in the 1870s, this defect became explicitly codified in formal theory and is replicated in the textbooks to this day. Instead of the characteristic features of a given socio-economic system, the starting point of neoclassical economics is the ahistorical, abstract individual. Axioms about human behaviour were derived by 'introspection' rather than investigation, leading to the construction of general theories, impoverished in terms of their concreteness, relevance and practical application. The features and institutions that characterise a given economy did not form part of the core analysis. Specific institutions and social relations were either forgotten or framed in terms of prior universals.

In starting from allegedly universal and ahistorical concepts, neoclassical economics fails to engage sufficiently with any specific socio-economic system. Its very generality becomes a barrier to a deeper understanding of capitalism or other systems. Instead of attempting to confront a particular economy, or *real* object, it becomes confined to a remotely abstract and artificial *idea* of an economy: the economy in general.

Influenced by both neoclassical and Austrian economists, Robbins (1932) encapsulated this approach with his influential but ahistorical definition of economics as the 'science of choice'. The 'economic problem' became one of the allocation of scarce means in the pursuit of given ends. Individuals are assumed to have fixed and given utility functions and they exchange resources with each other to maximise their own utility. Such a framework universalises the concepts of 'exchange' and relative 'price'. It is alleged that a wide range of social and economic phenomena – and in all types of present, past and future economy, as long as they afflicted with the seemingly ubiquitous problem of 'scarcity' – can be analysed in these terms. As Robbins (1932, p. 20) himself put it: 'The generalisations of the theory of value are as applicable to the behaviour of isolated man or the executive authority of a communist society, as to the behaviour of man in an exchange economy.' All differences between these systems are 'subsidiary to the main fact of scarcity'.[2]

Since Robbins, the universality of neoclassical assumptions has been pushed to enterprising extremes. Experimental work with rats and other animals (Kagel *et al.*, 1981, 1995) has 'revealed' that animals have downward-sloping demand curves, just like humans. Gary Becker (1991, p. 307) has argued extensively that: 'Economic analysis is a powerful tool not only in understanding human behavior but also in understanding the behavior of other species.' Similarly, Gordon Tullock (1994) has claimed that most or all organisms – from bacteria to bees – can be treated as if they have the same general type of preference function that is attributed to humans in the economics textbooks. Neoclassical economists thus assume that other animals and organisms are 'rational' too. Accordingly, core neoclassical concepts are not only applied to all forms of human society since we evolved from apes, but also to a large portion of the animal kingdom as well. Seemingly, we now have 'evidence' of the 'rationality' of everything from the amoeba upwards!

Even confined to human societies, this relentless quest for universality gives rise to what is fondly described by its practitioners as 'economic imperialism'. This refers to the invasion of other social sciences with the choice-theoretic methods of neoclassical economics. It is argued that the core assumptions of neoclassical economics can and should be applied to a wide variety of fields of study, including politics, sociology, anthropology, psychology, history and even biology, as well as economics itself. It is based on the belief that the idea of 'rational economic man' is appropriate to social science as a whole. The case for the conquest of other social sciences and biology by neoclassical economists rests on the presumed universality of such ideas as scarcity, competition and rational self-interest.[3]

As discussed further below, these allegedly universal assumptions have been controversial since their inception. Thus the deductive schema based on universal axioms found in Marshall's *Principles* was opposed by a group of economists and economic historians including William Cunningham (1892, p. 493) at the end of the nineteenth century:

> The underlying assumption against which I wish to protest is ... that the same motives have been at work in all ages, and have produced similar results, and that, therefore, it is possible to formu-

late economic laws which describe the action of economic causes at all times and in all places.

This same criticism resonates to this day. It remains relevant because of the seemingly imperishable, universalist approach of both mainstream and Austrian economics.

UNIVERSALISM VERSUS REALISM IN HAYEK'S ECONOMICS

Hayek, for example, despite his incisive criticisms of much of mainstream economic theory, followed both the neoclassical school and other Austrian school economists by insisting that the starting point of economic theory was the allegedly universal features of the economic situation, rather than the essential features of a specific type of socioeconomic system. Alluding to the German historical school (that had influenced Cunningham, Leslie and others), he criticised such an alternative approach in the following manner:

> To start here at the wrong end, to seek for regularities of complex phenomena which could never be observed twice under identical conditions, could not but lead to the conclusion that there were no general laws, no inherent necessities determined by the permanent nature of the constituting elements, and that the only task of economic science in particular was a description of historical change. It was only with this abandonment of the appropriate methods of procedure, well established in the classical period, that it began to be thought that there were no other laws of social life than those made by men, that all observed phenomena were only the product of social or legal institutions, merely 'historical categories' and not in any way arising out of the basic economic problems which humanity has to face.
>
> (Hayek, 1935, p. 12)[4]

Presumably, in Hayek's view, 'the basic economic problems which humanity has to face' concern choice and scarcity. But on their own, these presumed universals tell us very little about specific institutions, such as private property and markets. They tell us nothing, furthermore, of different types of socio-economic system. In fact, any 'basic economic problems' are never themselves institution-free. Accordingly, when discussing these problems, many neoclassical and most Austrian school economists assume that the 'basic economic problems' of choice and scarcity can be realised only through the operation of markets and private property. It has thus to be assumed that these institutions have existed, to some degree, since the dawn of humanity.[5]

This confusion over the question of universal and historically specific categories has persisted through Hayek's writings, despite important shifts over the years in his methodological stance (Caldwell, 1988; Fleetwood, 1995; Lawson, 1994, 1996, 1997). Probably, the refusal to get tied down to specifics partially accounted for Hayek's (1982, vol. 1, p. 62) disapproval of the word 'capitalism' to describe the existing or his ideal society. He wrote, with a degree of vagueness, of the 'free system' and the 'Great Society' but it is nevertheless clear that he was referring to a system dominated by market exchanges and individual private property. But in turn, these terms were not adequately defined.

The confusion is exemplified in Hayek's treatment of the market. In fact, two different conceptions of the market appeared in his work. In some passages Hayek (1982, vol. 3, p. 162) supported the conception of the market as the general context in which competitive selection takes place. In this view the market is simply the forum in which individual property owners collide. The market was itself seen as bereft of institutions or rules: these appear on the market simply through the trading actions of the individuals concerned. The crucial question was left open how this long-standing general context of competition and trade itself originally evolved.

Criticising Hayek on this point, Viktor Vanberg (1986, p. 75) pointed out that the market 'is always a system of social interaction characterized by a specific *institutional framework*, that is, by a *set of rules* defining certain restrictions on the behavior of market participants'. Whether these rules are formal or informal the result is that there is no such thing as the 'true, unhampered market', operating in an institutional vacuum. 'This raises the issue of what rules can be considered "appropriate" in the sense of allowing for a beneficial working of the market mechanism' (ibid., p. 97).

Notably, the market itself is not a natural datum or ether, but is itself a *social institution*, governed by sets of rules defining restrictions on some, and legitimating other, behaviours. Furthermore, the market is necessarily entangled with other social institutions such as the state, and is promoted or even in some cases created by conscious design.[6] Given that markets are themselves institutions, then they may grow or decline like other institutions, and compete with them for resources and hegemony.

In his last book Hayek (1988, pp. 38–47) took the view of the market as one institution among others, rather than the over-arching context of competition. This may have corrected his earlier error but it created further theoretical problems. Hayek argued that the market is not itself the context of evolution but an evolved structure or order: a specific outcome of evolution itself. However, this interpretation left open the nature of the context in which the market emerges. To assume that the market itself emerges in a market environment suggested the unacknowledged possibility of a nested set of market structures in which competitive selection occurs: a market for markets.[7] But if this was the case then there must be another market in which the selection for this market for markets occurs, and so on, indefinitely. Clearly, this cannot go on for ever: there must come a point where the market is superseded. There must be a context other than the market in which selection occurs. If, by contrast, it is assumed that the market is always there as a context for the competitive battle, then Hayek was guilty of the same error as the neoclassical economists: endowing the specific phenomenon of the market with a spurious universality.

If the market itself evolves, then it is reasonable to pay significant attention to the possibility of the emergence of different kinds of markets, with varied structures and constituent rules. Yet Jim Tomlinson found that Hayek, along with most other economists including neoclassicals and Marxists, treated the market as an abstract principle, independent of its institutional and cultural integument. However, as noted in the preceding chapter, markets are highly varied phenomena. Consequently, as Tomlinson (1990, p. 121) put it: 'the political desirability of markets *cannot* be judged separately from the peculiarities of the market concerned'.

Furthermore, it is reasonable to argue that such higher levels of competitive selection must involve the selection of different types of institution, including both market and non-market forms, of many coexisting varieties. To work at such higher levels, institutional competition must involve different types of ownership structure and resource allocation mechanisms, all coexisting in a mixed economy. This is quite contrary to Hayek's preferred policy stance.

At root, there is a methodological problem in the approach of the Austrian school. On the one hand, they attempt to replicate the neoclassical methodology of starting from allegedly enduring and universal features of the 'economic situation'. On the other hand, they point to the workings of real markets and examine the formation of beliefs and expectations in such a context. But to reconcile these principles they retain a half-formed, de-institutionalised notion of market that hangs together neither in reality nor in the imagination. They are torn between, on the one hand, some genuinely realist inclinations to study real social structures, and, on the other, a misguided belief in the universality of all 'economic' principles.

THE HIDDEN, IDEOLOGICAL SPECIFICS

Scarcity and competition are not as universal as neoclassical and Austrian economists presume. In extending the ideas of scarcity and competition to the natural world, the economic imperialists echo the Social Darwinists who were prominent in the later years of the nineteenth century and the early years of the twentieth. In reaction against the Social Darwinists, Petr Kropotkin drew on his own field experience to publish *Mutual Aid* in 1902, showing plentiful evidence from biology that competition and scarcity are neither universal nor natural laws. In addition, Herman Reinheimer (1913) rejected the universality of competition in both the social and the natural spheres. Since then, many subsequent studies attest to the view that there are plentiful cases of co-operation in both nature and human society, and relatively limited instances of direct competition over scarce resources. Neither biology nor anthropology give support to the universal presupposition of competition and scarcity.[8]

In a direct attack on Robbins and other neoclassical economists, Marshall Sahlins (1972) showed that tribal economies differ from capitalism in that they do not generate ever-increasing wants.[9] In addition, and again in contrast to capitalism, tribal, hunter–gatherer societies in tropical regions are faced with such an abundance of food and other necessities that resources are, for practical purposes, unlimited. Thus, to invert the neoclassical view, it is possible for there to be vast resources and scarce wants.[10] Even in a modern capitalist society, as Stephen Lea *et al.* (1987, p. 111) contended after a careful survey of the evidence: 'the axiom of greed must be rejected because real people, unlike *Homo economicus*, are not insatiable.'

There are other important examples of the scarcity law being broken that are highly appropriate to modern economies. Note that Robbins (1932, pp. 12–16) explicitly related the concept of scarcity to the notion of a resource that is 'limited'. The fact that a good or service may be wanted or needed by an individual is not enough to make it scarce, at least according to Robbins's definition. However, keeping faithful to Robbins's usage of the term, we may note that several important ingredients of socio-economic systems are not 'scarce'. For instance, trust, arguably so central to the functioning of an economy, is not a scarce resource in the sense that its supply is limited. Trust increases the more it is used or relied upon. Likewise, the reserves of honour or mutual respect do not diminish as they are put to use. Scarcity is hardly consistent with the enduring phenomenon of mass unemployment; in such circumstances labour power is far from limited or scarce.

A limitation of the neoclassical principle of scarcity is also – and crucially – exhibited with respect to the issue of information and knowledge. Information is a peculiar commodity because if it is sold it can be still retained by the seller. Neither skills nor knowledge are given or limited, because of the phenomenon of 'learning by doing'. As Albert Hirschman (1985, p. 16) pointed out: 'Use of a resource such as a skill has the immediate effect of improving the skill, of enlarging (rather than depleting) its availability.'

Especially in the growing and knowledge-intensive economies of modern capitalism the so-called universal 'law' of scarcity is thus broken. Even in the modern competitive and acquisitive age the concept of scarcity applies uneasily to important phenomena as information and knowledge. Knowledge and information are not scarce in the sense that they are a fixed resource. Even if neoclassical economics abandons its universalist claims, and applies itself to a more limited set of types of socio-economic system, it still ill-fits the modern age.

Admittedly, some things, like time, are universally scarce. The point, however, is that the alleged 'law' of scarcity does not apply to everything. And the exceptions include crucial phenomena such as knowledge.

In sum, the supposedly utility-maximising individual in a world of scarcity is not as universal as neoclassical economic theorists typically proclaim. A concept or argument that is seemingly typified in a capitalist society is extended without warranty by mainstream economics to all forms of socio-economic system. Although mainstream economics often claims to be universal, by stressing individualism, scarcity and competition its analysis reflects dominant ideological conceptions found in Europe and America in the modern age.

However, ideology does not necessarily correspond with reality. It is inaccurate to suggest that neoclassical economics strictly represents a capitalist or market economy, of any type. Although its theoretical representations emanate from the modern era of individualism and commerce, remarkably they fail to provide an accurate picture of the epoch.

Why is this so? A core theoretical construct in neoclassical economics is Walrasian general equilibrium theory. This relies on the notion of a Walrasian 'auctioneer' to co-ordinate the market. In this model, agents are not allowed to make binding contracts with each other until all markets are in equilibrium. This assumption is necessary for the theory to work but it is obviously unrealistic: traders in the real world do not wait for a market equilibrium before concluding contracts with each other.

Attempts to encompass time and change in the Walrasian model have followed the pioneering work of Kenneth Arrow and Gerard Debreu. The basic idea is to incorporate future products and future developments with the assumption of a complete set of futures markets. In addition, in the model there are markets for each possible 'state of the world'. Trading in all markets, present and future, is co-ordinated in one single event by the highly energetic and omnipresent auctioneer. However, dealing simultaneously in so many markets presents each agent with unmanageable computational problems. Accordingly, leading neoclassical theorist Kenneth Arrow (1986, p. S393) openly concluded: 'A complete general equilibrium system ... requires markets for all contingencies in all future periods. Such a system could not exist.'

Neither is money incorporated in a Walrasian model. As Arrow's collaborator and leading general equilibrium theorist Frank Hahn (1988, p. 972) wrote: 'monetary theory cannot simply be grafted on to Walrasian theory with minor modifications. Money is an outward sign that the economy is not adequately described by the pristine construction of Arrow and Debreu.' It has also been readily admitted by the prominent neoclassical theorist Fritz Machlup (1967) that the neoclassical theory of the firm is really a theory of market prices and costs, and is consequently not about firms at all. Accordingly, critics of neoclassical theory such as Brian Loasby (1976) and Neil Kay (1984) argued that in general equilibrium analysis, including its probabilistic or contingent-claims versions, there is no need in theory for any non-market form of organisation.

It is thus admitted – even by some leading exponents – that neoclassical economic theory, at least in its Walrasian version, does not satisfactorily encompass money, markets or firms. Such a theory can hardly be an adequate representation of any type of capitalist economy! This point is underlined by the fact that Walrasian theory was used by Oskar Lange and others – as related above in Chapter 2 – to build a model of a centrally planned economy with nationalised firms and without genuine markets at its core. Hence Walrasian theory is not specifically rooted in capitalism.

Neoclassical economics is not only strictly inaccurate but also insufficiently specific. Its universality is spurious and its specificity is unrepresentative of the characteristic relations and structures of modern socio-economic systems. The irony is that by attempting to erect a universal analysis of socio-economic behaviour, neoclassical economics ends up basing itself on a specific set of concepts seemingly associated with an individualistic and competitive market economy. That which is meant to be universal turns out in the end to be specific. Yet the specificity is not that of the real features of any actually existing capitalism. Such institutional textures are absent from the theoretical system. On the contrary, the picture portrayed is both specific and unreal.

THE LIMITS OF CONTRACTARIAN ANALYSIS

Remarkably, neoclassical theory itself demonstrates limits to markets and exchange. As noted above, if Walrasian general equilibrium theory is extended to cover all present and future markets then agents are presented with unmanageable computational problems. In a brilliant paper, Roy Radner (1968) showed that the informational demands on the auctioneer would be excessive in such a completely specified Walrasian system. For instance, with only one hundred commodities, one hundred possible states of the world, and one hundred present and future dates, there will have to be a million different markets. Agents are supposed to observe prices in all these markets and make appropriate bids. Clearly this is absurd. In line with Herbert Simon's (1957) concept of 'bounded rationality', Radner argued that the number of markets and the amount of information each agent is supposed to process has to be drastically reduced in anything approaching a feasible model. In an adequately realistic model it is impossible to accommodate a full list of futures markets, partly because of the escalating complexity and the information problems involved. Hence there will always be 'missing markets' in the real world.

For these and additional reasons, markets cannot be ubiquitous. However, neoclassical economics still considers all social relations as if they were potentially subject to contracts and exchange. This overwhelming contractarian emphasis neglects the practical limitations of contracts in the real world. Because contracts cannot be formulated to cover all eventualities, institutions play a crucial role in facilitating relations between people and aiding decision-making. The institution of money, for instance, provides reserves to deal with an uncertain future. We hold money precisely because we do not know all future exchanges: exact knowledge of the timings and amounts of future receipts and expenditures is impossible. Likewise, the employment contract in the firm is incompletely specified because employers are not able to predict all future eventualities (Simon, 1951, 1957). Institutions such as the firm and money arise when there are no adequate markets for all contingent commodities, because of uncertainty and because no one knows how to specify the contingency sets (Loasby, 1976). Money and the employment contract are examples of institutions providing reserves through time to deal with uncertainty and unknowledge.

Neoclassical theory, by pointing to 'missing markets', itself suggests the need for non-market institutions but cannot analyse them adequately because of its own core assumptions. Missing markets are sometimes treated as a result of the ahistorical limitations of the human psyche (Magill and Quinzii, 1996) rather than specific social structures. Some of the most important 'missing markets' within capitalism – the absence of futures markets for labour, skills and knowledge – are thus given insufficient emphasis. Uncertainty about the future – meaning that probabilities of events cannot be calculated – is assumed away, yet one of the vital functions of institutions is to help agents cope with this uncertainty. Although neoclassical economists have made some progress in incorporating institutions in their models, at least for this reason their success will always be limited.[11]

Consider the family or household. It has been traditional for neoclassical economic theory in the past to either ignore the family as an institution or to treat it as if it was a single individual: the paternal 'head of the household' personifying the family as a whole.[12] However, neoclassical theorists such as Becker (1976a, 1991) subsequently developed a theoretical model of the family that recognised the individuals within it, but treated the household as if it were itself a market and contract-based institution, essentially indistinguishable from the market or a capitalist firm. Although Becker's views are not shared by all neoclassical economists, they are illustrative of the institutional blindness of neoclassical theory.[13]

Without irony, Becker (1976a, p. 206) wrote that 'a *market* for marriages can be presumed to exist'. Note that, for Becker, markets are little more than means by which agents can transact in some vague way to each increase their own utility. At one stroke he thus confused five different things: (a) the non-existent sale of 'marriages' *per se* (marriages, as such, cannot be sold), (b) the possible sale of *permission to marry* by parents and others, according to specific custom, (c) the possible sale of the *information services* of *dating agencies* or *marriage bureaux*, (d) the possible sale of *sexual* or *partnering services*, with the expectation of possible marriage, explicitly in return for money or other commodities, and (e) offers and requests for *sexual partnerships*, possibly leading to marriage, not typically accompanied by demands in return for money or other commodities, hence not strictly 'supply' or 'demand' in the economic sense. Becker seemed blind to these important institutional distinctions. Yet modern cultural norms make a very strong differentiation between, on the one hand, domestic and sexual activities obtained by money payment, and, on the other, those obtained by non-commercial means. These differences are elided in Becker's analysis of the family. Neoclassical theory is generally heedless to these moral, cultural and institutional distinctions.

As a result, although modern neoclassical economists widely recognise the need to analyse the household in terms of the individuals composing it, the result is to treat all the relations between individuals along purely contractarian lines. Symptomatically, in this approach there is no conceptual dividing line between the family and the marketplace. Our relationship with our spouse is deemed to be conceptually equivalent to that with our grocer. Accordingly, neoclassical economics is unable to conceptualise the specific institutional features of the household and the special human relations within that sphere.

This conceptual blindness is a serious handicap. Apart from failing to recognise the difference between commercial and non-commercial institutions and practices within capitalism, the intrinsic limits to markets and contracts are neglected. This has devastating consequences for both the analysis of different types of capitalism and for the recognition of the limits to capitalism itself.

But the modern family is still not completely invaded by commercial relations, and cultural norms are still sensitive to this fact. Neoclassical economics either ignores the family or tries to force it into a purely contractarian analysis. This has been an enduring problem. As the great Irish economist T. E. Cliffe Leslie (1888, p. 196) pointed out, in criticism of the hedonistic, mainstream economics of his day:

> The family finds no place in a system which takes cognizance only of individuals, and of no motive save personal gain. Yet without the family, and the altruistic as well as self-regarding motives that maintain it, the work of the world would come almost to a standstill.

More generally, it has been argued in the preceding chapter that there are limits to the extension of market and contractual relations within capitalism. Indeed, an over-extension of market and purely contractarian relations would threaten to break up cultural and other bonds that are necessary for the functioning of the system as a whole.

Markets and exchange cannot govern all relations in a capitalist society. However, neoclassical economics fails to distinguish between commercial and non-commercial relations and thus side-steps the problem. Blind to the nature and boundaries of real markets, all relations are treated as if they were market transactions.[14] Yet the distinction between market and non-market relations is both indelible and central to the nature of capitalism. Significantly, as argued below, the precise boundaries of the demarcation profoundly affect the nature of the specific variety of capitalist system.

ACTOR AND STRUCTURE

Neoclassical economics places great emphasis on individuality and choice. However, it is arguable that free choice is in fact denied and that neoclassical theory makes the individual a prisoner of his or her immanent and often invariable preferences and beliefs.[15] In adopting an utilitarian analysis, neoclassical theory makes the individual a servant, to use Jeremy Bentham's (1823, p. 1) own words, of 'two sovereign masters, *pain* and *pleasure*'. In modern neoclassical economics the individual, in all their richness and complexity, is simply reduced to a well-behaved preference function that obeys textbook axioms. As the neoclassical economist Pareto (1971, p. 120) wrote in his *Manual of Political Economy*: 'The individual can disappear, provided he leaves us this photograph of his tastes.'

The possible origins of this preference function are left unexplained. In a miraculous immaculate conception, it is assumed that the individual comes into the world with a well-formed set of preferences, and continues through it to death with little or no fundamental change (Stigler and Becker, 1977). As argued at length elsewhere (Hodgson, 1988), this conception of the individual regards the person as detachable from the rich cultural world and the web of institutions upon which we depend. Instead, the individual is regarded as a self-contained, contracting atom. Institutions, in so far as they exist, are treated as the product of individual interactions and not as the moulders of individual purposes, preferences and capacities.

To make things worse, almost without exception, presentations of neoclassical general equilibrium theory not only assume that each individual's preference function is fixed, but that every individual's preference function is the same. This assumption has been found necessary to attempt to overcome the enormous problems of mathematical intractability. Amongst other things this denies the possibility of 'gains from trade arising from individual differences' (Arrow, 1986, p. S390). Thus, despite the traditional celebrations of individualism and competition, and despite decades of formal development, the hard core theory of neoclassical economics can handle no more than a grey uniformity of mechanical actors.

Neoclassical theory does not appreciate the way in which culture and institutions influence human character, preferences and capacities. It is thus unable to perceive some of the key differences between different forms of capitalism. For instance, in Japan there is a custom to ascribe guilt automatically to both sides in a legal dispute. Litigation is often regarded as a shameful way of attempting to enforce a contract or gain recompense. Such customs and cultural norms do not simply act as a constraint on individual activity: they entail a different way of perceiving contract and trade, involving mutual obligation and reciprocity. To take recourse to law is to abandon this interpersonal relationship and to lose hope in the understanding and potential generosity of the colleague. To operate in such a world, individuals must adopt a very different framework of meanings, perceptions and norms. Their goals and preferences are fundamentally altered. In contrast, in neoclassical theory the formative influences of specific cultures and institutional frameworks on individual preference functions are generally excluded.[16]

The Austrian school of economics has historically given more attention to the explanation of the nature and evolution of socio-economic institutions. One of the classic cases here is Carl Menger's celebrated theory of the 'organic' and spontaneous evolution of money from a barter economy. Barter is typically inefficient and traders face the problem of finding a double coincidence of wants. Some commodities become recognised by agents as being more frequently and readily saleable than others and thus begin to be used as money:

> As *each* economizing individual becomes increasingly more aware of his economic interest, he is led by this *interest, without any agreement, without legislative compulsion, and even without regard to the*

114

public interest, to give his commodities in exchange for other, more saleable, commodities, even if he does not need them for any immediate consumption purpose.

(Menger, 1981, p. 260)

Once a monetary unit begins to emerge, it establishes a 'convention'. Like other such conventions – such as language, or driving on the same side of the road – we are impelled to do something because it is done by others. The institution of money emerges as an undesigned result of individual interactions. The emphasis in this Mengerian account is on the evolution of institutions from the action and interaction of *given* individuals. The existence of institutions is explained primarily by reference to individuals and their interactions.

This is an important, but one-sided view of the nature and role of institutions. Insufficient emphasis is given to the way in which individuals are *changed and reconstituted* by the institutional context in which they operate. This point was made with regard to money by the 'old' institutional economist Wesley Mitchell. He emphasised that the evolution of money was not simply a result of individual interactions. Its emergence cannot be explained simply because it reduced costs or made life easier for traders. The penetration of money exchange into social life altered the very configurations of rationality, involving the particular conceptions of abstraction, measurement, quantification and calculative intent. It was thus a transformation of individuals rather than simply the emergence of institutions and rules:

> the money economy ... is in fact one of the most potent institutions in our whole culture. In sober truth it stamps its pattern upon wayward human nature, makes us all react in standard ways to the standard stimuli it offers, and affects our very ideals of what is good, beautiful and true.
>
> (Mitchell, 1937, p. 371)

The failure to consider fully the effects of institutions on human personality and purposes is a persistent defect in the writings of both the neoclassical and the Austrian schools.

However, on the question of agency there are important differences between neoclassical and Austrian economists. The conception of socio-economic evolution in the writings of Austrian school economists is not deterministic. The spontaneity and indeterminacy of human purposes and actions are emphasised. However, this does not mean that there is nothing in human agency requiring, or capable of, an explanation. Yet in emphasising the indeterminacy of human action the task of explaining what lies behind it is abandoned. Whilst Marx assumed that individuals are driven by their class position and interest, von Mises and Hayek were persistently reluctant to attempt to explain individual human actions. Both specific human motivations and systemic outcomes were indeterminate in their theory.[17]

Austrian school economists suggest that little or nothing can be said about the forces that mould individual preferences, purposes, capacities and action. The polar opposite position would be to suggest that structures and institutions completely determine human behaviour. Is some intermediate position possible? Elsewhere I have argued that it is (Hodgson, 1988).[18]

There are external influences moulding the purposes and actions of individuals, but action is not entirely determined by them. The environment is influential but it does not completely determine either what the individual aims to do or what he or she may achieve. The individual is ridden by habits of thought but not bereft of choice. There are actions that may be uncaused, but at the same time there are patterns of thought or behaviour that may relate to the cultural or institutional environment within which the person acts. Action, in short, is partially determined, and partially indeterminate: partly predictable but partly unforeseeable. The economic future is still uncertain, in the most radical sense; at the same time, however, economic reality displays a degree of pattern and order.

In sum, it is desirable to assert the importance of indeterminacy and spontaneity in human action but also to recognise its limits at the same time. In some ranges or dimensions, action may be indeterminate, but in others it is not. To assert indeterminacy is not to deny its limits: that action is also bounded and moulded by the influences of culture, institutions and social structures, all enduring and evolving from the past.

Both neoclassical and Austrian theorists start from universal assumptions about socio-economic systems and human behaviour. For both neoclassical and Austrian theorists, the transhistorical elements of theoretical analysis are individuals and 'the basic economic problems which humanity has to face'. The word 'market' is in their theoretical vocabulary. But the specific natures of these 'markets' are regarded as unproblematic and the prior existence of the market is often assumed. Because of the extreme generality of these perspectives, they can identify neither the specific features of the capitalist system nor the distinctive characteristics of any particular type of capitalism. On the abundant, actual or potential variety of forms of capitalism – and of varied human cultures and modes of behaviour within that system – these theorists have little of significance to say. By failing in this area, they are likewise unable to recognise key economic changes and are consequently unqualified to appraise different scenarios for the future. They are disabled by their presumptions of theoretical universality.

5

KARL MARX AND THE
TRIUMPH OF CAPITALISM

The bourgeoisie, by the rapid improvement of all instruments of
production, by the immensely facilitated means of communication, draws all, even the most barbarian, nations into civilization.
The cheap prices of its commodities are the heavy artillery with
which it batters down all Chinese walls. ... It compels all nations,
on pain of extinction, to adopt the bourgeois mode of production;
it compels them ... to become bourgeois themselves. In one word,
it creates a world after its own image.

Karl Marx and Frederick Engels,
Manifesto of the Communist Party (1848)

Karl Marx provided a impressive analysis of the dynamics of the capitalist system which remains valuable today. The first volume of *Capital*
includes a incisive analysis of the internal dynamics of the capitalist firm,
as well as a seminal theories of the trade cycle and of capitalist development. The second volume on the circulation of capital inspired Michal
Kalecki to develop a theory of effective demand prior to, and independently of, that of John Maynard Keynes. The third volume contains much
of the material which Nobel Laureate Lawrence Klein (1947) described as
'probably the origin of macroeconomics'.

Nevertheless, it is notable that Marx paid little attention to the analysis of different varieties of capitalist system. Perhaps we can excuse this
because of the sheer span of his analytical imagination, covering all the
social sciences and much of human history. However, the cost, as
explained below, is enormous: it is in the path dependence of institutional variety that different histories are preserved.

A key analytical question here is how variety is to be treated. Marx
readily acknowledged the existence of actual varieties of capitalism, but
saw an underlying, single, essence. In analysing this essence he thought
that the variety could be ignored. Marx adopted the prevalent analytical
view that variations were accidental, and were unnecessary theoretical
complications. On the contrary, the view promoted here is that the
essence of the system cannot be understood without understanding the

117

real basis and span of its potential and actual variety. Variety is not an accidental aberration: it is part and parcel of the potential evolution of the system. The argument for this standpoint is developed in this and the next chapter.

As noted in the preceding chapter, there is an important difference between the economics of Karl Marx and that of the classical, neoclassical and Austrian economists. Mainstream economists take the analytical starting point of the ahistorical, abstract individual. Marx's approach is different. As revealed in Marx's letter to Pavel Annenkov, written in 1846, the thrust of his criticism of Pierre Joseph Proudhon clearly applies to much of modern mainstream economics as well:

> Mr Proudhon, chiefly because he doesn't know history, fails to see that, in developing his productive faculties, i.e. in living, man develops certain inter-relations, and that the nature of these relations necessarily changes with the modification and the growth of the said productive faculties. He fails to see that *economic categories* are but *abstractions* of those real relations, that they are truths only in so far as those relations continue to exist. Thus he fails into the error of bourgeois economists who regard those economic categories as eternal laws and not as historical laws which are laws only for a given historical development, a specific development of the productive forces. Thus, instead of regarding politico-economic categories as abstractions of actual social relations that are transitory and historical, Mr Proudhon, by a mystical inversion, sees in real relations only the embodiment of those abstractions. Those abstractions are themselves formulas which have been slumbering in the bosom of God the Father since the beginning of the world.
>
> (Marx and Engels, 1982, p. 100)

In Marx's view, ahistorical categories such as 'utility', 'choice' and 'scarcity' cannot capture the essential features of a specific socio-economic system. His recognition of the processes of historical development led him to choose concepts that capture the essences of particular systems. Thus Marx claimed that the core categories in *Capital* were abstract expressions of real social relations found within the capitalist mode of production. Such categories are held to be applicable to reality as long as such social relations exist.

In the 'method of political economy' section of the *Grundrisse*, Marx (1973b, pp. 100–1) argued similarly that discussions of concrete socio-economic systems must ascend 'from the simpler relations, such as labour, division of labour, need, exchange value, to the level of the state, exchange between nations and the world market'. This, he saw, was the 'scientifically correct method'. Marx's primary aim was to analyse the type of economy emerging in Britain and Europe in the nineteenth century. Thus in the Preface to the first edition of *Capital* he made it clear that the objective of that work was to examine not economies in general but 'the capitalist mode of production'. It was the 'ultimate aim' of that work 'to reveal the economic law of motion of modern society' (Marx, 1976a, pp. 90, 92).

Accordingly, unlike the modern textbooks, *Capital* does not start with a general and ahistorical 'economic problem'. This procedure would ignore the historically specific and characteristic structures and relations of the object of study. Instead, Marx's economic analysis started from what he regarded as the essential social relations of the capitalist social formation. Marx (1976b, p. 214) himself explained: 'What I proceed from is the simplest social form in which the product of labour in contemporary society manifests itself, and this is as "commodity".' This starting point and its elaboration are clear from the key words in the titles of the opening chapters of *Capital*: 'commodities', 'exchange', 'money', 'capital', and 'labour power'. Marx did not aim to write a text on economics that would adequately reveal the workings of *all* socio-economic systems. No such work, he rightly argued, would ever be possible. Instead it was necessary to focus on a particular socio-economic system, and the particular relations and laws that governed its operation and evolution.[1]

A prior conceptual framework is necessary in order to understand the world. Contrary to empiricism, all empirical analysis presupposes a set of concepts and an implicit or explicit theory. All statements of fact are theory-laden. Accordingly, in their analysis of socio-economic systems social scientists are obliged to rely on something similar to 'ideal types'. Ideal types are abstract descriptions of phenomena that indicate the general features upon which a theorist will focus for purposes of explanation (Commons, 1934, pp. 719–48; Schutz, 1967; Weber, 1949, 1968). It is impossible to include all details and all features in such a venture because socio-economic systems are too complex. A process of abstraction must occur where the essential structures and features of the system are identified. The crucial question, of course, is which abstractions to make, or which ideal type is to be selected in the analysis of a given phenomenon.

Marx had a specific answer to this question, as we shall see below. All social scientists are likewise forced to make abstractions or simplifications, of one kind or another. Neoclassical theory, for instance, assumes given individuals with fixed preference functions. It is frequently admitted that the axioms of individual rationality may be violated in the real world. But rational behaviour is still taken to be a worthwhile and universal approximation. Socio-economic complexity is thus addressed through the universal 'ideal type' of a system based on atomistic, rational, utility-maximising individuals. Similar remarks apply to the widespread assumption of 'perfect competition' in neoclassical economics.

Marx considered several possible types of socio-economic system, such as feudalism and classical antiquity. In his view, capitalism would eventually be replaced by communism. In specifying such distinct socio-economic systems, he saw the need to develop specific analyses of the structure and dynamic of each one. In particular, he aimed to show that capitalism has inner contradictions, leading to its breakdown and supersession by another social formation. Writing in the 1870s, Frederick Engels (1962, p. 204) echoed Marx's methodological approach:

> Political economy is therefore essentially a *historical* science. It deals with material which is historical, that is, constantly changing; it must first investigate the special laws of each individual stage in the evolution of production and exchange, and only when it has completed this investigation will it be able to establish a few quite general laws which hold good for production and exchange in general. At the same time it goes without saying that the laws which are valid for definite modes of production and forms of exchange hold good for all historical periods in which these modes of production and exchange prevail.

The concept of a historically specific socio-economic system raises questions that are downgraded in neoclassical and other ahistorical approaches. For instance, the idea of historically specific socio-economic systems raises questions concerning the origin and transformation of each system. In turn, the accent on economic transformations and crises contrasts with the more static neoclassical preoccupation with economic equilibria and the theory of relative prices.

Clearly, the definition of each type of socio-economic system is crucial. This is pre-eminently the case with capitalism. Capitalism is essentially a type of market system involving extensive private property, capital markets and employment contracts. To examine this in more detail we first explore Marx's definition of 'the capitalist firm'. This is regarded by Marx (1976a, pp. 291–2) as an institution where:

1 'the worker works under the control of the capitalist to whom his labour belongs';
2 'the product is the property of the capitalist and not that of the worker';
3 further, such capitalist firms produce commodities for sale in the pursuit of profit.

Point 1, as Marx elaborated elsewhere in *Capital*, implies an employment relationship between employer and employee. Points 2 and 3 imply the existence of private ownership of the means of production. They also are tied up with the fact that the capitalists, rather than the workers, are the 'residual claimants': they take up the profits and losses from the sale of the products, after all other costs are paid. The definition has formal and legal, as well as cultural and informal, aspects. It entails an employment relationship and excludes co-operatives and one-person firms, as Marx himself made clear on repeated occasions.

The capitalist social formation was regarded by Marx as a system in which most production takes place in capitalist firms. Commodities were understood by Marx as goods or services that are destined for market or other contractual exchange. Exchanges involve the consensual transfer of property rights. By the above definition, the products of capitalist firms are commodities. Marx (1981, p. 1019) clearly identified a 'characteristic trait' of the capitalist mode of production as follows:

> It produces its products as commodities. The fact that it produces commodities does not in itself distinguish it from other modes of production; but that the dominant and determining character of its product is the commodity certainly does so. This means, first of all, that ... labour generally appears as wage-labour ... [and] the relationship of capital to wage-labour determines the whole character of the mode of production.

In short, for Marx, capitalism is generalised commodity production.[2] It is generalised in a double sense, first because under capitalism most goods and services are destined for sale on the market, that is, they are commodities. An important example is the existence of a market for capital. Second, because under capitalism one type of item is importantly a commodity: labour power, or the capacity for work.[3] In other words, an important feature of capitalism is the existence of a labour market in which labour is hired by an employer and put to work according to the terms of an employment contract. Within capitalism, there are markets for both capital and labour power, and these have crucial regulatory functions for the system as a whole. However, markets and private property are necessary but not sufficient features of capitalism: not all market systems are capitalist systems.[4]

Although Marx refers most frequently to capitalism in Britain, his aim is not to analyse any specific variety of capitalism but capitalism in general. Rather than any specific form of capitalism, capitalism *per se* is chosen as an ideal type because the dynamism of that system is attributed to its general relations and structures rather than national or cultural specificities. Cultural and structural variations were recognised by Marx, but they did not play a core analytic role in *Capital*. Instead of encompassing variation in his analysis, Marx focused on the unique, definitional essence. Relations that defined the capitalist system were used by Marx to validate the primary deployment of core concepts such as the commodity, exchange, money, capital, and labour power. In particular, the foremost use of the concept of the commodity was validated by the generality of the commodity-form under capitalism itself.

121

At least at first sight, such an approach seems eminently reasonable. If capitalism is a specific type of socio-economic system, with its own structural features and dynamics of development, then economics has to identify these specific features and dynamic processes. On the basis of their conceptualisation, a specific theory – with greater explanatory power than any theory based on universal and ahistorical presuppositions – could be constructed as a result.

An upshot of this methodological procedure is that Marxian economics is distinguished radically from classical, neoclassical and Austrian economics. Unlike the other approaches, Marxian economics is not based on ostensibly universal assumptions. Through this methodology, Marxism is connected with what could be regarded as the structural core of the mode of production that presently dominates our planet. Whatever the merits or flaws of Marx's analysis in *Capital*, no other theoretical system in social science has related itself so closely and directly to the general features of the capitalist socio-economic formation.

Marx's vision of history as a succession of different socio-economic systems was illuminated not only by the intellectual influence of Hegel but by his ideological commitment to a socialist future. Marx's strong political belief in the possibility and desirability of the revolutionary overthrow of the existing order, and in the construction of a quite different type of economy and polity, led him to focus analytically on what he thought were the distinctive features of the exploitative capitalist system. But whatever the impulse behind his thinking, his general idea that history has been a succession of different socio-economic systems, each to some degree with its own structure and dynamic, can be separated from the ideological energy that fuelled its creation, and even from the contentious question of the feasibility of socialism itself. Even if socialism is unfeasible – or undesirable – Marx's segmented vision of past history remains. His formulation of the problem of historical specificity remains relevant, to the past and the present, and to whatever future that we do indeed face.

THE HIDDEN, AHISTORICAL UNIVERSALS

However, there are major theoretical difficulties with Marx's particular approach to this problem. While the historically specific analytical system seems to support the key analytical concepts in the above manner, it does not validate its own meta-theoretical apparatus. *Some use of transhistorical and ahistorical concepts is unavoidable.* This is shown in Marx's own writing, but *not admitted explicitly in his own methodology*. The term 'transhistorical' applies to any concept or theory which is held to apply to a multiplicity of different historical periods, or different types of social formation. The term 'ahistorical' applies to any concept or theory which is alleged to pertain to *all* possible socio-economic systems. Both concepts transcend any single social formation. Close examination of *Capital* indicates that at crucial stages in his argument Marx himself had to fall back on both transhistorical and ahistorical concepts. Some of these concepts are as ahistorical as the allegedly universal concepts of mainstream economics, criticised in principle by Marx.

Hence, most obviously, the concept of capitalism itself had to invoke the ahistorical concept of a mode of production. But the problem goes further than that. For instance, in the very first chapter of *Capital*, Marx invoked the ahistorical concept of use-value in his discussion of commodities and exchange. It was recognised that specific use-values may be socially and historically conditioned. However, the concept of use-value, unlike the concept of a commodity, was taken as a universal, common to all possible socio-economic systems. Hence Marx himself did not follow his own blanket methodological injunction cited earlier: he did not see *all* economic 'categories as abstractions of actual social relations that are transitory and historical'.

Similar examples permeate his analysis. For instance the analysis of the production process in Chapter 7 of Volume 1 relied on a conceptual distinction between, on the one hand, labour in general – that is the idea of labour as an activity that permeates all kinds of socio-economic system – and, on the other, the organisation and processes of production that are specific to capitalism. Likewise, the distinction between labour and labour power is conceptually quite general, although the specific phenomenon of the hiring of labour power by an employer is far from universal and is an archetypal feature of the capitalist mode of production. There are many other examples, including the twin concepts of forces and relations of production and Marx's general and quite universal theory – outlined in his famous 'Preface' to the *Contribution to the Critique of Political Economy* – that socio-economic change is promoted when the developing forces of production come up against and break down allegedly antiquated productive relations.[5]

Indeed, the very generality and universality of the concept of labour in Marx's analysis helped him to sustain an ahistorical picture of labour as the life blood of all economic systems. As Marco Lippi (1979) has perceptively observed, despite the claimed historical specificity of Marx's analysis of 'value' in *Capital*, it rests essentially on an ahistorical and 'naturalistic' concept of labour. Similarly, Elias Khalil (1990) showed that Marx's ahistorical concept of social labour amounts to asserting that the actions of agents can be *ex ante* calculated according to a global rationality. The assumption of global rationality is itself a reflection of the specific Western intellectual culture of the nineteenth century and notably and ironically is prominent in neoclassical economic theory as well.[6]

To avoid any misunderstanding, Marx is *not* being criticised here for appealing to universal and ahistorical categories. On the contrary, such an invocation is unavoidable. Any study embracing the sweep of history must invoke general categories. Any attempt to establish historically specific categories must itself rely on a transcendent imperative. There is no way of avoiding this. However, Marx gave insufficient methodological attention to this problem and provided only a limited discussion of the meta-theoretical issues involved. In one rare passage Marx (1971, p. 214) gave a brief admission of 'general abstract definitions, which therefore appertain in some measure to all social formations'. In another he wrote of the 'simple and abstract elements' of the 'labour process' as being 'common to all forms of society in which human beings live' (Marx, 1976a, p. 290). The problem is not that Marx uses transhistorical or ahistorical categories but that he gives no *methodological* guidance on their importance, nor on the means of establishing them. Without such guidance, we might stumble on the abstract concepts – such as scarcity and utility – pertaining to neoclassical economic theory. Yet Marx criticised these alleged universals. Instead, Marx fell back on another set of questionable and ahistorical categories, without giving us sufficient reason for their use.

Again irony: but with double strength. Neoclassical economists attempted to construct a universal framework of socio-economic analysis but end up viewing the universe through the distorting lenses of a specific type of socio-economic system. The universality of their allegedly universal principles is thus questioned. Marx, on the other hand, knowingly reacted against this universalist type of approach and attempted to site his analysis of specific systems on specific concepts appropriate to each system. Yet, contrary to his own arguments, he ended up relying on concepts and theories that are in fact universal. Neoclassical economics aspired to universality but ended up being specific; Marxism aspired to specificity but ended up relying on the general.

THE PROBLEM OF NECESSARY IMPURITIES

Although he acknowledged their real existence, when analysing the capitalist system in *Capital*, Marx ignored all the non-capitalist elements in that system. This was not merely an initial, simplifying assumption. They were assumed away at the outset, never to be reincorporated at a later stage of the analysis. This was because he believed that commodity exchange and the hiring of labour power in a capitalist firm would become increasingly widespread, displacing all other forms of economic co-ordination and productive organisation. Thus, in *The Communist Manifesto*, Marx and Engels proclaimed:

The bourgeoisie, wherever it has got the upper hand, has put an end to all feudal, patriarchal, idyllic relations ... and has left remaining no other nexus between man and man than naked self-interest, than callous 'cash payment'. ... It has resolved personal worth into exchange value, and ... has set up that single, unconscionable freedom – free trade. ... The bourgeoisie has torn away from the family its sentimental veil, and has reduced the family relation to a mere money relation.

(Marx, 1973a, p. 70)

If the family is genuinely 'a mere money relation', then it logically follows that we may analyse money and ignore families in our theory. The statement was clearly an exaggeration for rhetorical purposes, but it attired a more serious analytical belief in the universal, corrosive power of markets and money. Marx acknowledged the existence of the family but gave it no more than passing reference in *Capital* (Marx, 1976a, pp. 471, 620–1). Engels went much further and published *The Origin of the Family, Private Property and the State* (1884). Nevertheless, both authors saw the family as rapidly becoming a wholly commercial institution, and they both failed to see its non-commercial features as essential for the survival of capitalism itself.

Confidence in the all-consuming power of capitalist markets was Marx's justification for ignoring impurities in his analysis of the alleged essentials of the capitalist system. Such impurities were regarded as doomed and extraneous hangovers of the feudal past, eventually to be pulverised by the ever-expanding market. Just as capitalism and commodity-exchange were assumed to become all-powerful, the Marxian theoretical system was built on these structures and relations alone.[7]

Yet it has been noted above that some of the crucial subsystems within capitalism are unlikely ever to become organised on a strictly capitalist basis. Consider the family. Contrary to Marx, there are practical and theoretical limitations to the operation of markets within that sphere. If the rearing of children were carried out on a capitalist basis, then they would be strictly owned as property by the owners of the household 'firm' and eventually sold like slaves on a market. Yet anti-slavery laws within modern capitalism prevent the possession and sale of one citizen by another.[8] Hence within capitalism the household can never typically be internally organised on the basis of markets, individual ownership and profit. Ironically, in both neoclassical and Marxian economics, the characteristic features of the family disappear from view. Just as the neoclassical economists treat all human activities as if they took the form of contracted exchange, Marx wrongly assumed that the entire capitalist system can be understood solely on the basis of commodity exchange and the exploitation of hired labour power.[9]

More generally, as argued in the preceding chapters, there are limits to the extension of market and contractual relations within capitalism. The views of leading heterodox economists such as Joseph Schumpeter and François Perroux have been noted already: the spread of market and contractarian relations can threaten to break up cultural and other enduring bonds from the past that are necessary for the functioning of the system as a whole. The role of the state has to be understood in this context. As Schumpeter and others have emphasised, the state is partly responsible for the bonding of society and the prevention of its dissolution into atomistic units by the corroding action of market relations. Accordingly, Polanyi (1944) showed that even in 'laissez-faire' Victorian Britain the state was necessarily intimately involved in the formation and subsequent regulation of markets.

The 'impurity principle' is proposed as a general idea applicable to all socio-economic systems. The idea is that every socio-economic system must rely on at least one structurally dissimilar subsystem to function. There must always be a coexistent plurality of modes of production, so that the social formation as a whole has the requisite structural variety to cope with change. Thus if one type of structure is to prevail (e.g. central planning), other structures (e.g. markets, private corporations) are necessary to enable the system as a whole to work effectively. As Michel Albert (1993, p. 101) wrote succinctly: 'Just as there can be no socialist society in which all goods and services are free, so can there be no capitalist society in which all goods and services may be bought and sold.' In particular, neither planning nor markets can become all-embracing systems of socio-economic regulation. In general, it is not feasible for one mode of production to become so comprehensive that it drives out all the others. Every system relies on its 'impurities'.

Although it cannot be formally proved, materials for a defence of this principle at an abstract level can be found in systems theory (Ashby, 1952, 1956; Beer, 1972; Luhmann, 1982). Further support can come from analyses of past socio-economic formations in history (Hodgson, 1984, 1988). Capitalism today depends on the 'impurities' of the family, household production and the state. The slave mode of production of classical times depended on the military organisation of the state as well as trade and an external market. Likewise, feudalism relied on both regulated markets and a powerful church. Finally, without extensive, legal or illegal markets the Soviet-type system of central planning would have ceased to function long before 1989. The system relied on an extensive network of black market dealers and illegal suppliers of materials and spare parts. In each of the four major modes of production after Christ (slavery, feudalism, capitalism and Soviet-type societies) at least one 'impurity', i.e. a non-dominant economic structure, has played a functional role in the reproduction of the system as a whole.

What is involved here is more than an empirical observation that

126

different structures and systems have co-existed through history. What is involved is an assertion that some of these economic structures were *necessary* for the socio-economic system to function over time. As I have shown elsewhere, additional and related arguments for the impurity principle can be derived from systems theory (Hodgson, 1984, pp. 106–9; 1988, pp. 257, 303–4).

The impurity principle is a theoretical guideline, based on ontological considerations. It is not itself a theory, and theoretical explanations have to be built upon it. It takes us only so far, and it would be a mistake to claim too much for it. Nevertheless, it does provide us with a yardstick to examine other theories, such as Marxism.

It should be emphasised that all perceptive Marxian economists have recognised the co-existence of different structures and forms within capitalism and the actuality of different forms of the capitalist mode of production. These are more-or-less sensible *empirical* statements. The empirical fact that social formations, including capitalism, have combined varied and dissimilar structures has been widely recognised. Their is a vast Marxist literature on the structural dissimilarities between capitalist industry and peasant agriculture, and so on. However, impurity principle concerns much more than the empirical existence of impurities. Above all it concerns their functional necessity for the system as a whole. The theoretical recognition of the *necessity* of such a co-existence of dissimilar socio-economic structures is entirely absent from the writings of Marx and his followers, a partial exception being the writings of Rosa Luxemburg. The impurity principle is incompatible with orthodox Marxism.[10]

In methodological terms, Marx's analytical procedure involved ignoring all necessary impurities. In the analysis they did not appear, even if their empirical existence was acknowledged. Nowhere did Marx announce any plan to incorporate key impurities – such as the family – into his subsequent analytical work on the capitalist system (although he did intend to write something on the state). His volume on 'capitalist production' is silent about the essential, functional role of the household in sustaining that system. There is no indication that he intended to rectify this particular omission.

Clearly, no-one can analyse everything at once, and it was quite reasonable for Marx to commence his analysis of capitalism with commodities, exchange and so on. But, as Tony Lawson (1997, p. 236) argued in a more general context:

> there is literally a world of difference between leaving something (temporarily) out of focus and treating it as though it does not exist. The achieving of an abstraction and treating something as though it existed in isolation are not the same thing at all.

For example, Marx was of course aware of the existence of the family, but because he saw it wrongly as 'a mere money relation' he analysed the capitalist system as though the family did not exist. This particular example is just an element in the more general analytical neglect of impurities in the analysis in *Capital*. Subsequently, in much of twentieth-century Marxism, the overwhelming analytical concentration on commodities and capital, ignoring the role of necessary impurities, has led to many similar errors and blind alleys.

Consider, for example, the work of Kozo Uno (1980). Although less known in the West, this was a highly influential attempt within Japan – with its strong support for Marxism among the intelligentsia – to clarify and systematise Marxian economics. At the most abstract level, Uno articulated the notion of 'pure theory' and identified a core concept of 'pure capitalism'. As Uno (1980, p. xxii) has elaborated:

> the pure theory of capitalism must presuppose the abstract context of a purely capitalist society. ... The pure theory, in other words, reproduces a theoretical capitalist society, the self-containedness of which conclusively demonstrates the ability of capitalism to form an historical society.

These ideas fit in closely with the writing of Marx. Uno suggested the possibility of a feasible and 'self-contained' capitalist system, without impurities. Obviously, the notion of such a purified system involves a denial of the *necessary* role of impurities. Marx and Uno willingly recognised the *empirical* existence of impurities, but not their functional role for the system as a whole. They recognised the empirical fact of diverse forms of capitalism but focused initially on a single, pure form. Allegedly, this form found its clearest empirical manifestation in England in the nineteenth century. Uno and his followers defended the concept of 'pure' capitalism by the argument that 'actual capitalism in its liberal stage of development demonstrated a tendency toward self-perfection, divesting itself more and more of pre-capitalist economic relations' (Sekine, 1975, p. 857).

At a more concrete level, Uno outlined a 'stages theory', arguing that in its development, capitalism passes through a number of successive stages. He saw the subsequent emergence, in the twentieth century, of less pure and varied, 'finance' and 'imperialist' stages of capitalism. Again, the diversity of empirical forms of capitalism was acknowledged but not the fact that impurities were necessary to sustain the system.

For these and other reasons, the problem of understanding the nature of modern Japanese capitalism has confounded Marxian economists for decades (Morris-Suzuki, 1989, pp. 103–30). Is modern Japan a highly developed form of capitalism? Or, on the contrary, is it a largely antiquated system in the process of shedding its feudal remnants and moving towards the 'purer' form of modern capitalism found in (say) the United States? Marxists have been unable to resolve these questions among themselves because they have been encumbered by the baggage of the concept (implicit in *Capital*) of 'pure capitalism'. Their vision has also been restricted by the widespread but mistaken notion that capitalism in all countries must necessarily go through the same sequence of stages.

In contrast, by adopting the impurity principle, we acquire a very different perspective. With it there is no difficulty accepting the idea that coexisting capitalist systems can develop in different ways, especially in different local circumstances. The evolution of a system depends on both its history and its context: path dependence is thus acknowledged. It is not even necessary to claim that one impure system is 'more advanced' or 'higher' than another. After all, what is dynamic or efficient in one context may be less dynamic or efficient in another.[11]

The impurity principle also admits the possibility that developments within particular socio-economic systems may depend to a significant extent on exogenous as well as endogenous changes. Because all socio-economic systems depend on impurities, there is the possibility that a system can rely in part on a geographically separate system, as well as dissimilar subsystems within the same social formation. For example, eighteenth-century British capitalism depended on the overseas colonies and the transatlantic slave trade. Modern Japan depends on its intimate political and trading relationship with the United States, both as a guarantor of political stability and as a huge market for Japanese exports. In contrast, Marxists have traditionally underestimated the importance of exogenous influences, seeing the dynamic forces of economic development as coming largely from within. The concept of a potentially self-sufficient 'pure' capitalism compounds this error.[12]

While the impurity principle contends that different kinds of subsystem are necessary for the system as a whole to function, it does not specify the particular kind of subsystem nor the precise boundaries between each subsystem and the system as a whole. Indeed, a variety of types of system and subsystem can feasibly be combined. For example, in many capitalist societies child-rearing is done within the non-capitalist institution of the nuclear family. But, in principle, alternative non-capitalist arrangements are possible for this purpose, such as collective households along the lines of the Israeli *kibbutzim*, or perhaps the rearing of children for sale on the market as child slaves (maybe gaining their legal freedom at their age of majority). Some such arrangements have existed in capitalist societies but they are not themselves capitalist. For example, before the Civil War, an extended system of slavery existed in the United States alongside capitalist institutions. Furthermore, in general – as illustrated by the particular case of subsystems of slavery within capitalism – the boundaries between subsystem and dominant system can be highly variable.

These points demarcate the impurity principle from functionalism. Some critics (Dow, 1991) have regarded the impurity principle as a case of functionalism and thereby invalid. Functionalism is typically defined as the notion that the contribution of an entity to the maintenance of a system is sufficient to explain the existence of that entity. In other words, the existence of an entity is fully explained by its function. However, the impurity principle does not purport to explain why any one given mode of production or subsystem may exist. To say that the household sustains the capitalist system, does not itself give an explanation of the existence of the household. As noted above, the capitalist mode of production could be sustained by a system other than the conventional household – child-rearing co-operatives for example. All the impurity principle asserts is that at least one such dissimilar subsystem is necessary for each system to survive. Because it does not purport to explain the existence of any one specific system or subsystem, it is not a case of functionalism.

The fact that the need for a dissimilar subsystem can be fulfilled by one or more of a variety of possible subsystems it is of particular significance for the argument here. The particular subsystem, the nature of the combination, and the precise boundaries of the demarcation profoundly affect the nature of the specific variety of capitalist system. *A corollary of the impurity principle is the contention that an immense variety of forms of any given socio-economic system can exist.* In particular, an infinite variety of forms of capitalism is possible.

ACTOR AND STRUCTURE

Another acute problem in Marx's perspective is that human motivations are not explained in any detail: they are assumed to spring in broad and mysterious terms from the relations and forces of the system. Consider the following passage by Marx:

> The principal agents of this mode of production itself, the capitalist and the wage-labourer, are as such *simply* embodiments and personifications of capital and wage-labour – specific social characters that the social production process stamps on individuals, products of these specific social relations of production.
>
> (Marx, 1981, pp. 1019–20, emphasis added)

Similar ideas appear in the following extract:

> The functions fulfilled by the capitalist are *no more* than the functions of capital ... executed consciously and willingly. The capitalist

130

functions *only* as personified capital, capital as a person, just as the worker is *no more* than labour personified.

(Marx, 1976a, p. 989, emphasis altered)

It is clear from these passages that Marx saw individual actions as 'no more' that the working out of objective, structural powers.[13] Accordingly, when discussing the mechanisms of change at the individual level, Marx was extremely vague. There was frequent reference to 'productive forces', as if technology itself were a driving force, unmediated by individuals. In general, he saw individuals as 'simply embodiments and personifications' of social relations. Thus, under capitalism, it was assumed that workers will typically struggle for higher wages and shorter hours, and capitalists for enhanced profits. But these are little else than expressions of the principles of maximisation also common to neoclassical theory.[14] What is missing is an explanation of the historical origin of such calculative behaviour and the mode of its cultural transmission from individual to individual. Marx assumed that values and motives are simply functional to the pursuit of class and economic interests.

Thus Marx believed that the class position of the workers as employees, coupled with the tendency of capitalism itself to bring workers together in larger and larger firms and cities, would lead to the eventual combination and revolt of the working class against the capitalist system. For him, such a process was an expression of the irresistible logic of economic development. Yet well over a hundred years after Marx's death there still has not been a single successful socialist revolution in any advanced capitalist country. Marx's faith that class positions and relations themselves were largely sufficient to impel the designated actions has to be questioned.

An important case study confirms the point. In his classic study of production workers in the United States, Michael Burawoy (1979) showed that hierarchy and authority on the shop floor are themselves unlikely to lead to the production of socialist ideology or revolt. Burawoy further demonstrated that, despite the over-riding *de jure* power of the management, there was a sphere of autonomy on the shop floor in which a specific sub-culture survived. It consisted of 'game playing' to maximise production bonuses and the modification of work processes and rules to overcome management inefficiencies.

Such a workplace culture would help to fill the analytical vacuum in Marx's theory. This culture may express the autonomy and even the resistance to authority of the workers. However, detailed examination of its typical features showed that there is no necessary, nor even likely, transmission belt from the condition of wage labour to the event of socialist revolution. Contrary to Marx, a given social structure or class system does not imply a tendency towards particular patterns of behaviour. This, as

Abram Harris (1932, p. 743) has rightly noted, 'is the weakest link in his chain of reasoning'.[15]

Marx seemed to suggest that human agents will gravitate to a single view of the truth simply on the basis of empirical evidence and rational reflection. In making this assumption, Marx was reflecting a prominent tendency in nineteenth-century thought. As C. Wright Mills (1953, p. 326) has observed: 'both Marxism and Liberalism make the same rationalist assumption that men, given the opportunity, will naturally come to political consciousness of interests, of self, or of class'.

Of course, Marx argued that 'false consciousness' often obscured the truth. Yet his view was that this ephemeral and temporary 'false consciousness' could be readily dissolved in the concentrated acid of reason and scientific analysis. What Marx ignored was that *any* form of consciousness, be it 'true' or 'false', is made up of deeply-rooted habits of thought, and based on culturally given concepts and values. Reason and science themselves are never entirely culture-free. If they are stripped of culture they are stripped of meaning.[16]

The class position of an agent – exploiter or exploited – does not imply that that person will be impelled towards any particular view of reality or any particular pattern of action. Later Marxists such as Vladimir Ilich Lenin and Antonio Gramsci wrestled interminably with these issues. Lenin's attempt to deal with the problem involved his theory of the energising and inspirational revolutionary party. However, this solution was almost entirely in terms of revolutionary agitation and propaganda. Allegedly, by these means, the proletariat would be aroused from its conservative slumbers, brought under the banner of socialism and given the confidence to revolt. However, Lenin underestimated the longevity of traditional habits of thought and the elusive but powerful role of social culture. He still assumed that once the facts had been revealed and assimilated, people would then reach a single understanding of their situation.

In his *Prison Notebooks*, Gramsci (1971) went much further than Lenin, probing the deep cultural roots of conservatism and fascism in his native Italy. The result is a Marxism very different from that of Marx or of Lenin, freed of much of its former determinism and its teleological excesses. In the recognition of the profound and diverse role of culture in human life, Gramsci's Marxism comes much closer to institutionalism. It is to the perspective of institutionalism that we now turn.

6

INSTITUTIONALISM AND VARIETIES OF CAPITALISM

The economic life history of the individual is a cumulative process of adaptation of means to ends that cumulatively change as the process goes on, both the agent and his environment being at any point the outcome of the last process. His methods of life to-day are enforced upon him by his habits of life carried over from yesterday and the circumstances left as the mechanical residue of the life of yesterday.

Thorstein Veblen, *The Place of Science in Modern Civilization* (1919)

We live in a world full of contradiction and paradox, a fact of which perhaps the fundamental illustration is this: the existence of a problem of knowledge depends on the future being different from the past, while the possibility of the solution of the problem depends on the future being like the past.

Frank Knight, *Risk, Uncertainty and Profit* (1921)

Having reviewed neoclassical, Austrian and Marxian economics in the context of the variety of forms of actually existing capitalism, we now turn to the alternative framework of the 'old' institutional economics of Veblen and his followers. Although this intellectual tradition has the means to overcome some of the aforementioned problems, the institutionalist solution remains incomplete and underdeveloped.

VEBLEN'S CRITIQUE OF MARX

Veblen highlighted the analytical gap in Marx's analysis between actor and social structure. Although sympathetic to much of Marx's analysis of capitalism, he noted that it failed to connect the actor with the specific structures and institutions, and failed to explain thereby human motivation and action. Veblen's analytical solution to this problem, inspired by Charles Sanders Peirce and the pragmatist philosophers, was based on the key concept of habit. Veblen thus followed the pragmatists in breaking from the rationalist conception of action that had dominated nineteenth-century Western thinking, including both Marx and the founders of neo-classical economic theory.[1]

Veblen saw that Marx's rationalistic concept of action was connected with his transhistorical concept of social labour and the implicit idea that labour can be evaluated according to a global rationality. Forest Hill (1958, p. 139) summarised Veblen's critique of Marx as follows:

> In Veblen's opinion, Marx uncritically adopted natural rights and natural law preconceptions and a hedonistic psychology of rational self-interest. On these bases Marx elaborated his labor theory of value, with labor as the source and measure of value, and the corollary doctrines of labor's right to its full product, of surplus value, and exploitation of labor. He attributed rational self-interest not only to individuals but to entire classes, thereby explaining their asserted solidarity and motivation in class struggle. Veblen rejected the concept of rational class interest and the labor theory of value, along with its corollaries and natural rights basis.

Marx saw his scientific analysis of capitalism in *Capital* as a potentially revolutionary instrument in helping the working class both to analyse and end its own exploitation. However, Veblen rejected the view that if working people reflected rationally upon their situation they would be impelled to criticise and revolt against the capitalist system. He rejected this underlying assumption of potential rational transparency and saw how, within Marxism, it was connected to a strain of fatalistic and teleological thinking. Stephen Edgell and Jules Townshend (1993, p. 728) have explained this connection clearly:

> Marx's portrayal of humankind as potentially rational also resolves the puzzle as to why Marx could simultaneously entertain the idea of an historical telos, with its deterministic implications, and uphold the voluntaristic and reflexive notions of praxis or practical activity. He assumes that workers – through rational thought, through reflecting on their experience of capitalism, and notably through their increasing immiseration and growing collective strength, will inevitably want and be able to overthrow it.

In Marxism, the process of rational reflection is seen to drive the working class to the same unavoidable outcome (Cohen 1978, 1989). Even if we stress a more open-ended and less deterministic account of capitalist development than the one found in the famous 'Preface' to the *Contribution to the Critique of Political Economy*, 'we are still left with a highly teleological theory of capitalism, with its downfall being the inevitable result of its inner contradictions' (Edgell and Townshend, 1993, p. 729).[2]

Veblen's critique of these rationalistic premises owed a great deal to the pragmatist philosophers. By attacking the rationalistic conception of action, the pragmatist philosophers undermined the foundations of Marx's view. As John Commons (1934, p. 150) put it, Peirce dissolved the antinomies of rationalism and empiricism at a stroke, making 'Habit and Custom, instead of intellect and sensations, the foundation of all science.' Habits of thought provide and reproduce the conceptual frameworks through which we understand and attribute meaning to the world. For Peirce (1934, pp. 255–6) habit does not merely reinforce belief, the 'essence of belief is the establishment of habit'. Through the concept of habit, as the pragmatist philosophers realised, thought is linked with action and the Cartesian division of the world between the mental and the physical is dissolved. Peirce had a crucial influence on Veblen and on Commons.

Veblen (1934, p. 88) wrote: 'A habitual line of action constitutes a habitual line of thought, and gives the point of view from which facts and events are apprehended and reduced to a body of knowledge.' Veblen rejected the continuously calculating, marginally adjusting agent of neoclassical theory and emphasised inertia and habit instead. Institutions are defined by Veblen (1919, p. 239) as 'settled habits of thought common to the generality of men'. They are seen as both outgrowths and reinforcers of routinized thought processes shared by a number of persons in a given society. Institutions thereby help sustain habits of action and thought:

> The situation of today shapes the institutions of tomorrow through a selective, coercive process, by acting upon men's habitual view of things, and so altering or fortifying a point of view or a mental attitude handed down from the past. ... Institutions are products of the past processes, are adapted to past circumstances, and are therefore never in full accord with the requirements of the present.
>
> (Veblen, 1899, pp. 190–1)[3]

Importantly, Veblen also emphasised the importance of novelty and human creativity and distanced himself from cultural or institutional determinism. Furthermore, it was recognised by Veblen and Commons that institutions are not simply constraints. For example, when Commons (1934, p. 73), wrote of the dual presence of 'liberation' and 'control' he clearly saw institutions as a liberating as well as a constraining force. As in the modern social theory of Roy Bhaskar (1979, 1989), Anthony Giddens (1984) and others, it is argued that institutions enable as well as constrain action.

The importance of institutions in shaping thought and action was implied in Veblen's attack on Marx's 'materialist conception of history'. This, according to Veblen (1919, p. 314):

> has very little to say regarding the efficient force, the channels, or the methods by which the economic situation is conceived to have

its effect upon institutions. What answer the early Marxists gave to this question, of how the economic situation shapes institutions, was to the effect that causal connection lies through the selfish, calculating class interest. But, while class interest may count for much in the outcome, this answer is plainly not a competent one, since, for one thing, institutions by no means change with the alacrity which the sole efficiency of reasoned class interest would require.

Veblen suggested that the mere class position of an individual as a wage labourer or a capitalist tells us very little about the specific conceptions or habits of thought of the individuals involved.[4] Even if the worker's interests would be served by joining a trade union, or voting for a political party that proclaimed common ownership of the means of production, there is no necessary reason why the worker's position as an employee would necessarily impel him or her to necessarily take such actions. Individual interests, whatever they are, do not necessarily lead to accordant individual actions. Hence Veblen criticised the implicit rationalism of many Marxists in the following terms:

> it must be held that men's reasoning is largely controlled by other than logical, intellectual forces; that the conclusion reached by public or class opinion is as much, or more, a matter of sentiment than of logical inference; and that the sentiment which animates men, singly or collectively, is as much, or more, an outcome of habit and native propensity as of calculated material interest. There is, for instance, no warrant ... for asserting *a priori* that the class interest of the working class will bring them to take a stand against the propertied class.
>
> (Veblen, 1919, p. 441)

Marxism has often been insensitive to the existence and relevance of divergences between actors' interpretations. As Veblen (1919, p. 442) pointed out, and as sophisticated Marxists such as Antonio Gramsci (1971, pp. 163–5) later emphasised, the members of the working class could perceive their own salvation just as much in terms of patriotism or nationalism as in socialist revolution. In general, the assumption of a class interest and rational calculation tells us nothing about the habits, concepts and frameworks of thought which are used to appraise reality, nor about the mode of calculation used to perceive a supposed optimum. As noted above, and contrary to what seems to be implied by Marx, human agents will not gravitate to a single view of the truth simply on the basis of empirical evidence and rational reflection.

Such arguments have a wider relevance than Marxism and apply to other calculative or rationalistic conceptions of action. Accordingly, a critique is implied of the optimising rationality of neoclassical economics. In models of the use of information by rational agents, it is generally assumed that all will interpret the same signals in the same way. In the extreme case of the 'rational expectations hypothesis', it is held that through mere data-gathering, agents will become aware of the basic, underlying structure and mechanisms of the economy. This hypothesis likewise neglects the conceptual framing involved in the perception of data and the theory-bound character of all observation.[5]

In general, neither class interest nor rational reflection upon circumstances will typically lead to a single outcome in terms of either perceptions or actions. For instance, although the capitalists' interests may be best served by striving for ever-greater profits, this tells us little about precise corporate strategy, the mode of management or the precise structure of the firm. In the case of the capitalist, the Marxian response to this argument is familiar: capitalist competition will *force* capitalists to follow the more successful route to profit and the accumulation of capital. Lucky or shrewd capitalists will follow this imperative and the others will become marginalised or bankrupt. Thereby the strategy, structure and goals of the firm are uniquely determined by competition. Uncannily, a very similar argument is advanced by the far-from-Marxist, Milton Friedman (1953) in a famous paper, where he argued that competitive 'natural selection' is bound to ensure that most if not all surviving firms are profit maximising.[6]

Similar arguments pervade both economics and sociology. Consider the following statement by Douglas Porpora (1989, p. 208):

> actors are motivated to act in their interests, which are a function of their social position. Again, this doesn't mean that actors always with necessity act in their interests, but if they don't they are likely to suffer. A capitalist who shows no concern to maximise profits is liable to cease being a capitalist.

Once more this implies some kind of competitive selection process, by which those that do not aspire to maximise profits and act accordingly will go under, leaving a population of maximisers and near-maximisers. Again, the means by which 'social position' leads inexorably to specific ideas and 'motivations' is left unexplained. There are two further problems, concerning profit maximisation. The first is that, in a dynamic context, it is not at all clear what 'maximising profits' means. It would be pointless to maximise profits one year if profits collapse the next. Reasonably, 'maximising profits' would involve future years. It might mean 'maximising the expected value of a future net income stream', where expectations are on the basis of estimated probabilities. But the problem here is that expectations and estimates are necessarily imperfect. *Also they are always culturally and historically conditioned.* 'Maximising profits' leads us to no single or obvious value. The second problem is that in any market economy, competitive selection is haphazard and imperfect, and also depends on cultural norms and interpretations. Firms that go bankrupt are typically organisations that fail to obtain credit. The granting of credit depends, once more, on the *assessment* of the bank or other financial institution of the *future* profit-owning potential of the company. Once again, we are in a bounded but open territory, where culture history and prejudice have their reign. In sum, the *making* of profits is ignored by a capitalist firm at its peril, but the *maximising* of profits is an ambiguous objective, always subject to culture and history. And *even if* it were a clear and singular objective then attaining it would not guarantee survival. The grain of truth in Porpora's statement is the recognition that eschewal of the profit objective is a treacherous venture for a capitalist firm: the options are bounded. However, within these bounds, both maximising and making profits imply a significant plurality of possible options, conditioned by culture and by history.

Likewise, Jim Tomlinson (1982) pointed out that profit cannot act as a simple regulator of the growth or decline of firms. Even if firms are trying to maximise their profits this does not imply a single strategy as to how this maximisation is to be achieved. 'Firms like generals have *strategies*, a term which itself implies room for manoeuvre, room for diverse calculations, diverse practices to be brought to bear on the objective' (p. 34). More concretely, case studies reveal a varied repertoire of strategic responses by firms. Note the study by Richard Whittington (1989) of the varied strategic behaviour of firms enduring a common recession, and the remarks about firm discretionary behaviour made by Richard Nelson (1991). Richard Cyert and James March (1963) and others have argued that firms are generally profit seeking, not strictly profit maximising. Within limits, and being no longer driven towards a single maximum, a variety of profit-seeking behaviours are possible. This gives scope for varied behaviour by capitalist firms. Conceptions of the sources of greater profit, as well as modes of calculation and appraisal, are always coloured by the cultural context in which firms act. Crucially, institutions and culture vary from firm to firm and from country to country. The objectives of firms are culturally and institutionally specific.

To understand the actual and potential diversity of firm behaviour it is necessary to escape from the strait-jacket of equilibrium theorising. In a dynamic perspective the exclusive focus is no longer on equilibrium outcomes. Out of equilibrium, greater diversity of structure and performance is possible. As Jack Downie (1955), Edith Penrose (1959), Wilfred Salter (1966) and Joseph Steindl (1952) have indicated – in four classic studies that have suffered unwarranted neglect – there can be enormous and sustained variations in productivity between different firms in the same industry. This contrasts with the textbook picture of firms being driven towards the same long-run equilibrium where costs (and revenues) are typically the same across firms. A dynamic and open-ended approach challenges the relevance of a long-run equilibrium and admits an ongoing diversity of outcomes. Penrose in particular took on board the central importance of firm heterogeneity and related it to the notion of firm-specific knowledge accumulation. Along with the equilibrium framework of mainstream economics, the Marshallian hypothesis of the 'representative firm' was discarded. The emphasis on dynamics and learning in a non-equilibrium context enabled a more satisfactory accommodation of the real world fact of firm heterogeneity (Eliasson, 1991; Metcalfe, 1988).

Veblen's answer to the Marxian argument that for the firm only one strategic response is possible, and also his rebuff to the neoclassical concept of equilibrium, was his theory of cumulative causation. He saw both the circumstances and temperament of individuals as part of the cumulative processes of change. For Veblen – inspired by Darwin – the idea that all kinds of socio-economic system should converge to one ('natural') type, was as absurd as a presumption that all animal species should eventually evolve into one.

Directly or indirectly influenced by Veblen, the notion of cumulative causation was developed by Allyn Young (1928), Nobel Laureate Gunnar Myrdal (1957), K. William Kapp (1976), Nicholas Kaldor (1967, 1972, 1978, 1985) and others. It relates to the modern idea that technologies and socio-economic systems can get 'locked in' – and sometimes as a result of initial accidents – to relatively constrained paths of development (Arthur, 1989, 1990). Hence there is 'path dependence' rather than convergence to a given equilibrium. History matters.[7]

Veblen's concept of cumulative causation is an antidote to both neoclassical and Marxian economic theory. Contrary to the equilibrium analysis of neoclassical economics, Veblen saw the socio-economic system not as a 'self-balancing mechanism' but as a 'cumulatively unfolding process'. As Myrdal and Kaldor argued at length, the processes of cumulative causation suggest that regional and national development is generally divergent rather than convergent. Young and Kaldor suggest that economies of scale imply divergent patterns of corporate growth leading to the domination of a small number of large firms. This contradicts the typical emphasis within neoclassical economic theory on processes of compensating feedback and mutual adjustment, via the price mechanism, leading to greater uniformity and convergence.

Contrary to some Marxist and neoclassical thinking, Veblen argued that multiple futures are possible. Equilibrating forces do not always pull the economy back onto a single track. This exposes a severe weakness in Marx's conception of history. Although Veblen had socialist leanings, he argued against the idea of finality or consummation in economic development. Variety and cumulative causation mean that history has 'no final term' (Veblen, 1919, p. 37). In Marxism the final term is communism or the classless society, but Veblen rejected the teleological concept of a final goal. Furthermore, for Veblen, socio-economic evolution was idiosyncratic and imperfect, and carried the conservative baggage of its past. This meant a rejection of the ideas of the 'inevitability' of socialism and of a 'natural' outcome or end-point in capitalist evolution. There is no natural path, or law, governing economic development. Accordingly, and in rejecting any predetermination in capitalist evolution, Veblen accepted the possibility of varieties of capitalism and different paths of capitalist development. Not all paths lead inexorably to the same equilibrium. Historical explanation was given a place and a role.[8]

There is some consideration of specific varieties of capitalism in Veblen's works, particularly in his *Imperial Germany* (1915). In general, however, it was not a prominent or sustained project. Furthermore, and contrary to the recognition of the flowering of diversity, some of Veblen's writings may suggest a logic of technological domination, and others the idea of the irresistible triumph of a pecuniary culture. Veblen's own insights into the future, like his vague and unelaborated brand of anarcho-syndicalist politics, are much less significant in comparison with his other insights. What stands out is his anti-teleological message.

Subsequent institutionalists, notably Commons, recognised actual and potential variety within capitalism. Commons argued that the United States was impelled by its own distinct history to evolve organisations and structures quite different from that in Europe. Commons observed (1893, p. 59), for example, that:

> The English economists have taken the laws of private property for granted, assuming that they are fixed and immutable in the nature of things, and therefore need no investigation. But such laws are changeable – they differ for different peoples and places, and they have profound influence upon the production and distribution of wealth.

In addition, as Dorothy Ross (1991, p. 203) pointed out, in her extensive study of US workers: 'Commons's central argument was that American labor organization was unique, the product of competitive market conditions and America's unique historical circumstances.'

SPECIFICITY AND UNIVERSALITY

Neoclassical economists have criticised institutionalism – along with the German historical school – for failing to discover general economic laws. Thus Lionel Robbins (1932, p. 114) wrote: 'not one single "law" deserving of the name, not one quantitative generalisation of permanent validity has emerged from their efforts'. Yet many institutionalists would be reluctant to admit that 'generalisations of permanent validity' exist, due to the manifestly varied and changing nature of socio-economic reality. In doubting their existence, they should not be condemned outright for failing to discover them. Unlike physics and chemistry, the ultimate objects of investigation in economics undergo evolution and fundamental change.[9]

It has been noted in preceding chapters that neoclassical and Marxian economics get trapped in obverse types of problem when it comes to assumptions about specificity or universality in economic analysis. Neoclassical economics is built on allegedly universal assumptions about choice, competition and scarcity. We discover that they are not, in fact, universally applicable and that they reflect the specific ideology of a particular moment of capitalist development. The analytical starting point of Marxian economics is the specific features and relations of the capitalist mode of production. We discover that the analysis ends up relying on concepts and theories that are in fact ahistorical. Neoclassical economics aspires to universality but ends up being specific; Marxism aspires to specificity but ends up relying on concepts that are ubiquitous.

Two broad conclusions may be drawn out of the preceding discussion. The first is that the theoretical analysis of a specific socio-economic system cannot rely entirely on concepts drawn exclusively from that system. This is because the very organisation and extraction of these concepts must rely on other categories of wider applicability. To talk of capitalism we must refer to other socio-economic systems; if we speak of socio-economic systems we are using that ahistorical concept; and so on. The very meta-theoretical terms of this discourse are themselves ahistorical. Whilst historical and institutional specificity is important, we are obliged to rely to some degree on the transhistorical and ahistorical.

The second conclusion is that the entire analysis of any given system cannot and should not be based on universal concepts alone. The first levels of abstraction must be quite general, but if those universalist layers are extended too far – as in the case of neoclassical theory – then the danger is that we end up with conceptions that are unable to come to grips with reality. The scope of analysis of the first levels of abstraction should be highly confined.[10]

The same problem has been addressed within sociology. Emile Durkheim (1982, p. 109) rejected universal laws in favour of an approach which recognised that 'between the confused multitude of historical societies and the unique, although ideal, concept of humanity, there are intermediate entities: these are the social species'. Max Weber too shunned attempts wholly to understand society through universalistic, master-key theories. Yet at the same time it was appreciated that an understanding of social reality requires a system of theoretical priors. As Richard Ellis (1993, p. 98) put it: 'Weber's ideal types, like Durkheim's

141

social species ... occupy a middle ground between the uniqueness of concrete history and the universality of covering laws.'

The concepts of specific historical analysis have to be grounded in some way, by appealing to a transhistorical and more abstract level of analysis. This is a problem which Marx ignored. A possible framework at a very high level of generality is provided by systems theory (Bertalanffy, 1971; Emery, 1981; Laszlo, 1972; J. Miller, 1978), such as developed and applied to economics by Janos Kornai (1971) and to sociology by Niklas Luhmann (1982, 1995). Recent systems thinking has moved on to encompass evolution within its unifying set of principles (Laszlo, 1987).

Although Veblen did not provide an adequate methodological discussion of the problem of historical specificity, he recognised the need for a general, meta-theoretical framework. For Veblen the transhistorical analytical framework is evolution. The idea of evolution spans both the biotic and the socio-economic spheres and grounds social theory in some general metaphors and principles. This does not mean that biology has to be slavishly imitated in the social sciences (Hodgson, 1993b). Instead, some careful use can be made of ideas and principles that span both the social and the biotic domains, without adopting the reductionist view that social explanations have to be framed in biological terms. In Veblen's (1899, 1919) writings the objects of evolutionary selection are institutions.

The concept of evolution provides a ground plan for the general foundations. Inspired in particular by Charles Darwin and Charles Sanders Peirce, Veblen saw the importance and ontological priority of both variation and continuity (Hodgson, 1992b, 1993b). First, there must be sustained variation among institutions, and the sources and mechanisms of renewal of such variation must be considered, whether they are causal, random or purposive. Veblen considered such sources, including his principle of 'idle curiosity' (Veblen 1914; Dyer 1986). Second, there must be some principle of continuity by which institutions endure and some principle of heredity by which succeeding institutions resemble their precedents or ancestors. The self-reinforcing and 'conservative' (Veblen, 1899, p. 191) features of habits and institutions are relevant here, as are the ideas of imitation and 'emulation' (ibid., p. 23). Note that these two 'evolutionary' principles are very general and much broader than the specific mechanisms of evolution outlined by Darwin. The issues here are at root ontological, concerning the sources of novelty and the mechanisms of persistence, and do not themselves involve adherence to a specific evolutionary theory taken from biology or elsewhere (Foss, 1994).[11]

INSTITUTIONS AS UNITS OF ANALYSIS

However, transhistorical principles are not enough. Theoretical analysis must build a conceptual bridge with a real object. The theoretical analysis of a real object must begin by abstracting its basic features. Abstraction entails the identification of what is essential to, and enduring in, an entity, ignoring the accidental and superficial. More fundamentally, the identification of features, relations and structures depends upon acts of taxonomy and classification, involving the assignment of sameness and difference. Classification, by bringing together entities in discrete groups, must refer to enduring common qualities. However, as Alfred Whitehead (1926) argued, abstractions are essential but they always do some violence to the complex, changing reality. Also, as Nicholas Georgescu-Roegen (1971) has insisted, operational concepts have a contradictory or dialectical quality and cannot correspond precisely with real phenomena. All acts of categorisation and abstraction must, therefore, be provisional. All theoretical foundations must forever be under scrutiny.

The problem is to develop meaningful and operational principles of categorisation on which analysis can be founded. These principles must identify relatively durable entities, from which categorisation and analysis may proceed. The neoclassical and Austrian approaches thus start from the given individual. A crucial problem in this approach, as we have seen in preceding chapters, is that it does not account for the evolution of individuality itself. In contrast, the institutionalist tradition has a different answer to this problem, locating invariances in the (imperfect) self-reinforcing mechanisms of (partially) stable social institutions.

The institutionalist Walton Hamilton (1932, p. 84) defined an institution as

> a way of thought or action of some prevalence and permanence, which is embedded in the habits of a group or the customs of a people. ... Institutions fix the confines of and impose form upon the activities of human beings.

Because of their relatively stable and self-reinforcing qualities, institutions are chosen as relatively invariant units. Institutions have a stable and inert quality, and tend to sustain and thus 'pass on' their important characteristics through time. Institutions are both outgrowths and reinforcers of the routinised thought processes that are shared by a number of persons in a given society.

The power and durability of institutions and routines are manifest in a number of ways. In particular, with the benefit of modern developments in modern anthropology and psychology it can be seen that institutions play an essential role in providing a cognitive framework for interpreting sense data and in providing intellectual habits or routines for transforming information into useful knowledge (Hodgson, 1988). The cultural and cognitive functions of institutions have been investigated by anthropologists such as Mary Douglas (1987) and Barbara Lloyd (1972).

Reference to the cognitive functions of institutions and routines is important in understanding their relative stability and capacity to replicate. Indeed, the strong, mutually reinforcing interaction between social institutions and individual cognition provides some significant stability in socio-economic systems, partly by buffering and constraining the diverse and variable actions of many agents. Institutions become cumulatively 'locked in' to relatively stable and constrained paths of development.

Hence the institution, as Philip Mirowski (1987, p. 1034n.) has suggested, may be regarded as 'a socially constructed invariant'. On this basis, institutions can be taken as key starting units in any concrete analysis. This contrasts with the idea of the individual as the irreducible unit of analysis in neoclassical economics, and applies to both microeconomics and macroeconomics. How is this principle manifest? It would suggest, for instance, that theories based on aggregates become plausible when based on corresponding social institutions. Money is a legitimate unit of account because money itself is an institutionally sanctioned medium; aggregate consumption functions should relate to a set of persons with strong institutional and cultural links; and so on. Again this contrasts with the approach based on reasoning from axioms based on the supposed universals of individual behaviour. An approach based largely on institutional specifics rather than ahistorical universals is characteristic of institutional economics, and has parallels in some of the economics of the Marxian and Post Keynesian schools.

Of course, this does not mean that institutions are regarded as immutable. Institutions themselves may change. We may consider 'institutional evolution' as a process, and even use biological metaphors in such a discourse. But when compared with biological evolution, institutions have nothing like the degree of permanence of the gene. What is important is to stress the *relative* invariance and self-reinforcing character of institutions: to see socioeconomic development as periods of institutional continuity punctuated by periods of crisis and more rapid development.

Notably, institutions fill the key conceptual gap that we have identified in neoclassical, Austrian and Marxian theories. Institutions simultaneously constitute and are constituted by human action. Institutions are sustained by 'subjective' ideas in the heads of agents and are also 'objective' structures faced by them. The concept of an institution connects the microeconomic world of individual action, of habit and choice, with the macroeconomic sphere of seemingly detached and impersonal structures. Actor and structure are thus connected in a spiral of mutual interaction and interdependence:

> The economic life history of the individual is a cumulative process
> of adaptation of means to ends that cumulatively change as the

process goes on, both the agent and his environment being at any point the outcome of the last process.

(Veblen, 1919, pp. 74–5)

The above remarks on the analytical significance of institutions are general and ahistorical. Yet we have moved from the general principles of evolutionary and systems theory towards a type of theoretical framework which can be used to categorise and dissect specific economic structures. There is much more methodological and theoretical work to be done here, but ostensibly the gap can be filled by institutional economics. This theoretical work is far from complete but institutionalism does seem to offer a favourable basis for further theoretical development, with its core concept of an institution and its deployment of the evolutionary metaphor. The grounds for this judgement include considerations such as the following.

Notably, the very concept of an institution points from the sphere of general principles to the study of the specific. Although some general principles regarding institutions can and have to be established, these tell us very little about the nature and dynamics of specific institutions. However, the approach being advocated here is not the 'add-social-context-and-stir' method found in some 'economic sociology' and rightly criticised by Viviana Zelizer (1993, p. 194). Institutions are not merely constraints, bearing upon a pre-existing and 'non-institutional' economy or market. Institutions and culture are not the context of a pre-given economy because the economy is not pre-given without institutions and culture. Economies and markets are themselves constituted as collections of institutions, and are not merely constrained by them. The market, for instance, as Harrison White (1988, p. 232) rightly stressed, is 'intensely social – as social as kinship networks or feudal armies'. The market, in short, is itself an institution (Hodgson, 1988).

Consider the theory of market price as an illustration. The concept of relative price in institutionalism is quite different from that in both Marx and the neoclassicals. Marx relied on the labour theory of value. Neoclassical economics proceeds from the concepts of supply, demand and marginal utility. By contrast, in institutionalism prices are social conventions. Such conventions are various and reflect the varied types of institution, mode of calculation, pricing process and commodity under capitalism. As Richard McIntyre (1992, p. 47) noted: 'There is no "general" theory of price because there is no general process of price formation.' Nevertheless, some common features of the price formation process in modern capitalism, such as markets, consumers and capitalist firms, can be used to develop some general outline principles, just as an even more general theory of conventions can be elaborated.[12]

Institutional economists have rightly argued that it is essential to focus on specific institutions and to understand their nature and dynamics. However, there is a danger that the need for general theories and concepts is lost in the search for specificity. In the past, the concentration on the specific and concrete, to the detriment of abstract and systematic theory, became a problem in institutional economics in the 1930s when according Gunnar Myrdal (1958, p. 254) – himself a strong devotee of institutionalism – it degenerated into data-gathering and 'naive empiricism'. Having failed to develop its theoretical foundations sufficiently, institutionalism cracked and subsided.

There are clearly two temptations to be avoided here. One is to erect an ahistorical theory: 'theory without data'. The other is to eschew theory and a system-building for data-gathering: 'data without theory'. But it must be emphasised that this is not a matter of finding a golden mean between such extremes. The very ideas of 'theory without data' and 'data without theory' are misconceptions. They are both false navigational poles. It cannot be a question of the appropriate mixture of the two basic ingredients of theory and empirics because data cannot be considered or appraised independently of a theory. All statements of fact are theory-laden. All attempts to gather data are informed unavoidably by a set of classificatory concepts and implicit or explicit theories. As well as the importance of concrete data, the primacy of theory has to be emphasised.[13]

Clearly, institutional economics needs to be further developed to deal with the important issues raised here. This requires methodological work and conceptual analysis to supplement the foundational work of Veblen and other early institutionalists. An important supplementary idea discussed here is the impurity principle.

VARIETY AND THE IMPURITY PRINCIPLE

It has been argued above that every socio-economic system must rely on at least one structurally dissimilar subsystem to function. Capitalism in particular, according to this 'impurity principle', depends on its impurities. As we have seen, Marxian, Austrian and neoclassical economists all fail to recognise this point, although it is accepted by a number of other writers. Incorporating no conceptual distinction between commercial and non-commercial activity, neoclassical economics applies the same choice-theoretic framework to all kinds of social institution and is thus blind to the demarcation between contract-based and other social relations. Austrian economics, by contrast, recognises the significance of property and contract and is able to differentiate them from other social relations. But it believes unrealistically – and with strange silences on the question of the family – in the possibility and even necessity of a vast extension of commercial contracts and individual property rights.

146

Finally, although Marx recognised the co-existence of capitalist with non-capitalist social structures in any capitalist society, he shared with Hayek and von Mises the view that commodity and market relations could grow to the eventual exclusion of all non-capitalist features.

Neither neoclassical, Austrian nor Marxian economics recognise the functional *necessity* of non-capitalist structures and relations within capitalism. The critique implied in the impurity principle thus applies to Marxian, Austrian and neoclassical economists with substantial force. In contrast, the impurity principle clearly dovetails with the ontological emphasis on variety in institutional economics. If every system relies on structurally dissimilar impurities, then some degree of variety will always be with us.

It is necessary to adopt a system of analysis that recognises both different modes of production and the fact that no single mode can triumph overall. All socio-economic systems are unavoidably a combination of multiple types of subsystems or modes of production. Unlike neoclassical economics, the theoretical system of Marx is sufficiently sophisticated to recognise some key differences between one type of mode of production and another. However, the failure to recognise the functional necessity of a combination of different modes of production with a single socio-economic system has to be rectified.

The corollary of the impurity principle, outlined above, should be stressed here. This corollary goes further than the assertion that no pure socio-economic system is viable. The stress is on the potential variety of impurities. By accepting the possible variety of combinations of subsystems with given systems, it is recognised that an immense diversity of forms of any given socio-economic system can feasibly exist. The denial of the impurity principle would involve the denial of such a potential variety of combinations.

In dynamic and evolutionary terms, the impurity principle is testimony that all systems carry, and to some extent depend upon, residues of that which preceded them. All systems depend on impurities, and are further obliged to make use of those impurities bestowed by history. It is thus illegitimate to abstract from those impurities, either by assuming that modern economies are asymptotically approaching the purified ideal of a market economy (as in much of mainstream economics) or by assuming that each social revolution makes irrelevant much that had gone before (as in Marxian theory). On the contrary, each system is obliged – as institutionalists have emphasised – to build out of the remaining bric-à-brac of the past. All development is a process of creatively 'making do' with the historical legacy of institutions and routines. We can never build entirely anew.

It is strange that two authors who have provided us with the deepest understanding of the workings of modern capitalism, Marx and Hayek, have little to say about specific economic policies. Marx advocates the broad but undetailed policy of central or collective planning and public ownership. Hayek's policy stance is diametrically opposed to that of Marx but is hardly less bland: we are offered the generalities of more market competition and extended private ownership. Hayek, like Marx and his followers, has very little to say in detailed, policy terms. The common blindness to varieties of capitalism disables their theoretical systems in policy terms.

The way out of this difficulty is to place the detailed analysis of capitalist institutions and of national and corporate cultures at the centre of the stage. Institutional economics thus provides a fruitful approach to the formulation of relevant and operational economic policies. With the notable exception of Veblen, many leading institutionalists in the past have been deeply involved in the development of economic policy. Much of this work was based on empirical study, but there is no reason why work in the future should not be guided by the deepest theoretical and methodological insights. Instead of empty formalism there is the possibility that economics may thus be capable of providing inspiration and sagacious guidance for those in government, finance and business.[14]

VARIETIES OF ACTUALLY EXISTING CAPITALISM

Given the potential variety of systemic combinations, and the reality of path dependence and cumulative causation, an immense variety of institutions and forms are possible (see Table 6.1). As Michael Storper and Robert Salais (1997, p. 18) have asserted: 'There is a great diversity of possible conventions for organizing productive activity, and also a great diversity of possible, conventionally agreed-upon economic tests of whether an economic activity is economically viable or "efficient".'

The argument concerning actual and potential variety is buttressed by the rich evidence of diversity even within modern capitalism. Such evidence encompasses specific institutions, such as corporations, as well as whole nations. Nelson (1991, 1994) has argued that, even within the same industry, firms typically differ in several respects, including their propensities to commit resources to innovation and imitation, their success in developing and adopting new products and organisational forms. (See also Dosi, 1988b; Freeman, 1982.) There is also substantial evidence that profit differentials between firms are quite persistent over time (Geroski and Jacquemin, 1984; Mueller, 1986). Differences in productivity are also pronounced in international comparisons (Pavitt and Patel, 1988; Prais, 1981; Pratten, 1976) and are particularly prevalent in manufacturing sectors (Bernard and Jones, 1996). Similar divergences and path dependence can result from varied corporate or other organisational structures, especially given the persistence and durability of

Table 6.1 Varieties of analysis and varieties of capitalism

	Neoclassical economics	*Austrian economics*	*Marxian economics*	*Institutional economics*
General unit of analysis	given individuals	given individuals	socially formed and socially related individuals	institutions
Capital-specific unit of analysis	—	—	maximising individuals	institutions in capitalist systems
General analytical concepts	utility, scarcity, choice, equilibrium	individual purposeful behaviour, scarcity, choice	labour, labour process, forces of production, relations of production, mode of production	habit, emulation, labour, creativity, cumulative causation, economic relations and systems
Capital-specific concepts	—	—	commodities, exchange, money, capital	transactions, money, capital
General micro-motive forces	utility or profit maximisation	purposeful individuals	socially conditioned individuals	habit, emulation, curiosity
Capital-specific micro-motive forces	—	—	capital accumulation, profit maximisation and worker resistance	specific cultural and institutional manifestations of capital accumulation, trade union activity, etc.
General micro-macro link	—	—	—	institutions
General macro-motive forces	—	—	forces of production	technological change, institutional inertia
Typical analytical outcome	unique general equilibrium, macroeconomic convergence	spontaneous order	typical or common path of historical and capitalist development, leading to communism	cumulatively divergent historical and capitalist developments with no asymptotic state

organisational cultures and routines (Binger and Hoffman, 1989; Dosi and Marengo, 1994; Langlois, 1988; North, 1990; Ruigrok and van Tulder, 1995).

Charles Sabel and Jonathan Zeitlin (1985) have argued on the basis of historical evidence that in Europe there was an alternative path to industrialisation based on small-scale firms and flexible specialisation. Maxine Berg (1991) compared explanations based on the supposed dictates of technology with the idea of such an alternative road. She concluded that industrialisation could have taken many possible pathways and occurred in different sequences. Broadly in line with this perspective, the literature on the Emilia-Romagna 'industrial districts' of modern Italy has addressed an alternative and very different mode of capitalist organisation, based on a number of closely networked and highly flexible small firms. These have been a significant departure from the presumed capitalist norm of large-scale, mass production (Best, 1990; Brusco, 1982; Dei Ottati, 1991; Goodman and Bamford, 1989; Piore and Sabel, 1984; Pyke *et al.*, 1990).

The literature on 'national systems of innovation' (Freeman, 1987; Lundvall, 1992; Nelson, 1993) has been based on the premise that 'basic differences in historical experience, language, and culture will be reflected in national idiosyncrasies' (Lundvall, 1992, p. 13) in the internal organisation of firms, the types of inter-firm relationship, the role of the public sector, the structure of financial institutions, and the nature, organisation and volume of research and development.

One of the most obvious and highly relevant comparisons is between the Anglo-American capitalisms and the capitalist system in Japan. The key to the difference lies in history. Capitalism in Britain emerged after a very long period of gestation. Three hundred years separate the disintegration of English feudalism in the fifteenth century from the beginning of the Industrial Revolution in the late eighteenth. Private property relations and an individualistic culture took well over three hundred years to develop. In contrast, the inception of capitalism in Japan was sudden and dramatic. The Meiji Restoration of 1868 marked an abrupt transition from a variety of feudalism to a Western-inspired capitalist society. Hence Japan today still bears the clear hallmarks of its relatively recent feudal past. The Japanese corporation has replaced the feudal estate but codes of loyalty and chivalry are still paramount. Long-standing, Confucian ethical doctrines are now expressed in terms of loyalty both to the capitalist firm and to the nation as a whole.

The comparative literature in this area is enormous and informative. In a classic and seminal study, Ronald Dore (1973) traced the development of a quite different system of industrial relations in Japan. This has led to a large comparative literature on Japanese industrial relations, a recent example of which is by Benjamin Coriat (1995). Chalmers Johnson

(1982) examined the evolution of a distinctive type of industrial policy in Japan. Masahiko Aoki (1988, 1990a) has theorised the peculiarities of the Japanese firm. Michio Morishima (1982) saw the origins of the Japanese economic 'miracle' in distinctive cultural traits formed through the inter-action of religious, social and technological ideas and practices. Maureen McKelvey (1993) surveyed the different kinds of Japanese institutions supporting technological innovation. Marco Orrù (1993) compared different forms of institutional co-operation in Japanese and German capitalism. Radical differences in financial structure between Germany and Japan, on the one hand, and Anglo-American capitalism, on the other, gave rise to a policy debate about the virtues of 'stakeholder' versus 'shareholder' capitalism (Albert, 1993; Blair, 1995; Dore, 1993; Hutton, 1995, 1997; Kelly et al., 1997). Kyoko Sheridan (1993) argued that Japan is not on a convergence route to Western-type capitalism but is sustained on a different track by a distinctive type of politico-economic formation. David Williams (1994) turned Fukuyama's view of an 'end of history' in the shape of American capitalism on its head: in his view Japan is not only a quite distinctive type of capitalist formation but also offers a far greater long-term challenge to Western theories and values than the fallen systems of Eastern Europe have ever represented.[15]

Stuart Clegg and S. Gordon Redding (1990), and Charles Hampden-Turner and Alfons Trompenaars (1993) surveyed the enormous diversity of cultures within modern capitalist countries. Varieties of capitalism are also the subject of works by Henk De Jong (1995), John Groenewegen (1997), Jerzy Hausner et al. (1993), Winfried Ruigrok and Rob van Tulder (1995) and Lester Thurow (1992). Richard Whitley (1992, 1994) has provided detailed examinations of the distinctive forms of corporate structure and firm-market relations found in East Asia.

Western observers have sometimes wrongly assumed that because the East Asian economies have exhibited increasing productivity and growth, then they must have been free market economies. It is generally presumed that only a free market economy could be so successful. In fact, the state has played a quite central role in these economies, and in varied ways. And markets there are generally not as 'free' as is often believed. Typically, state intervention and industrial policy are paramount (Amsden, 1989; Chan, 1995; Fransman, 1995; Gerlach, 1992; Lim, 1983; Tabb, 1995; Wade, 1990; Westphal, 1990; G. White, 1988).[16]

The recent literature on the emerging capitalist economies of post-1989 Eastern Europe also confirms that path-dependent and historically contingent processes are leading, not to convergence to a presumed unique 'Western' model, but to historically located and specific varieties of capitalism in each country (Roland, 1990; Zon, 1995; Chavance, 1995; Chavance and Magnin, 1995, 1997; Kozul-Wright and Rayment, 1997).

Applied economic analysis gives us a rich picture of diversity. Much economic theory, by contrast, is insensitive to these variations. At the level of its theoretical foundations, economic analysis cannot afford to remain blind to the immense and persistent variety of forms within modern capitalism.

THE SPECTRES OF GLOBALISATION AND CONVERGENCE

However, the modern socio-economic system is globally integrated to a degree that has no historical parallel. Transport and communications have evolved and cheapened to the extent that massive international transfers of people, goods, money and information are possible on an hour-to-hour basis. This is leading to some notable homogenisation of languages, ideas, technology, products, services, cultures and organisational forms. Does this mean that the days of persistent variety within capitalism are numbered, as diversity is drowned by the tides of globalisation?

The short answer is no. Admittedly, forceful processes of integration and homogenisation are likely to persist, and even accelerate. However, this does not mean that they will overwhelm the counteracting forces of divergence, or eradicate all important differences. There are several reasons for this judgement. First, as Paul David (1975) argued in a seminal study, learning always builds cumulatively on its past. Hence the centrality of learning to technological change renders economic development a path-dependent process. Similarly, as Paolo Saviotti (1996, pp. 199–202) has elaborated, innovation promotes divergence and institutional rigidities restrain convergence. Storper and Salais (1997) not only have cited evidence of specialisation and product diversification but also have argued convincingly that different national production systems are embedded in diverse and durable institutional frameworks that endure the growth the world trade. Accordingly, contrary to some pronouncements, globalisation is not about to eradicate national and supra-national boundaries and institutions. Some of the arguments concerning 'globalisation' are little more than the anarcho-liberal dreams of multinational entrepreneurs concerning the withering away of the taxing and interfering national state. On the contrary, international trade always depends on projections of national or supra-national state power, to provide it with military, legal, and financial stability. There is an ongoing debate about the extent to which globalisation is eroding national powers or differences, but there is no evidence that they are fast reaching insignificance (Amin and Thrift, 1994; Berger and Dore, 1996; Boyer and Drache, 1996; Dunning, 1993; Hirst and Thompson, 1996; R. J. B. Jones, 1995; Radice, forthcoming). In particular, the tacit and institution-bound character of much technological knowledge places severe limits on global transfers of technology, making national technology policies far from obsolete (Archibugi and Michie, 1995; Fransman, 1995). Overall, national cultures and institutional divisions endure, and there remains substantial scope for both national and supra-national economic policies.

Second, any socio-economic system is a *structured combination of partially complementary dissimilars*. Even substantial global forces of organisational convergence are likely to act upon individual elements of the system in different ways, and are unlikely to bring about the required structured combination of complementary institutions. For example, the Japanese system is a 'dual economy', combining large corporations with high productivity rates and enduring labour contracts, with smaller, less productive, enterprises which are much more flexible in their hiring and firing of labour. Each sector is dependent on the other. When advanced Japanese forms of organisation and management spread to other countries they do not always have the adjoining network of smaller and more flexible firms. Furthermore, reigning macroeconomic policies and performance may lead to a climate of slower growth and economic instability in which the Japanese-type corporation does not prosper to the same degree. For instance, it may be less able to shed labour in a recession. As a result, an organisational form which is highly efficient in one national context does not always readily spread with similarly impressive results to another national socio-economic system.

Third, even when convergence occurs, change is often slow and elements of the old system can persist indefinitely. Sometimes this is simply because of a time lag – the time taken to replace one set of reigning habits of thought with another. In other cases it is because elements of the old system are so deeply rooted that it is impossible to change them without endangering the system itself. The paths of convergence may have a narrowing gap, but may never meet. There are instructive examples of this in the natural world. The Eurasian wolf and the Tasmanian wolf are superficially similar in appearance and habit. But the former is a mammal and the latter a marsupial. These differences will persist, and continue to have significant effects. Similar remarks apply to socio-economic systems.[17]

The idea of the 'end of history' – along with the socialism of Owen or Marx, and the market individualism of Hayek or Friedman – is deeply connected to an Enlightenment principle. This is the idea of an universal history: the notion of an universal destination, underpinned by absolute, rational principles. Whether or not convergence is in process in any discrete period is largely an empirical question. By contrast, the absolute goal in Enlightenment thought suggests the dissolution of all cultural and institutional variations, and of all separate historical paths and identities. John Gray (1995, p. 125) has characterised this Enlightenment conception: 'Distinct cultural identities, along with their constituted histories, were like streams, whose destiny was to flow irreversibly into the great ocean of universal humanity.'

The interplay between divergent and convergent forces is thus a matter for empirical investigation and causal analysis, rather than grand, universal schemas. To some degree, the differences will always matter. Any practical policy must recognise these differences, and the historical and causal chains that have led to them. As we look into the past, and consider the roads not travelled, we must recognise alternative possibilities as we face the future. More than one outcome is feasible: there is no unique possibility. Actual outcomes are rarely predictable. If utopians are still to find a place in the modern world then they must escape from their singular futures. If there is a role for utopians in the uncertain and unpredictable global system, it is not to design one Jerusalem but to understand and imagine a whole set of contrasting and unfolding possibilities, and the social forces that could lead to them. The remainder of this book is concerned with the development and application of this kind of thinking.

Part III

BACK TO THE FUTURE

7

CONTRACT AND CAPITALISM

Is the theory of labour as a commodity anything other than a theory of disguised bondage? ... To claim that human life is a commodity, one must, therefore, admit slavery.

Eugène Buret, *De la misère des classes laborieuses en Angleterre et en France* (1840)

If the servant can get a better place, he is free to take one, and the master can only tell what is the real market value of his labour, by requiring as much as he will give. This is the politico-economical view of the case, according to the doctors of that science; who assert that by this procedure the greatest average of work will be obtained from the servant, and therefore, the greatest benefit to the community, and through the community, by reversion, to the servant himself. That, however, is not so. It would be so if the servant were an engine of which the motive power was steam, magnetism, gravitation, or other agent of calculable force. But he being, on the contrary, an engine whose motive power is the Soul, the force of this very peculiar agent, as an unknown quantity, enters into all the political economist's equations, without his knowledge, and falsifies every one of their results. The largest quantity of work will not be done by this curious engine for pay, or under pressure, or by help of any kind of fuel which may be supplied by the chaldron. It will be done only when the motive force, that is to say, the will or spirit of the creature, is brought to its greatest strength by its own proper fuel; namely, by the affections.

John Ruskin, *Unto This Last* (1866)

Stories of the possible end of capitalism, and of the future beyond, have been with us for a long time. Some, from time to time, have seen the end of the system as imminent. More widely there has been a view of immanent transformation, working itself through at a greater or lesser pace. The end of capitalism has thus been portended on the basis of perceived events. For instance, for well over a hundred years, it has been widely believed that capitalism has been transforming itself into an oligopolistic

157

system dominated by just a few firms, and with ever-increasing economic intervention by the state. According to this account, capitalism itself has created the preconditions for the transformation of the system into a planned, socialist society.

In its essentials, this view was advanced by Karl Marx and Frederick Engels, but also widely accepted by non-Marxists and anti-socialists, such as Joseph Schumpeter. For much of the twentieth century, few people challenged the assumption of greater and greater monopoly power within capitalism.[1] Many saw the perceived future trends as evidence of socialism's inevitability. It was believed that monopoly would prepare the ground for state ownership and socialism. Such developments have been seen as the 'tide of history'.

In line with this notion, Marxists of different hues have seen twentieth-century capitalism as being the system in its 'late' or most mature form. This 'stage' of capitalism, which is alleged to prefigure socialism in some respects, has been described by various Marxists as 'monopoly capitalism,' 'state capitalism,' 'late capitalism' or 'state monopoly capitalism'. Despite some petty rivalry among these descriptions, in general, the 'centralisation of capital', and the associated 'combination' or 'socialisation' of labour, have widely been seen to prefigure the centralised and unitary aspects of the socialist economy.

Today, the previously assumed fact of increasing corporate concentration and 'centralisation of capital' is challenged.[2] Nevertheless, it is still probably the case that state intervention – by some appropriate measure – in most developed and many developing capitalist economies has increased significantly during the twentieth century.[3] However, it shall become evident below that these particular empirical issues, despite their obvious implications, do not deflect the argument in the present book.

Whatever the true facts, for much of the twentieth century the 'tide of history' thesis was widely accepted. However, by the 1980s and 1990s, the confidence in such developments had diminished dramatically. Especially after 1989, fewer people believed that tendencies within modern capitalism were in any sense leading to, or prefiguring in some way, the kind of planned economy traditionally favoured by socialists. Even European social democracy lost much of its former faith in its own chosen future, and conceded much intellectual ground to free market thinking. There has been a pronounced loss of faith in the possibility of socialism itself. It is now widely concluded among former radicals that the most that can be hoped for is a more humane and egalitarian form of capitalism.

Alongside this, views have been developed by some academics concerning the historical longevity of market societies. It has been alleged that markets and other proto-capitalist institutions go back into classical antiquity and have a much longer history and more significance than is sometimes supposed.[4] If these claims are true, and various forms of capitalism and proto-capitalism have been around for two thousand years or more, then what basis is there for the belief that capitalism will disappear in the next thousand?

It has been argued in Chapter 2 of this book that 'socialism', in the traditional and widely used sense of collective planning and common ownership, does have insurmountable problems of both economic and political feasibility. However, this does not mean that capitalism is immortal. The idea of an inevitable, global, capitalist *Reich*, stretching for thousands of years into the past or future, is challenged here.

Capitalism has only a limited past. Markets and money existed in ancient and medieval societies, but capitalism proper was a non-existent or extremely marginal system of production. Capitalism, as defined in this book and elsewhere, involves the widespread existence of markets for both capital and labour power, encompassing employment relationships within capitalist firms. As a dominant or widespread system of production it is emphatically a relatively recent phenomenon. It has existed in England for, at the very most, four hundred years. In most other countries it did not become prominent until the nineteenth or the twentieth centuries.

Whatever the other limitations of his thought, Marx's basic idea of history as a succession of different types of economic structure or system still has a lot going for it. This should not, however, be taken to imply that history is a deterministic series of stages, where one system 'inevitably' is transformed into another 'higher' system. History is not the unrolling of a scroll: it has no teleology. It is possible to extract a non-teleological, kernel of truth from Marx's notion of different socio-economic systems. This amounts simply to the proposition that different systems are possible, depending in part on the context, and that history exhibits structural variety and change. This kernel can be accepted without suggesting that socialism is feasible, necessary or inevitable.

If socialism is problematic, but the idea of past history as a succession of systemic transformations is retained, then the following question is raised. What other kind of system could possibly succeed capitalism? Many different options are possible, not all of them optimistic or progressive. Nuclear war or a super-virus could conceivably throw humanity back into the Dark Ages. With rapid and unabating population growth, the industrial economies could recklessly exhaust global reserves of vital raw materials, and collapse into an era of choking pollution and ecological devastation, with awesome consequences for the survival of both democracy and capitalism (Meadows *et al.*, 1974, 1992). Such catastrophes are frighteningly possible. Attempts to assess their probability shall be left to others. Instead, a number of alternative and less apocalyptic scenarios are mooted here.

What is more to the point in this non-catastrophic analysis is whether or not capitalism itself has immanent transformative tendencies, or 'contradictions' that in some way create or enhance some of the preconditions for another feasible and highly productive socio-economic system. Emphatically, it is not insinuated here that the collapse of capitalism is predestined, nor that it shall inevitably be replaced by any feasible successor. It is simply suggested that developments within contemporary capitalism may be giving rise to economic structures and institutions that could form part of the basis of a new type of system that may replace it. In a similar manner, several hundred years ago, the development of markets and private property rights within English feudalism assembled some of the foundations for the later establishment of capitalism. But the creation of such foundations did not make the construction of capitalism inevitable.

It is argued here that within modern capitalism such transformative tendencies do exist. A possible and prominent direction of future and post-capitalist development will be outlined. However, before this possibility is summarised, it is necessary to establish some reasonably clear and precise definitions. Some people find such word-chopping tiresome. However, in any rigorous argument, precise definitions are unavoidable: partly as classifiers and markers. Precision is required to address and analyse a complex and changing reality. Without it, we remain with a fuzzy and clouded view of the world, without means of clarification, measurement or comparison. Even a complex and murky reality requires precise scientific instruments to aid analysis, detect variation and identify change. We cannot understand the future without laying down clear markers at the present. As Max Weber (1949, p. 107) argued:

> Indeed, it is *because* the content of historical concepts is necessarily subject to change that they must be formulated precisely and clearly on all occasions. In their application, their character as ideal analytical constructs should be carefully kept in mind, and the ideal-type and historical reality should not be confused with each other.

Aided by such definitions, we may consider some possible future developments. In the following chapters we engage in an exercise of long-term 'scenario planning'. Arguably, if there is a place for utopians in the modern, complex and uncertain world, it is not as the drafters of fixed blueprints, but as the seers of various socio-economic scenarios for the future. The greater impetus, and indeed necessity, for such speculations are due to the rapid pace of technological and institutional change in modern society. At first, however, we turn to questions of definition, before moving on to the discussion of plausible scenarios in the next chapter.

THE DEFINITION OF CAPITALISM REVISITED

Capitalism has already been defined in this book as a socio-economic system in which markets and commodity production are pervasive, including a labour market and a capital market. Under capitalism most production takes place in capitalist firms. A capitalist firm is an institution in which products are made for sale in the outside world, and workers are employed under the supervision of the management. Capitalism is generalised commodity production. It is generalised in a double sense, first because under capitalism most goods and services are commodities. Second, because under capitalism the capacity to work is itself a commodity. An important feature of capitalism is the existence of labour markets and the hiring of workers by employers. In addition, the capital market performs a crucial regulatory function in allocating other resources within the economy. Capitalism is a market system but not all economies involving markets and private property are capitalist systems. A necessary feature of capitalism is the widespread use of the employment relationship, involving employer control over the manner and pattern of work.[5]

This definition is consistent with that of Marx and those of many other social and economic theorists. For instance, the sociologist Anthony Giddens (1994, p. 11) wrote of 'capitalism, defined as a competitive market system in which goods and labour power are commodities'. This definition can be accepted by capitalism's supporters as well as by its opponents.

It is important to emphasise the centrality of the employment relationship to the above definition. In other words, without the sale of labour power to an employer there can be no capitalism. Firms in which there is no such employment relationship are not capitalist firms, even if they have other attributes (hierarchy, control, exploitation, alienation, or commodity production) which are also found in capitalist corporations. Some would regard this definition of capitalism as excessively narrow. But it is perfectly consistent with Marx (1981, p. 276) who wrote: 'Let us suppose the workers are themselves in possession of their respective means of production and exchange their commodities with one another. These commodities would not be products of capital.' In other words, if the workers own their respective tools and machinery on an individual or co-operative basis, and trade their products as commodities, then the system is not capitalism. It is different from capitalism principally because the workers are not employed by the owners. In the same volume, Marx (1981, p. 1019) further emphasised that, under capitalism, 'the relationship of capital to wage-labour determines the whole character of the mode of production'.

In practice, the definition proposed here is not that narrow: it is wide enough to identify all developed economies today as 'capitalist'. The overwhelming majority of workers in developed economies earn most of their income through an employment relationship. The precision of the definition helps us focus on this crucial fact. Clearly, the definition of capitalism adopted here refers to a type of productive system which currently dominates the globe.

A capitalist may be defined as someone whose main income is from the ownership of the means of production in capitalist firms, as defined above. In practice it is much more important to be able to identify clearly a capitalist firm than to assign the capitalist epithet to individuals. Indeed, by comparison with the vast amounts of ink and paper devoted to the elusive 'sociological' issues of class and status, the literature devoted to clear and historically specific categorisations of the basic 'economic' structures and institutions of modern capitalism is regrettably small by comparison.[6]

Peter Drucker (1993) has argued that Western economies are no longer capitalist, because ownership of the means of production is largely in pension funds, and the pension funds are owned by the workers, not the capitalists. However, capitalism does not necessarily involve two mutually exclusive social classes, where each individual can be unambiguously assigned to one social class or the other. It is an economic structure with two important sources of income: one from ownership of the means of production, and the other from employment for a wage or salary. It has always been possible, in principle, for individuals to receive income from both of these sources. If a person receives a substantial income from both, then this may put difficulties in the way of attaching the single label 'capitalist' or 'worker' to that individual. But it does not undermine the reality of two quite different types of income, and of their underlying structural sources.

Even if capitalism evolved to the extent that all firms were owned by pension funds, and the traditional capitalist class no longer existed, then the system would still remain capitalism, at least by the definition adopted in the present book. Although it is far from being realised in practice in any country, we should not deny the theoretical possibility of a capitalism with much more dispersed ownership of the means of production and consequently a more equal distribution of wealth and income. The utopian vision of such a 'people's capitalism' has long existed in the United States, and it caught the imagination of a Thatcherite Britain in the 1980s. Contrary to Drucker, however, such a system would still be capitalism.

The contemporary pension fund phenomenon has not blurred the traditional class divisions as much as Drucker has suggested. Typically, pension funds are not under the direct control of their owners, nor subject to their free disposal. In addition, substantial income and power

162

for a rich minority still derive from property outside of pension funds: from individual and corporate ownership of the means of production. Admittedly, the growth of pension funds and the spread of individual share ownership in several advanced capitalist countries are important developments. But these substantial changes are nevertheless *within* the capitalist system.

Today, most people in industrial economies live wholly or primarily by hiring their capacity to work in return for a wage or a salary. For the overwhelming majority, any pension funds or shares will generally yield a much lower accumulated income than their lifetime income from their employment. In the European Union well over 80 per cent of the working population live wholly or mainly off income gained from employment, and in the United States the figure is more than 90 per cent. Furthermore, the proportion of wage or salary earners has increased substantially during both the nineteenth and the twentieth centuries.[7]

On the other hand, the proportion of what are described in official statistics as 'manual workers' has declined slightly, to below 40 or 50 per cent in several advanced countries.[8] In addition, the service sector accounts for an increasing fraction of employment, at the expense of industry and agriculture (Rowthorn and Wells, 1987). Often, in common usage, the term 'working class' is associated with manual or industrial workers only. However, for Marx and other social and economic theorists, the most fundamental issue in determining social class is whether the income is gained from employment or otherwise, not the details of the work itself, nor the self-description of social status. Nevertheless, although more than 80 per cent of the population in many industrial economies are 'working class' according to a Marxian definition, many of them would reject the varied and often misleading connotations of manual labour, struggle, propertylessness, collectivism, inferiority or cultural unrefinement that in popular parlance are widely associated with the label in many countries and subcultures. There may have been a decline in 'working class' self-identification and subculture, and also a diminution in the proportion of workers in industry in developed countries. But the proportion of workers whose main income is derived from employment in capitalist firms has increased rather than declined throughout the world.

The percentage of the workforce organised in trade unions has fallen since 1979 in the United States, Britain, Japan and elsewhere; but it has risen in Scandinavia (Blanchflower and Freeman, 1992). Overall, these issues of formal membership, subculture and popular description are not our primary concern here, even if they are important for any modern political party attempting to mobilise enduring popular support. What is most relevant for our purposes is to note the enduring and very widespread use of the contract of employment in modern society. Against this, questions of working class self-identification and subculture are of secondary importance.

In general, contracts concerning the buying and selling of commodities involve the exchange of property rights, as well as services or physical goods, as John Commons (1950, pp. 48–9) stressed some time ago. These rights must be sufficiently clear to the parties involved for exchange to function properly. Accordingly, for contracts to operate, adequate legal and other rules concerning property and ownership are necessary. As Friedrich Hayek (1948, p. 18) has insisted: what are needed are 'rules which, above all, enable man to distinguish between mine and thine, and from which he and his fellows can ascertain what is his and what is somebody else's sphere of responsibility'.

Like all contracts, the employment contract involves attempts to define spheres of responsibility. But there are peculiar difficulties here, as we shall see below. Nevertheless, the capitalist system depends upon the assumption that these agreements and responsibilities are sufficiently well defined for a valid and proper employment contract to be concluded.

To take a contrasting example: the modern family and household is not a capitalist firm. Although marriage entails a legal contract between husband and wife, it is not a contract of employment. Further, the children produced as a result of the union are not owned as property by one or both of the parties. These factors differentiate the household from the capitalist firm. This does not deny that significant and economically fruitful activity – often done by women – takes place in the household. The household is part of the modern capitalist economy, but that does not make it a capitalist institution. If definitions are to be useful, they must draw distinctions between quite different institutional arrangements such as marriage, feudal bondage, slavery and employment. Distinctions must be drawn, despite the fact that one institution is often tainted by the values, preoccupations and habits of another.

THE NATURE AND IMPORTANCE OF THE EMPLOYMENT RELATIONSHIP

However, one crucial element in the above definition of capitalism remains to be clarified. That is, what is meant by an employment relationship? Answering this question is vital, but not as easy as it might seem. An employment contract is very different from enslavement, but there are some common features. Both slaves and employees are placed under the potential or actual control of a manager or supervisor. Like the slave, the employee does not have the right to the possession of the fruits of his or her labour, and is also not liable for any costs while incurred carrying out the instructions of the employer during the work process.

On the other hand, employees have legal rights not enjoyed by the slave. They are legal persons, entitled to own and trade property in their own right. Employees, unlike slaves, are entitled under contract law for some agreed remuneration for their work. Employment contracts are also limited in their scope: the employer does not have the legal right to require the employee to do work outside the terms of the contract. Also employees have the legal right to terminate the contract with the employer. These differences concerning rights, between slavery and employment, are of substantial economic significance. The self-employed also enjoy similar rights that are denied to slaves.

We now consider the distinction between employment and self-employment. In practice there is a very fuzzy line between the two; both legal practice and economic theory find it difficult to identify the boundary in precise terms. Nevertheless, the boundary is very important. Despite the practical difficulties involved, the distinctions between an employment contract and a contract for services, and between an employment contract and self-employment, are attempted today by legal and welfare systems in most advanced capitalist countries. Accordingly, as well as being central to the definition of capitalism adopted above, modern legal and welfare systems accept these distinctions as real.

In an employment contract the worker agrees, within limits, to work under the authority of an employer. This authority involves potential, but not always actual, direct or indirect control. This control typically concerns such matters as the manner and specification of the work to be performed. Crucially, this power of control is not itself specified in detail; it is implicit and to some extent open-ended. But at the same time there are legal and contractual limits to what the employer can require of the employee. In return, the employer agrees to pay the worker by the hour, day, week or month, or by the quantity of output produced.[9]

In contrast, if we hire a window cleaner, typically we are not employing that person; instead we are purchasing window cleaning services. The person cleaning the windows can be self-employed, or employed by a window cleaning company. In neither case are *we* employing the window cleaner. To make the window cleaner our employee we would have to hire directly that person; we would have to assume the right of detailed control and interference in the manner and pattern of work. The manner of this control would not have to be fully specified in advance. In an employment contract it is the fact rather than the detail of control that is taken for granted. A distinctive feature of the employment relationship is the *potential* power of employer control over the manner and pattern of work in all sorts of contingencies.

Modern English law makes a distinction between a 'contract of service' (employment) and a 'contract for services' (sales contract). A servant or employee 'is any person who works for another upon the terms that he is subject to the control of that other person as to the *manner* in which he shall do his work' (James, 1966, pp. 322–3). In contrast, with a contract for services, the worker is an independent contractor, and not an employee of the person purchasing the services. The law 'of master and servant' applies to an employment contract where the master has 'the right to control the servant's work. ... It is this right of control or interference ... which is the dominant characteristic in this relation and marks off the servant from an independent contractor' (Batt, 1929, p. 6).[10]

This is not to deny the abundance of difficult and intermediate cases. 'The difference between the contract of service and "contract for services" has taxed the ingenuity of judges' (Wedderburn, 1971, p. 53). In modern legal practice, the aforementioned 'control test' (concerning who is in control of the manner of work) is often unclear and inconclusive. Additional criteria are often used, particularly whether the worker owns or provides the instruments of work, or whether the worker is genuinely working 'on their own account' or is part of an organisation (Deakin and Morris, 1995; Kahn-Freund, 1983; Wedderburn, 1971, 1993). Nevertheless, despite the real-world muddle, the demarcation of legal ideal types is a necessary means of dealing with an important distinction within the capitalist system.

The distinction is often confused by use of language. If we 'hire' a lawyer who has an independent practice to deal with our affairs then that lawyer does not become our employee. In contrast, if a corporation 'hires' a lawyer onto its own legal staff then that person becomes an employee of that firm. Although the term 'hire' can be applied to both cases, they are in fact quite different. Other routines can muddle the issue. A contractor may invoice us for repairs to our washing machine, showing the required payment being made up of new parts and so many hours of labour. This does not mean, however, that we have purchased the labour, nor that the plumber has become our employee. The calculations used to justify the price of the job have simply been made explicit.

At this stage we have at least three distinct categories: (a) employment (b) self-employment, and (c) a contract for services. Note that (c) can be offered by both a self-employed worker and by a capitalist firm. Furthermore, (b) may result in the production of goods rather than services. Hence (b) is neither necessary nor sufficient for (c). Taken literally, there is also a slight distinction between (c) and a sales contract (d), in that the latter covers goods as well as services. Above all, there are two vitally important distinctions to consider: between (a) and (b) and between (a) and (c or d).

The distinction between (a) employment and (b) self-employment is essential to the analysis of modern socio-economic systems. If employment was indistinguishable from self-employment, then capitalism would be indistinguishable from a community of self-employed producers. Marx referred to the latter as 'simple' or 'petty' commodity production. Quite reasonably, he regarded capitalism and 'petty commodity production' as two quite different modes of production.

Just as there are varieties of capitalism, there are also different configurations of self-employment. At one extreme there is the case where the self-employed workers own all the means of production necessary for their work. In turn, this ownership can be on an individual or a group basis. Still more cases are possible, including one that notably bears some resemblance to capitalism. But it is not capitalism. In order to further clarify the definition of capitalism we shall briefly dwell on this imaginary case. Assume that all employment contracts within capitalism today are magically transformed into contracts with self-employed workers. Workers are contracted to provide the same labour services as before. They do the same work but the *form of the contract* changes. The employer still owns the means of production but no longer has the power of control over the manner of work; the pattern and content of the work are agreed in the contract itself. Emphatically, this is no longer capitalism, because there is no employment relationship and no potential or actual power of detailed control over the manner and pattern of work.

For a century or more the employment contract has survived and eventually prevailed. There are complex historical and practical reasons for this, including the provision of a degree of necessarily flexibility at work. Nevertheless, a significant minority have remained self-employed. Over time, the boundary between the employed and the self-employed workforce has shifted back and forth. In some firms self-employment has replaced employment. The construction industry, for example, has shifted from one kind of contract to another. Freight trucking companies have sometimes encouraged their drivers to become self-employed and to take out loans to purchase their lorries. There is the real possibility of an extension of self-employment, even in modern socio-economic systems. There is nothing forcing the system towards inevitable and complete proletarianisation.

We now come to the vital point. By definition, firms largely using genuinely self-employed workers are no longer capitalist firms. If such a practice became general then the socio-economic system would no longer be capitalist. This would not mean that we have moved in the direction of socialism: markets and private property would remain. There is no reason to assume at this stage that the workers would inevitably be better, or worse, off. Non-capitalism is not necessarily better than capitalism. The point is instead one of analysis and definition: the erosion of the employment relationship means the erosion of capitalism.

A possible response to this – which may find adherents among both Marxian and mainstream economists – would be to say that such changes in the legal form of the contract are surface phenomena, and the underlying relationships between bosses and workers would remain essentially unaltered, even if the workers were formally 'self-employed'. The grain of truth in this argument is that legal formalities are never adequate or accurate summaries of economic relationships. The flaw in the argument is to detach the alleged 'underlying reality' entirely from the 'surface' phenomena, failing to recognise that content is affected by form, and form by content. Each direction of causality requires us to recognise the reality, if not importance, of the legal form. Marx (1976a, p. 178) himself wrote:

> The juridical relation, whose form is the contract, whether as part of a developed legal system or not, is a relation between two wills which mirrors the economic relation. The content of this juridical relation (or relation of two wills) is itself determined by the economic relation.

Accordingly, the legal form of the contract gives us clues about the underlying economic relation, even if the mirror to which Marx alludes is always in fact a distorting one.

We all tend to take the existence of the capitalist system for granted. Hence it is important to realise the possibility of modern socio-economic systems that are neither capitalist nor socialist, even if some of these systems may still resemble capitalism in many respects. Assume that the workers are self-employed but do not own all the means of production. In this case there still may be powerful owners of factories, offices and machines. Even in a competitive equilibrium the owners of the means of production would still receive an income, emanating from that ownership. In bargaining with these owners, the workers would be required to concede the claim of these owners to an income, as they would be unable to produce without making use of the means of production owned by others. Hence the workers would still be deprived of what Marx described as 'surplus value'. Profits would still derive from ownership of the means of production. The differences with capitalism would be less to do with questions of income distribution, and more to do with matters of control over the work process.[11]

Hence we retain the employment relationship as central to the definition of capitalism, and maintain the important distinction between employment and self-employment. This conceptual demarcation is important not only in Marxian economics. For example, the famous discussion of 'the nature of the firm' by Ronald Coase (1937) relied importantly on what could be described as a 'thought experiment' involving, in part, a variety of self-employment. He compared two (real or hypothetical) ways in which production could be organised:

1 To organise production like a 'market', with a number of self-employed producers individually trading half-finished products and components with each other – or via some intermediary – during the production process. Even if they worked in close proximity, there would be no overall supervision by a manager or employer. Instead, production would be co-ordinated informally by a whole series of independent contracts and exchanges between self-employed individuals.

2 For an employer to set up a corporation, enter into an employment contract with each worker, and arrange for the supervision of the production process. For Coase (1937, p. 389) the key feature of the firm is its internal 'supersession of the price mechanism' and the allocation of resources by command rather than through price. Coase argued that this latter option emerges when an overall net reduction in the cost of contracting is involved.[12]

Hence the employment contract is central to Coase's (1937) notion of the firm: 'Within a firm, these market transactions are eliminated and in place of the complicated market structure with exchange transactions is substituted the entrepreneur-co-ordinator, who directs production' (p. 388). Labour and other 'factors' agree in return 'for a certain remuneration ... to obey the directions of an entrepreneur *within certain limits*' (p. 391). As a result, *if* one was unable to distinguish between employment and self-employment then much of Coase's account of the 'nature of the firm' would collapse, and he would be unable to distinguish between firms and non-firms.[13]

However, few economists during the twentieth century have paid much attention to the specificities of the employment contract or, until the 1970s, to the internal organisation of the firm. The emphasis has been on pure exchange rather than on production and its peculiarities. This criticism applies both to neoclassical and Austrian economists. Even today the conceptual issues involved here are only partially addressed under the more abstract formula of 'principal-agent theory'. However, principal-agent theory primarily concerns asymmetries of information and problems of monitoring rather then the distinction between employment and self-employment. Much of economic theory is regrettably blind to the institutional distinctions and issues elaborated here. Their real world importance is in no way diminished by this failure of mainstream economic theory.

THE INCOMPLETENESS OF THE EMPLOYMENT CONTRACT

Consider the distinction between (a) and (c or d) above. In an important

article on the topic, Herbert Simon (1951, p. 294) argued that the employment contract differs 'fundamentally from a sales contract – the kind of
contract that is assumed in ordinary formulations of price theory'. In a
sales contract a 'completely specified commodity' is exchanged for an
agreed amount. In contrast, in the employment contract the worker
agrees to perform one of a mutually agreed and limited range of patterns
of work, and allows the employer to select and allocate the tasks from a
known set. In addition, the worker accepts the authority of the employer,
notably concerning the specification of the work to be performed.

A key element in Simon's model is the fact that the outcomes (such as
costs, profits or work satisfaction) for each pattern of work are not
known precisely at the time of contracting. Simon formalises this by
considering the probability density function of outcomes for each
feasible pattern of work. At the time of contracting both employer and
employee are assumed to know the relevant probabilities but not the
precise outcomes.

Simon's formal 1951 model was a useful thought experiment but it
exaggerated the prior specification involved in the employment contract.
Neither the possibilities nor the probabilities are known to the extent that
Simon suggested. His model did not adequately encapsulate the ignorance, complexity and uncertainty that are associated with modern
production processes. Arguably, such situations of uncertainty or ignorance make the attachment even of subjective probabilities implausible.

Production processes involving human beings depend vitally upon
dispersed, uncodifiable and tacit knowledge. The complexity and inacces-
sibility of much of this knowledge mean that no worker nor manager can
know fully what is going on. All production involves learning; and in principle we do not know now what is yet to be learned in the future. Further,
production processes are generally complex to the degree that precise analysis and prediction are often confounded. In particular, they involve
human actors, who are sometimes unpredictable. Finally, they are subject
to uncertain shocks and disturbances from the outside world. Overall, key
outcomes are uncertain, in the Keynesian and Knightian sense, and also
many events and innovations are both unenvisaged and unforeseen.

For these reasons, employment contracts are imperfectly and incompletely specified. The terms of the contract cannot in practice be spelt out
in full detail because of the complexity of the work process, and the
degree of unpredictability of key outcomes. These problems of
complexity and uncertainty are found to some degree in other contracts,
but with employment contracts they are particularly severe. This is
because of the complexity and uncertainty of the work process, and the
fact that it continuously and directly involves conscious and capricious
human agents. Accordingly, we are in a strange Heisenbergian world
where the use-value of labour power is not known fully until it is used.

170

Employment contracts are always messy and incomplete. Employment contracts typically rely on trust and 'give and take' rather than complete or strict legal specification (Fox, 1974). Typically, employment contracts involve intensive social interaction and rely acutely on cultural and other non-contractual norms. The dual dependence upon both formal rules and informal norms is widely accepted in organisation theory (Levitt and March, 1988; Powell and DiMaggio, 1991). As a result, one of the most subversive instruments that can be used by trade unionists in dispute with their employers is 'working to rule'. It does not necessarily involve breaking the contract, but carrying it out in pedantic rather than conciliatory mode, tediously observing each letter and detail of its specification, and breaking the unwritten cultural norms that are the fabric of co-operation and goodwill. With these informal supports removed, the formalities of the contract become more of an encumbrance and less of an asset.

Likewise, one of the most dangerous and potentially counterproductive of managerial practices is to attempt to specify an employment contract in every detail. Such measures typically fail, partly because of the degree of complexity and unpredictability of the phenomena they attempt to describe and control. Furthermore, they undermine trust and co-operation, and create a punitive and corrosive atmosphere of litigation within the firm.[14]

Emile Durkheim's argument concerning *all* contracts is relevant here. As noted in a previous chapter, Durkheim argued that 'in a contract not everything is contractual'. There are factors, not reducible to the intentions or agreements of individuals, which have regulatory and binding functions for the contract itself. These consist of rules and norms that are not necessarily codified in law. The parties to the agreement have no alternative but to rely on institutional rules and standard patterns of behaviour, which cannot for practical reasons be established or confirmed by detailed negotiation. A point that is significant about employment contracts is the much greater degree to which such problems arise, and the much greater reliance on inexplicit and semi-explicit norms and rules. Because of the more extensive and intense social interactions involved, they rely even more on social conventions and norms. Likewise, employment relationships rely even more on the cultural cement of loyalty and trust. The practical limits to contractual specification are especially severe, and uncodifiable intangibles such as duty and precedent must fill in the gaps.

Among others, Joseph Schumpeter (1976), Karl Polanyi (1944) have noted that relations of employment cannot be completely reduced to explicit contracts. Schumpeter, for example, stressed that capitalism depended upon norms of loyalty and trust inherited from the former feudal era. Employment contracts are thus only partially successful attempts to encapsulate a messy and complex situation in contractarian terms. The difficulties outlined by Schumpeter, Polanyi and others cast severe doubt on the possibility of a purified capitalism operating through individual self-interest and explicit contract alone. As noted in preceding chapters, capitalism depends on its 'impurities'. This is especially the case within the employment relationship.

To recapitulate, in an employment contract the employer has the power of control over the pattern and manner of work. This extensive 'right of control or interference' by an employer distinguishes the employment relation from a contract for services. If we enter into a contract for services with an individual or a firm then we have no power of detailed control over the manner and pattern of work, even if that work is carried out by an employee of the contracting firm. The individual, self-employed contractor has much more detailed control than the employee over their work. Making this distinction in practice between employment and a contract for services is sometimes difficult and tangled but it is no less real or important for that. It hinges, essentially, on the existence or otherwise of the power of detailed control by an employer over the work performed by an employee.

BUYING TUNA AND CONTESTING EXCHANGE

To further clarify some of the underlying issues, we shall now consider ways in which the key distinction elaborated above can be under-emphasised, avoided or obscured. First we address the tendency of Samuel Bowles and Herbert Gintis (1988, 1993b) to treat the employment contract as just a specific case of a more general phenomenon that they have described as 'contested exchange'.[15]

Their starting point was quite different. Following Harry Braverman (1974) and others, Gintis (1976) and Gintis and Bowles (1981) originally began by stressing the importance of Marx's analytical distinction between labour (the activity of work) and labour power (the capacity or potential for work). Under capitalism, the capacity for work is hired by the hour or the day. Marxian 'labour process' theorists have concerned themselves with the specific social arrangements and practices used by employers to extract the maximum possible amount of labour out of a given quantity of labour power. They have asserted, quite rightly, that no single quantity or quality of labour flows automatically from the contracted labour power. Instead, the outcome depends on a struggle and trial of strength between management and employees, as well as the letter and legalities of the contract itself. It was this 'contested terrain' – to use the popular phrase of Richard Edwards (1979) – that lay at the centre of the work by Bowles and Gintis in the late 1970s and early 1980s on this topic.[16]

In response to Bowles, Gintis, Edwards and others, Victor Goldberg (1980a, p. 253) argued that, in respect to the distinction between labour power and labour, the 'employment relationship is not, as the radicals suggest, unique' because:

Most exchange relationships will entail, in varying degrees, the type of gap between promise and execution implicit in the labor-labor power distinction. The appearance of uniqueness arises from the fact that the assumptions of conventional microeconomic analysis preclude the existence of such a gap.

As if in acknowledgement of Goldberg, the emphasis of Bowles and Gintis then began to shift. After the early 1980s they saw class struggle in employment as a special case of a much more general phenomenon which they called 'contested exchange'. They explained that it was based on incomplete specifications and crucial information asymmetries between the parties to the contract, as in similar work by prominent mainstream authors such as Joseph Stiglitz (1987). In principle, 'contested exchange' could cover a wide variety of exchanges for goods or services, as long as they featured a significant degree of incompleteness of information. While the peculiar features of the employment contract were not denied by Bowles and Gintis, they were not emphasised nor elaborated fully. Instead, foremost emphasis was put on the characteristics of the general power relationship common to all forms of contested exchange.

Although specific features of the employment contract remained in sight, the analytical emphasis shifted to 'contested exchange' in general. Although the employment relationship was still seen as a power relationship, power was also discovered in everyday exchange. The value of the Bowles–Gintis contribution was to show that standard Walrasian theorising ignored the problem and cost of enforcement of contracts. Exchange was recognised as a relationship of power. However, the danger is to see employment as merely an example of contested exchange and to ignore its peculiar features. Production is not merely a special case of (contested) exchange.

In making the concept of 'contested exchange' central to their analysis of all these diverse phenomena, Bowles and Gintis reproduced the contractarian bias of much of Enlightenment social theory. Contract – albeit disputed, with imperfect information – became in their work the analytical centrepiece. 'Contested exchange' was seen as a way of reintroducing the concept of power into economic analysis. However, this involved a narrow and contractarian concept of power, defined in terms of the explicit threat or actual imposition of sanctions. Power and conflict were regarded as involving a clash of wills, perhaps with asymmetric information and resources, but with each party aware of its own purposes or preferences.

This is described as an incomplete and 'one-dimensional view of power' in the important work of Steven Lukes (1974, p. 15). This notion of power is limited to 'a focus on *behaviour* in the making of *decisions* on *issues* over which there is an observable *conflict* of (subjective) interests'. This one-dimensional view ignores the fact that an individual may exercise power over another 'by influencing, shaping or determining his very wants. Indeed, is it not the supreme exercise of power to get another or others to have the desires you want them to have ...?' (Lukes, 1974, p. 23). In this more subtle case, power is exercised, but typically without open contest or conflict.

The exercise of power, even in a contract-ridden economy, is as much a result of non-contractual phenomena such as 'taking things for granted' or of unthinking conformism to established custom and practice. Such matters cannot be understood adequately in terms of explicit disputes over the details of any contractual agreement. As John Westergaard and Henrietta Resler (1976, p. 144) have argued: 'Power is to be found more in uneventful routine than in conscious and active exercise of will.' Similarly, Marx (1976a, p. 280) emphasised that the 'silent compulsion of economic relations sets the seal on the domination of the capitalist over the worker'. John Commons (1934, p. 701) noted that on those rare occasions 'when customs change ... then it is realized that the compulsion of custom has been there all along, but unquestioned and undisturbed'. The concept of 'contested exchange' misleads us by suggesting, on the contrary, that these issues are much more to do with continuous and open altercation between agents.

In reality, the exercise of power is often uncontested. The employment contract offers no exception to this rule. What is essential to the employment contract is not a gap between promise and execution, nor information asymmetries, nor imperfect specification of the contract itself. All these features are important but found elsewhere. What is essential to the employment contract is the actual *or potential* exercise of the power of detailed interference, by an employer, into the manner and pattern of work of an employee.

Rather than being fully recognised, and treated as a matter of strategic calculation, this power of detailed service is often taken for granted. Such power may be exercised within the scope afforded by the employee's acceptance of an ethic of service or deference. In such cases it is neither 'contested', nor accurately described as a contractual 'exchange'. On the whole, the terminology of 'contested exchange' misleads us by suggesting that both open conflict and highly cognizant trade are general and universal features of the employment relationship, whereas, in fact, they are historically and culturally specific, non-essential associations with this social relation. They are manifest more in modern American culture than elsewhere.

There are other important cases where key differences between employment contracts and other contracts have been overlooked. In an analysis in most respects inferior to that of Bowles and Gintis, Armen Alchian and Harold Demsetz (1972, p. 777) argued that:

> It is common to see the firm characterized by the power to settle issues by fiat, by authority, or by disciplinary action superior to that available in the conventional market. This is a delusion. The firm ... has no power of fiat, no authority, no disciplinary action any different in the slightest degree from ordinary market contracting between any two people. ... To speak of managing, directing, or assigning workers to various tasks is a deceptive way of noting that the employer continually is involved in renegotiation of contracts in terms that must be acceptable to both parties. Telling an employee to type this letter rather than to file that document is like my telling a grocer to sell me this brand of tuna rather than that brand of bread. I have no contract to continue to purchase from the grocer and neither the employer nor the employee is bound by any contractual obligations to continue the relationship.

Unlike Bowles and Gintis, Alchian and Demsetz imagined markets all around them, including within firms. In this case, the desire to establish the universality of 'market contracting' obscures the difference between employment and other contracts. However, there are important reasons why an employment contract is different from a sales contract, or contract for services. First, 'telling a grocer to sell me this brand of tuna rather than that brand of bread' is simply choosing to enter into one contract rather than another. The power of choice and direction being exercised in the Alchian and Demsetz example is in the choice *of* contract, not *within* each individual contract. Second, although the consumer has some power of a sort, the purchaser has no significant power over the *manner of execution* of a sales contract. It would be like the customer asking the grocer to smile when passing the tuna and to consider dressing more smartly in the future. Such commands are possible during the execution of an employment contract but not within a sales contract: the customer has no such power over the grocer. In a sales contract we have the power only of 'exit' – to choose another grocer. In an employment contract the boss has *both* the power of 'voice' (that is, within limits, to command the worker) *and* the power of 'exit' (that is, to end the contract, by firing the worker).[17] It is the power of detailed control over the manner of work that is crucial and distinctive.

Alchian and Demsetz assumed that when control over the detailed manner of work is being exercised in an employment contract then the contract is (implicitly) being 'continuously renegotiated'.[18] However, this is a mere fiction to save appearances. It entails a false assumption, designed to restore the conceptual symmetry between employment and sales contracts. The falsity is because the renegotiation is fictional rather than real. In general, neither the contracting participants nor the legal system will recognise that any renegotiation is going on. It is bad practice to assume that people are negotiating and coming to agreements when they are themselves aware of no such thing. Indeed, in real life it would be a recipe for despotism. The despot could simply claim that agreement had been reached with someone to perform some unwelcome task, even if the victim was unaware of the agreement. A liberal system of exchange and contract depends to a significant degree on explicit and voluntary consent. In reality an employment contract is not continuously renegotiated. Instead, it involves the actual or potential exercise of power and it is incompletely specified to the degree that it covers a large range of possible tasks and ways of doing them. [19]

Despite its traditional ideological support for the rights of property and contract, mainstream economics typically slides over questions concerning the existence or non-existence of voluntary consent in some crucial areas. The reckless imputation of 'implicit contracts' is a case in point. An equivalent in law would be to suggest that the victim of rape had given implicit consent to sexual intercourse, despite giving no indication of assent. Thankfully, the legal system is more careful in such matters: the question of the existence or non-existence of explicit contract or consent is crucial in the courts. But, regrettably, economists are not generally so careful.

The fiction of continuous renegotiation is an attempt to force the power relationship of the employment contract into a contractarian analysis. The language of 'contested exchange' has a different immediate purpose but a similar effect. In reality, however, by forcing the employment contract into purely contractarian framework we neglect some of the fundamental, and essentially non-contractarian features of that relationship, as well as vital differences between labour and capital, and between production and exchange.

There are other reasons why buying tuna is quite different from employing a worker. There are, for instance, fundamental differences between the ownership of labour services and of other commodities. These break the symmetry assumed in most economics textbooks between the ownership of 'labour' and of 'capital'. Both are seen as 'factors of production' differing in little else but name. In contrast, a peculiar quality of labour was noted by the political philosopher Thomas Green (1888, p. 373): 'Labour, the economist tells us, is a commodity exchangeable like other commodities. This is in a certain sense true, but it is a commodity which attaches in a peculiar manner to the person of man.'

Alfred Marshall (1949, p. 471) also noted the asymmetry between factors of production in his famous textbook. He wrote:

176

when a person sells his services, he has to present himself where they are delivered. It matters nothing to the seller of bricks whether they are to be used in building a palace or a sewer: but it matters a great deal to the seller of labour.

These authors thus noted that even when hired out to another, labour necessarily remains united with its original owner. The same cannot be said for physical 'capital' goods when purchased or hired. When we buy a bag of potatoes they pass from the hands of the seller, and we may thus part company. When we hire a car we drive the vehicle away and the hirer is free to do other business. On the contrary, the worker, after hiring out his or her capacity to work, is obliged to enter and remain in the purchaser's domain. The act of hiring a worker necessarily involves an ongoing relationship between the buyer and seller, the employer and employee. The employer does not simply hire labour power, but also the inseparable time and attention of its original owner.[20]

What is also neglected by many economists is a key difference between production and exchange. In contrast to purchases of tuna, and to other contracts simply involving the exchange of goods, production encompasses the use of labour and the intentional and ongoing involvement of the worker. Production is the intentional creation by human beings of a good or service, using appropriate knowledge, tools, machines and materials. The fact of intentionality is important. Labour differs from capital goods because *people act but things do not*. As David Ellerman (1973, 1992) has reminded us, the modern legal system rightly recognises that the murderer alone, not the murderer plus his gun, was responsible for the killing. In the legal judgements concerning a crime there is no symmetry of responsibility between 'factors'.

Exchange itself creates no additional good or service. Those economists who attempt to gloss over this obvious distinction between production and exchange typically do so by assuming that exchange 'produces' marginal subjective utility for both buyer and seller. True or not, it does not actually produce additional goods or services. Mainstream economics typically focuses exclusively on the allocation of given sets of goods or services, neglecting the analysis of their creation or accumulation.

To sum up: incomplete and asymmetric information means that all sorts of contracts are potentially contestable in their detail and substance. Furthermore, some degree of power and control can be manifest in sales contracts as well as in employment contracts. However, what distinguishes the employment contract from other contracts is the legally sanctioned, power of detailed control by an employer over the manner and pattern of work of an employee.

Part of the difficulty in these matters is that the real world is muddled and complicated. As a result, legal and other authorities sometimes have difficulty distinguishing between employment, contracts for services and self-employment. Some people would take this as a reason for abandoning the analytical distinctions between employment, contracts for services and self-employment. Not so. As long as these concepts relate to important, underlying social relations then there is a justification for retaining the distinctions, no matter how murky and messy the phenomena may appear. Furthermore, even if these social relations disappear, the distinction will still be important to understand the nature of the former socio-economic system.

In general, an apparently blurred continuum of possibilities must be defined in terms of co-ordinates generated by distinctive polarities or ideal types. A muddled reality is no excuse for a muddled model. Likewise, a mutable reality is no justification for elastic ideas. Accordingly, even if the boundaries between employment and self-employment are breaking down in reality, the conceptual distinction between these two terms is still necessary to make sense of such a statement. In order to describe such a tangled reality we need carefully determined abstractions and clear ideal types to guide us. Without them we are conceptually blind. Clear and unmuddled concepts are necessary to penetrate a muddled world.

8

KNOWLEDGE AND
EMPLOYMENT

We will win and you will lose. You cannot do anything about it
because your failure is an internal disease. Your companies are
based on Taylor's principles. Worse, your heads are Taylorized
too. You firmly believe that sound management means executives
on the one side and workers on the other, on the one side men
who think and on the other side men who can only work. For you,
sound management is the art of smoothly transferring the executives' ideas into the workers' hands. We have passed the Taylor
stage. We are aware that business has become terribly complex.
Survival is very uncertain in an environment increasingly filled
with risk, the unexpected, and competition. Therefore, a company
must have the constant commitment of the minds of all of its
employees to survive. ... We know that the intelligence of a few
technocrats – even very bright ones – has become totally inadequate to face these challenges. Only the intellects of all employees
can permit a company to live with the ups and downs and the
requirements of its new environment. Yes, we will win and you
will lose. For you are not able to rid your minds of the obsolete
Taylorisms that we never had.
Konosuke Matsushita, founder of the Matsushita Electric
Industrial Co., 'The Secret is Shared' (1988)

In the preceding chapter, capitalism has been defined, and its dependence on
employment contracts established. In turn, the employment contract has
been distinguished from slavery, self-employment and contracts for
services. Essentially, what distinguishes employment from slavery is that
employees have legal rights not enjoyed by the slave. (They are legal
persons, entitled to own and trade property in their own right. They are entitled under contract law for some agreed remuneration for their work. They
have the legal right to terminate the contract with the employer.) What
distinguishes the employment contract from self-employment is the potential in the former case for detailed and ongoing control by an employer of the
manner and pattern of work. It was admitted, however, that in reality this
particular distinction is often blurred. The conceptual and legal distinction
between the two forms of contract is often difficult to enforce in practice.

Nevertheless, as argued above, precise definitions are necessary to make sense of variety and change. Aided by such definitions we may consider some possible future developments. In this and the following chapters we engage in an exercise of long-term 'scenario planning'. The time horizon here is longer than in the scenario planning typically used in business. However, the analysis shares with the established philosophy of scenarios a rejection of the pervasive notion that the best way to deal with the uncertain future is by building a deterministic or probabilistic model in an attempt to make a single 'best' forecast. Such methods are rejected in part because of the insurmountable difficulties in making forecasts in complex and open systems. In addition, there are practical as well as analytic reasons for not placing much emphasis on predictive modelling or probabilistic forecasts. Proponents of scenario planning regard forecasting as an encumbrance to strategic flexibility. This is partly because forecasts may attain an air of unwarranted authority in human affairs, based on a misplaced fatalism or determinism. Furthermore, people act within the terms of the forecast, and subsequently blame the forecaster rather than themselves if things go wrong. Strategic innovation and flexibility are not encouraged. Hence scenario planning has both an analytic and a practical rationale.[1]

Within the philosophy of scenarios, how is a scenario defined? Brian Loasby (1990, pp. 52–3) answered this question in the following terms:

> A scenario is an imagined future: a coherent set (or sequence) of possibilities to the realisation of which no fatal obstacle is perceived. One might conceive of a scenario for a specific project being assembled from a particular combination of values included within a sensitivity analysis, justified by a particular set of possible outcomes to the problems and threats identified, potential synergies (positive or negative) achieved, and particular contributions to the organisation's objectives.

It is scenarios of this type that are explored here, but applied to the socio-economic system as a whole rather than to any single organisation. Given that they depend to large degree on intuition and creative imagination, scenarios may sometimes seem to have an arbitrary quality. However, they become more meaningful and useful if they are rooted in the conditions of the present. Scenarios, like the 'utopian realism' advocated by Anthony Giddens (1990, pp. 154–5), are connected to 'institutionally immanent possibilities'. Scenario building is not idle speculation, but the investigation of *plausible future causal chains*, stemming from the conditions and forces of the present. The most powerful scenarios depend upon deep understanding and analysis, as well as creative intuition.

The particular scenarios considered here are born of the belief that modern, developed economies have entered, in the last two decades of the twentieth century, a long process which can lead to immense trans-formations, of historical proportions comparable to the Industrial Revolution itself.

THE ADVANCE OF COMPLEXITY AND KNOWLEDGE

In this chapter we shall discuss a connected set of developments which are currently manifest to some degree in all developed capitalist coun-tries. In particular, it shall be argued that if these developments continue on their present course they shall make the distinction in practice between employment and self-employment all the more difficult to uphold. Current legal difficulties in making this differentiation will be greatly exacerbated. In turn, this could lead to the emergence of a new types of legal and social relations between the worker and the firm. These changes will portend the metamorphosis of the entire social formation. If they proceed, these transformations in the underlying structure will bring all sorts of other changes in the patterns of life and work. Initially, the following broad and interlinked developments within modern capitalism will be assumed:

1 In core sectors of the economy, the processes of production and their products are becoming more complex and sophisticated.
2 Increasingly advanced knowledge or skills are being required in many processes of production. Skill levels in many sectors are being raised to cope with the growing degrees of difficulty and complexity.

Increasing economic complexity, in a meaningful and adequate sense, will entail a growing diversity of interactions between human beings, and between people and their technology.[2] Like all complex and open systems in changing environments, modern economies are subject to unpredictable changes and discontinuous structural transformations.[3]

What is meant by *increasing* complexity and *more advanced* knowledge? Acknowledging the difficulties involved in the definition of complexity, a rough-and-ready approach to such ordinal measures of change is proposed. By definition, as complexity increases, more and more 'bits' of information are required to specify interactions and changes within the structured system. To cope with increasing complexity in an economy, higher levels of skill and adaptability are required of workers. The level of skill is determined by the minimum amount of time taken to acquire the capacity to perform that skill. (This definition will be refined and elaborated in Chapter 10.)

Emphatically, it is not being suggested that any of these developments are inevitable. Indeed, for the sake of the argument in this section, it need not even be assumed that the above developments are real. The thesis can simply be treated as deductive and self-contained: *in so far* as those developments may occur, *then* such-and-such an outcome may be envisaged as a prominent possibility, based on a plausible chain of feasible causes and effects. However, the importance of the following argument derives largely from the fact that the above developments have been manifest in the general evolution of capitalist development over the last one or two centuries. Furthermore, in the last fifty years, they have become enhanced on a global scale and have gained substantial momentum. The knowledge-intensifying scenario discussed here has a high level of plausibility.

The idea of a 'law' of increasing complexity in both natural and social systems is found in the nineteenth-century writings of Herbert Spencer (1862). It has twentieth-century defenders but it has remained highly controversial. There is an important, long-standing and unresolved debate within modern biology as to whether evolution produces increasing complexity in nature.[4] However, it is not necessary to take sides on all these intricate issues in order to accept the thesis concerning the possible 'end of capitalism' to be elaborated below. What concerns us here is not some general evolutionary law, relevant for all complex systems, human and non-human, but a manifest tendency in modern industrial economies. As Thomas E. Cliffe Leslie (1888, p. 224) observed, well over a hundred years ago: 'the movement of the economic world has been one from simplicity to complexity, from uniformity to diversity, from unbroken custom to change, and, therefore, from the known to the unknown'. In broad terms this comment befits the modern world.

Robert Carneiro (1972, 1973) and Niklas Luhmann (1982, 1995) have also argued that increasing complexity in modern societies is an empirical fact and have given some reasons for its manifestation. Some of these reasons concern the increasing capacity for information storage and communication in modern economies, and the increasing possibility to build upon and process the acquired knowledge. If these arguments are correct, then the 'end of capitalism' thesis to be advanced here would acquire even greater force and significance. It would become more than a mere possibility.[5]

What are some consequences of assumptions 1 and 2 above? Consider the following points, all of which result from the former two assumptions:

3 Alongside general skills, there is an increasing reliance on specialist and idiosyncratic skills.
4 The use and transfer of information are becoming ever more extensive and important in economic activities.
5 Uncertainty is intruding increasingly into economic life.

Increasing complexity in an open and dynamic system brings with it the need for increased organisational and individual flexibility and adaptability. As complexity increases, and the required levels of skill rise, workers require more intensive training. New specialisms emerge to deal with the multiplying facets of the increasingly complex socio-economic system. But it becomes more difficult and costly to transfer readily from one specialism to another. Workers with advanced and transferable skills, and with enhanced capacities to rapidly learn and adapt, are more and more at a premium. We have a scenario of enhanced skills and growing knowledge intensity.

The increasing use of information is partly a result of growing complexity within an integrated system, and advances in information and communications technology. Uncertainty increases because calculable estimates of future events are more difficult in a more complex world (Beck, 1992). Democratic institutions also have difficulty coping with the complexity, bringing further uncertainty (Zolo, 1992). The pace of scientific and technological advance quickens, but brings increasing uncertainty along with its benefits. We are assured by the promise of future knowledge, but what future knowledge may bring is uncertain in principle.

Accordingly, increasing complexity is associated with greater 'knowledge intensity' in socio-economic systems. The growing importance of knowledge in the modern world has been marked by the use of terms such as the 'knowledge society'.[6] Some commentators have gone so far as to recognise the extent to which the growing importance of knowledge 'challenges property and labor as the constitutive mechanisms of society' (Böhme and Stehr, 1986, p. 7). The further exploration of this challenge is the theme of this chapter and much of the remainder of this book.

The importance of rapid learning is stressed in the modern strategic management literature. Michael Porter (1990, p. 73) argued that much modern competitiveness involves enhancing the capacity to learn of the corporation. Ray Stata (1989, p. 64) argued that 'the rate at which individuals and organizations learn may become the most sustainable competitive advantage'. Porter and Claas van der Linde (1995, p. 98) summarised the evidence on this issue: 'Detailed case studies of hundreds of industries, based in dozens of countries, reveal that internationally competitive companies are not those with the cheapest inputs or the largest scale, but those with the capacity to improve and innovate continually.'

In a complex and evolving, knowledge-intensive, system, agents not only have to learn, they have to learn how to learn, and to adapt and create anew (Bateson, 1972; Boisot, 1995; Drucker, 1993; J. Marquand, 1989; Senge, 1990). Workers and managers require more and more of the sophisticated cognitive abilities identified as essential to the cohesion and operation of the capitalist firm (Cartier, 1994; Choo, 1998; Fransman, 1994; Nonaka and Takeuchi, 1995). The economy becomes relatively less 'machine-intensive', and more and more 'knowledge-intensive'.

An important feature of the knowledge-intensive economy is the dematerialization of much production, and the shift from action-centred to intellective skills. For many people, the nature and form of work change radically: 'Immediate physical responses must be replaced by an abstract thought process in which options are considered, and choices are made and then translated into the terms of the information system' (Zuboff, 1988, p. 71). The growing knowledge intensity of work is expressed in such a shift of emphasis, from physical power and dexterity to the processing and evaluation of ideas (Reich, 1991). All human activity involves some use of both muscle and brain. But as the balance shifts radically from action to intellect, and from the manipulation of materials to symbols, work undergoes a fundamental transformation.

In the above discussion, not much use has been made of the crucial distinction between, on the one hand, codifiable or explicit knowledge, and on the other, tacit, incorporated or practical knowledge (Giddens, 1984; Nelson and Winter, 1982; M. Polyani, 1967). This does not mean that the difference is unimportant. It simply means that with the general growth of knowledge in an increasingly complex economy, it is not clear how the boundaries between codifiable and tacit knowledge will shift. In any case, whatever the relative balance, the absolute importance of tacit knowledge will not diminish with these developments. Tacit knowledge remains an indispensable foundation of all knowledge.[7]

WHERE MARXISM GOT IT WRONG

This scenario of declining machine intensity, and increasing knowledge intensity, is the reverse of the developments portrayed in *Capital*. There Karl Marx (1976a, pp. 546–7) argued that the technical development of machinery within capitalism was leading to a reduction in the time taken to acquire the specialist skills of a machine operative. Consequently, the development of machinery would undermine the division of labour. He continued:

> The special skill of each individual machine-operator, who has been now deprived of all significance, vanishes as an infinitesimal quantity in the face of the science, the gigantic natural forces, and the mass of social labour embodied in the system of machinery.
>
> (Marx, 1976a, p. 549)

Accordingly, Marx (1976a, p. 788) wrote:

> the development of the capitalist mode of production ... enables the

capitalist...to set in motion more labour... as he progressively replaces skilled workers by less skilled, mature labour-power by immature, male by female, that of adults by that of young persons or children.

Overall, Marx perceived an inexorable process of de-skilling under capitalism. He paid inadequate attention to the growing complexity of socio-economic systems and the increasing need for knowledge-based skills.

Furthermore, Marx inherited from Adam Smith an emphasis on the material and manual aspects of work. For Marx, like Smith, labour was primarily an engagement of human mind and muscle with machines, tools and materials. Instead of information and knowledge, Smith (1976, p. 17) wrote principally of 'the increase of dexterity in every particular workman'. Thus Smith saw the benefit of learning-by-doing as being primarily one of manual dexterity. Wider notions of learning and knowledge were not prominent. True, he considered the mental as well as the manual division of labour. However, his implicit separation of the processes of conception and execution in the labour process robbed manual labour of tacit or and other knowledge and denied the unity of knowing and doing. Furthermore, although Smith put technological change to the forefront, this was not linked explicitly and primarily to an increase in knowledge but to an increase of physical capital goods. Marx inherited these traits from Smith and other classical writers.

This conception of labour, as being engaged first and foremost with material objects, ignores an important point, evident even in the times of Smith or Marx, but much more obvious today. The point is that work is not necessarily centred on the materiality of machines, tools and raw materials but is also engaged with *other minds*, whether these be human minds or their pale and partial computer surrogates. Action always takes place in a material and natural integument, but it deals more and more with intersubjective discourses, concerning the interpretations, meanings and uses of information. It has always been more than the manipulation of material objects. Labour requires judgement, and all judgement unavoidably involves the deployment of both tacit and explicit knowledge. And it is a social and cultural process, engaging with the interpretations and judgements of others.[8]

Inadequate conceptions of labour prevailed for more than a century after the first volume of *Capital* and for almost two centuries after *The Wealth of Nations*. Taking his cue explicitly from Marx, the influential theorist Harry Braverman (1974) asserted that modern capitalism had an inherent and unavoidable tendency towards the de-skilling of work. His argument was that craft-based and other skills were being replaced by machines and that the workers were being reallocated to relatively unskilled tasks. But, despite its influence, his argument was flawed. It is not clear why the re-tasked worker will *necessarily* be placed in jobs involving a lower level of skill. Based on a one-sided theoretical argument and inadequate empirical evidence, the prediction has failed to materialise (Ashton and Green, 1996; Attewell, 1992; Cutler, 1978; Rubery and Wilkinson, 1994; S. Wood, 1982, 1989). In particular, 'there is no substantial evidence to show that the overall skill level of the U.S. labor force has declined through the twentieth century' (Nyland, 1996, p. 988). Historical evidence suggests that machines can enhance skills rather than reduce them (Goldin and Katz, 1996). At least throughout the twentieth century, in many major sectors of modern capitalist economies, skill levels have increased rather than decreased.

Braverman overlooked the fact that the capitalists can have opportunities and incentives to mechanise unskilled as well as skilled work. There are greater and cheaper possibilities for creating machines to do simple and repetitive work, compared with getting machines to carry out sophisticated, analytical and creative tasks. For the capitalist, the net benefit from replacing relatively unskilled labour by machines could be greater than that obtained by mechanising skilled work. Braverman and his followers have not shown otherwise, and the argument that capitalism *necessarily* involves de-skilling falls. Indeed, many of his illustrations related specifically to US institutions and cannot be readily transposed elsewhere. Instead of an immanent, inevitable and universal tendency within capitalism, Braverman identified just one possible scenario. The alternative *possibility* of de-skilling is discussed within the so-called 'omega scenario' below.

However, despite its errors, Marxism should at least be credited with engaging with possible futures. By contrast, mainstream economics has paid relatively attention to the underlying forces of transformation that challenge contemporary socio-economic systems. It is one thing to say something interesting and to get it wrong. It is another to avoid committing error by saying nothing. We learn from conjecture and error, rather than from silence.

COMPLEXITY AND COMPUTER TECHNOLOGY

The assumptions here regarding increasing skill levels concern the most knowledge-intensive, technologically advanced and dynamic core of the capitalist system, in parts of the manufacturing and service sectors. We are addressing developments at the dynamic core of the economy, not in its every niche or recess. This does not rule out the possibility, as today, of a substantial underclass of unskilled or unemployed workers.[9] Today, many workers in developed countries are confined to low paid, part-time, insecure or menial 'McJobs', often in the service sector. To some degree this may result from, as well as persist alongside, the above

186

developments. Some technological innovations, such as the fork-lift truck, have put thousands of manual workers out of work. Other developments in information technology may enable increased surveillance of – and power over – sections of the workforce, undermining further their flexibility and autonomy: an 'information panopticon' (Zuboff, 1988, Chapter 9). Nevertheless, at first we are considering a scenario where the developments at the dynamic core overwhelm and dominate other tendencies. Ways in which this dominant scenario could be blocked or undermined will be considered later.

Furthermore, what happens in the dynamic core is not sufficient to determine outcomes in the remainder of the economy. For example, studies of the impact of computers and other technological changes indicate a diverse set of possible outcomes on the overall level of unemployment and the structure of the labour force, depending much on the institutional forms prevailing in the countries involved (Appelbaum and Schettkat, 1990).

Technology has an effect on the nature, pattern, organisation and context of work, but alone it does not determine them. It can be used in different ways, leading to different outcomes. For instance, technology can be used to increase automaticity: to routinise human work by making it even more mechanical and inflexible. But this is a precarious and impermanent outcome because it makes the humans more readily substitutable by machines. Neither does it use the powers of modern technology to the full.

Will increasingly sophisticated computers and artificial intelligence take over some of the functions of the intelligent human in the production process? Possibly, but only to a very limited degree. Computers can mimic some aspects of intelligent behaviour through their data-processing powers. But they cannot replicate key features of human intelligence. Crucially, they lack intuition and sophisticated judgement (Dreyfus and Dreyfus, 1986). Such skilled competences cannot be taken over by machines. In so far as computers can take over some functions, the overall, net outcome in terms of the balance of skills in the workforce is not necessarily towards de-skilling (Levy and Murnane, 1996; S. Wood, 1989). The scenario being discussed here is thus compatible with the development of computer technology.

Consistent with this scenario, it is possible that a growing population of intelligent machines will be associated with a growing team of versatile, creative, problem-solving human beings. In the past, the introduction of machines has often meant an increase in skill levels, rather than the reverse: machines and skilled workers have often been complements rather than substitutes (Goldin and Katz, 1996). Humans are required to perform the more intuitive, complex and human-interactive tasks for which machines are less suited. But it remains to be seen whether these capacities will be restrained or enhanced. With proposition 2 above we are assuming the latter rather than the former. Although it cannot be simply extrapolated from existing data, nor does technological advance necessarily bring this result, we are nevertheless assuming a process of 'upskilling' in this particular scenario.[10]

In some contexts, the automation of aspects of production can challenge managerial control. Computers may free up skilled workers for tasks of a more evaluative and judgmental character. In turn, critical judgement involves asking questions, and saying 'no' when things do not seem right. However, probing questions can be inimical to managerial authority, especially when leading to suggestions that established procedures should be changed. As Shoshona Zuboff (1988, p. 291) has elaborated, in her extensive study of the impact of computer technology on work:

> Obedience has been the axial principle of task execution in the traditional environment of imperative control. The logic of that environment is reproduced when technology is used only to automate. When tasks require intellective effort, however, obedience can be dysfunctional and can impede the exploitation of information. Under such conditions, internal commitment and motivation replace authority as the primary bond between the individual and the task.

In this way, traditional work organisation and managerial authority are challenged:

> The explication of meaning that is so central to the development of intellective skills requires that people become their own authorities. ... Without the consensual immediacy of a shared action context, individuals must construct interpretations of the information at hand and so reveal what they believe to be significant. In this way, authority is located in the process of creating and articulating meaning, rather than in a particular position or function. Under such conditions, it is unlikely that a traditional organization will achieve the efficiencies ... that have become mandatory.
> (Zuboff, 1988, p. 308)

The developments outlined above thus present a challenge for the future. However, a generalised failure of organisations to transform their structures to meet these challenges will frustrate the unfolding of the knowledge-intensive scenario. The developments of the past and coming decades offer alternative paths into the future. We must thus consider alternative scenarios, alongside the main one considered here.

AN ALTERNATIVE ROUTE: THE OMEGA SCENARIO

If the growth of knowledge intensity is thwarted – possibly by a failure of organisations to transform themselves to meet the challenges – a technologically sophisticated economy may evolve in which, nevertheless, human innovation and learning have stagnated. In the place of humans, many production processes would be administered largely by artificially intelligent machines. Technology would be used extensively, not to enhance human creative powers, but by as much as possible to replace them. Some economic growth occurs but it would not result from substantial human learning or innovation. It would emanate largely from a growing output of physical goods and automated services.

In this alternative scenario, the population would generally occupy a life of leisure, with some of them lucky (or unfortunate) enough to have a few hours' work a week in the restaurant or retail sector, serving customers who value human interaction. A few others would be active as the occasional, remaining managers within production, artists, or craft manufacturers of fashionable artefacts. In such a society, power and wealth would emanate largely from ownership of the intelligent machines. Being disengaged from productive activity and satiated by an adequate supply of entertainments and material goods, the general culture of aspiration becomes one more of conspicuous consumption than of productive emulation. Status would be conferred on people according to what they consume, rather than what they create or achieve.[11]

This brave new world of McJobs, unemployment and robots will be referred to in this book as the 'omega (ω) scenario'. (It could also be reasonably described as the 'Braverman scenario'.)[12] It is consistent with proposition 1 above, but it is a scenario quite different from any entailing proposition 2. The omega scenario is not being ruled out as impossible. It is simply the case that our foremost concern is to pursue scenarios involving all five propositions, without attaching any probabilities to any outcome. Notably, the omega scenario remains squarely within capitalism, as employer control of the work process, as well as shareholder ownership of the corporation and its products, are not further undermined to any great degree. The omega scenario will be discussed further in the next two chapters. We now return to the main scenario discussed here, involving all five of the above propositions.

THE ARROW PROBLEM, THE KNIGHT PARADOX AND THE DISSOLUTION OF CONTROL

We now focus on proposition 4 above, and on the increasing use of information in modern economies. Attempts to fit information and knowledge into neoclassical economic analyses typically treat it as something 'out there' which is costly to obtain or produce. The mainstream 'economics of information' handles information much like any other commodity (Stigler, 1961). But this is illegitimate, for several reasons. Clearly, each new piece of information must be different from every other, otherwise it would not be new or useful information. Information is clearly non-homogeneous, and consequently cannot be traded on competitive markets, where broadly similar commodities compete on price terms. As Kenneth Boulding (1966, p. 3) pointed out: 'the intrinsic heterogeneity of its substance, makes it very difficult to think of a price of knowledge as such'. For several additional reasons, some of which are explored elsewhere in this present volume, information and knowledge do not readily fit into the analytical framework of neoclassical economics.[13]

Furthermore, as explained below, the growth of knowledge and information raises questions concerning the nature of property, trade and markets. As knowledge and information become more important in modern economies, the very meaning of core ideas such as property and exchange are challenged, and their continued existence may even be undermined. It is sometimes argued that the development of scientific knowledge is to some extent hindered by too much reliance on private property rights and markets (Arrow, 1962a; Nelson, 1959; Wible, 1995). This may be true or false. The separate point being made here is causally in the reverse direction: that the integrity of property and the functioning of the market are being undermined by the growth of knowledge (Callon, 1994). This fact is somewhat ironic, as the very twentieth-century economists – such as Frank Knight, Ludwig von Mises and Friedrich Hayek – who most persistently emphasised problems of knowledge and uncertainty, were among those most wedded to a free market ideology. It seems that they did not know the full content of the Pandora's box that they had successfully opened.

Unlike other commodities, the contractual transfer of information has some curious features that challenge and possibly impair the standard contractarian framework. Some of these contractarian oddities were pointed out several years ago by Richard Nelson (1959, p. 306) and developed by Kenneth Arrow (1962a) in a famous article. Implicitly, Arrow confined his discussion to explicit and transferable information: this excludes tacit knowledge. Nevertheless, in reality, much information is codifiable and transferable, and the following points are of some importance.

First, once acquired, codifiable information can often be easily reproduced in multiple copies by its buyer, and possibly be sold to others. This places the seller at a disadvantage. Accordingly, there may be licences, patents or other restrictions to prevent the buyer from selling it on to others.

Second, codifiable information has the peculiar property that, once it is sold, it also remains in the hands of the seller. Information is not a 'normal' commodity that changes hands from seller to buyer when it is purchased. Thomas Jefferson allegedly likened knowledge to the light of a candle: even as its flame is passed on to another candle, its own light is not weakened.

Third, and crucially for our purposes here, Arrow (1962a, p. 616) wrote: 'there is a fundamental paradox in the determination of demand for information: its value for the purchaser is not known until he has the information, but then he has in effect acquired it without cost'. If we knew what we were going to buy then we would no longer need to buy it.

As a result, in an economy involving substantial flows of information, it is *not* always possible, to use Hayek's (1948, p. 18) symptomatically possessive phraseology, to establish clear 'rules which, above all, enable man to distinguish between mine and thine'. As Arrow suggested, information challenges the bounds of exclusive and individual property. For instance, what is sold as information remains also the property of the seller. Outside the restrictions of patent laws, what is possessed cannot always be clearly defined, because to define it is to give it away. It is often unclear as to who owns what information. It is not always possibly to break up information into discrete pieces and give each one an ownership tag. It is often difficult to determine who 'discovered' the information in the first place, and who can thus claim legal title to its 'ownership'. Far from being transparent, in an information-rich society what is 'mine' and what is 'thine' may become increasingly mysterious.[14]

In particular, the crucial problem of not knowing what we are buying until after we have bought it is clearly manifest in many modern employment contracts. This is especially the case with highly skilled employees: note propositions 2 and 3 above (pp. 181, 182). With skilled workers, the hirers do not know what they have hired. The persons interviewing the potential employees for the job may not be versed in the particular skills being sought, and will thus be unable to make a fully-informed judgement of their abilities.

Even if the interviewing panel *did* have these skills, it would be extremely unlikely that the people appointing the members of the panel would have them as well. Who judges the judgement of the judges? At some stage the judgement would be imperfect. This kind of information problem was explored by Knight (1921) in his classic work on the firm. He identified the intractable problem of 'judgement of judgement' (p. 311) in a climate of unknowledge and uncertainty. How do we judge the capabilities of others to make good decisions, with regard to matters with which we are ourselves unfamiliar? Knight argued that the task 'of selecting human capacities for dealing with unforseeable situations involves paradox and apparent theoretical impossibility of solution' (p. 298). In other words, the purchase or allocation of knowledge or competence itself requires knowledge or competence, and there is a potential problem of infinite regress (Pelikan, 1989). Knight thus suggested that not all economic competences – particularly that relating to the exercising of judgement in a milieu of uncertainty – are contractible. As a result, a complete market for all skills is impossible in principle.[15]

Typically it will be assumed that the potential employee will learn many of the particular skills after he or she is appointed. Such learning will often depend on imitation and close interaction with others at work. But it is impossible to specify fully in advance the skills that a worker may acquire while working on the job, or to detail the information that may be transferred and the learning experiences that may occur.

Difficulties of this kind do not arise simply at the selection and appointment of an employee. They remain during the subsequent period of employment. By definition, employment involves potential control and supervision by others. However, as Drucker (1993, p. 107) asserts, 'the organization is increasingly composed of specialists, each of whom knows more about his or her own speciality than anybody else in the organization'. This creates a supervisory problem. If the worker has the highly specific and idiosyncratic skills that are needed in a complex economy, then the extent of proficient supervision and control of the worker depends also on the possession of relevant capabilities by the supervisor. In an increasing number of cases, these capabilities will be lacking. Close and highly evaluative supervision, based on a hierarchy of command, will be less viable, simply because the nominal supervisors will not know the best way of doing the job – or even the precise purpose of the specialist job itself – and the worker will know better.

The shift from physical to intellectual work also compounds the problem. Even though managers lacked complete knowledge of the idiosyncratic skills required in action-centred work, at least they could observe the physical activity and its output, and make semi-informed judgements concerning the efficiency and aptitude of the worker. In contrast, with intellective skills, meaningful supervision is less viable. We can observe manual work, but it is impossible to see what is going on in someone's head (Zuboff, 1988).

Admittedly, developments in information technology would in some respects make sophisticated surveillance of the workforce possible. However, such surveillance would mainly concern the location and visible engagement of the workers, not the workings of the mind, nor the evaluation of the details of knowledge-intensive work. If managers cannot know what their workers know, then neither can a video- or computer-based monitoring system. Furthermore, the installation of surveillance systems is likely to undermine the culture of trust and co-operation which is necessary for the full development of the learning economy. As work becomes more complex and knowledge-intensive, then these problems are compounded.

Detailed direction, concerning what to do and how to do it, will become less viable and productive. Without finding evaluators with similar expertise, the possibility of assessing the worker's capacities and performance will be limited. Detailed and effective supervision is thwarted by problems of complexity. As Nelson (1981, p. 1038) has argued:

> management cannot effectively 'choose' what is to be done in any detailed way, and has only broad control over what is done, and how well. Only a small portion of what people actually do on a job can be monitored in detail.

Consequently, in the employment contract, the key characteristic of detailed managerial control is increasingly bounded and impaired as a result of the growing complexity of the production process.

To some degree, problems associated with a degree of complexity existed in early industrial capitalism, even when manual workers were operating looms, digging ditches or sharpening pins. Workers have always possessed some tacit and other skills beyond the reach of managerial comprehension. But in modern, complex, knowledge-intensive capitalism the predicament has become immensely more compounded and severe. In particular, what were formerly regarded as exclusively managerial, administrative or organisational capabilities are more and more being expected of other workers, not nominally described as managers. The old distinctions between the conception of a task and its execution, as elaborated in the 'scientific management' of Frederick Winslow Taylor (1911), are breaking down. In practice, the division between the two is increasingly difficult to enforce or sustain (McGregor, 1960; Vroom and Deci, 1970).[16]

The flattening of the traditional hierarchies, with the blurring of the boundary between managers and workers, is bound up with the increasing complexity and knowledge intensity of the processes of production. Responsibility is diffused more throughout the organisation, instead of being concentrated at the top. With flatter hierarchies, there is less vested interest in the status bestowed by rank, and in the status quo. There is thus less resistance to change, and flatter structures may facilitate learning (Fligstein, 1990; Hamilton and Feenstra, 1995; Hammer and Champy, 1993; Perrow, 1986, 1990; Wikström and Norman, 1994).

TOUCHING THE INTANGIBLE

A further consequence of an increasing reliance on advanced skills and knowledge is that these become relatively more important, compared with the physical instruments of work, such as tools and machines. This shifting balance is likely to be expressed in changes in relative costs. Today, some specialist skills can command very high prices on the market, whereas – despite massive improvements – computers and many other high-technology components have become progressively cheaper in real terms. It is being assumed here that the balance of strategic importance and economic value will shift further in favour of human knowledge and skill.

To understand ideas, it is important to see how they have evolved, and with what they have been contrasted. In this section we examine some of the precedents for the opposing views on this question, as well as developing and clarifying the ideas further.[17]

The relative importance of the physical means of production in the production process, compared with knowledge and other 'intangible assets', has typically been over-stressed by mainstream and non-mainstream economists alike. Mainstream economists have long depicted the contribution of physical 'capital', alongside 'labour', to production, treating them both as inputs into a mechanistic function.[18] Although Marx differed in one respect, by seeing labour alone as the source of all 'value', he also stressed tangible rather than intangible assets. Further, in his theory of the falling rate of profit he argued that the overall value of the physical means of production would tend to increase, relative to the value of the living labour.[19] In addition, an exclusive focus on physical assets is also found in the input–output matrices of Wassily Leontief (1966) and Piero Sraffa (1960).[20]

Against this overwhelming trend, Thorstein Veblen was one of the first to stress the relative importance of immaterial assets, including the 'knowledge and practice of ways and means' (Veblen, 1919, p. 343). For Veblen (ibid., pp. 185–6) production relied on 'the accumulated, habitual knowledge of the ways and means involved … the outcome of long experience and experimentation'. The production and use of all material and immaterial assets depend on elusive, immaterial circumstances and combinations of skills, which are often difficult to identify and own. These capacities reside in the institutions and culture of the socio-economic system, and they are built up over a long period of time. Accordingly, 'the capitalist employer is … not possessed of any appreciable fraction of the immaterial equipment' that is drawn upon every day in the process of production (ibid., p. 344).[21]

Veblen invited his readers to consider what would be worse for a community: the loss of all the capital goods used in production, or the loss of all knowledge and skills. The latter sacrifice, he contended, would be much more destructive, because without the relevant knowledge it would not be possible to use much of the remaining equipment. On the other hand, while the loss of capital goods would be substantial and destructive, production could be built up to former levels in a much shorter period of time, using the knowledge retained.[22] Veblen thus argued that 'the substantial core of capital is immaterial wealth, and that the material objects which are formally the subject of the capitalist's ownership are, by comparison, a transient and adventitious matter' (ibid., p. 200). As he rejoined in another work:

> This immaterial equipment is, far and away, the most important productive agency in the case; although, it is true, economists have not been in the habit of making much of it, since it is in the main not capable of being stated in terms of price, and so does not appear in the statistical schedules of accumulated wealth.
>
> (Veblen, 1915, p. 272)

These important arguments were taken up and developed by the American institutional economist John Commons (1924, pp. 235–82; 1934, pp. 649–72). Furthermore, aspects of Veblen's standpoint were eloquently summarised by the neglected British institutional economist John Hobson (1936, p. 67):

> The productivity of workers on the soil or in the factory depends for its amount and quality not entirely and not chiefly upon their working energy, but upon economic conditions under which they work that lie outside their personal control. First and foremost among these conditions is the state of the industrial arts, a rich social inheritance of long accumulation, which is the basis of all skilled workmanship. No living worker or group of workers can properly lay claim to this accumulated knowledge as his private possession, though he is entitled to utilize it in order to increase his productivity.

The distinctiveness of this conceptual viewpoint should not be underestimated. Mainstream explanations of economic growth have stressed changes in factor inputs, on the one hand, and technological changes driven by research and development, on the other. Emphasis on such tangible inputs and measures has often obscured the importance of learning, and the accumulation of social knowledge. Kenneth Boulding was one of a number of heterodox economists who questioned mainstream treatments of information and knowledge. He wrote that:

> economic development ... is essentially a knowledge process ... but we are still too much obsessed by mechanical models, capital-income ratios, and even input-output tables, to the neglect of the study of the learning process which is the real key to development.
>
> (Boulding, 1966, p. 6)

There is a tendency to treat knowledge and skill as identifiable substances, stored up and possessed by individuals, alongside and akin to their material wealth. For example, the widespread use of the term 'human capital' often misleads us by suggesting that accumulated knowledge and skills are readily measurable in monetary terms and generally tradable on the market.[23] On the contrary, they are complex, intangible, tacit, elusive, socially embodied, multi-faceted and largely unmarketable. Above all, why should we ennoble 'capital' with human qualities? As David Ashton and Francis Green (1996, p. 18) remark, instead of the 'theory of human capital':

> It might have been more accurate to speak instead of 'the theory of capital humans' as this would capture the fact that it is humans whose skills are being objectified, rather than physical capital which is being dignified with humanity.[24]

Since the time of Veblen and Hobson, capitalism has become much more knowledge-intensive and reliant on socially accumulated knowledge. Consequently, in the knowledge-based economy of today, the importance of the earlier insights of Veblen and Hobson is much the greater. From them we may draw a number of implications. First, in so far as the physical means of production have become relatively less important, the question of who owns them has become less consequential to a similar degree. Accordingly, the possession of useful knowledge and skills by the worker has increased in relative significance, compared to the tangible instruments of work.

It is not being suggested that we should disregard the question of who owns the means of production. What is being argued is that in this scenario the changing balance between intangible and tangible assets, and the growing reliance on knowledge and skill, should be taken into account. It means, for instance, that the relative bargaining power of the skilled employee has increased, and the gap in this respect between the skilled and the unskilled worker has widened substantially. These differences are manifest in growing differences of income, and the severe shortages of skilled labour in many industrialised countries, compared with the widespread mass unemployment of unskilled labour. The skilled worker carries knowledge as a significant tool, signifying possession of an important but immaterial part of the means of production.[25]

It also means that the emphasis made by Marx and his followers on the *de facto* separation of the worker from ownership of any of the 'means of production' has to be modified. As knowledge-intensive skills become more prominent, then more and more workers will be in possession of valuable set of conceptual, analytical, administrative and other skills.[26] The term 'proletarian' – referring literally to those that possess nothing but their children – has become even more of an exaggeration. The mental means of production have become much more important, in both relative and absolute terms. Under capitalism, these personal skills may be hired but not owned by others. Of course, this does not mean the abolition of divisions between social classes, nor necessarily a reduction in material inequality. Today, the skilled worker carries valuable, inalienable, accumulated knowledge, even if they are relatively deprived in terms of income, wealth, control and power.

These developments are not an embarrassment for Marxism alone. They create increasing practical problems for the legal enforcement of the distinction between employment contracts and contracts for services. The legal system has already experienced severe difficulty in identifying clear criteria to identify whether or not the worker is under the 'control' of another person. As a result, as noted above, the question of whether or not the worker owns or provides the instruments of work is often used as a surrogate criterion. But this alternative test is itself in severe difficulties. For example, some corporations are making increasing use of allegedly self-employed management experts and consultants. These skilled managers often move on from one problem-shooting exercise to another, and receive substantial fees. However, these rewards have little or nothing to do with the physical instruments of production used (and perhaps owned) by the consultant. Essentially, what is being hired is intangible: the knowledge and highly developed capabilities of the skilled manager. As a consequence, the surrogate legal criterion will mistakenly fail to identify this person as self-employed, even if the perceptions of both consultant and client are to the contrary.

COLLECTIVE KNOWLEDGE AND CORPORATE CULTURE

Propositions 2 and 3 above suggest that education, training and on-the-job learning are of increasing significance. Here we shall concern ourselves primarily with on-the-job learning, where much productive and practical knowledge is acquired. It will be contended that much of this learning is of a group character. Such a proposition may seem odd, given the presumption that ideas and knowledge surely reside in the heads of individuals, not somehow in groups. Methodologically individualist economists dismiss the notion of group knowledge as untenable. Nevertheless, ideas of group and organisational knowledge are widely established, in a number of literatures, from organisational learning to the theory of the firm. Again we shall examine some relevant pieces of intellectual history. It will be shown also that key ideas in this area were prefigured in earlier work by institutional economists, from Veblen to Edith Penrose. These prescient ideas were relevant in the past, but much more so today. Their importance has increased rather than declined.

Learning from experience involves, by imitation and repetition, the acquisition of both tacit and explicit knowledge (Penrose, 1959, p. 53). Partly because of the extent and importance of imitation, on-the-job learning is very much an interactive and group activity. The knowledge is largely uncodified, so often we learn by closely observing and imitating others. As Bart Nooteboom (1992, pp. 295–7) has elaborated:

> To change one's ideas one needs to interact with others ... one needs interaction with users, suppliers and competitors in order to acquire or develop appropriate or novel categories of perception, interpretation and evaluation. In the case of tacit knowledge, interaction facilitates the transfer of knowledge ... that would not otherwise be possible.

For the above reasons, a view arises in this literature that competences within the firm are both context-dependent and organically related to each other. As Penrose (1959, p. 52) has explained in her classic book on the firm:

> When men have become used to working in a particular group of other men, they become individually and as a group more valuable to the firm in that the services they can render are enhanced by their knowledge of their fellow-workers, of the methods of the firm, and the best way of doing things in the particular set of circumstances in which they are working.

Another passage made a similar point:

> Businessmen commonly refer to the managerial group as a 'team' and the use of this word implies that management in some sense works as a unit. An administrative group is something more than a collection of individuals; it is a collection of individuals who have had experience in working together, for only in this way can 'teamwork' be developed. Existing managerial personnel provide services that cannot be provided by personnel newly hired from outside the firm, not only because they make up the administrative organization which cannot be expanded except by their own actions, but also because the experience they gain from working within the firm and with each other enables them to provide services that are uniquely valuable for the operation of the particular group with which they are associated.
>
> (Penrose, 1959, p. 46)

Competences do not reside merely in individuals because they are dependent on the organisational context (Argyris and Schön, 1978). Typically they have an interdependent and organic quality, many depending on the shared experiences and interactions within the firm.

That the knowledge within a corporation relates essentially to the organisation and the group, rather than to the individuals composing them, has also been emphasised by Sidney Winter. He wrote that: 'it is undeniable that large corporations are *as organisations* among society's most significant repositories of the productive knowledge that they exercise and not merely an economic contrivance of the individuals currently associated with them' (Winter, 1988, p. 170). As Winter (1982, p. 76) elaborated elsewhere:

> The coordination displayed in the performance of organizational routines is, like that displayed in the exercise of individual skills, the fruit of practice. What requires emphasis is that ... the learning experience is a shared experience of organization members ... Thus, even if the contents of the organizational memory are stored only in the form of memory traces in the memories of individual members, it is still an organizational knowledge in the sense that the fragment stored by each individual member is not fully meaningful or effective except in the context provided by the fragments stored by other members.
>
> (Winter, 1982, p. 76)

Accordingly, 'it is firms, not the people that work for firms, that know how to make gasoline, automobiles and computers' (ibid.). Note also that Masahiko Aoki wrote of the collective nature of employee knowledge in the firm. Since 'learning and communication of employees take place only within the organizational framework, their knowledge, as well as their capacities to communicate with each other are not individually portable' (Aoki, 1990b, p. 45). Similar points were stressed by Dosi and Marengo (1994, p. 162): 'organizational knowledge is neither presupposed nor derived from the available information but rather emerges as a property of the learning system and is shaped by the interaction among the various learning processes that constitute the organization'. Teece and Pisano (1994, pp. 544–5) elaborated a similar theme:

> While individual skills are of relevance, their value depends upon their employment, in particular organizational settings. Learning processes are intrinsically social and collective and occur not only through the imitation and emulation of individuals, as with teacher-student or master-apprentice, but also because of joint contributions to the understanding of complex problems. Learning requires common codes of communication and coordinated search procedures.

Contrary to the view of information and knowledge as portable and readily transmissible, knowledge is embedded in social structures and in general is not immediately transparent. This is partly because opportunities for learning within the firm are transaction and production-specific

(Teece, 1988). Also, learning is an instituted process of interpretation, appraisal, trial, feedback, and evaluation, involving socially-transmitted cognitive frames and routinised group practices which are often taken for granted. Organisational knowledge interacts with individual knowledge but is more than the sum of the individual parts. It is context-dependent, culture-bound and institutionalised. Organisational learning entails a process of inquiry, reflection and evaluation in which the model that is shared by several people is revised and becomes embedded in the regular practices of the organisation.

For these reasons and more, the values and culture of a corporation are all-important. As Chester Barnard (1938, p. 282) wrote long ago: 'Organizations endure, however, in proportion to the breadth of the morality by which they are governed. This is only to say that foresight, long purposes, high ideals, are the basis for the persistence of cooperation.' For such reasons, analysts such as Gary Miller (1992) suggest that firms succeed in so far as they transcend narrow, individual opportunism by an ethic of mutual co-operation.

However, the cultivation of trust and co-operation is just one part of the story. Another key point is that the firm acts as a relatively durable repository and transmission belt through time of a corporate culture. This cultural transmission facilitates group and individual learning and therefore increases productivity within the firm. Having rejected the analytical starting point of the given individual, it is possible to conceive of learning as a developmental and reconstitutive process. Corporate culture is more than shared information: through shared practices and habits of thought, it provides the method, context, values and language of learning and the evolution of both group and individual competences.

Corporate culture is not sustained of its own accord. The firm survives and functions on the basis of both formal and informal relations. Legal contracts and property rights, sustaining human relations of command and authority, are essential in keeping the firm together as a unit and motivating the individuals within it. This is because individuals cannot always be relied on to co-operate together in a way which serves the objectives of the organisation as a whole. A degree of opportunism may be a partial reason for this, but it is not necessary to exaggerate its importance, or paint a picture in the genre of Oliver Williamson (1975, 1985) of a collection of wholly devious and self-seeking individuals. Opportunism exists, but plentiful evidence exists that it is not the single most important characteristic of human nature (Brown, 1954).

Informal relations involving cultural norms, established routines, trust and so on, are also essential to the integrity of the firm. The legal framework of contracts and property rights is not enough to integrate the firm as a unit. Containing individuals from different backgrounds, with diverse occupations and duties, the firm has to attempt to generate a unifying and integrative culture to survive. As Michael Dietrich (1993, 1994) outlines, typically, a firm's culture will combine diversity – reflecting different contexts, practices, goals and beliefs – with the binding threads of a culture of corporate oneness and unity. The relative coherence of this integrative culture parallels the administrative unity of the firm. Within this integrated institution, the corporate culture affects the storage and transmission of information, the acquisition and retention of knowledge, the framing of decisions and the nature and extent of human learning.

The acquisition and use of knowledge depend typically on cues and circumstances provided in the immediate social and material environment (Bruner, 1973; Clark, 1997). Appropriate cues call forth bursts of activity, which in turn create a new situation, and new cues for action. Thought and action are inseparable from their context. The skilled writer will not compose without writing materials at hand. *A fortiori,* the tacit knowledge of the computer technician will not be deployed without engagement with the physical surroundings of computer technology. Knowledge involving extended social interaction with others will rely on the cues and triggers of social behaviour, using a common language with shared meanings. This gives much relevant knowledge a group or organisational quality, even if social groups lack brains apart from the individuals of which they are composed. Accordingly, as Ikujiro Nonaka and Hirotaka Takeuchi (1995) explain at length, on the basis of case studies of Japanese and American companies, the creation and use of knowledge in modern economies involve intensive interaction and conversation between people, sharing to a degree a common vision and purpose.

Note that the group-based character of technological and productive knowledge was recognised by Veblen, long ago, albeit in a less elaborated form. He wrote with a high degree of conceptual and methodological sophistication. Contrary to some interpreters, Veblen's standpoint was not informed by a crude holism in which the individual was submerged in the collectivity. His insights have increasing relevance in the modern, learning economy. Consider first the following passage, written in 1908:

> The complement of technological knowledge so held, used, and transmitted in the life of the community is, of course, made up out of the experience of individuals. Experience, experimentation, habit, knowledge, initiative, are phenomena of individual life, and it is necessarily from this source that the community's common stock is all derived. The possibility of growth lies in the feasibility of accumulating knowledge gained by individual experience and initiative, and therefore it lies in the feasibility of one individual's learning from the experience of another.
>
> (Veblen, 1919, p. 328)

It is striking that the modern view that 'possibility of growth lies in the feasibility of accumulating knowledge' could have emerged so long ago. Veblen saw *both* the focus of knowledge in individual experience *and* its dependence upon social relations. As he explained in 1898:

> Production takes place only in society – only through the co-operation of an industrial community. This industrial community ... always comprises a group, large enough to contain and transmit the traditions, tools, technical knowledge, and usages without which there can be no industrial organisation and no economic relation of individuals to one another or to their environment. The isolated individual is not a productive agent. ... There can be no production without technical knowledge; hence no accumulation and no wealth to be owned, in severalty or otherwise. And there is no technical knowledge apart from an industrial community.
>
> (Veblen, 1934, p. 34)

Again, in 1908, Veblen (1919, p. 186) argued: 'The great body of commonplace knowledge made use of in industry is the product and heritage of the group.' In a number of works, Hobson argued along similar and complementary lines. For example, he wrote:

> every conscious corporate life is accompanied and nourished by some common consciousness of will and purpose which feeds and fortifies the personal centres, stimulating those that are weaker and raising them to a decent level of effort, reducing dissent and imparting conscious unity of action into complex processes of cooperation.
>
> (Hobson, 1914, pp. 302–3)

Clearly, the social basis of knowledge, and the ideas of group and organisational learning, were established by American and British institutional economists, long before they appeared in the recent business economics and management literatures.

Given these arguments, it is very difficult to conceptualise or identify the separate contribution of each individual worker to the production process. Social and organisational knowledge, and knowledge spillover and seepage throughout the system, also make it difficult to establish, in terms of intellectual property, what is 'mine and thine' for much of the tacit and codifiable knowledge in the economy. Accordingly, Veblen (1934, p. 34) argued: 'Since there is no individual production and no individual productivity, the natural-rights preconception that ownership rests on the individually productive labor of the owner reduces itself to absurdity, even under the logic of its own assumptions.' Veblen saw this conclusion as destructive for the neoclassical theory of distribution – as developed by John Bates Clark and others – based on the presumption of defined ownership of 'factors of production'. Both Veblen and Hobson argued instead that productivity could not be explained wholly in terms of the 'factors' owned by individual agents.

Note that, despite a superficial similarity, this is a much more radical conclusion than that advanced by Alchian and Demsetz (1972) in their famous paper on the firm. Alchian and Demsetz argued convincingly that because of the interrelated and 'team' character of production it is typically very difficult for management to *identify and monitor* the contribution of each worker. However, this does not go so far as to suggest (as is done here) that there are productive inputs that are not individually owned. Alchian and Demsetz did not deny the fact that each individual worker contributes a marginal product, they simply argued that it cannot readily be measured apart from the team. In contrast, Veblen and Hobson argued that production is an emergent and socially embedded activity which in principle cannot wholly be reduced to discrete and identifiable individual contributions, although, in a very real sense, individuals and their contributions matter. The combination of individual contributions leads to emergent properties that are not reducible to individuals. As a result, the 'fiction' of production resulting purely from the combination of individually owned 'factors' is unacceptable. This fiction denies the emergent properties of the whole.[27]

SOME IMPLICATIONS FOR THE EMPLOYMENT CONTRACT

This has important implications for the employment contract. A contract of employment is notionally an agreement between an individual worker and an employer, where the worker agrees to make a productive contribution of some kind, under the direction of the management, in return for a stipulated wage or salary. Work is contracted and the right of employer control is accepted, in return for an agreed remuneration. However, the group and team character of work suggests that this is not in essence a straightforward 'exchange' of atomistic rights and contributions at all. Furthermore, monitoring and control are made much more difficult by the complex and interrelated character of production. In sum, *the employment contract is in large measure a convenient fiction, couched in the individualistic categories of modern contract law, which in fact masks the social and co-operative character of all productive activity.*

Within capitalism, has this always been the case? Many of the above arguments have a generality that indicates that the fictional character of the individualistic employment contract is no recent development. Has there always been a mismatch between the productive realities and the formal framework of contract law? To a degree this is true, but this does not mean that legal formalities can be disregarded. Legal formalities are part of the reality itself, although they do not constitute or reflect it in its entirety.

It has been noted in the preceding chapter that the explicit formulation of the employment relationship in terms of a contract has been a relatively recent phenomenon. In Britain, as late as the early part of the twentieth century, employment was seen as a relationship of service or obligation, even with the master having a proprietary right in his servant. The struggle to dispense with these outdated notions and to modernise employment law had very real effects. In ideological terms, there was a clash between the Enlightenment notions of individual contractual rights and the older but surviving, quasi-feudal notions of obligation and service. Nevertheless, despite significant legal developments, what has endured throughout the history of employment within capitalism over two centuries is potential or actual employer control over the manner and pattern of work. It is the survival or otherwise of this underlying reality that in part determines the lifespan of the capitalism system.

The history of employment law helps us to understand the possible future changes to, and even the supersession of, the employment contract under the pressure of changing institutions and work relations. The history suggests that, when considering such matters, both the *de facto* and the *de jure* aspects have to be considered in tandem, without exclusive emphasis on one or the other. Although the enduring basis of the employment relationship is a matter of power and control, the ideologies, the legalities and the realities of power in the workplace are in fact enmeshed and inseparable.

The increasing complexity of the production process would arguably widen the mismatch between individualistic formulations of the employment contract and productive realities. It can be further argued that with the increasing dependence on advanced and knowledge-intensive skills comes the increasing reliance on the group as a forum for imitative and other learning. Production becomes more interrelated and social in its character, not less. Production assumes more and more of an organic quantity: it cannot be broken down and analysed in terms of individual components, exchanges and contributions.

It is curious that the individualistic formulations of contract law have been most appropriate for a relatively short period of capitalism's existence. In both Britain and America they have been confined largely to the twentieth century. The epoch of individual contract coincides remarkably with the epoch of collectivist socialism. To a large extent, both individualism and collectivism are based on shared presuppositions. As these joint assumptions are challenged, the supersession of both individualism and collectivism should therefore not surprise us.

9

THE END OF CAPITALISM?

Labour itself cannot be bought nor sold for anything, being price-less. The idea that it is a commodity to be bought or sold, is the alpha and omega of Politico-Economic fallacy.

John Ruskin, *Munera Pulveris* (1898)

If this tendency to de-manage continues, the distasteful trappings of authority ... will in time disappear. Some people, according to ability and inclination, will have more responsibility than others. But everyone will have essentially the same *kind* of responsibility. A new kind of elemental equality will prevail. A company will become an association of equal specialists. Some will specialize in steering the company. ... But no one will boss anyone else. Authority, in the sense we now know it, will disappear.

Richard Cornuelle, *De-Managing America* (1976)

We have seen in the preceding chapter that the move from machine-intensive to knowledge-intensive capitalism is tied up with the complex and organic developments in the sphere of production which cannot be readily encapsulated by the notions of property and contract. The gap between the *de facto* organicism of economic life, and the *de jure* mechanics of the contractarian stipulation, widens to critical proportions.

This does not mean that the stipulations of employment or property law are irrelevant and can be readily disregarded. The system of contract law – as Emile Durkheim has shown – in principle depends on its non-contractual elements. Capitalism essentially relies on its 'impurities', hidden beneath the surface expressions of contract law. To understand capitalism, we have to understand *both* aspects, and not only how each depends on and sustains the other, but also how each may corrode the other at the same time.

As long as its delimiting framework of private property, contract and employment law remains, then capitalism is still capitalism. It may, however, harbour within it structures and processes which are increasingly antagonistic or corrosive to the dominant system. There is nothing necessarily cataclysmic about this. To some degree, all systems contain internal strains of this type. They can persist for long periods of time and can lead to varied outcomes.

Consider an illustration from an earlier type of socio-economic system. In English feudalism, serfdom declined rapidly after the 1300s, to be replaced by various types of land tenancy and casual labour. Markets and urban manufactures grew steadily in importance. The feudal economy benefited enormously from these changes, and it entered a period of relative prosperity in the fifteenth century. Yet these developments were to some degree corrosive of feudal social relations: its principles of inherited divine right and duty based on a hierarchy of land tenure. The norms of allegiance that were crucial in the old order were undermined. Rich and powerful, non-aristocratic interest groups emerged, including the merchants and the landed gentry. These were eventually to pose a fatal threat to the feudal system.[1]

But these developments took hundreds of years. Furthermore, it was far from a monotonic and direct transition. As the crisis within the structures of feudalism evolved, the first substantive structural outcome was not the ascendancy of the *nouveau riche* but a sustained – and for a long time successful – attempt by the monarchy to centralise and strengthen its own power. The direct reaction to the feudal crisis was the development of the absolutist state: a vigorous attempt to preserve rather than to dispense with the old feudal order, but where expedient making compromises with powerful groups and interests. Hence, from the victory of Henry Tudor at Bosworth Field in 1485 to the opening shots in the English Civil War in 1642, a system of absolutism prevailed, organised around the monarchy and the London-based central state apparatus. Furthermore, elements of this absolutist system survive in Britain still to this day: including the monarchy and its limited prerogatives; and an over-centralised state apparatus, lacking in countervailing national, regional and local political powers. Remnants of feudal law, with their complexes of rights, duties and qualifications to absolute ownership, also survive in modern English land law.

History indicates that politico-economic systems can muddle through and survive for a very long time, despite their internal contradictions. It also tells us that the existence of specific types of impurity within a system does not necessarily foreshadow a new system in which those impurities are somehow more prominent.

Consider, nevertheless, a (real or notional) variety of capitalism where the aforementioned tendencies – connected with propositions 1 to 5 in the preceding chapter – have become prominent. The use of knowledge becomes more intensive. Specialist expertise subdivides into a variety of forms. In the face of this increasing complexity and parcellised knowledge, the 'bounded rationality' of management becomes increasingly apparent. *Accordingly, managerial control of the work process is progressively undermined.* As Peter Drucker (1993, p. 65) put it: 'Knowledge employees cannot, in effect, be supervised.'

Higher knowledge intensity makes the worker a prized possession, but one that depends on (essentially partial and limited) evidence of acquired skills to become marketable. The worker knows more than before, but not many will know what he or she knows. This undermines the efficacy of supervisory control but creates a problem of accreditation for the worker. If knowledge skills are specialist and idiosyncratic, then the possibilities for self-employment may be limited by the fact that few would know what skills they are purchasing. The services of a self-employed teacher, for example, may not find many buyers, simply because the absence of accredited organisational affiliations means the buyers do not in principle know what they are buying. We are judged in part by the organisations that admit us. For this reason, the knowledge worker may depend to a great degree on access to an organisation, in order to exercise and validate his or her skills.

There are additional reasons why the process of organisational valida-tion or accreditation is important. With advanced information technology and an information-oriented culture, the whole system faces the problem of information overload. Greater use is made of information screening agencies and systems of selecting appropriate information and knowledge. As Anthony Giddens (1990, p. 83) pointed out, such 'expert systems' are essential to modern institutions, as means to establish credi-bility and trust. In particular, the marketing of knowledge-intensive skills depends on mechanisms of accreditation: the academic qualification, the institutional certification, the expert's testimonial. These are the imper-fect means by which we attempt a semi-informed judgement of the knowledge, and judgement abilities, of others, whose skills we can neither fully fathom nor understand.

Like Frank Knight's (1921, pp. 298–311) puzzle concerning the judge-ment of judgement – discussed in the previous chapter – the processes of accreditation face the problem of infinite upward regress: who accredits the accreditors? It is not possible for everyone to accredit everyone else. Apart from being too time-consuming, it would depend upon an unattainable diffusion of specialist knowledge. A hierarchy of evaluating and accrediting agencies may emerge, but this an incomplete solution. Some institution has to act as the quality assurer of last resort. Failing a solution to this problem, there is a danger of degeneration into a semi-anarchy of competing propositions with questionable credentials.

Faced with an ever-more technical and sophisticated array of goods and services for sale, the consumer faces a similar problem. To some degree, we cope with our lack of appropriate technical information, concerning the goods and services we buy, by a reliance on brand name reputation. We place a precarious trust in a product, based on our tentative confidence in the integrity of the corporate producer. Alternatively, we rely on the advice of consumer groups and associations.

The worker becomes more like an independent contractor, possessing the prized, knowledge-based skills; but one that owns neither the material means of production nor the product of the work performed. Further, as well as owning the material means of production, the capitalist remains in control of many of the (imperfect) procedures of quality assessment and authentication. Given the collective nature of much knowledge, the worker often requires an organisation in which to work. In such cases, the knowledge worker depends on the organisation just as the organisation depends on the worker. And the organisation may still be owned by capitalists or other shareholders.

As a result of the increasing knowledge-intensity of production, however, the boundary between conception and execution becomes increasingly blurred. Within the organisation the titular division between management and worker becomes more and more an anachronism. Hierarchies within the firm become even flatter, with a reduction of layers of management. Going even further, some progressive corporations may develop schemes of worker participation, especially in regard to decision-making in process-related and day-to-day matters. Worker involvement in some management decisions may become a matter of employment law, as already in Germany. These extensions of worker participation and codetermination may yield substantial benefits in terms of enhanced productivity and profitability for the firms involved.[2]

There is also the possibility of the growth of lifetime employment rights, as part of a package of measures attempting to secure employee dedication and commitment. Forms of lifetime job-tenure have already been established in some large Japanese corporations. They also exist in many universities throughout the world. In some quarters, such arrangements bring fears that the removal of the potential threat of redundancy may undermine worker discipline. However, on the other hand, such measures may help to enhance vital feelings of community and belongingness at work. Such feelings can improve motivation and enhance productive social interaction in the workplace.

As the boundary between manager and employee breaks down, and formal control is eroded, a kind of quasi-self-employment will develop. Strictly, in many cases, it will not be self-employment, but it will have some of its features. By owning part of the intangible means of production, in the form of specialist knowledge, and having a considerable degree of control over his or her work process, in some respects the employee will resemble a self-employed worker. On the other hand, the employing corporation will retain ownership of the goods or services that are produced, of the physical means of production, and some of the crucial mechanisms of knowledge accreditation. For these reasons the worker does not become fully self-employed, in either a *de facto* or a *de jure* sense. Nevertheless, the possession of highly specialist knowledge, and the control of the work process by the employee, can develop to the extent that the worker is virtually a autonomous agent. We can find examples of this quasi-self-employment today, in many public and private universities, and even in some research units in large, knowledge-intensive capitalist corporations.[3]

Furthermore, as Charles Handy (1984) has pointed out, with the increase in the relative and absolute cost of specialist skills, there may be more cases of employment contracts being replaced by *de facto* and *de jure* self-employment, where the skilled worker contracts explicitly for specific services, not hours of work. The relatively high cost of skilled labour provides a strong push towards the hiring of the services of skilled, professional individuals or groups, on the basis of a contract for services rather than an employment contract. Handy thus argued that the 'gathered organisation' where all skills are possessed by the form on the basis of employment contracts, typically organised together in specific localities, will be gradually replaced by the 'contractual organisation', relying heavily on subcontracting and contracts for services, often with people working from home or from other dispersed locations.

Along with the increasing role of specialist and idiosyncratic knowledge, the emergence of real and quasi-self-employment, and the decline of the 'gathered organisation' in one locality, the stipulation in the employment contract of a number of hours to be worked loses much of its operational significance and meaning. Even if he or she remains formally an employee, the knowledge worker may require periods of contemplation, reading, research or study that cannot always be confined to official office hours. Conversely, scheduled hours spent out of the office can often assume a ritualistic vacuity. Work will be taken home, performed for hours or days in a domestic rather than a supervised environment. These developments make the concept of 'hours worked' less and less operational and meaningful. The boundary between work and leisure becomes blurred, making a temporally bounded contract of 'employment' an anomaly.[4]

Further, the specialist and idiosyncratic nature of work makes detailed regulation or supervision of defined periods of knowledge work difficult or impossible. As has already become common in many professional and managerial positions, employment contracts do not stipulate a minimum or guideline number of hours to be worked. Instead, the tasks required in the job are vaguely and broadly specified.

These developments bring dangers as well as positive possibilities. Yet more alternative scenarios and sub-scenarios unfold. For instance, on the negative side, the nature of knowledge-intensive work, and the difficulty of regulating it by specifying a fixed number of hours, bring the concomitant risks of overwork, resulting from social pressure or addiction to work itself. By its nature, knowledge work means a shift from time-keeping to normative control, permitting indefinite extension and intensification. Today, overworked knowledge workers are prevalent in both the West and Japan.[5]

In the history of capitalism, managerial authority has been legitimated by various ideological appeals, including divine right, natural law, the survival of the fittest and meritocratic entitlement (Zuboff, 1988, Chapter 6). At its contractual core, it has been legitimated as a delegated power, stemming from ownership of the means of production. As skilled knowledge, embodied in people, becomes relatively more important, the most resistant legitimation of managerial power, based on the authority of capital ownership, itself begins to be eroded.

Considering all such developments, the meaning of the employment contract is stretched to the limit, creating normative and legal tensions that may suggest its radical reformulation into something quite different. In so far as these developments spread, this bodes the end of the classical employment relationship, the transformation of the capitalist firm, and the demise of capitalism itself.

It must be emphasised that the above is a very broad-brush account of possible future developments in a knowledge-intensive economy. Not only is there no inevitability about them, they can themselves be expressed and sustained within a number of quite different institutional frameworks. These range from formal legislation, such as German code-termination law, to the much looser acceptance of rules and legalities within a solidaristic social culture. Many such institutional frameworks have already emerged within modern capitalism, challenging the boundaries and definitional formalities of the system.

LIBERTARIANISM VERSUS RESPONSIBILITY

It has been shown above how the growth of knowledge-intensive production in modern capitalism challenges aspects of contractual law and brings legal formulations within the employment contract under increasing strain. This raises the possible alternative scenario of a libertarian–contractarian reaction to attempts to protect and extend inalienable rights. Just as there was a regressive reaction to the growing power, wealth and influence of the English peasantry under feudalism, leading to the creation of an absolutist state, a reaction can occur to the erosion of the formal employment contract within capitalism.

A libertarian–contractarian reaction to the increasing complexity of the socio-economic system would stress the importance of explicit contractual legalities and attempt to restore managerial authority, especially by diminishing the organised power of the workforce. To some degree, such neo-liberal measures have been promoted by governments in the United States and Britain, under Ronald Reagan and Margaret Thatcher, in the 1980s. If the above argument is correct, then such developments will constrain the development of a knowledge-intensive economy and lead to a lower rate of growth of labour productivity.

Such a reaction would involve the extensive use of contract and labour law. It would entangle itself in endless further legislation, attempting to deal with the contradictions within the employment contract and the contractual problems involved in a knowledge-intensive economy. Just as the state extends rights of contract and trade and attempts to remove all barriers to free exchange, the state needs to place more and more controls on the forces it has unleashed. Far from the libertarian ideal of a diminished state, there would be once again the 'double movement' – described by Karl Polanyi (1944) with regard to the early nineteenth century. Furthermore, the inability to break free from the endless tangle of legislation and legal meddling creates the conditions for an authoritarian threat. Frustrated by the omnipresent barriers to the mythical libertarian ideal, the state takes upon itself authoritarian power, complemented by a growing bureaucracy of limited political accountability.

We have noted the growing problems of containing the growth and use of knowledge, within a contractarian framework in general and the employment relation in particular. Although it has precedents in the Thatcher–Reagan era, a further libertarian–contractarian reaction to this development is not inevitable. Such a development can be resisted. One possible antidote to this reaction may be the existence of a powerful and enlightened group of business leaders, aware of the kind of democratic culture and participatory industrial relations that facilitate productivity growth in a knowledge-intensive economy. As well as stressing the importance of a participatory culture within firms, the importance of enduring collaborative and co-operative relationships between firms could also be emphasised, against the neo-liberal insistence on fierce, price-driven, market competition. Such a progressive movement of business people could find valuable allies among trade unionists and the population as a whole. Emphatically, the outcome is not predetermined. But upon it may depend the possibility of moving beyond capitalism itself.

BEYOND CAPITALISM: THE EPSILON SCENARIO

It is difficult to determine the precise point at which a corroded employment contract and a transformed employer–employee relationship become sufficiently different from their capitalist archetype: then to proclaim 'the end of capitalism'. Equally, it is difficult to identify the date or even the period when capitalism emerged from a preceding order. These problems do not affect the argument, however. We are using a methodology of ideal types, as a means of understanding a direction of development and mapping a continuum of possibilities.

It is suggested that one possible ideal type, which could reasonably be described as beyond capitalism, is encapsulated here in what is called the epsilon (ε) scenario. In these circumstances a form of employment contract remains, but it is a mere shell of its former capitalist self. In the work process, the degree of control by the employer over the employee is minimal. Instead, to engender dedication and commitment, reliance is placed on the corporate culture and on the socialisation processes within the workplace. By and large, the workers manage the production processes themselves.

However, in this scenario a residual form of employment contract remains. This contractual agreement governs the entry, exit and boundaries of the employment period and process. The hiring of the worker is a potentially long-term and even lifetime decision. It is still a contract between employer and worker, but the employee retains much control of the process of work. In return for the perceived potential commitment and capabilities of the worker, the employers give an immediate or delayed offer of a substantial degree of job security. Similarly, contractual stipulations will govern the mode of exit from the firm's employment. In addition, the contract is likely to mention some boundaries concerning the sphere of work, and may also stipulate some forms of unacceptable behaviour.

Other than these issues, the relationship is largely extra-contractual, and based instead on mutual trust. Within the firm, not only is the market absent, but also the pressure of formal contract is marginalised. With trust relations being dominant, the formal, contractual element in the employment relationship enters as a necessary 'impurity', in the sense of the 'impurity principle' discussed in Chapters 5 and 6. Its role is simply to regulate the temporal and behavioural boundaries of the activity, not the activity itself. In day-to-day practice, trust and commitment, rather than legal obligation, are the central motivating norms. Managers become more mentors and leaders, rather than controllers. The relationship still depends on the interest of each party, and in a very loose sense it may be seen as a 'trade'. However, this is no longer a contract involving extensive control of the manner of work. *Essentially, this is not an employment contract in the classical and legal sense.*

Accordingly, the firm will no longer be a capitalist firm. It may still be associated with major inequalities of wealth and power. The corporation will still be owned by its shareholders. The corporation, rather than the workers, will own the goods or services produced. There may be no significant changes in the distribution of ownership of the *material* means of production. However, the workers will possess significant immaterial and knowledge-based assets. To distinguish these formations from capitalist corporations, we shall describe them as 'shareholder knowops': the pun on 'co-ops' being deliberate.

There is always the possibility that some sectors of the economy undergo the transformation outlined here, accompanied by de-skilling and a major reduction in the knowledge requirements of workers in other sectors. This is a dual scenario that places further complications upon the analysis. An important point to note here is that such a dual economy will face impediments to the full development of the institutional and trust relationships associated with the epsilon scenario. This scenario will unfold fully only if these relationships become dominant and pervasive throughout the system.

What if the epsilon scenario has played out to the full? The socio-economic system would not be socialist, in any common sense of the word. Furthermore, it is an economy still dominated by private property relations, and largely regulated by the market. Nevertheless, it is not capitalism. Capitalism means *more* than private property and markets. The existence of the market is a necessary but not a sufficient condition for the existence of capitalism. The system outlined above is not capitalism, even if it may contain capitalist 'impurities'. 'Market knowledgism' or 'market cognitism' (from the Latin *cognitio*, referring to knowledge, study and recognition) are some of the best labels for this system that I can come up with. The term 'learning economy' is rather loose and less specific, but perhaps it is more appealing.

Clearly, such a system requires a high social valuation of trust-based and extra-contractual relationships. A capitalist society with an ideological history of individualism, and a highly developed culture of litigation, will find it all the more difficult to accommodate these embryonic, non-contractual forms and develop in the direction outlined. The epsilon scenario may thus be blocked. Such a system could remain locked into capitalism, possibly with a relapse into the omega scenario as outlined above.

The epsilon scenario (ε) is laid out and compared with others in Table 9.1. A brief summary of these scenarios is appropriate here. Note, first, that in much of its essential structure, the omega scenario differs little from the alpha system; hence they are placed in the same column.

The alpha (α) scenario is reminiscent of the machine-intensive capitalism of the second half of the nineteenth, and the first half of the twentieth, century, in such countries as Britain, Germany and America, whereas the omega (ω) or 'Braverman' scenario relates to the 'brave new world of McJobs, unemployment and robots' discussed above.

The beta (β) scenario relates to many of the actually existing developments in the advanced, knowledge-intensive capitalism of the late

Table 9.1 Comparison of the epsilon, zeta and other scenarios

Scenario	α and ω	β	γ	δ	ε	ξ
1. Technology and organisation of production	machine-intensive capitalism	knowledge-intensive capitalism	machine intensive state socialism	machine-intensive worker co-ops	share-holder knowops	worker knowco-ops
2 Essential systematic form	capitalism	capitalism	state socialism	market socialism	market cognitism	market socio-cognitism
3 Owners of the corporation	shareholders	shareholders	the state	workers	shareholders	workers and other shareholders
4 Strategic significance of ownership of physical means of production	high	medium	high	high	medium	medium
5 Strategic significance of brand labels and control of knowledge accreditation	low	high	low	low	high	high
6 De facto controllers of the production process	shareholder-appointed managers	shareholder-appointed managers and workers	state-appointed managers	worker-appointed managers	chiefly the workers, as managers	chiefly, the workers as managers
7 Typical mode of control and management	Taylorism	partial worker participation	Taylorism	workers' self-management	workers' self-management	workers' self-management

twentieth century. High productivity is not possible without a degree of worker participation, despite the survival of traditional corporate ownership structures.

The gamma (γ) scenario is described here, loosely, as 'state socialism'. It relates to a centrally planned economy under public ownership, with the machine-intensive technology of the second half of the nineteenth, and the first half of the twentieth, century. To some degree, this scenario evokes the experience of the centrally planned economies in the former Soviet Bloc, although there is no need to take these regimes as representative or typical.

The delta (δ) scenario, with machine-intensive production and worker co-operatives, is the type of genuine 'market socialism' discussed above, and manifest to some degree in the former Yugoslavia from the 1950s to the 1980s, and in Mondragon in Spain.

As discussed above, in the epsilon (ε) scenario a form of employment contract remains, but it is a mere shell of its former capitalist self. Technology and organisation are knowledge-intensive, leading to minimal control by the employer over the employee.

The zeta (ζ) scenario is discussed more below. It is a further post-capitalist development of the epsilon scenario, involving further increases in the knowledge-intensity of production, of human skills, in the economic power of the workforce, and in the broadening of share ownership.

Note especially how the parameters of ownership in the second and third rows (2 and 3) change through the other five scenarios. For example, from α to β their importance diminishes slightly, showing that the focus upon the question of ownership thus can become relatively less important *within* capitalism. However, the move beyond capitalism to scenario ε involves less change in the ownership related aspects of the system. The more significant changes in the move from β to ε concern the control of the production process.

By contrast, the direct transition from machine-intensive capitalism to machine-intensive state socialism – from α to γ without any intermediate stage – involves little else here in this table than the change in the identity of the owners. Concerning the transition to the epsilon scenario, actual and informed employer control has become more important.

As noted above, and given its characteristics, the epsilon scenario is neither capitalism nor socialism. Markets and private property still play an extensive role, but the classical employment contract with significant employer control has been marginalised. The workers do not individually own all the means of production, so the system is not 'simple commodity production' in Marx's terms. The physical means of production are owned by the shareholders, not by the workers. The firm is not a worker co-operative, and the system as a whole cannot reasonably be described as a form of market socialism. It is, nevertheless, a possible future.

BEYOND THE EPSILON SCENARIO

If we speculate a little further, however, we can see beyond the epsilon scenario. Assume a further increase in the knowledge-intensity of production, of human skills, and other associated developments, as outlined above. These further developments lay the basis for what shall be called here the zeta (ζ) scenario.

As skills increase the economic power of the workforce increases. This power is manifest in influence over the production process and in bargaining strength on the market. We can imagine also the growth of employee share ownership schemes (ESOPs) or management buy-outs, leading to a situation where the employees, either collectively or individually, own a large proportion of the shares of leading corporations.[6]

Given the interrelated and collective nature of much productive knowledge within the corporation, it is likely that schemes for pooling employee shareholdings will emerge. Forms of common ownership could develop alongside private ownership. Furthermore, a significant degree of ownership by external agencies and individuals could be retained. These external agencies could be 'stakeholders': that is, institutions that are affected by the behaviour of the corporation in some way (Hutton, 1995, 1997). In addition, there could be some degree of share ownership by the general public. Nevertheless, forms of pooled employee ownership could increase alongside other shareholdings, as the collective integration and economic power of the workforce increases.

The extension and interlocking of ownership rights in the firm, involving the workers themselves to substantial degree, create incentives for longer-term employment. This would help to enhance investment in human learning, and begin to overcome the problem – identified by Marshall (1949, p. 470) among others – that the capitalist employer has insufficient incentive to invest in employees' skills.

Overall, in these circumstances something resembling in some respects what has been described as 'market socialism' may emerge. However, it has already been noted that this term has a legacy of deep ambiguity. It is used to refer to a variety of quite different things, including the planning model developed by Oskar Lange and others (Lange and Taylor, 1938). However, the models developed by Lange and his collaborators involved a degree of centralised co-ordination and knowledge that was incompatible with any real-world market. At best, it was an attempt to mimic the market through central controls. Hence, the term 'market socialism' is more appropriately used to refer to a decentralised, market-based system in which corporations are owned as co-operatives by the workers within them, and the products of the co-operative are sold on the market, with an appropriate exchange of property rights. In the latter system there are real, not simulated, markets. This differs from capitalism in two important respects. First, the workers in a co-operative collectively own and control the means of production. Second, the workers do not sell their labour power for a wage or salary. The members of the co-operative work for a share of its income and not for a wage. A market socialism of this type, with machine-intensive production and worker co-operatives, is incorporated in Table 9.1 as the delta (δ) scenario.

The zeta (ζ) scenario being discussed here is slightly different from this, however. First, it does not necessarily involve common, complete and exclusive ownership of the corporation by the workforce. Second, knowledge is more sophisticated and has an enhanced role. Hence the outcome of the zeta scenario would be better described – even by such awkward terms – as 'market quasi-socialism', or 'market cogni-socialism', or 'market socio-cognitism'. Despite the lack of complete common ownership, it is not necessarily less co-operative than idealised socialism in its prevailing cultural values, nor necessarily any less egalitarian in its economic outcomes. In fact, the question of the actual ownership of the physical means of production is relatively less important in such a knowledge-intensive socio-economic system. However, compared with the epsilon scenario, in the zeta scenario the balance of ownership of the corporation shifts crucially from the shareholders to the workers and managers.

Consider, within the zeta scenario, a mixed economy consisting of various forms of enterprise, including state-owned corporations and capitalist firms, but where a large and dynamic sector of the economy consists of worker knowco-ops. It is not market socialism in a strict sense, nor is it any form of state socialism. State planning may exist, but primarily in the forms of fiscal regulation, interventionist industrial policies or indicative guidance: examples of which are already found in many capitalist countries today. In the zeta scenario, state planning based on central directives or on state ownership of the means of production is, at most, confined to a relatively small segment of the economy. However, such a system is socialistic and co-operative in its dominant ethos, and close in structure to some notions of market socialism.

Nevertheless, markets and commodity exchange retain a crucial co-ordinating role in the system. Competitive and commercial values may appear antagonistic to the co-operative ethos inside the worker knowops and knowco-ops. However, it has been argued in preceding chapters that it is wrong to universalise the market and thereby exaggerate its anti-co-operative or other features. The character of the market depends very much on the prevailing social culture through which it is constituted. Although markets are often corrosive of co-operative social values and traditions, to a large degree these effects can be neutralised by a strong co-operative and trust-intensive culture.

Most importantly, furthermore, commodity exchange does not centre exclusively on markets proper, and often depends on long-term 'relational contracting' between buyers and sellers. This refers to a situation where firms build up relatively longstanding ties between each other and develop close bonds of mutual understanding and loyalty, rather than going to the open market (Dore, 1983; Goldberg, 1980b; Richardson, 1972). Many, if not most, transactions between corporations in modern capitalism are done in this manner. Such relations are often facilitated by modern business networks (Best, 1990; Dei Ottati, 1991; Ford, 1990; Goodman and Bamford, 1989; Grabher, 1993; G. F. Thompson *et al.*, 1991).

In part, relational contracts and business networks reflect the degree of knowledge intensity of the system. Knowledge-intensive production requires close mutual understanding between firms and their suppliers. The firm supplying services or components has to know in detail what the buying firm requires. In a complex economy this involves long-standing relationships and the building up of common norms of evaluation, shared values and objectives, and matching cognitive frameworks. Sometimes this common culture of communication is so complex and important that the vertical integration of the firms is the only answer. Where relational exchange is possible, it is often superior in these respects to the open market (Foss, 1993; Sah, 1991).

The open, competitive market may exist alongside more intimate and less anonymous forms of exchange. Markets proper may even be confined or marginalised by the growth of relational exchange. In any case, however, there will be extensive use of private property, including private property owned by corporations. In many cases these corporations will be worker co-operatives. But, in this scenario, nationalised or state-owned corporations will be less widespread than either co-operatives or privately owned companies. In so far as the system can be described as 'socialist' (if that term is appropriate at all), it will be first and foremost in the strength of its co-operative and communitarian culture and values, and the strength of the co-operative and quasi-co-operative sectors in production. For the system overall, the elimination of exchange and private property is not possible. However, at the subsystemic level, substantial spheres of economic life will be organised outside of both.

Furthermore, as is already happening within modern capitalism, contract law itself will be increasingly circumscribed. Contracting activity will be further limited to agreements that are deemed not to undermine social cohesion, human dignity, the rights of unborn generations or ecological sustainability. Recognising the increasingly specialist nature of knowledge, contracts will not be made without regard to the ability of each party to understand relevant details. The 'classical' system of contract law will come to an end (Atiyah, 1979; Slawson, 1996).

Conventional Marxists will be uncomfortable with this argument, challenging as it does their standard picture of capitalism being replaced by traditional socialism. Remarkably, however, in conceptual terms, there is some common ground with Marx's analysis, and some of his ideas can be adapted to fit this quite different scenario. For example, Marx (1976a, pp. 1019–38) made a distinction between the 'formal' and the 'real subsumption of labour under capital'. He argued that 'formal subsumption' occurred in a pre-capitalist state of affairs when moneyed interests took ownership of the means of handicraft or peasant production, but work itself carried on as much as before. Hence subsumption was then not 'real'. Historically, 'real subsumption' came later, when these moneyed interests directly or indirectly took *control* of the labour process and transformed it, both organisationally and technologically. According to Marx, it is only with the real subsumption of labour, and the control of work by an employer, that capitalism proper became established.

The argument in the present work is that in some respects the historical sequence outlined by Marx is now being reversed. The real subsumption of labour is being undermined while formal subsumption survives. The basic formalities of employment law and the employment contract remain. But actual or possible control of the manner of work by the employer becomes increasingly difficult and counterproductive. This is the epsilon scenario. Eventually, the degree of control of the work process by the employer becomes closer to that of a contract for services, rather than an employment contract. This is the zeta scenario. It signals, according to Marx's own definition, the end of the capitalist system. In turn, formal subsumption is ended as well.

Where this analysis differs from Marxism is in its treatment of the concept of knowledge, seeing labour no longer as the single, undifferentiated, commensurable substance, driving production. Furthermore, Marxism emphasises the differences between types of ownership or contract, such as the difference between state and private ownership, between employment and self-employment. Instead, what is being stressed here is the radical transformation of ownership and contract themselves. Some of the Enlightenment assumptions upon which the laws of property and contract were based are being eroded.

Similar objections apply to mainstream economics as well. It has been argued in preceding chapters that mainstream economic theory, like Marxism, has inadequate conceptions of both knowledge and learning. Likewise, mainstream theory does not see beyond the assumptions of classical contract and property law: social relations are seen wholly through contractarian lenses. Both mainstream economics and Marxism are ill-equipped to understand or examine the possible futures being outlined here.

It is important to emphasise that normative questions are not being

219

raised at this stage. The argument in this chapter should be examined on the basis of analytical, rather than normative, considerations. It is vital not to put the normative cart before the horse of theoretical analysis, even if the two are typically connected. It is beyond the immediate point whether this post-capitalist situation is desirable or undesirable, liberating or constraining, exploitative or unexploitative. The crucial points are (a) the epsilon–zeta scenario involves a *plausible causal chain*, and (b) the chain leads to a system that it is not capitalism. Whether the system is desirable is a different matter.[7]

At the risk of excessive repetition, some key propositions involved in (a) and (b) may be restated. First, by a reasonable definition, capitalism necessarily entails the widespread use of the employment relationship. Second, for reasons given above, transformative processes within capitalism itself are undermining this relationship. We are thus facing the possibility – no matter how long it may take – of modern capitalism being transformed into a system in which the employment relationship is no longer central. By common definition, such a system would no longer be capitalism.

The following appendix discusses theoretical models of the co-operative and knowco-op systems. The next chapter analyses some of the issues involved in the advance of knowledge in a learning economy. Subsequently, the final chapter addresses the policies involved in promoting further moves towards the epsilon and zeta scenarios and avoiding the omega (ω) alternative.

APPENDIX: ARE WORKER KNOWCO-OPS EFFICIENT?

The neoclassical economic analysis of self-managed, worker co-operatives, concludes that these firms are less efficient than their capitalist rivals. This appendix asks if the same alleged comparative inefficiency would also apply to the worker knowop or knowco-op.

Economic models of worker co-operatives were first devised by Benjamin Ward (1958, 1967), Jaroslav Vanek (1970, 1975) and others.[8] Using the methods and assumptions of neoclassical economics, Ward and Vanek compared a worker co-operative with a capitalist firm, assuming identical technology. A capitalist firm was assumed to be profit maximising whereas, in contrast, a worker co-operative was assumed to be maximising the average net income of the workers. Standard textbook assumptions, such as diminishing returns from the labour input, were also invoked in their analyses. For much of their analyses, the behaviour of the firm was considered in the short run, which, by definition, means that the amount of capital input is fixed, leaving the labour input to vary.

According to the above assumptions the theory proceeds as follows.

In the (profit-maximising) capitalist firm the level of employment would be adjusted to the point where the marginal revenue product of labour equals the wage rate (w). At that point there would be no incentive for the capitalists to increase or decrease employment. This is shown by point A in Figure 9.1. The wage rate is the gradient of the line that is tangential to the revenue product curve at A.

In contrast, in the worker co-operative, the workers as a whole are making the employment decisions. Given the price of the product (p) and the rate of interest (r) the objective of the worker co-operative is to maximise

$$y = (pq - rK)/L$$

subject to $q = f(L,K)$, with first order conditions $y = pf_L$, $r = pf_K$. In Figure 9.1 the revenue product function is pq. Its gradient decreases as the labour input increases, reflecting diminishing returns. To maximise their average income, the level of employment is fixed where the marginal revenue product of labour equals the net average income per worker. The line DB is drawn tangentially to pq from ordinate at OD (where $OD = rK$). Its slope gives y and the point of touching pq gives the level of employment in the firm. At that point the workers would not increase their average income by either shedding or recruiting workers.

In a capitalist firm, net income is divided between profits and wages. The objective of the capitalist firm is to maximise

$$y = (pq - rK)$$

For the firm to make a profit, the wage rate must be lower than the net average income per worker ($y > w$). Then, because of the assumption of

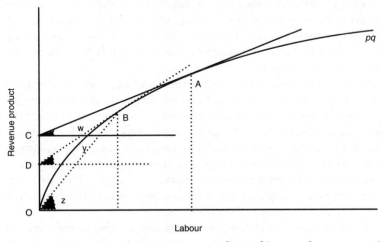

Figure 9.1 Optimal employment in a capitalist and in a worker co-operative firm: decreasing returns

diminishing marginal returns, the capitalist firm will then reach its short-run equilibrium at a higher level of employment and output than its co-operative counterpart. It must be further up the revenue curve at a point with a lower gradient, equal to the (lower) wage rate. This is the first part of the Ward–Vanek story, illustrated in Figure 9.1. The net average income per worker is the gradient of the line that is tangential to the revenue product curve at point B. B is the optimum point for the worker co-operative under these assumptions.

Under the adopted assumptions, it can be shown that there will be 'perverse' effects. In a worker co-operative, in the short run, any upward (downward) shift in the revenue product function or reduction (increase) in the interest rate leads the co-operative to reduce (increase) equilibrium membership and output in order to raise average earnings. Hence, for example, a worker co-operative, in contrast to its capitalist counterpart, will respond to an increase (or decrease) in the market price of its product with a decrease (or increase) in output and employment. Furthermore, the worker co-operative will respond to decreases in capital costs also by cutting employment. In such circumstances, the co-operative is likely to employ less or invest less, compared to the capitalist firm.

An intuitive explanation of these results is as follows. By assumption, the co-operative is assumed to be maximising its average net income per worker. To obtain this maximum, two opposing pressures must be balanced. The first concerns the average gross revenue per head of the co-operative. (Average gross revenue per head is shown by the gradient z of the ray from the origin to point B in Figure 9.1.) With the above assumptions, the average revenue per head of the co-operative will increase as the membership declines. In fact, by the assumption of diminishing returns, the maximum *gross* output per worker is approached as employment gets closer to zero. Any increase above that level involves a diminished return. However, the co-operative is assumed to be maximising *net* rather than gross income.

This brings us to the second, and countervailing, pressure. The co-operative has to cover a number of fixed capital costs. As employment increases, these costs are shared between more workers, and thus fixed costs per worker decrease. Per capita, these fixed costs are inversely related to employment. As employment approaches zero, fixed costs per worker approach infinity. Accordingly, the maximisation of average net worker income must balance these two opposed pressures. It is not z that must be maximised but y, within the constraint of the revenue product curve.

As a result, decreasing the fixed capital costs reduces the upward pressure on employment and the number of workers is reduced. Increasing the price of the product increases revenue per unit and increases the downward pressure on employment. Other results can be derived from similar and appropriate reasoning, using the counter-vailing pressures idea. (The reader seeking more formal treatments may consult Estrin (1983), Bonin and Putterman (1987), and other references cited above.)

In contrast, with a capitalist corporation, the shareholders are assumed to be maximising the net value of the corporation, not the average net income of the workers. Consequently, decreases in fixed capital costs do not reduce the upward pressure on employment. Neither does a reduction in the product price or the cost of the fixed capital have this effect. Instead, the level of employment is fixed at the point where the marginal revenue product of labour equals the wage rate. As long as the marginal revenue product of labour and the wage rate remain unchanged, then the level of employment at the short-run equilibrium will remain at this equilibrium point.

The outcome for the worker co-operative is quite different. Under the assumptions of the model, the co-operative workers will not maximise the short-run returns from the labour input in this way. This is because they are simultaneously concerned with the return on their share of the capital in the corporation. They cannot separate their equity in the corpo-ration from their ownership of their work input, and they are presumed to be primarily concerned with their own net remuneration, more than the net value of the corporation as a whole. Hence these 'perverse' results occur. From the point of view of society, it is argued, it is best that a mechanism exists to maximise the net value of the corporation, rather than simply the income of a sectional interest within it.[9]

Accepting the assumptions, the logic is flawless. However, the assump-tions have been contested on both theoretical and empirical grounds. It is possible to change some of the assumptions in the model and get quite different results.[10] Furthermore, if workers get more satisfaction from working in a co-operative than in a capitalist firm, then, using the standard Paretian criterion of 'economic welfare', the co-operative firm may be superior, even if the same 'perverse' results obtain (Pagano, 1985).

At root, and crucially, the Ward–Vanek model wrongly assumed that social relations and technology are separable; that the production function itself does not change shape when co-operative relations are introduced to replace capitalist ones. Yet we have much evidence (cited above) to support the contention that participation and co-operation can increase technological efficiency. Production involves people – their ideas and aspirations – and not simply machines operating under the laws of physics. It seems that, in their search of pretty diagrams and tractable mathematical models, mainstream economists often forget this.

Much of the evidence that we do have about the behaviour of real-world worker co-operatives is that they respond to changes in market prices in a similar manner to the capitalist firm (Horvat, 1982, pp. 339–44). Accordingly, the basic assumptions in the model are questioned by the evidence. However, despite this evidence to the contrary, the idea of the general inferiority of the worker co-operative retains a tenacious hold even on educated opinion.[11]

Nevertheless, we shall press on with the analysis, and for a while in terms conceived by mainstream economists, in order to reveal further problems and internal flaws in the argument. Consider a knowop or knowco-op, with decreasing returns, that is maximising net worker income rather than the firm's profit. Assume that this knowop or knowco-op has less physical capital equipment than a comparable co-op. This would seem to diminish the upward pressure on employment. With the countervailing pressure diminishing in relative terms – as a result of the diminishing relative costs of fixed capital – decreasing returns would force employment downwards. As the fixed cost of capital was reduced relative to labour, the net-income-maximising knowop or knowco-op would reduce the size of its labour force. If this process continued it would have just one employee, and the system as a whole could transform into an economy of self-employed producers.

However, this argument is inappropriate, for several reasons. It ignores the importance of collective knowledge within the firm and neglects the learning synergies that accrue from working together. In addition, the neoclassical models of market socialism often assume homogeneous labour, and the point here being stressed is that the workers in knowledge-intensive systems have specialist skills. These points make the formal modelling of knowops or knowco-ops much more complicated.

Indeed, once specialist skills become more important, relative to the physical capital, then further problems arise for the conventional capitalist firm. Because, employees are employees, not slaves, then they cannot claim legal title to the future skills acquired by the worker. There is a 'missing market' for future skills. Even in terms of neoclassical economic analysis, therefore, it has to be recognised that investment in what is described as 'human capital' will be suboptimal. As Kenneth Arrow (1962b, p. 168) has noted:

> the presence of learning means that an act of investment benefits future investors, but this benefit is not paid for by the market. Hence, it is to be expected that the aggregate amount of investment under the competitive model ... will fall short of the socially optimum level.

The capitalist can own a machine, and hence may have an interest in investing in new machine technology. By contrast, the capitalist may reap considerable rewards from the knowledge worker, and will wish that their productive skills are retained by an ongoing employment contract, but cannot legally extend the employment contract more than a few weeks into the future. As Alfred Marshall (1949, p. 470) noted long ago, this diminishes the incentive of the capitalist to invest in the worker's future skills, and to devote adequate resources to employee education and training.[12]

In so far as a worker knowco-op is better at retaining its own work-force, and gives greater incentives for them remaining with the same organisation, then, other things equal, it does not have this problem of skill underinvestment to the same degree. This advantage may offset any relative disadvantages of the knowco-op firm.

Further, with knowledge-intensive work, it seems no longer reasonable to assume that there are decreasing returns, with respect to the labour input. The assumption of short-run decreasing returns from labour is suited to a machine-intensive system but not a knowledge-intensive one. In a machine-intensive system the argument would go as follows. We consider a fixed number of machines. As the labour input increases incrementally from zero, output increases. Sooner or later, however, there is not enough machinery to occupy each worker adequately, and a point of decreasing returns to each increase of labour input sets in. Decreasing returns may also result from the more-than-proportionate need for management bureaucracy in the larger firm. This is the usual textbook justification of the assumption of short-run diminishing returns.

Concerning the physical capital equipment, with a knowledge-intensive system similar problems may arise. Each worker requires a personal computer and an office desk. However, these items are relatively cheap, and their effects on unit costs are likely to be swamped by other factors. For example, there are possible 'Smithian' effects from an increasing division of intellectual labour, allowing the development of more specialist, detailed and productive knowledge. The collective and interactive nature of much knowledge – as discussed by Veblen, Hobson, Penrose, Winter, Teece and Pisano above – also may mean that *increasing* rather than decreasing returns dominate.

Furthermore, in so far as knowops and knowco-ops bring greater worker participation in management, and flatter management hierarchies, the idea of more-than-proportionate growth in management bureaucracy is challenged. The traditional argument that the large and growing firm will eventually come up against the barrier of increasing and disproportionate bureaucratic costs may no longer pertain. The bureaucratic costs may not increase at the same rate as the firm itself. Alternatively, they may be swamped by the positive benefits of scale in a knowledge-intensive firm.

Overall, the arguments for decreasing returns are much weakened in the case

225

of the knowop or knowco-op. If we add the assumption of 'learning by doing' (Arrow, 1962b) then we move even further away from the conventional textbook picture. Learning brings 'endogenous growth': that is, growth even without an increase in factor inputs, such as the number of employees or in capital investment (Romer, 1986, 1990, 1994).[13]

Assuming increasing returns from a (unrealistically homogeneous) labour input, then what happens to the short-run theory of the self-managed firm?[14] The answer is that the firm no longer reduces its level of employment in response to a cheapening of capital equipment or an increase of prices. Rather than downsizing, the response of the firm is to expand its level of employment and output. In fact, it is easy to build a model in which in all circumstances it expands indefinitely: ever upwards in search of an elusive point where net income per worker is maximised. At least in the short run, a net income maximising equilibrium is not reached. Furthermore, if the system is sufficiently dynamic, in terms of learning by doing, technological innovation and other productivity increasing effects, then an equilibrium may never be reached, even in the long run. The firm may grow forever. The 'perverse' results of the Ward–Vanek models thus disappear.

We have just compared a knowledge-intensive co-operative firm (with increasing returns) with a machine-intensive co-operative firm (with decreasing returns). Perhaps the most important comparison, however, is between a knowledge-intensive capitalist firm (with increasing returns) with a knowledge-intensive worker knowco-op (with increasing returns). The former may be assumed to be maximising profits, the latter to be maximising the average net income of the workers. As we have seen, this difference can be important in the case of decreasing returns. But in the case of increasing returns, the profit-maximising capitalist firm and the income-maximising knowco-op are both forever ascending the same upward slope, in a vain attempt to find a short run equilibrium. The outcome in this model, therefore, is similar for the capitalist firm and the knowco-op.

There is thus no *a priori* reason to assume that net income maximising knowops or knowco-ops are less efficient than capitalist firms. The assumption of increasing returns is sufficient to demonstrate this point. However, there are additional factors to be taken into account, suggesting that knowops or knowco-ops may outperform their capitalist rivals. For instance, there is much empirical evidence, from the West to the East, indicating that the more participatory knowledge-intensive firms within capitalism are often more productive and bring higher rates of growth. Production is a social process, and technology is itself conditioned by its cultural and institutional integument. For this reason, it is not to make comparisons between capitalist and post-capitalist systems while assuming that the underlying technology does not change.

Furthermore, the objectives of firms, and the relationships between them are likely to evolve in the type of scenario discussed here. A knowledge-intensive economy depends on networking and co-operation, rather than atomistic competition. The exclusive pursuit of profit becomes increasingly an anachronism. Firms have to devote themselves to the unquantifiable enhancement of future knowledge as much as to profit. Their objectives necessarily become multiple and diffuse, qualitative as well as quantitative. If they were to concentrate solely on their pecuniary 'bottom line' then they would lose out to their innovating and dynamic rivals. In such circumstances, the unrealism of the standard textbook model of the profit-maximising firm is further underlined. The alleged 'proof' of the superiority of the profit-maximising firm becomes not only questionable but irrelevant.

10

THE LEARNING FRONTIER

The higher the degree of intelligence and the larger the available body of knowledge current in any given community, the more extensive and elaborate will be the logic of ways and means interposed between ... impulses and their realisation. ... The apparatus of ways and means available for the pursuit of whatever may be worth seeking is, substantially all, a matter of tradition out of the past, a legacy of habits of thought accumulated through the experience of past generations. ... Under the discipline of habituation this logic and apparatus of ways and means falls into conventional lines, acquires the consistency of custom and prescription, and so takes on an institutional character and force. ... The typical human endowment of instincts, as well as the typical make-up of the race in the physical respect, has according to this current view been transmitted intact from the beginning of humanity. ... On the other hand the habitual elements of human life change unremittingly and cumulatively, resulting in a continued proliferous growth of institutions.

Thorstein Veblen, *The Instinct of Workmanship* (1914)

The late twentieth century has witnessed an explosion in this ability to store knowledge in our culture rather than in our brains.

Jack Cohen and Ian Stewart, *The Collapse of Chaos* (1994)

KNOWLEDGE AND SKILLS

It has been assumed in the preceding chapters that increasingly advanced knowledge and skills are being required in many processes of production. In the context here it is appropriate to treat knowledge as consisting of skills or capacities. How is the level of advancement of knowledge or skill to be measured? What factors lead to a change in this measure?

Not all skills may be useful. The medieval alchemist had a set of intricate procedures believed to convert inferior matter into gold. Trainee alchemists had to learn this art, perhaps over several years. Likewise, some strange religious rituals may seem worthless to the outsider. We

228

may thus distinguish between those skills that serve human needs, and those that do not (Doyal and Gough, 1991). However, the techniques of measurement proposed in this chapter do not depend upon such a criterion. Instead of need, it is possible to consider those skills that are called upon by market demand, or by any other rule that may be chosen.

This chapter is devoted to issues of measurement and analysis. We are concerned primarily with the measurement of skills and capabilities. A first approximation is: *the measure of a skill is the amount of time it takes to achieve that level of skill*. Knowledge and skills take time to acquire and that duration is their magnitude.

Consider an example: a brain surgeon. Overall, the acquisition of such a skill requires something in the order of (say) thirty years. All necessary education from birth is included in this calculation, including primary socialisation in the household, elementary literary skills, basic schooling and specialist education at university and elsewhere. In contrast, a manual labourer may be able to acquire the necessary skills for labouring work in about half the time. In general, the shift from action-centred to intellective abilities involves a substantial increase in the time taken to acquire the required skills.

Note that this is not the same as the Marxian method of computing and assessing skills. Marx saw skill as being enhanced by the labour of the instructor. For Marx, labour time was a 'substance' that flowed around the economy. He saw learning as the flow of labour from teacher to student, into a stock of congealed talent. Factors such as the student–teacher ratio are relevant in this approach, because the total labour outflow from the teachers has to be divided among the students. In the Marxian approach there is a conservation principle; as long as it is not wasted, labour time is conserved in the transfer process.

Here the approach is quite different. There is no notion of labour embodied, or of labour as a substance being transferred to and embodied in the commodity output. Furthermore, unlike Marx, no direct account is taken of the labour time of the teachers or trainers passing on the skills, nor the materials used in the education process. There is no flow, nor conservation, of a labour substance. Instead the picture is of the building up of skills and capabilities through time. Skill is here measured as a stock, not as a flow. Although a temporal measure is being proposed here, it is not the same as the Marxian concept of labour time.

The first difficulty that we may address concerns the existence of different physical and mental talents and aptitudes. Not all people may have the ability to become brain surgeons within thirty years. Some may never be capable of such work, just as some may not be able to develop an adequate ability to become a manual labourer. In the Marxian approach this difficulty is dealt with by considering the potential of the *average person*, ignoring any variation about the mean. The essentialism of this approach is rejected here, in part because of its neglect of the ineradicable variety of human ability and skill.[1]

Instead, the proposed solution to this difficulty is as follows. First, we address the division of labour within the economy at a given level of development. The division of labour will depend on the composition of final output, including the pattern of consumption. A proportion of the working population will be allocated to each skill. We assume that training procedures have been optimal in allocating human abilities to jobs, in the sense that any change in the allocation of people to training schemes, or subsequently to jobs, would eventually reduce the net output the economy.[2]

Accordingly, the metric of skill is amended in the following manner. *The measure of a skill is the minimum amount of time that it takes the proportion of the population allocated to that skill to acquire that skill, given the currently optimal allocation of labour.* This is measured on a per capita basis for each skill. For each person involved, the minimum amount of time required to acquire that skill will be calculated. The measure of a particular skill will be the mean value of these minima.

The above formulation can be amended to deal with cases of team production, where the output is the product of a group, rather than a whole economy. The skills may be complementary and inseparable, and it may not be possible to identify the contribution of each individual. In this case the measure of the skill of the team is the average amount of time it takes for each member of the currently most efficient possible team to acquire the skill that is used within the team.

The approach developed here can also be applied to organisations and firms, as well as to whole economies. By tracking human skills and capabilities down to a quantifiable metric it could serve as an important analytical instrument for what is now known as the 'capabilities', 'resources' or 'competence-based' theory of the firm (Foss, 1993; Foss and Knudsen, 1996; Hodgson, 1998b, 1998c; Penrose, 1959; Senge, 1990; Teece and Pisano, 1994). Like much of this literature, there is a stress on capacities and potentialities and not simply immediate, manifest performance. However, we must leave the development of this application, as well as various technical problems involved in the comparison of a sector of the economy with the economy a whole, to a future study.

For the remainder of this chapter we shall consider the skill level in the economy as a whole. We also add a further complication at this stage, concerning the dynamics of development through time rather than static, cross-sectional variation. The measure of each skill is likely to change, as the economy develops. A number of factors may be considered here. The first is innate ability. We shall then move on to discuss the educative and cultural environment, the changing efficiency of the processes of education and training, and the effects of technical change.

230

Consider innate ability. In the modern, Darwinian view of human evolution, the innate potential of human beings has changed little in thousands of years. Contrary to the Lamarckian view, characteristics acquired during the development of each human individual are not passed on in the genetic make-up of the next generation. Accordingly, the human genetic stock can change only very slowly, by the processes of natural selection. As a result, changes in innate ability are too small to be significant in the much shorter time scale to be considered here.

In contrast, human culture and human institutions change relatively rapidly. Much can happen in a few hundred years that cannot be explained in terms of the much slower changes of human genetic material. The changes in culture and institutions create the potential for human learning and human development. With a more sophisticated technological and scientific culture, even greater human learning is possible, not because of the changes in genetic make-up or innate ability, but because of the possibility of a more advanced education. What changes with the advance of science, technology and human institutions is not genetically endowed human nature but the greater social capacity for educative nurture.[3]

The major effect of these cultural and institutional advances is to increase the educative and skill potential of the population. An increase in the level of skill and relevant knowledge of a human population will be represented as an upward movement in the *learning frontier*. By definition, at that frontier the system as a whole has reached the maximum level of learning and skill, given its level of development and state of scientific and technological knowledge. No further overall productivity improvement is possible via some reallocation of labour.

The extent of the learning frontier is measured by the average amount of time it takes the population to reach the levels of skill that are deployed at this optimal position. The upward movement of the learning frontier is the main quantitative representation of the general advancement of human knowledge and development in the system.

As the learning frontier moves upwards, individuals enjoy enhanced possibilities of educative development. These enhanced possibilities do not result from significant changes in innate capacity but from changes in the social culture, socio-economic institutions and the level and availability of knowledge. To use the appropriate biological terms, phylogenetic evolution (involving changes in the genetic material) is much too slow to have any significant influence on socio-economic evolution. Nevertheless, the rapid changes in the social environment are a moving ceiling for the ontogenetic development of each human individual. (Ontogeny is the development and growth of a single organism, without genetic changes.) The actual (that is, 'phenotyopic') development of any particular organism depends, additionally, on the stimulation and nutrition it receives from its environment. And a movement in the learning frontier provides the possibility of this stimulation.

A secondary effect of the aforementioned cultural and institutional advances is to increase the efficiency of education in each specific skill. These advances may not simply improve the general potential, but also the time taken to reach any point up to that potential. In particular, a stimulating and educative cultural environment will increase the rate at which many people – of given innate capacities – can acquire a skill.

The effect here is similar to that of Alfred Marshall's (1949) notion of 'external economies'.[4] Like the concept of 'external economies' in the classic text of Allyn Young (1928) and the subsequent work of Nicholas Kaldor (1972, 1978, 1985), they cannot be encompassed by the standard textbook concept of increasing returns. Increasing returns are manifestations of a given and static production function. Instead, 'external economies' are cases of interdependence, the results of which are not manifest instantaneously, but only through adequate time. In part to avoid this confusion, and to further the conceptual separation from the increasing returns phenomenon, they shall be termed here as *learning externalities*. We are referring to the reduction of the time taken in the learning of a skill due to a more stimulating or appropriated cultural, intellectual, scientific or technological environment. This environment is itself the product of the general improvement in the level of knowledge and skill throughout the economy. Typically such improvements have externalities, or spillover effects.

In addition, people may stumble upon quicker and more efficient ways of doing things themselves. The sum total of all reductions in the time taken to acquire a skill, with given tools, machines and equipment, will be referred to as *learning efficiencies*. Learning efficiencies are made up, in part, of learning externalities.

In quantitative terms, such improvements in the efficiency of skill acquisition have the effect of deflating the measure of the skill. Unless due correction is made, over time the skill level – measured by the minimum amount of time it takes to acquire the skill – will appear to be less than it is, measured consistently by former standards. Improvements over time in the efficiency of skill acquisition mean that skills are being measured with units of changing size.

Technical changes that replace specific skills will also have a negative effect. For example, the development of the mechanical or electronic calculator may render unnecessary the skills of mental arithmetic. The invention of the automatic gearbox reduced the number of skills that were necessary to drive a car. Harry Braverman (1974, p. 225) cites a study which showed that, due to the introduction of more numerous and accurate measuring and monitoring instruments, the additional time taken to train a coal-tar distiller was reduced from six months to three weeks. In general, as a result of technical advances, less training and education of human operatives will be required to reach the same level of productive capability.

At this stage it is useful to make a distinction between a *skill* and a *capability*. A capability is a specific task, whether aided or unaided by tools, machines or other technological devices. Skills are the direct human contributions to capabilities. Skills empower the work that is directly performed by the human agents involved in that task.

If an accountant no longer requires the ability of mental arithmetic, and can use a calculator instead, then the measure of the skill of an accountant may be reduced but the capability to perform the task of accounting remains undiminished. The chores of mental arithmetic can be replaced by electronic calculators, thus diminishing the skill of accounting, but not diminishing accounting capabilities. Similarly, much of the growth in the use of machines over the last two hundred years has been to substitute for human muscle and effort. There would thus be losses in physical strength, dexterity and stamina. In both cases some skills have declined will capabilities have been constant or enhanced.

Both skill-replacing technical changes and learning efficiencies lead to a diminution of the time required to acquire the skill. However, the *capability level* or *capability frontier* has not declined. The system still has the same level of capability. Furthermore, learning efficiencies arguably represent no reduction in the true skill level, but merely a reduction in the time taken to acquire the skill. Some method must be found to compensate for this measure, to bring it into line with the true skill level.

Consider the following example. We start from a representative sample or 'basket' of established capabilities and skills at a given point in time. At t_0 the average time taken to acquire the skills involved in these capabilities would be measured. Let us assume that the result is 20 years (of time taken to acquire the skills). At this point we do not attempt a numerically separate measure of capabilities, despite the fact that were it not for technical aids the time taken would be greater, because we are primarily interested in changes through time rather than absolute amounts. Hence this difference is disregarded in the first instance. We could imagine an 'early and rude state of society' where production was accomplished with bare hands, unaided by tools or machines. However, in practice it would neither be practical nor meaningful to obtain the data going back to those prehistoric times. It would be more sensible to start from a base year, in the modern period, and trace the contributions of technical changes and acquired skills from that date on. This base year is t_0.

One decade later the same calculation is performed on the same representative sample of capabilities. Let us assume that a decrease of time taken of two years takes place and that the resulting measure at t_{10} of the skills involved in the same sample of capabilities is thus 18 years. This reduction is due to both increased efficiencies in learning the skills and better technical aids, replacing skills. In this illustrative example, it will be assumed that skill-replacing technical changes cause half of this decline and learning efficiencies account for the other half. Overall, the crude skill measure has deflated by 10 per cent. Nevertheless, in reality, there has been no change in the capabilities being delivered. Accordingly, a 10 per cent upwards adjustment is required to the value at t_{10} to take account of the fact that the two values at t_0 and t_{10} are in fact measuring the *same* capabilities.

The crude measure of skill, which was 20 years at t_0 and 18 years at t_{10} we shall call the *unadjusted skill level*. With the same capabilities, the capability level is constant. The capability frontier would thus be horizontal, at 20 years. The learning frontier is a third measure, which must reflect the real de-skilling involved. In this example, the learning frontier has moved from 20 years at t_0 to 19 years at t_{10}, representing a 5 per cent decline due to skill-replacing technical changes alone. In other words, at t_{10} a 5 per cent *upwards* compensation to the *unadjusted* skill level is required to take account of learning efficiencies.

We also have to take into account the fact that representative basket of capabilities may change through time. Although these factors create difficulties for the proposed measures of the skill and capability levels, they do not render the methods of measurement invalid. Problems concerning the inflation or deflation of a unit of measure are commonplace in socio-economic systems and a whole set of techniques have been developed to deal with them. The formulation of the widely used index of retail prices is a prominent example.

We now amend this example to take account of the fact that new skills and capabilities have become established in the economy in that decade, because of qualitative economic developments. Hence at t_{10} the representative sample of capabilities has to be altered. Assume that the new representative basket of capabilities has an average time of acquisition at t_{10} of 21 years. The representative level of skill of 21 at t_{10} is the new unadjusted skill level. Taking this into account, the new unadjusted skill level has moved from 20 years at t_0 to 21 years at t_{10}.

According to the original measure of skill at time t_0, this unadjusted figure of 21 (pertaining to t_{10}) must be inflated by 5 per cent to make it commensurate with the former measure (pertaining to t_0), and to recognise the effect of learning efficiencies, giving a result of about 22.[5] Hence, by this method of computation, in the 10 years the learning frontier has risen from 20 to about 22. This rise is powered by the emergence of new skills and learning efficiencies, but not by any skill-replacing technological changes.

A further compensation is required to update the capability frontier. The figure of 21 (pertaining to t_{10}) must be inflated by 10 per cent to make it commensurate with the former measure (pertaining to t_0), and to recognise the effect of both learning efficiencies and skill-replacing technological changes, giving a result of 23.5. Hence, by this method of computation, in the 10 years the capability frontier has risen from 20 to 23.5. This rise is powered by both new skills and skill-replacing technological changes.

An analogous method of adjustment is used in the computation of the price index in modern economies. In a similar manner, a regularly updated basket of goods is chosen as the standard. Likewise, a scalar index is derived and used to obtain comparable values over time.

To repeat: the learning frontier is a comparative and intertemporal measure of the skills of the population. The capability frontier is a measure of average productive capacity or sophistication of the economy as a whole, taking into consideration both human beings and the means of production. The unadjusted skill level is a measure of the time per capita devoted to education and training. Hence the unadjusted skill level is equivalent to the *mean training time* for the population. Assume that it is possible to measure these three regularly, involving periodic updates of the representative basket of capabilities. Three time series of data will result, capable of diagrammatic representation. Two possible scenarios are presented in Figures 10.1 and 10.2. Figure 10.1 shows a picture consistent with the advance of complexity and human knowledge in the socio-economic system.

It is now possible to represent the omega scenario – as discussed in the preceding two chapters – in the above framework. According to the omega scenario, technical changes involving machines, computers and robots lead to a replacement of mental and manual human labour in some areas. There is an overall stagnation in the level of learning in the economy, even if the economy as a whole is growing in output, measured conventionally (Rifkin, 1995). The periodic update of the basket of representative capabilities shows that some highly-skilled jobs are disappearing, as they are taken over by machines. The average time taken to acquire the representative basket of capabilities is decreasing.

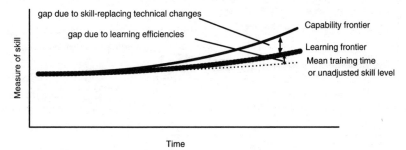

Figure 10.1 The learning frontier

This is represented in Figure 10.2. This figure also shows a picture consistent with the advance of complexity in the socio-economic system. Accordingly, there may also be advances in human knowledge. However, for much of the population there is substantial human deskilling.

In Figure 10.2 both the unadjusted skill level and the learning frontier decline, even when the capability frontier moves upwards. Overall, the economy is growing in technological sophistication and output, but, on the average, enhanced human skills are not being deployed. Furthermore, human learning is diminishing in its extent, requiring less and less time to train the average worker. By this measure, assumption 2 in Chapter 8 is no longer valid, even if assumption 1 remains.

As noted above, many of the technological advances over the last two hundred years have substituted primarily for human muscle and effort. Production has been revolutionised as a result. However, in the terms explored here, machines substituted for muscles that did not take much time to strengthen. If a machine simply substitutes for muscular effort, then the reduction in time for skill acquisition is simply the amount of time that no longer has to be devoted to reaching the level of physical fitness to work efficiently. The loss of training time due to that replace-ment would not have been that great. These losses could have readily been compensated by the acquisition of new skills that would require training, in equal or greater measure.

However, in the last two hundred years the time taken to obtain repre-sentative and widely used skills has increased significantly. Many of the innovations of the late twentieth century, such as the computer, may lead or have led to a greater proportionate reduction in the time required to acquire the skills associated with specific capabilities. This is because such innovations substitute for a wide range of relatively sophisticated mental abilities which originally would take a longer time to acquire. It is very likely that intellective skills have a greater metric. Accordingly, many of the technical innovations of the late twentieth century may have lead to a proportionately greater destruction of specialised skills, measured by the time required to achieve that skill.

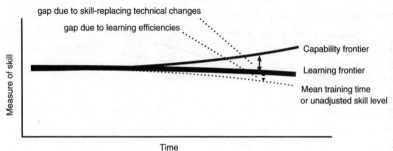

Figure 10.2 The omega scenario

For example, the development of computer-aided design and manu-facture (CAD-CAM) has made obsolete a whole range of skills from technical drawing to manual lathe operation, that each took many years to acquire. They are often replaced by computer programming and oper-ating skills, perhaps of similar measure. But whatever the gain or loss after replacement, consider the scale of destruction of specialist skills involved in the transition. The dimension of the loss of skill involved in CAD-CAM is much greater than that associated with, for example, the earlier and highly consequential transition from the horse-drawn plough to the tractor. As the measure of skills increases, there is more retraining to be done as the skills are replaced. The march of technical progress thus imposes increasing costs of transition, and requires increasing education and (re)training to compensate for the destruction of old skills. The costs of change increase in proportion.

Overall, in the modern economy, the gap between the capability and the learning frontiers may widen more rapidly because of the increasing relative and absolute contribution of technical change. Without other counteracting forces, this greater gap can be associated with a stagnation or decline in the net and unadjusted skill levels. Accordingly, the omega scenario emerges as a much greater threat in the modern than in any former era. Contrary to the thrust of Braverman's (1974) *Labor and Monopoly Capital*, modern technical change threatens to de-skill mental more than manual labour, at least by the measures of skill adopted in the present work. The antidote to this scenario does not sensibly involve a slowdown in the rate of technical change, nor the stifling of learning effi-ciencies, but a greater rate of growth of the unadjusted skill level. Quite simply, this means more time spent on education and training, sufficient to outpace the accelerating and combined impact of technical aids and improving learning efficiency.

Alternatively, it could be argued that it is sufficient to halt the omega scenario by an upward move in the learning frontier, rather than the unadjusted skill level. This means that human skills are increasing but the time taken to acquire those skills is possibly being reduced. This would be a dangerous economy in resources, because it would involve a contraction in the time, routines and institutions dedicated to education and training. For its success it would depend on ongoing improvements in learning efficiencies which are often delayed and unreliable. Furthermore, it would involve a severe constraint on the growth of human skill: a worthy end in itself. It would be far better to expand the unadjusted skill level, as well as the learning capability frontiers, and use the gains made by learning efficiencies for improvements in the level and scope of human knowledge. Some further policy implications of this analysis are taken up in the next chapter.

As well as being quite different from the Marxian focus on embodied labour time, the approach here also contrasts with the neoclassical idea of flows of factor inputs – involving symmetrically both labour and capital – being responsible for economic growth. Instead, the analysis centres asymmetrically on levels of human knowledge and skill – often misleadingly described as 'human capital'. Furthermore, the measure of economic development is not in terms of the value of the produced output of goods and services. Instead the primary measure is of human knowledge and capabilities, embodied in individuals and institutions.

This is consistent with Thorstein Veblen's (1915, p. 272) view that this 'immaterial equipment is, far and away, the most important productive agency'. In consonance with this standpoint, material products are no longer the main focus and measure of economic growth. Machines and tools are important, but products of, and subservient to, the advance of human learning. The symmetry between 'capital' and 'labour' in mainstream economics is broken. Humanity, rather than material goods, becomes the centrepiece of economic science.[6]

Accordingly, the gap between the capability frontier and the learning frontier should not be interpreted simply or primarily as the 'contribution' of machinery and equipment to economic capability or development, just as the learning frontier is seen to represent the contribution of human labour. A reading based on the assumed symmetry of 'factors of production' with each supposedly making a 'contribution' to output is inappropriate. This is not simply because what is involved here is a measure of capabilities rather than output. It also should be noted that some capabilities – such as the ability to fly and travel at high speeds – will not be expressed in the capability frontier because they are not human skills that have been *replaced* by machines. The significance of the capability frontier is as a relative measure, changing through time. The gap between the capability and learning frontiers is a measure of de-skilling of *human* labour; it partially represents what is no longer necessary and what has been *lost* in human skills.

In the history of civilisation, the invention of writing diminished the skill of memorising and relating from memory; the invention of printing diminished the skill of oral storytelling; the machine diminished the exercising of our muscles; the typewriter diminished the skill of calligraphy; the radio and television diminished the arts of home self-entertainment; the pocket calculator diminished our aptitude in mental arithmetic; the computer spellcheck program may diminish the knowledge of correct spelling and the computer thesaurus may decrease our instantly recallable vocabulary. Simultaneously, however, these developments created new specialist skills and professions such as the clerk, printer, publisher, mechanical engineer, mechanic, telecommunications engineer, electronic engineer, and computer programmer. They created a new knowledge – not held by all but nevertheless accessible to some – within a more complex set of social relations and division of labour. In a sense, for most of us, this knowledge is held on our social culture but not in our brains.

These developments represented both a loss and a liberation. On the positive side, not only did they create new professions and skills, they also freed up the processes of human work and created possibilities for the development and acquisitions still more skills. The diminution of the burden of manual work by the machine in the nineteenth and the twentieth centuries has liberated an enormous amount of human time for much more creative activity, as well as created the threats of an ill-exercised and obese population. The new information technology will likewise bring new possibilities for and threats to our intellectual and mental progress. The advance of the capability frontier can stimulate further learning, as well as stunt its development. This, perhaps, is a crucial dilemma for the new millennium.

11

SOME NORMATIVE AND POLICY ISSUES

Where there is no vision, the people perish.

Proverbs, xxix, 18

Only by abandoning the philosophical premises of the seventeenth and eighteenth centuries; by reformulating and enlarging the meaning of its basic concepts of wealth production; and by supplementing its study of market prices by a study of social value, will economic science finally achieve an impartial and critical comprehension of the economic process which will be relevant to any form of economic organization.

K. William Kapp, *The Social Costs of Business Enterprise* (1978)

All detailed policy prescriptions, of any degree of viability, depend upon detailed analyses of particular circumstances and institutions. For that reason, and due to pressing constraints of space, it is not possible here to elaborate detailed policies for any single country or group of countries. The brief, normative, discussion here must remain at a much more general level. This does not mean, however, that important things cannot be said. Policy has to engage with, and build upon, generalities, although emphatically it should not be confined to them.

In very general terms, a challenge for the twenty-first century is not the construction of a fixed and final utopia but of *evotopia* – a system that can foster learning, enhance human capacities, systematically incorporate growing knowledge and adapt to changing circumstances. The very fact that there is learning to be done, and human capabilities to be enhanced, means that no fixed blueprint of a desired future is possible. However, for similar reasons, it is likewise impossible to remain satisfied with existing attitudes and values. The partial resolution of this dilemma is an 'evotopian' scheme of thought, embracing the following principles:

- Reigning uncertainty and incomplete knowledge make any fully rational, social or economic, policy or design impossible. All policies

240

are fallible, and hence they must be explicitly provisional and practically adaptable.

- Much policy should be formulated by experimentation, and with a variety of routines, institutions and structures. Only on the basis of such a variety can policies and institutions be given any comparative and pragmatic evaluation.
- In-built variety is important for helping the system deal with and adapt to unforeseen changes: variety is essential to learning and adaptability at both the systemic and the individual level.
- The impossibility of omniscience, in both institutions or individuals, means that neither can be relied upon as a final judge of what is needed. A learning and adapting system enjoins a democratic and participatory dialogue, covering both scientific and normative issues, in which the prevailing policies, and principles of morality and justice, are repeatedly scrutinised.

THE FOUNDATIONS OF EVOTOPIA

This book is not one of intellectual history, but occasionally a brief historical digression is in order. It is useful to sketch out some of the past threads of evotopian thinking, in order to place any new developments in their context. Prior to Charles Darwin, we find inspiration for evotopian thought in the writings of Thomas Robert Malthus (1766–1834) and John Stuart Mill (1806–1873), among others. Both these writers stressed the role of diversity in progressive change. Let us start with Malthus. His writings are often ignored because he is regarded as a reactionary. Like it or not, however, Malthus's ghost has returned to haunt us: world population is currently doubling every forty years, and we face an uncannily Malthusian ecological crisis in the twenty-first century.

Malthus's relevance is heightened for additional reasons. It is not widely known that one of the main reasons why Malthus published his famous *Essay* on population in 1798 was to counter radical and utopian ideas concerning the perfectibility of society that had emerged in the period of the French Revolution. Indeed, the full title of the first edition is *An Essay on the Principle of Population, as it Affects the Future Improvement of Society, with Remarks on the Speculations of Mr. Godwin, M. Condorcet, and other Writers.* It is notable that two rationalistic utopians were mentioned so prominently, and singled out for criticism.

Malthus suggested a sophisticated line of argument that can be used to criticise later utopian proposals, such as those advanced by both Karl Marx and Friedrich Hayek. Paradoxically, it is the anti-utopian writings of Malthus that give us an insight into a modern utopia; while being described elsewhere as immoral they in fact sustain a moral vision upon which the modern utopia or evotopia can be based.

In his *Essay*, Malthus addressed a key problem faced by all believers: why should a wise and caring God plan or allow the existence of such wickedness and suffering in the world? Malthus's answer is that the intended role of evil is to energise us for the struggle for good. Malthus did not tolerate evil. He simply explained the existence of such sufferings and wrongs in terms of their function in arousing humanity to strive unceasingly for virtuous ends. He warned that without evil to struggle against, the virtuous may become complacent or inert. Goodness in this way depends upon imperfection.

A similar argument applies to the existence of diversity and imperfection in the natural sphere. Malthus (1798, p. 379) saw 'the infinite variety of nature' which 'cannot exist without inferior parts, or apparent blemishes'. This diversity was seen as having an essential and ultimately beneficial role in God's creation. The function of such diversity and struggle was to enable the development of improved forms. Without such a contest, no species would be impelled to improve itself. Without the test of struggle, there would be no successful development of the population as a whole. Malthus thus hints at the essential, dynamic function of diversity and variety. This idea was a key inspiration for Darwin in his development of the theory of evolution by natural selection.

Although Malthus accepted some reforms, he insisted that the creation of a perfect social order was impossible. Furthermore, as well as offering no solace for radicals, there was no comfort in the *Essay* for Panglossian conservatives either. In opposition to Malthus, both the conservatives and the radical utopians believed in harmony and perfectibility; they simply differed in their idea of perfection. Similar remarks apply to the utopias of centralist socialism and market individualism. Malthus's conception of endless struggle, diversity and impurity within a population ruled out any such optimal outcomes.

Malthus's doctrine of the imperfectibility of the world thus had two important by-products. First, no kind of economic mechanism, including the market, could ever bring about an optimal order. Second, given that no optimum was possible, and that every result necessarily contained bad elements in opposition to the good, then no means or outcome should be denied moral evaluation. The utilitarian device of disregarding the morality of the means, by assuming that they served clear and specified ends, did not work for Malthus. Regrettably, neither ends nor means could be entirely cleansed of evil, and both were thus subject to moral vigilance and scrutiny. His utilitarianism was thus qualified, and his ideas were in contrast to the more pronounced utilitarian drift of much subsequent economic theory; he provided a place for ethical assessment of both policies and outcomes.

Even his theory of population was not fatalistic; he advocated the limitation of the birth rate. Further, his theory of gluts involved a denial of the existence of effective equilibrating mechanisms and pointed to some limitations of the free market. For such reasons, Malthus's views were subsequently an important infusion for John Maynard Keynes's (1936, pp. 362–4) theory of unemployment, in which the market is not regarded as a necessarily self-righting and optimising mechanism. For Malthus, neither self-interest nor the invisible hand had unqualified virtue. While Malthus endorsed the idea of the global benefits of the pursuit of self-interest, he added the reservation that an individual should so act only 'while he adheres to the rules of justice' (Malthus, 1836, p. 2). In contrast, few such qualifications are found in the writings of Adam Smith and other classical economists.

Turning to John Stuart Mill, his 1859 tract *On Liberty* put forward parallel arguments encouraging diversity of opinion and behaviour. Like Malthus, Mill recognised the functional role of error. Unless a received and true opinion is

> vigorously and earnestly contested, it will ... be held in the manner of a prejudice, with little comprehension or feeling of its rational grounds ... the meaning of the doctrine itself will be in danger of being lost, or enfeebled, and deprived of its vital effect on the char-acter and conduct.

Furthermore, given the possibility of a received opinion being false, to deny any contrary opinions any outlet is to wrongly 'assume our own infallibility' (Mill, 1964, pp. 111–12). Mill goes on to extend such princi-ples, not only to thought, but to behaviour. 'As it is useful that while mankind is imperfect there should be different opinions, so it is that there should be different experiments of living ... the worth of different modes of life should be proved practically' (ibid., pp. 114–15). Mill thus argued for multiple experiment and comparison in socio-economic design.

The common recognition of the functional role of diversity and error in the writings of both Malthus and Mill undermines a fixed notion of utopia derived by reason, or containing a uniformity of structures or institutions. Instead therein we find the roots of evotopia: a mixed economy where variety and impurity are essential to test all structures and systems on a pragmatic, experimental and evolutionary basis.

Crucially, Malthus inspired Darwin. In the *Origin of Species*, Darwin emphasised that biotic diversity provided natural selection with its evolutionary fuel. In turn, Darwinism inspired social science, and in particular Thorstein Veblen and other American institutionalists in the 1890s and thereafter. Malthusian insights thus took root within institu-tional and evolutionary – as well as Keynesian – economics. Veblen criticised both communists and pro-marketeers for proposing that history could, would or should reach a fixed or perfect outcome. Veblen rejected as pre-Darwinian the doctrinal and teleological concept of a final goal, be it communism, capitalism or whatever. Like Malthus and Darwin, Veblen stressed the positive role of human diversity. He also attempted to analyse the sources of institutional and economic variation. He saw individuals as largely moulded by their circumstances, and thus capable of learning and advancement.

Similar ideas were advanced at about the same time by John A. Hobson, the pioneer of institutional economics in Britain. In terms similar to Veblen, he criticised the fixed utopia and 'free trade' market individualism of the nineteenth-century 'Manchester school':

> Manchesterism ... takes a purely statical and mechanical view of society. The conviction that there is one structure of industrial society right for all nations and all ages was generally accepted. ... The evolutionary idea had not yet been assimilated, either from the study of history or of the natural sciences. Even to-day the tendency to construct rigid and absolute 'ideals,' and to seek to impose them upon the world of phenomena as practical reforms, is the commonest of errors.
>
> (Hobson, 1902, pp. 30–1)

Hobson rightly suggested that a rigid utopian scheme ignored the possibility of its own fallibility: it did not recognise the importance of evolutionary ideas. He warned against the kind of utopian thinking built upon 'rigid and absolute' principles. But at the same time he advanced flexible and pragmatic reforms.

Hobson placed emphasis on 'organic' moral values and on the limitations of atomistic self-interest. Hobson combined the basic 'old' institutionalist tenet of the malleability of human purposes and preferences – prominent in the history of institutionalist writing from Veblen to John Kenneth Galbraith – with an assertion of the centrality of social norms and moral values to economic policy. Hobson also insisted on the importance of material and pecuniary incentives to motivate individuals. To some degree economic policy has to appeal to self-interest, but at the same time it has to transcend it by considering the 'organic' interests of society as a whole.

John Dewey also expressed what are described here as 'evotopian ideas'. Writing from the perspective of a radical, social liberalism, he stressed the ongoing importance and interconnection of both individual education and social reform. He rejected fascism, market individualism and centralised socialism. Like Hobson he eschewed fixed utopias, embracing a 'method of experimental and coöperative intelligence' based on science. He looked forward to the time when 'the method of intelligence and experimental control is the rule in social relations and social direction' (Dewey, 1935, p. 92).

The rejection of Benthamite individualism and utilitarianism is important within an evotopian perspective. Benthamite utilitarianism falls back on the individual as the best judge of his or her own interests, thus failing to accommodate the full possibility of future individual learning and education. This defect of utilitarianism troubled John Stuart Mill, when he questioned the utilitarian conclusion that 'pushpin and poetry' were morally and aesthetically equivalent if they led to the same degree of individual satisfaction. Contrary to Bentham, Mill thus suggested that some normative values could not be reduced to individual satisfactions. But Mill was never able to resolve this difficulty, for he remained in an utilitarian framework based on individualist foundations.

Influenced by the social organicism of the German historical school, and writing towards the end of the nineteenth century, the Irish economist John Ingram warned of the theoretical and ethical dangers of an excessive individualism and subjectivism, in the then emerging neoclassical economics:

> The radical vice of this unscientific character of political economy seems to lie in the too individual and subjective aspect under which it has been treated. Wealth having been conceived as what satisfies desires, the definitely determinable qualities possessed by some objects of supplying physical energy, and improving the physiological constitution are left out of account. Everything is gauged by the standard of subjective notions and desires. All desires are viewed as equally legitimate, and all that satisfies our desires as equally wealth. ... The truth is, that at the bottom of all economic investigation must lie the idea of the destination of wealth for the maintenance and evolution of a society. And if we overlook this, our economics will become a play of logic or a manual for the market, rather than a contribution to social science; whilst wearing an air of completeness, they will be in truth one-sided and superficial. Economic science is something far larger than the Catallactics [science of exchange] to which some have wished to reduce it.
>
> (Ingram, 1915, p. 295)

Writing in 1933 along similar lines, Keynes (1972, pp. 445–6) went further than Mill in his critique of Benthamism, seeing it as corrosive to civilisation itself:

> I do now regard that [Benthamite tradition] as the worm which has been gnawing the insides of modern civilisation and is responsible for the present moral decay. We used to regard the Christians as the enemy, because they appeared as the representatives of tradition, convention and hocus-pocus. In truth it was the Benthamite calculus based on an over-valuation of the economic criterion, which was destroying the quality of the popular Ideal.

Keynes's ideas fit in with an evotopian perspective for an additional reason: his advocacy of a mixed economy. Broadly, Keynes accepted a market-based socio-economic system. He saw the market as 'the best safeguard of personal liberty in the sense that, compared with any other system, it greatly widens the field for the exercise of personal choice. It is also the best safeguard of the variety of life' (Keynes, 1936, p. 380). However, at the same time, he noted the limitations of the market, particularly in regard to questions of long-term investment. He thus noted that: 'When the capital development of a country becomes the by-product of the activities of a casino, the job is likely to be ill-done' (ibid., p. 159). As a result he argued 'that a somewhat comprehensive socialisation of investment will prove the only means of securing an approximation to full employment; though this need not exclude all manner of compromises and devices by which public authority will co-operate with private initiative' (ibid., p. 378). Consequently, he laid out a broad path to a mixed economy, criticising Hayek in particular for greatly underestimating 'the practicality of the middle course' between markets and planning and between private and public enterprise (Keynes, 1980, p. 386).

As exemplified in these writings, the necessity of variety is the first principle of an evotopian analysis. After the Second World War, this idea found its way into systems theory, and the writings of those influenced by it. It is argued that a functional justification for variety is to cope with a degree of unforeseen change (Ashby, 1952, 1956; Beer, 1972; Luhmann, 1982; Hodgson, 1984). We have to conceive of 'a system that would continue to operate despite radical changes in its environment' (Boguslaw, 1965, p. 142). As a result, it is necessary to ensure that 'some degree of variability' is continuously generated. Also necessary is the capability to detect changes in the system's environment, and to find solutions to the new problems that emerge. However, this principle does not inform us about the nature and range of such variety. It is a task of evotopian discourse to address this question.

The point, however, is that there never can be a final answer. Our bounded understanding of all complex systems and our ignorance of future events and possibilities render all such analysis as provisional. Goals are necessary, but they too will evolve. Much work is required to derive detailed policy conclusions, and in time they will require amendment, but that does not mean that we should not start the process.

EVOTOPIA AND THE LEARNING ECONOMY

The above ideas provide no more than a general framework within which a whole range of policy scenarios and normative arguments are possible. For much of this chapter we focus on a policy priority that has emerged in this book, and which is a desirable element of evotopian thinking. Much of economics since Adam Smith has tacitly adopted his dictum that: 'Consumption is the sole end and purpose of all production' (Smith, 1976, p. 666). In contrast, it is argued here that a major end and purpose of economic activity is to safeguard and develop human capabilities, including human enlightenment and learning. The ultimate end is not simply consumption, but human education and the production of useful and warranted knowledge. It is also necessary to ensure that economic activity is sustainable in future generations. This too requires knowledge. Above all we are concerned with knowledge that serves human needs, enhances the human life process and helps humanity adapt to, and live in harmony with, its natural environment. Not all human needs are reducible to knowledge, but knowledge serves an essential role in understanding and meeting them.

Learning does not simply mean the implantation of ideas in the head; it also means the adaptation and replication of habits and behaviour. At the socio-economic level this entails changes in routines and institutions. The development in human learning over the last two hundred years has to a large degree been the result of such changes. Many of these institutional developments have been a matter of deliberate policy by governments, from the extension of basic literacy and numeracy in several advanced countries in the nineteenth century to the immense growth of vocational training and higher education in the twentieth.

A principal locus of learning is in production. Although academic courses and qualifications play an important role, much learning is contextual and rooted in the specificities of productive work. This is especially true in a knowledge-intensive economy. As Shoshana Zuboff (1988, p. 395) has remarked: 'learning is the heart of productive activity … learning is the new form of labour.'

An essential policy conclusion is the need for growing investment in education and training, at all stages and levels. In order to move the learning frontier – discussed in the preceding chapter – on a steady upward curve, substantial and increasing investment in educational institutions and training programmes is required. Progressively expanding expenditure on academic and technological research is necessary to extend the horizons of knowledge and to serve human needs. The evotopian emphasis, however, is not exclusively or primarily on quantitative measures. Quantity can never fully express quality. A huge variety of adaptable skills and capacities are required to deal with complexity.

To repeat, learning is not simply the acquisition of information. The rapidly changing world in which we live highlights the importance not simply of learning, but of 'second-order learning', that is, learning how to learn. There are some general principles and techniques that are useful in that respect, but education for flexibility and adaptability requires in

247

general the development of the powers of intuition, comparison, analogy and experimentation. Such second order learning requires the protection and development of individual autonomy, within a secure but stimulating environment.

This point is important, because there is a prevailing view today that a flexible workforce is attained through 'flexible labour markets'. But human adaptability and the capacity to learn are not the same thing as a flexible market. Indeed, overly flexible markets may create a climate of insecurity that is deleterious to learning. Furthermore, high levels of labour mobility may deter managers from investing in and enhancing the skills of their own workforce, for fear that once the workers have become trained they will move on elsewhere. On the contrary, flexibility of skills and second order learning may be best promoted with a climate of employment security and lower levels of labour turnover within the firm. There is also evidence that the creation of a flexible labour market will not necessarily reduce unemployment (Freeman, 1995). For unemployment to be reduced, the workforce must have appropriate skills, and the economy must be buoyant enough to create sufficient effective demand for those skills. Unemployment means the decay of skills. The unemployed worker is thus often an unattractive employment prospect, even at a low price. Flexibility and adaptability are not necessarily achieved by maximising the role of markets. Instead, flexibility is the result of enhanced learning.[1]

The transformation and enrichment of work are an end as well as a means. Work has to be transformed from a drudgery, to a means of expression of human potential and creativity. The repetitive and stultifying aspects of work should be replaced by computers and machines. Work has to organised, financed and motivated in a manner that serves the interests of both the worker and of society at large. In future studies, attention should be given to the specific designs of the knowops and knowco-ops discussed briefly in Chapter 9.

More generally, the market has a necessary but limited role in an evotopian economy. One of its functions is to help to provide scope for diversity and experimentation. Another is to act as a processor and signaller of much price information. However, the market is not relied upon as the single and supreme regulatory institution. Not only is such a policy implausible, for reasons discussed earlier in this book, but also it neglects the necessary and complementary function of other institutions and regulatory policies. It is important to realise that government economic involvement and regulatory policies can provide opportunities rather than mere constraints. Carefully constructed frameworks of regulation can increase the capacity of the economy to innovate and adapt, and even improve the functioning of markets themselves. As Franz Traxler and Brigitte Unger (1994, p. 2) have pointed out: 'some regulatory institutions enhance, rather than decrease, the adaptive capacity of economies'. One reason for this, they argued, has been

> the secular trend of more functional differentiation and specialization in modern societies. This implies that societal subsystems (e.g., economy, education, science, and politics) become ever more idiosyncratic in their functioning principles, such as goal-setting, criteria of success, or language. This produces more and more problems of communication and coordination between subsystems. ... Such problems require institutional bridges between different subsystems.
>
> (Traxler and Unger, 1994, p. 17)

Accordingly, flexibility and adaptability are not necessarily gained by giving markets full rein. A complex economy has a diversity of idiosyncratic goals and functioning principles, requiring over-arching, non-market frameworks of communication and regulation. Dynamic growth and flexibility can be thwarted by making all subsystems the subject of the pecuniary and contractarian dictates of the market. For reasons discussed earlier, this is true *a fortiori* with the growth of education and knowledge.

For developed countries keen to sustain economic growth and to diminish unemployment, education-centred economic policies have a special and additional significance today. In the last two decades of the twentieth century there has been rapid economic growth in a number of developing countries. New technologies have taken root and there have been substantial advances in levels of skill. This has led to the situation where a huge global workforce in the developing world can now take on, at much lower wage costs, much of the manufacturing work formerly confined to the developed countries. The developed world now imports cheap but sophisticated manufactured goods and computer software from India or East Asia. Accordingly, in the West there has been a dramatic loss in employment opportunities for workers in manufacturing and elsewhere (A. Wood, 1994, 1995).

In developed countries and elsewhere, the acquisition of alternative, viable skills, for which there is sufficient local demand at higher wage costs, is necessary to reduce this unemployment. Given the institutional and cultural conditions of the developed world, it is not possible to compete with the newly industrialised countries in terms of lower costs. Instead, the strategy must be to concentrate on knowledge-intensive, high quality, goods and services. In pursuit of this approach the developed West has no acceptable alternative but to invest massively and continuously in education and training.

Since the 1970s, there has been a substantial rise in income inequality in several developed countries, particularly the United States and

Britain. This is not a 'natural' outcome decreed by economic 'laws': there is little evidence to suggest that inequality is a necessary price for economic efficiency (Kenworthy, 1995). Although many factors, including institutional changes, lie behind this growing inequality, there is a wide consensus view that rising skill differentials, and rising relative wages for skilled and experienced workers, are a major force behind the change (Danzinger and Gottschalk, 1995).

Some have suggested employment subsidies for the less skilled as a means of tackling the problem. This would be little more than a short-term ameliorative measure, using government financial resources merely to augment the demand for labour. Comparative evidence between countries indicates that legislation to establish a substantial minimum wage and to enable greater trade union bargaining power would help to reduce inequality (Fortin and Lemieux, 1997). But such measures could not match the rapidly growing demand for skilled or educated labour nor restrain the global forces of low-cost competition. They would bring some short-term benefits, but not a lasting solution.

Whatever complementary measures are deployed, the only substantial and enduring strategy must involve heavy investment in education, to increase the relative and absolute supply of skilled and educated workers (Gottschalk, 1997; Johnson, 1997; Topel, 1997). In the face of rapid and dramatic global and technological changes, massive increases in effective expenditure on education and training are required to reduce both unemployment and inequality. Countries that have travelled more than others down this road, particularly Germany, have not witnessed a significant increase in income inequality since the 1970s, and have been more able to train and relocate workers of relatively lower skill (OECD, 1993; Nickell and Bell, 1996).

Education does not exist in isolation. Without the satisfaction of prior social, physiological and psychological needs – such as food, health, shelter, security, nurture, care, interaction and affection – education cannot thrive or progress. The mere provision of learning opportunities is not enough. The personality of the individual, including the capacity and motivation to learn, are largely formed in childhood. Social and material conditions are crucial, especially in the early years of life. It must be a priority to ensure that the material, social and cultural conditions of both children and adults are conducive to learning. Clearly, learning cannot be effective unless such primary needs are addressed. People learn much less effectively when they are hungry and when they lack self-esteem. The learning economy must necessarily address and gratify all human needs.

In general, a need can usefully be defined as that which 'persons must achieve if they are to avoid sustained and serious harm' (Doyal and Gough, 1991, p. 50). The avoidance of harm involves the protection and enhancement of human life and knowledge. Furthermore, needs are distinguished from wants, the latter term being reserved for desires, which are not necessarily individually or socially beneficial. Instead of subjective desire or utility, such needs are progressively revealed via some instituted social process of technical or scientific enquiry. They are a matter of objective and ongoing discussion, not merely subjective gratification. As the institutional economist K. William Kapp (1978, p. 297) wrote: 'social choices are made not in terms of subjectively experienced deficiencies and wants but in terms of objective requirements or scientifically determined standards'.[2]

This is not to deny the problematic nature of this venture, or indeed of science itself. There is no fixed or final set of standards for the identification and evaluation of human needs. Partly for this reason, the better writings in this tradition emphasise the ongoing, fallible and open-ended nature of enquiry, and address the problem of designing flexible institutions that are appropriate for the ongoing democratic evaluation and revision of declared needs (Doyal and Gough, 1991; Tool, 1979). As a result, the evaluation of need depends on the advancement of learning, just as the advancement of learning depends upon the satisfaction of other needs. Learning and needs each depend on the other. The development of the learning economy not only depends upon, but also itself enhances, our understanding and gratification of human needs.

On the negative side, the general development of the learning economy would be thwarted by the social exclusion of, or discrimination against, any disadvantaged group. Social exclusion means lack of access to the institutions and facilities of learning. Efforts to end social exclusion involve policies against poverty and unemployment and the outlawing of ethnic and gender discrimination. Women, even if they stay at home, require access to modern electronic learning facilities and the education, incentives and encouragement to use them. The learning economy is necessarily an inclusive economy. It nurtures and thrives upon an endless diversity of human skills and talents, but it is infused throughout with an egalitarian morality of rights.

The approach to formal education must be neither narrow nor doctrinal. Education is not essentially the transmission of information but the adaptation and enlargement of human potential. Dewey (1935, p. 47) repeated throughout his life that education was more than the mere 'acquisition of information': it was the 'expansion of the understanding and judgement of meanings'. Judgement, flexibility and adaptability are required to deal with the unforeseen. There is a need, above all, to learn how to learn (Bateson, 1972; Drucker, 1993; Nonaka and Takeuchi, 1995; Senge, 1990). Useful learning is not the assimilation of masses of given facts. This would be both interminable and of little use. Neither is it the acquisition by training of fixed skills. These rapidly become obsolete. As well as some specific, functional skills, learning must involve general and transferable components. It has been shown that such basic but transferable aspects of learning, such as the use of analogy and the consideration of broader context, can be taught (J. Marquand, 1989).

Necessarily based on a strong sense of individual autonomy, effective learning generally involves a questioning attitude to received wisdom and the development of critical capacities. In turn, this implies the development of a pluralism of competing approaches within academic disciplines, not least within economics itself (Salanti and Screpanti, 1997). Innovation in general depends on variety.

Detailed studies of the growth and application of knowledge by managers and engineers suggest that innovative developments result from the ability to perceive and select routines and devices from a rich and varied repertoire of possibilities (Vincenti, 1990). In this respect, the growth of knowledge is an evolutionary process, depending and thriving on variety. Within the context of this variety there is a process of selection, based on expert intuition, perception, analysis and experiment (Campbell, 1974).

Variety and pluralism are important in both teaching and research. In Britain, for example, large-scale research funding is currently dominated by too few agencies. This has led to a damaging narrowness of scope and viewpoint, and the increased danger of exclusive domination by vested interests. It is possible, for example, that the public policy disaster of BSE, or 'mad cow disease' in the 1980s and 1990s could have been diminished or avoided, thus saving human lives, if research in the area had not been so exclusively dominated by the agricultural ministry and the vested interests of large-scale, industrial farming. With a greater tolerance of different investigative approaches, and with informed challenges to the scientific *status quo*, it is likely that the dangers could have been recognised and understood much earlier. Research thrives on competing viewpoints in a questioning culture. As Alfred Whitehead argued persuasively (1926) long ago, a science that loses the ability to question its own basic assumptions is doomed.

The capacity for self-questioning and self-criticism, of mainstream as well as other views, is not simply an individual matter, nor state of mind. It has to be built into the institutions, culture and practices of science and education, starting from the highest level. It has to permeate the university system, where alas it does not always thrive. It has to permeate the practice of government, instead of the widespread habit of commissioning the advisors most likely to confirm and endorse existing policy. Institutionalised pluralism within academia is not a luxury. It is a necessity, arising from the fallibility of all knowledge, made all the more vital in the face of growing complexity.

INFORMATION OVERLOAD: FILTERING AND ACCREDITATION

The recognition of the institutional character of knowledge suggests a policy emphasis on the development of a learning culture, involving shared material and immaterial resources. Organisations have to invest in such resources, just as they exist society-wide, from the public library to the Internet. Recognition of the importance of such issues is now commonplace, but, by comparison, insignificant attention has been given by policy-makers to the problems of an information-rich society, where a huge amount of information is available in the public domain. In particular, there are the important problems of *selection* in the context of information overload and of the *accreditation* of the selected information.

The problem of information accreditation has become particularly relevant on the electronic media. With the reduction in publication costs and the growth in number of books and journals, the problem has intensified in more traditional media as well. A huge and rapidly expanding amount of information is available, but its quality and reliability are often open to question. Until quite recently, the filtering and accreditation of information were maintained largely by universities, libraries and a few commercial publishers, each keen to select the most important and reputable items, and to protect its own academic and institutional reputation. By contrast, in the last few years, the explosion in scale of the electronic media, and the growth in the number of academic journals and publishing institutions, have made the verification and accreditation of information all the more difficult. It is not enough to find the information somewhere within the enormous electronic and paper haystack. The information cannot be relied upon unless it stems from some reliable authority, or its origins are verified.

The problem of information overload faced by any decision-maker has now reached acute proportions. It is simply impossible to analyse or make use of all the relevant information that is available. Simple, streamlined methods of communication – such as electronic mail – approach congestion due to over-use. In response, it is often complacently assumed that the system will sort itself out. Or perhaps, with the help of customised and artificially intelligent computer software, we shall learn to select the information that is useful to us, and safely ignore the rest.

However, such responses are somewhat over-optimistic and ignore key issues. Unavoidably, all methods of dealing with these problems involve selection criteria which are both normative and cursory. Normative issues are raised later; let us address the problem of cursoriness first. Whether we use our own judgement, or that of a sophisticated computer program, the use of relatively superficial criteria is unavoidable. In a situation of complexity and information overload, it is not possible to scrutinise all information fully. As suggested in Chapter 9, as the information explosion continues, greater use will be made of information screening agencies and systems of selecting appropriate information and knowledge, involving institutional certification and the testimonials of experts. These are the unavoidably imperfect means by which we attempt an inevitably semi-informed judgement of the value of the knowledge that we have yet to assimilate, and could no more than partially assimilate in principle.

Take financial markets as an example. With sophisticated information technology, leading to the widespread availability of information, the trader faces the problem of selecting, screening and evaluating a huge amount of changing information. In this situation of overload, institutions or individuals are able to select only a subset of all available information for closer scrutiny or evaluation. As a result, traders rely on widely publicised but highly selective indicators, such as the Dow-Jones and the *Financial Times* indices of share prices. Despite the abundance of readily available information, the interpretative work of the financial advisor becomes highly valued and lucrative.

As already noted, faced with an increasing choice of complex goods and services for sale, the consumer faces a similar problem. To cope with the abundance of choice and lack of appropriate technical information, reliance is made on brand name reputation. In this case the private corporation becomes the accreditor of quality, with all the attendant problems and dangers in this solution.

It was also noted in Chapter 9 that the processes of selection and accreditation face the problem of infinite upward regress: who accredits the accreditors? A hierarchy of evaluating and accrediting agencies may emerge, but some institution has to act as accreditor of last resort. This is a necessary but a dangerous solution. The state may be suited to take the place at the top, as the ultimate quality assurer. However, this solution is only viable if the state has, and is seen to have, both competence and legitimacy. Failing the existence of these qualities, there is the danger of totalitarian control and consequence abuse of the information by this ultimate assuring institution. On the other hand, in the absence of adequate institutions by which information can be accredited, there is a danger of degeneration into a semi-anarchy of competing claims with questionable credentials. The dilemma between institutional power and degenerative anarchy is unavoidable.

Arguably, the state could play the role of accreditor of last resort *but only on the basis of its own openness towards information and its full, democratic legitimacy.* Furthermore, there should be a system of checks and balances, involving appraisals of the quality assurance procedures and the promotion of supplementary agencies of accreditation. The existence of multiple accrediting and advising institutions, both public and private, is consistent with the evotopian approach.

COMPLEXITY, INFORMATION AND ETHICS

An interesting paradox is dramatised in a world of complexity. The learning economy is one which is necessarily reflective and self-critical. However, a complex society is required to rely also on trust, and less on explicit contracts, sanctions and rewards. In a complex and rapidly changing world, we are unable to make fully-informed judgements and we sometimes have to trust the opinions even of strangers. New commodities which are all the more complex and knowledge-intensive are all the more difficult to scrutinise and evaluate. Attempts to gain recompense for faulty goods by litigation are possible, but they are potentially costly to both sides. Paradoxically, for the wheels of commerce to run smoothly we have to take more and more for granted, even in a questioning society.

But trust that is blind and universal loses its meaning and value. The habit of trust has to be conditional upon appropriate conditions and triggers. In social life we always rely on a multiplicity of such indicators, often without full awareness of our own use of them. In particular, if we are led to believe that the other person is purely motivated by their own self-interest then trust is undermined. A soil in which trust can grow is one made fertile with moral considerations beyond calculative self-interest. As noted in Chapter 3, trust itself is undermined by the over-use of contractual negotiation and of the cost calculus. To repeat the words of Kenneth Arrow (1974, p. 23): 'If you have to buy [trust], you already have some doubts about what you've bought.' Even a market economy depends on values and commitments which are not tradable. Concerns about such issues of commensurability or pecuniary reduction stretch beyond institutional economists. Warren Hagstrom (1965, p. 20) has argued that commitments to values cannot best be engendered by offers of incentives or rewards:

> In general, *whenever strong commitments to values are expected, the rational calculation of punishments and rewards is regarded as an improper basis for making decisions.* Citizens who refrain from treason merely because it is against the law are, by that fact, of questionable loyalty; parents who refrain from incest merely because of fear of community reaction are, by that fact, unfit for parenthood.

Robert Frank (1993, p. 172) has argued along similar lines:

> it appears odd to use the label 'trustworthy' to describe someone whose co-operation is motivated only by fear of future retaliation; it

would be much more accurate to call such a person 'prudent.' Our ordinary understanding of trustworthiness involves honoring one's obligations even when material incentives clearly favor defection.

Accordingly, there are values or commitments held by individuals which are not in principle reducible purely to matters of incentive or deterrence. Attempts to reduce moral issues and values solely to matters of individual incentive or disincentive precisely betray such values or commitments (O'Neill, 1993). Some leading game theorists have come to the conclusion that, in many situations, a pair of cold-blooded, rational, calculating individuals will come off worse than those bound by considerations of fairness, of conscience and of reciprocity by others (Shubik, 1982, p. 294; Schelling, 1984, p. 209). Pursuing self-interest may be self-defeating unless there is a sense of social commitment (Frank, 1988).[3]

Within capitalism this leads to a further contradiction. The achievement of profit is necessary for the survival of business enterprise. However, a business that makes the maximisation of its own profits its explicit and exclusive objective is likely to fail. This has been described as the 'paradox of profit' (Bowie, 1988). The more a business becomes obsessed with profits, the less likely it is to achieve them. This is similar to what sages call the 'hedonistic paradox' – the more one seeks pleasure, the less likely one is to find it.

A self-centred obsession with profit will cultivate mistrust in the eyes of its suppliers and customers. In an open and information-rich society this problem becomes more severe, as any indicators of unworthiness can be more widely and readily publicised. The firm has to compete not simply for profit but for our confidence and trust. To achieve this, it has to abandon profit-maximisation, or even shareholder satisfaction, as the exclusive objectives of the organisation. Its explicit mission has to lie elsewhere: in product quality, customer satisfaction, ethical business practices and environmentally friendly policies, for example. Mission statements, and other such moral window dressing, are not enough: the efficient functionaries of the firm have to *believe* in its higher and fuller aims.

There is a dangerous tendency in the modern era to downplay the role of values and morality in economic and social life. In the expanding era of liberal capitalism, the growth of contract and commerce seemingly makes the individual the judge of worth and value. In general, a contract is legitimated on the basis of the fact that it is the result of free agreement between individuals. As a result, a contractarian society must tend to make the free individual the source of moral evaluation. All other sources of moral legitimacy are swept aside, for fear that the sanctity of the contract may be eroded. As a result, the individual appears as the sole moral arbiter. Alasdair MacIntyre (1985) has described the situation in which moral values are rendered relative and subjective, the gratification of emotions is seen as paramount, and the notion of the good is deemed to be a purely private matter. Each person is declared free to judge the moral good for herself, and is deemed to be at liberty to pursue that private vision subject to the constraint that it does not impinge on those like freedoms for others. Ironically, the abandonment of the search for a greater 'common good' has tragically been proclaimed as the era of freedom and human liberation. As Brian Crowley (1987, p. 18) argued:

> Having dispensed with any claim to be able to judge the goodness of the ends that men pursue, the moral interest of society in individual or collective action turns from the ends to be achieved to focus exclusively on the means chosen to achieve them.

Nevertheless, as argued earlier in this book, the relegation of moral judgements simply to the individual can never be absolute or complete. As Hector put it in Shakespeare's *Troilus and Cressida*: 'value resides not in particular will'. Logically, individuals alone cannot legitimate the individual as the exclusive source of moral authority. Paradoxically, ethical individualism cannot be validated by individuals alone. Functionally, the exclusive pursuit of self-interest is ultimately destructive and self-defeating.

This is a persistent but important theme. In the last century, John Ruskin warned prophetically in his book *Unto This Last* (1866, p. 17) that economic policies that appealed simply to hedonistic motives were doomed to failure. Writers such as Hobson, Mahatma Gandhi and Richard Tawney were influenced by Ruskin and see the importance of appeals to moral values in economic and social policy. Many twentieth-century social scientists, including Joseph Schumpeter (1976), Karl Polanyi (1944), Fred Hirsch (1977) and Amitai Etzioni (1988) have emphasised that even a competitive, capitalist economy itself depends on widely accepted moral norms.

Mainstream economics typically downplays or ignores questions of moral value in its discourse. Anything but the most superficial discussion of ethical philosophy is absent from the mainstream textbooks on economic policy. Yet ever since the rise of the 'dismal science', warnings have been raised that the teaching of economics purged of wider and deeper moral considerations is blinkered, misconceived and potentially destructive. The fact is overlooked that both economic activity and economic policy always depend upon evaluative and thereby moral judgements that transcend individuals alone.

Even in our basic theoretical assumptions we purvey a moral vision, of what is important or what is desirable. This is not least the case in the textbook picture of self-interested, 'economic man' maximising his own utility. As Gunnar Myrdal (1978, p. 5) repeatedly emphasised:

Valuations are always with us. Disinterested research there never has been and can never be. Prior to answers there must be questions. There can be no view except from a viewpoint. In the questions raised, and the viewpoint chosen, valuations are implied.

There is no retreat from wider ethical issues, in economic theory or policy. A view, found in economic writings from Malthus to Keynes, is that economics must be relatively less a mere technical or mathematical exercise and more a science involving moral judgement and the development of policy. The early institutionalists expressed similar concerns, and criticised the hedonistic presumptions of much economic theory. Veblen (1914, p. 47 n.) argued that while self-interest is prominent in modern society 'this self-seeking motive is hemmed in and guided at all points in the course of its development by considerations and conventions that are not of a primarily self-seeking kind'. Karl Polanyi (1947, p. 114) similarly criticised the concept of selfish 'economic man':

> In actual fact, man was never as selfish as the theory demanded. ... In vain was he exhorted by economists and utilitarian moralists alike to discount in business all other motives than 'material' ones. On closer investigation, he was still found to be acting on remarkably 'mixed' motives, not excluding those of duty towards himself and others – and maybe, secretly, even enjoying work for its own sake.

It is thus of some concern that economists today preach unquestioningly the doctrine that it is sufficient to assume that all people are motivated solely by the maximisation of their own utility, self-interest or greed to millions of students around the world. Accordingly, generations of workers, business people, journalists and politicians have become disposed to belittle public moral values and to favour policies based on such hedonistic presumptions. By assuming the ubiquity of selfishness, such behaviour is legitimated, in turn encouraging more greed and adding to other forces of social, economic and environmental disintegration. Not only is the depiction of the individual, solely maximising their own satisfaction, unrealistic and unfounded. As Keynes put it: this doctrine is a 'worm which has been gnawing the insides of modern civilisation'.[4]

Abandoning this hedonistic view of the individual does not mean adopting an equally naïve belief that people are wholly self-disregarding and virtuous. Human beings are often selfish and all-too-frequently capable of morally outrageous acts. This is not simply, or even mainly, a dispute between an 'optimistic' and a 'pessimistic' view of human nature. Instead, the key issues are best put in different terms.

Whatever their failings, humans are not *entirely* motivated by self-interest. Even criminals, dictators, gangsters and mass murderers generally live by a moral code, albeit one that is often defective. Second, the pursuit of policies based solely on an appeal to self-interest is ultimately self-defeating. As well as the established mainstream views, economics has to be conceived as a 'moral science' and fortified by the study of alternative positive and normative approaches. Amartya Sen (1987), in particular, has argued that too much weight has been given to the 'engineering' tradition in economics since the 1870s, and the moral tradition, going back to Adam Smith, has to be strengthened.

A prominent policy conclusion is clear. Appeals to appropriate moral values and not merely perceived self-interest should become part and parcel of economic policy. The economy is far too important to be left to the technocratic amorality of the mainstream economists. Hirsch (1977, p. 12), for example, has argued eloquently that instead of reliance on 'the self-interest principle' economic policy should pay much more heed to 'the role played by the supporting ethos of social obligation both in the formation of the relevant public policies and in their efficient transmission to market opportunities'. In an information-rich era of increasing complexity this is ever more true.

This does not mean that policies based on pecuniary and monetary incentives have no place. Indeed, such proposals can be reinforced by complementary appeals to moral values. Indeed, it could be argued that appeals simply to moral duty, on the one hand, or reliance on perceived self-interest, on the other, are likely to be of limited effect as they are employed alone. Carefully structured combinations working on both levels are likely to be more successful.

Contrary to frequent suggestions that they are ephemeral, values are difficult both to build and dislodge. Observe, for example, (a) the two centuries of tenacity of American individualism, (b) the grounding of Japanese social and corporate solidarity upon the foundation of a feudal epoch and (c) the stubbornly persistent British deference to class and status. These are quite different in their role and sustance. Despite the globalisation of the capitalist system and strong pressures of convergence and conformity, unique customs, cultures and systems of values still remain in each nation. These depend upon hundreds of years of history. An appeal to values is no easy or superficial policy fix. Yet once norms such as co-operation and fairness become established they can be self-reinforcing, and their effects can span both current and future generations.

THE FUTURE OF CONTRACT AND CORPORATION

In the development of the learning economy, or more particularly the 'market cognitism' discussed in Chapter 9, there are many zones of transformation. One is social culture. Another is the legal system. Already, within capitalism, as noted in Chapter 9, the classical system of contract law is beginning to be surpassed (Atiyah, 1979; Slawson, 1996). Under this classical system, the agreement of two parties to a deal was sometimes sufficient to ensure the legality of the contract, although restrictions and caveats were common. A key issue in the transformation and supersession of classical contract law is the decreasing use of mutual agreement between a limited number of parties as the exclusive basis of legality. Legal contracts increasingly are required to satisfy other criteria of 'reasonableness' or 'public policy', such as social cohesion, human dignity and ecological sustainability. The legitimation of contract by individual or collective agreement is not enough. Increasingly, the legal system sanctions and embodies moral values that are not reducible simply to the wishes of individuals or organisations.

This is especially the case in employment law. Even prior to the rise of wage-labour, the prohibition of voluntary bondage or slavery meant placing restrictions on the legality of agreements between master and worker. In Britain, from 1833 onwards, restrictions were put on the legality of agreements between employer and employee, with regard to child labour, female labour, night working, and the length of the working day. The twentieth century has seen a huge extension in the number and type of restrictions on free contract in the sphere of employment. The employment contract is central to capitalism and its contract system, yet in developed countries it is the sphere where the law of contract is typically most circumscribed.

It has been argued in preceding chapters that the growth of knowledge-intensive production in modern capitalism challenges aspects of contractual law and brings further restrictions on the legal formulations and agreements within the employment contract. The growth of restrictions, especially on the powers of employers, raises the possible scenario of a libertarian–contractarian reaction and forlorn attempts to preserve the individualistic norms of pure and unsullied contractual agreement between employer and employee. This was an ideological feature of governments in the United States and Britain in the 1980s. Although this libertarian–contractarian reaction was possibly slowed, or even halted, by later developments in the 1990s, it could return with renewed vigour, especially if the political pendulum was again to swing back against government economic regulation and intervention.

The argument in the present book is that the growth of complexity within the knowledge-intensive economy is breaking the confines of classical, individualistic, contract law, and recognising the necessity of irreducible and over-arching values to social and economic development. As a result, a policy aimed at the development of the learning economy must guard against any libertarian–contractarian reaction. While protecting individual rights and autonomy, an ethos of community and obligation to others has to be stressed, and preserved in our practices and institutions.

The future of contract is in these terms. No longer legitimated by individual agreement alone, the culture and legalities of the contractual transaction can evolve further by requiring the satisfaction of additional criteria of social and moral acceptability. In the epsilon and zeta scenarios discussed in Chapter 9, such considerations impinge increasingly upon all aspects of economic and social life.

The evolution of the modern corporation is an especially pertinent example. With the increasingly complex and knowledge-intensive development of the economy, the exclusive pursuit of profit becomes not only impossible but self-defeating. Both corporation law and corporate culture can develop further to reflect the complex and multi-faceted goals of productive activity. The social nature of knowledge itself can become reflected more in both the aims and the statutes of the organisation. Furthermore, there has to be extensive experimentation with other forms of corporate structure, in addition to the conventional, hierarchic firm under nominal shareholder control. Participatory management structures, co-operatives, and worker share ownership schemes are all relevant here. Furthermore, workplace law has to evolve to reflect the decreasing power and efficacy of employer control.

Moral considerations have always been present in family law, and in the law governing sexual activities such as prostitution. In these spheres the mere agreement of two parties has never been regarded as sufficient legal justification. The social and economic changes of the twentieth century have tested these issues relentlessly. We are familiar with complex debates concerning surrogate parenting, human fertility treatment, one-parent families and divorce. The technological capacities of the twenty-first century will probe such moral questions still further. We face the issues of genetic engineering, genetic screening of the unborn, human cloning, revamped eugenics, animal organ transplants into humans, foetal experimentation, euthanasia, and protracted longevity. It is not possible even to attempt to deal with all the complex ethical issues here. The point being raised is that all these problems challenge the relatively narrow, contractarian principles of the Enlightenment. Neither the dictates of the market nor the wisdom of the central planners can adequately resolve these issues. The approach has to be pragmatic and evaluative, involving prominent, sustained and scientifically informed moral debate within society (Radin, 1996).

FINAL REMARKS

The progressive development of the learning economy requires both a social culture and a set of social institutions that are infused with a democratic and open spirit, sustaining dialogue on the nature and extent of individual rights and duties, and fostering experimentation and careful evaluation of many new procedures and organisational forms. The guiding principles are the satisfaction of human need and the enlargement of human potential. We must also live in harmony with our natural environment: without undermining its variety or sustainability. But both the exploration and the implementation of these principles and constraints require an open, participatory and informed dialogue, itself sustained by democratic institutions. The normative goals for humanity – of knowledge, economic development, democracy, and need-satisfaction – are all entwined together. They are both ends and means at the same time.

Knowledge, in particular, is both a means and an end. This book has examined how the growth of knowledge can lead to a radical transformation of socio-economic systems. But there is nothing inevitable about this. Nor is knowledge the single engine of socio-economic change. However, as argued above, the growth of knowledge in a learning economy is a important and necessary feature of development.

Yet in one of our most poignant and enduring myths, God in the biblical Garden of Eden warned Adam and Eve not to taste the fruit of the tree of knowledge. Disobedience of God's order led to the Fall, to pain and suffering, and to the ongoing process of procreation of generations of progeny. Perhaps the truth in the scripture is that, unlike other animals, humanity is forever both cursed and blessed by knowledge. It is the original sin, for which there is no clemency and from which there is no release. No longer innocent, we are collectively afflicted by an unavoidable and endless imperative to pursue wisdom, almost as if for its own sake.

However, what the book of Genesis failed to mention was that the growth and spread of knowledge can help to expose injustice, break down obsolete barriers and bring human empowerment. Indeed, since the Fall, knowledge is no longer something to be forbidden: it is a formidable necessity. Stored in our institutions, it is a means of both individual self-realisation and social emancipation. Used properly, it is a basis for the enlargement and institutionalisation of other worthwhile human values. In turn, upon these common values, a better – but nevertheless varied and adaptable – socio-economic system may be built.

This book is an exercise in meta-utopian analysis and does not claim to highlight a detailed utopia or evotopia, or to derive detailed political or economic policies. Any attempt to do so must enter into much more empirical and historical detail than is conceivable in a work of this scope. Nevertheless, it has been possible to adduce some central principles and to touch upon some issues of contemporary relevance. Once we realise that we are not at the end of history then we can begin, with eyes open, the task of making it.

NOTES

PREFACE

1 Some observers have preferred to describe Soviet-type socio-economic systems as 'capitalist' or 'state capitalist'. This is not consistent with the (narrower) definition of capitalism adopted in this book. This leaves unanswered the quite separate question of whether or not they were properly described as 'socialist'. The reader is left to make up his or her own mind on the latter point. Although it is an important question, nothing major hinges on it here. In contrast, the argument in this volume depends crucially on a forensically precise definition of capitalism.

2 Furthermore, in the West, in a climate of intellectual intolerance charmingly reminiscent of Sino-Soviet totalitarianism, all varieties of non-mainstream economics – including Marxism, Post Keynesianism and the 'old' institutionalism – have systematically been driven out of university departments in several countries in the 1980s and 1990s. Contrary to the more pluralistic state of affairs in the 1950s and 1960s, non-mainstream economists are increasingly rare in economics departments in Britain, the United States, Germany and elsewhere. Against such developments, 'A Plea for a Pluralistic and Rigorous Economics' was signed by 44 leading economists – including four Nobel Laureates – and published in the May 1992 edition of the *American Economic Review*. This plea included the words:

> We the undersigned are concerned with the threat to economic science posed by intellectual monopoly. Economists today enforce a monopoly of method or core assumptions, often defended on no better ground than it constitutes the 'mainstream'. Economists will advocate free competition, but will not practice it in the marketplace of ideas.

For an excellent discussion of the issue of pluralism in economics see Salanti and Screpanti (1997).

3 The author has long been a strong critic of aspects of Marx's analysis, including the labour theory of value and the theory of the falling rate of profit. See Hodgson (1974a, 1974b, 1977, 1982, 1984, 1988, 1991, 1993b). Furthermore, as elaborated below, the author's projections concerning possible patterns of capitalist and post-capitalist development are very different from those supposed by Marx.

4 Works in the 1990s include: Albert (1993), Albert and Hahnel (1990), Amin (1996), Anderson (1992), R. Archer (1995), Åslund (1992), Bardhan and Roemer (1992, 1993, 1994), Boswell (1990), Bowles and Gintis (1993a), Bowles

et al. (1993), Bresser Pereira *et al.* (1993), Cockshott and Cottrell (1993), G. A. Cohen (1996), Cowling and Sugden (1994), Daly and Cobb (1990), Doyal and Gough (1991), Drucker (1993), Ellerman (1992), Gibson-Graham (1996), Giddens (1994), Gough (1994), Groenewegen and McFarlane (1995), Hain (1995), Hirst (1994), Hutchinson and Burkitt (1997), Hutton (1995, 1997), Itoh (1995), Jacobs (1991), Lipietz (1992), Lukes (1995), D. Marquand (1993), McCarney (1993), McNally (1993), Meade (1993), D. Miliband (1994), R. Miliband (1995), Nove (1991), Nove and Thatcher (1994), O'Neill (1993), Pagano and Rowthorn (1996), Patnaik (1991), Pierson (1995), Piore (1995), Prychitko (1991), Przeworski, (1991) Roemer (1994), Rose (1991), Rustin (1992), Scharpf (1991), Schweickart (1993), Screpanti (1992), Sik (1991), Skidelsky (1995), Stiglitz (1994), Thurow (1996), Van Parijs (1995), Wainwright (1994), Webster (1995), Yunker (1992, 1995) and Zadek (1993).

5 In particular, the idea of the 'impurity principle' is developed further in later chapters. A preceding hint of the impurity principle was in Hodgson (1982, pp. 179, 231–2) but the idea is developed more fully in Hodgson (1984, pp. 85–109, 220–8) and it is summarised in Hodgson (1988, pp. 167–71, 254–62).

1 INTRODUCTION

1 There are many examples of this time-leaping genre. The famous astronomer Hoyle (1966) offered a novel along these lines, as does Hollywood, with its television series *Sliders*.

2 Praise for More's work is not confined to socialists. The economist Schumpeter (1954, p. 207) rightly described this as a 'rich book of mature wisdom'.

3 The term is used occasionally in the present work, but only where required for stylistic reasons. The caveat here must always be borne in mind. Furthermore, as explained in Hodgson (1988), not all exchange takes place in markets, as markets are a particularly organised and institutional form of commodity exchange. The distinction between markets and 'relational exchange' will be made later. Nevertheless, considerations of style inhibit repeated recognition of the point, and invite the occasional, unqualified use of the term 'market'.

4 Medvedev (1989, p. 9) made this Soviet estimate. A more precise figure is emerging now that the former Soviet archives are being opened up for historical research. The tendency has been for estimates of deaths to increase rather than to decrease, as new information is revealed. Furthermore, Lenin has been found to be responsible for some atrocities, but on a much smaller scale relative to Stalin.

5 See Ashton *et al.* (1984) and MacFarquhar and Fairbank (1987, 1991).

6 Nozick (1974, pp. 309–12) refers to the 'utopia of utopias' or 'meta-utopia' as an order of many communities, each serving different values or conflicts of values.

7 The term 'Austrian economics' primarily refers to the works of Hayek and von Mises, secondarily to their intellectual tradition going back to Menger, and tertiarily to successors such as Lachmann and Kirzner.

2 SOCIALISM AND THE LIMITS TO
INNOVATION

1 There were differences, however. Fourier advocated a communistic city–state or *phalanstère*, Blanc saw a greater role for the central state. Saint-Simon advocated the abolition of inheritance, but not of all private property. For Saint-Simon, while the means of production were to be pooled in 'one central social fund', private ownership of goods would be tolerated. Both Owenites and Marxists saw Saint-Simon's proposals as inadequate.

2 For a discussion of the relatively sparse pronouncements of Marx on his desired future communist society see Ollman (1977). Both Kumar (1987) and Geoghegan (1987) rightly insist that Marxism has an incompletely formulated – but unavoidable – utopian vision of its own.

3 A flaw in Moore's argument is to the term 'socialism' differed clearly and substantially from 'communism' in terms of the final goal, and that 'socialism' can readily be seen to accommodate markets. Although Moore is writing for an American audience with extreme sensitivities on these issues, he should not have evaded the historical fact that traditionally, and until quite recently, 'socialism' has avoided all market associations.

4 Writing in 1923, Lenin (1967, vol. 3, p. 763) began to take a more positive view of worker and peasant co-operatives. Nevertheless, Lenin saw co-operatives as socialist enterprises if 'the land on which they are situated and the means of production belong to the state'. Whether the market would remain, as a means of coordinating these state-owned but co-operatively managed enterprises, was not made clear. And if it did remain, would this be a transitional phase rather than a final goal? Lenin died shortly afterwards, before these questions could be answered.

5 Among the influences on Heimann's thinking was the version of guild socialism promoted at the time by Karl Polanyi. Heimann actually proposed a decentralised system in which semi-autonomous publicly owned corporations could sell products to each other and to the consumer, *but at prices regulated by the central planners*. He thus anticipated the quasi-markets of Lange and others. Heimann was later to see additional (proto-Keynesian) roles for the central state: the direction of investment and the avoidance of recessions. See Halm (1935), Landauer (1959, pp. 1643 ff.), Nuti (1992).

6 Although cited as a supporter of von Mises's views on the importance of markets, the Russian emigré Brutzkus (1923) was more moderate in his views, and actually supported a form of mixed economy, involving private, public and co-operative sectors. However, despite these precedents, and even today, there is no developed and adequate theoretical rationale for a varied and mixed economy. Crosland (1956) presented the 'mixed economy' more as an ethical ideal, not as a functional necessity. The justification for a public sector in post-war mainstream economics, based on the idea of 'public goods' has been contested and largely abandoned. Kornai (1971) and Nove (1983) provided, but only in outline, sketches of an alternative theoretical approach. Just as Marxism and traditional socialism have suffered from under-theorisation concerning their proposed future, so too has modern social democracy.

7 Freed somewhat by his own movement away from orthodox Marxism, Kautsky (1925) was later more explicit in favouring a role for markets, money and prices in a future socialist economy. For this and other reasons he has often been treated by socialists as a heretic.

8 See Caldwell (1997), Hayek (1935), Hoff (1949), Lavoie (1985a, 1985b), Murrell (1983), Steele (1992), Vaughn (1980). Although he does not acknowledge the full force of the Austrian argument on the need for markets, Itoh (1995) also summarises some of the later debates over so-called 'market socialism'.

9 In explicit terms, these British and American writers wished to magnify freedom and democracy, and minimise bureaucracy, in their ideal socialist society. Dickenson applauded the full flowering of 'individualism' and described his model as a 'libertarian socialism'. Durbin and Lerner both applauded democracy, Lerner (1944, p. 1) making it a more supreme socialist value than the abolition of private property. However, the question of whether their liberal and democratic ideals were actually *in practice* compatible with their proposals for a huge concentration and centralisation of *de facto* economic power in the hands of the state, was a different matter. The road to totalitarianism is paved with good intentions.

10 See Hodgson (1992a) for an elaboration of this point. Neoclassical economics may be conveniently defined as an approach which first, assumes rational, maximising behaviour by agents with given and stable preference functions, second, focuses on attained, or movements towards, equilibrium states, and finally excludes chronic information problems. Notably, some recent developments in modern mainstream economic theory – such as in game theory – reach or even lie outside the boundaries of this definition. Stiglitz (1994) defined 'neoclassical' more narrowly, as the general equilibrium approach characterised by Arrow and Debreu. He was thus able to characterise his own approach as non-neoclassical, whereas it is much closer to satisfying the criteria in the broader definition given above. Although Stiglitz has advanced significantly the treatment of information in mainstream economics, he still has not embraced uncertainty in the Knightian or Keynesian sense, nor problems of divergent cognitions of the same data, nor the distinction between sense-data and information.

11 The very same charge, of being influenced by the dreaded institutionalists and the German historical school, had also been levied by Hayek against the socialists. Clearly, both sides in the debate were agreed upon one thing – the worst term of abuse to hurl against the other. In fact, as indicated in later chapters, institutionalism offers a ostensible resolution of some of the key problems facing Austrian, neoclassical and Marxian theory.

12 For a powerful criticism of this mainstream methodology, see Lawson (1997).

13 Several proposals for market socialism with genuine markets have been developed. Note the contributions of Bardhan and Roemer (1992, 1994), Le Grand and Estrin (1989), Meade (1993), D. Miller (1989), Nove (1991), Roemer (1994), Sik (1991) and others. See also the good overall discussion in Pierson (1995). Note, however, that there are huge variations in the degree of state planning and regulation of markets in the different proposals for genuine market socialism that are advocated by these authors. Some, like Nove, proposed extensive intervention and planning alongside the use of markets. Others preferred to leave the market as an invisible hand to co-ordinate the worker co-operatives, with little additional guidance.

14 Three examples will suffice. In a prominent journal published by the American Economic Association, two critics of 'market socialism', Shleifer and Vishny (1994, p. 166) have stated that the objections of von Mises and Hayek to socialism 'were effectively rebutted by Lange'. Another author, the American institutional economist Yunker (1995, p. 686), has written: 'Despite its theoretical attractiveness, Lange's proposal has been shrugged off on the

basis of various more or less extemporaneous and off-the-cuff objections.'
Finally, Patnaik (1991, p. 25) has asserted that 'Lange provided an extremely
subtle and powerful counter argument, which undermined the logical
validity not only of the Mises attack but also of the attack by Hayek and
Robbins.' The view taken here – supported by the analyses of the debate by
Lavoie (1985a, 1985b), Murrell (1983), Steele (1992), Vaughn (1980) and others
– is that these three appraisals of the outcome of the socialist calculation
controversy are false. Lange did not rebut the Austrians effectively, neither
did he provide a workable model of socialism.

15 Throughout this book, uncertainty is defined in the radical sense of Knight
(1921) or Keynes (1936). It concerns events in relation to which it is impossible to calculate a probability, and is thereby distinguished from risk.

16 Foss (1996a) criticised both O'Neill (1989) and Adaman and Devine on the
question of the nature of markets.

17 Adaman and Devine claimed inspiration for this distinction between statics
and dynamics in the writings of Maurice Dobb. However, Dobb (1969, p. 122)
himself seems in turn to have been partly inspired on this issue by Hicks
(1965, p. 32), who wrote: 'In statics there is no planning; mere repetition of
what has been done before does not need to be planned.' What is controversial here is not simply the allusion to the planning of dynamic processes, but
also the possibility in reality of an entirely static system. The distinction
between statics and dynamics is more a matter concerning economic models
that any real socio-economic system. In reality, no socio-economic system can
stand completely still.

18 Equally undetailed and problematic are their considerations of the pricing
process. For instance, Adaman and Devine (1996b, p. 533) write, without any
further elaboration: 'Enterprises would set prices equal to long-run average
cost, calculated on the basis of labour costs, a centrally determined capital
charge, and the prices of producer goods used as inputs.' Yet it is far from clear
how firms would find the appropriate point on the supposed long-run average
cost curve, or have any incentive or capability to minimise any cost or input,
especially when all relevant decisions, including their scale of their output, are
supposedly determined by an external network of negotiation committees.
Adaman and Devine seem to take it for granted that all such problems can be
sorted out simply by sufficient measures of discussion and goodwill.

19 See also Adaman and Devine (1997, p. 75): 'a process of cooperation and
negotiation ... would enable tacit knowledge to be articulated'.

20 Michael was a younger brother of the institutionalist Karl Polanyi, who also
figures prominently in this present work. Although their political standpoints
were dissimilar, they both made important theoretical contributions to social
science which are of relevance here.

21 The fact that Marx and Engels had little recognition of the importance of tacit
knowledge and the inevitability of specialist skills was evident in their
support for the idea that the division of labour could and should be abolished. In his Critique of the Gotha Programme, Marx (1977, p. 569) argued that
in the future communist society 'the enslaving subordination of the individual to the division of labour' would vanish. In a famous passage in The
German Ideology, Marx and Engels opined that:

> in communist society, where nobody has one exclusive sphere of
> activity but each can become accomplished in any branch he wishes,
> society regulates the general production and thus makes it possible for

me to do one thing today and another tomorrow, to hunt in the morning, fish in the afternoon, rear cattle in the evening, criticize after dinner, just as I have a mind, without ever becoming hunter, fisherman, cowherd or critic.

(Marx, 1977, p. 169)

Marx's widely employed analytical concepts of abstract and social labour also neglect the specificity and incommensurability of skills. For a relevant discussion see Khalil (1992).

22 See also Margolis (1994).

23 Major capitalist countries such as Britain, Germany, Japan and the United States have very different histories in terms of innovative success. More generally, see the illuminating comparative studies of the varied performances of 'national systems of innovation' (Edquist, 1997; Freeman, 1987; Lundvall, 1992; Nelson, 1993).

24 Notably, in a collection of essays published to commemorate the centenary of Marx's death, the leading Marxian economist Mandel (1983, pp. 217–18) similarly remarked that 'Von Mises' objection that you couldn't solve millions of equations ... has in the meantime been taken care of by the computer.'

25 For the record, I made these calculations in 1982. The typescript of *The Democratic Economy* was submitted to the publisher in January 1983.

26 A sparse matrix is one with lots of cells containing zeros, enabling a faster iterative method to be used. I had not assumed that the matrix was sparse in my 1982 calculation. Furthermore, as a much more serious confession, I devoted too much attention to the problem of *calculations* performed on accessible data in my 1984 book, and too little to the dynamic issues of learning and creativity.

27 Arguably, the propositions here concerning the nature of institutions and knowledge are foundational for institutional economics. They certainly were prominent for the pragmatist philosopher Peirce (1934), who taught Veblen. See also Hodgson (1997).

28 This act of intellectual escapology is often accomplished by the misleading description of the Soviet-type regimes as 'capitalist'. According to the definition of capitalism adopted in this book, such regimes cannot be so described. Much of production within them was not destined for the market, and, in particular, they lacked developed capital markets. Accordingly, *commodity* production was not general. However, if these regimes were not capitalist, this does not necessarily mean that they should be described as 'socialist'. An alternative option is to search for a third and distinctive label. But that is a further issue of categorisation that we need not enter into here. Indeed, it is suggested that *all* the proclaimed 'socialisms' of Owen, Marx, Lenin, Stalin, Mao or the Webbs, offered a dead end. This chapter establishes and uses the traditional, nineteenth-century meaning of socialism, without entering into a debate whether or not it was ever exemplified in China or the Soviet Bloc.

29 Similarly, purveyors of non-socialist economic doctrines also carry some responsibility for their intended or unintended consequences. For example, unemployment is not a sufficient and immediate cause of crime, but it creates circumstances in which theft and personal violence are all the more likely. We cannot hold the politicians and economists, who have endorsed and enacted policies leading to higher unemployment, legally responsible for every crime carried out by the unemployed. But they carry part of the blame for helping

to create the conditions of poverty, degradation and desperation in which crime was all the more likely. Likewise, Marx and others may be criticised for helping unintentionally to create the circumstances in which totalitarianism was more likely, although they have no blood on their hands. As Samuel Johnson put it: 'The road to hell is paved with good intentions.'

3 THE ABSOLUTISM OF MARKET INDIVIDUALISM

1 As Lukes (1973) has elaborated, 'individualism' has acquired a variety of meanings. They are not simply confined to the 'market individualism' that is scrutinised here. In an alternative, largely German, tradition developing in the latter part of the nineteenth century, 'individualism' or 'individuality' mean the true realisation of the unique capacities of the individual. Furthermore, in the writings around the turn of the century – for example, of Oscar Wilde and L. T. Hobhouse in Britain and of Thomas Mann in Germany – 'individualism' in such a sense was seen as entirely compatible with a form of socialism (Lukes, 1973, pp. 17–22; 35–8). In contrast, in the present chapter, we largely address what was described by Lukes as 'economic individualism': the idea that most economic and social arrangements are best mediated by individual property, contract and trade.

2 For mainstream discussions of these issues in the context of environmental problems see, for example, Baumol and Oates (1988), Helm and Pearce (1991), Pearce and Turner (1990).

3 There is a technical distinction between markets and exchange which is of marginal importance to the argument here. Commodity exchange is defined as the agreed contractual transfer of a property right to a good or service, in return either for money or a bartered good or service (Commons, 1950, pp. 48–9; Hodgson, 1988, pp. 148–9). A market is defined as a set of institution-alised and recurrent exchanges of a specific type (Hodgson, 1988, p. 174). Markets are institutionalised exchanges, where a consensus over prices and other information may be established. Clearly, with this strict definition, not all exchange takes place in markets. An important exception is 'relational exchange' where exchange is based on on-going ties of loyalty rather than competitive, open-market deals (Dore, 1983; Goldberg, 1980b; Richardson, 1972). However, the term 'market' is often used to refer more loosely to all commodity exchanges. To avoid cumbersome linguistic formulations, the term 'market' is sometimes used in the looser sense here. The more precise definition, with its distinction between market and non-market exchange, is raised only when strictly necessary.

4 This is denied by the transaction cost approach developed by Williamson (1975, 1985). For critiques of Williamson and evidence that trust is important see Berger et al. (1995), Arrighetti et al. (1997), Burchell and Wilkinson (1997), Lyons and Mehta (1997), Nooteboom et al. (1997).

5 For discussions and explorations of trust in this context see Arrighetti et al. (1997), Barber (1983), Beal and Dugdale (1975), Burchell and Wilkinson (1997), Campbell and Harris (1993), Fukuyama (1995), Gambetta (1988), C. Lane (1997), Lyons and Mehta (1997), Misztal (1996), Sako (1992), Kramer and Tyler (1996), Zucker (1986).

6 What is striking, however, is the degree of qualification that Hayek was obliged to introduce, in his own individualistic rhetoric here. He wrote that

'individuals should be allowed, *within defined limits*, to follow their own values and preferences ... *within these spheres* the individual's system of ends should be supreme and not subject to any dictation by others' (emphasis added). He seemed further to admit that we can appraise more than the needs of ourselves and as much as 'a sector of the needs of whole society'. After all, Hayek himself proclaimed a universal need for human liberty. Implicitly, Hayek had to claim, therefore, that in some things he was allegedly a better judge of our own interests than ourselves unaided by his insights.

7 Consider briefly the relationship of this issue to methodological individualism: 'the doctrine that all social phenomena (their structure and their change) are in principle explicable only in terms of individuals – their properties, goals, and beliefs' (Elster, 1982, p. 453). Likewise, Lachmann (1969, p. 94) asserted that methodological individualism means 'that we shall not be satisfied with any type of explanation of social phenomena which does not lead us ultimately to a human plan'. I have argued elsewhere (Hodgson, 1988, 1993) that if cultural or institutional influences are always present in the explanation of the behaviour of every individual then we can never reach a stage in the explanation where there are given individuals, free of all such influences. Furthermore, *if* we could reach an explanation of social phenomena in terms of human plans, why should we then be 'satisfied'? Surely we would be obliged as social scientists to consider the terms and conditions under which such plans were conceived and moulded? Contrary to widespread belief, such considerations do not necessarily lead us to a determinist account of human agency. However, this methodological source of disagreement is not the central concern of this chapter, which is concerned with the theoretical arguments for the utopia of market individualism.

8 We are reminded of Plato's theory of knowledge and its postulate of an immortal soul. As Georgescu-Roegen (1966, p. 25) put it: 'The pivot of Plato's epistemology is that we are born with a latent knowledge of all ideas ... because our immortal soul has visited their world sometime in the past. Every one of us, therefore, can learn ideas by reminiscence.'

9 The work of Romer (1986, 1990, 1994) departs significantly from equilibrium theory. A similar focus on increasing returns and disequilibrium has been readily used to undermine unqualified free-market conclusions (Krugman, 1990, 1994). Romer's amends the neoclassical 'production function' by including increasing returns and endogenous technical change through 'learning'. However, the lip-service to learning is largely through the formalisation of 'learning by doing' in the production function. As Storper and Salais (1997, p. 12) have observed, endogenous growth theorists have modelled growth but without exploration of its substance: 'The economy consists of mechanisms but is without practices; there is no content to what is made, how people make it, or how they think about and react to the world around them in so doing.'

10 For discussions of the character of learning see, for example, Argyris and Schön (1978), Berkson and Wettersten (1984), Boisot (1995), Campbell (1974), Cartier (1994), Choo (1998), Cohen and Levinthal (1990), Cohen and Sproull (1996), Dosi and Marengo (1994), Gregg (1974), Lundvall and Johnson (1994), J. Marquand (1989), Nonaka and Takeuchi (1995), Popper (1972), Rutherford (1988), Senge (1990), Storper and Salais (1997), Tomer (1987), Vincenti (1990).

11 Note that Lawson (1994, 1996, 1997) and Fleetwood (1995) interpret Hayek, despite his subjectivism, as a type of positivist. Positivism is a variety of empiricism involving the view that all knowledge is based on sense data.

Hayek emphasised that enquiry into social reality had to be based on the subjective conceptions of human agents. Hayek's empiricist conception of learning is consistent with his 'subjectivised positivism'.

12 Marshall's point was developed in different ways by J. M. Clark (1923), Arrow (1962b). See also Stabile (1996).

13 However, Hayek (1944, 1960) in fact accepted a significant degree of public intervention in the economic sphere, and his detailed policy stance was inconsistent with his own rhetoric against a mixed economy.

14 Of course, in some modern societies babies may be adopted, in return for payment. However, as Posner (1994, p. 410) has rightly pointed out: 'The term *baby selling*, while inevitable, is misleading. A mother who surrenders her parental rights for a fee is not selling her baby; babies are not chattels, and cannot be bought and sold. She is selling her parental rights.' In contrast, Becker (1991, pp. 362 ff.) was more sloppy in his use of language; he wrote of babies being sold when in fact what was involved was the sale of parental rights.

15 Many critics have noted that there is an unreconciled tension in Hayek's writings 'between a conservatism advised by an unqualified reverence for the traditional and an institutional reformism inspired by the idea of a spontaneous order' (Kley, 1994, p. 169). For similar and related evaluations see Forsyth (1988, p. 250), Gray (1980, 1984, pp. 129–30), Ioannides (1992), Kukathas (1989, pp. 206–15), Paul (1988, pp. 258–9), Roland (1990), Rowland (1988) and Tomlinson (1990, pp. 64–5).

16 A firm is defined as an integrated and durable organisation of people and other assets, set up for the purpose of producing goods or services, with the capacity to sell or hire them to customers, and with associated and recognised legal entitlements and liabilities. These entitlements and liabilities include the right of legal ownership of the goods as property before they are exchanged, the legal right to obtain contracted remuneration for the services, and any legal liabilities incurred in the production and provision of those goods or services. Note that the term 'legal' always has a strong customary element, and that the phrase 'legal or customary' could just as well replace 'legal' in this definition. A sense in which a firm is integrated is that it itself acts tacitly or otherwise as a 'legal person' – in a legislative or customary sense – owning its products and entering into contracts. The sense in which a firm is durable is that it constitutes more than a transient contract or agreement between its core members and it incorporates structures and routines of some expected longevity. A *capitalist* firm is a specific type of firm where its workers enter into an employment relationship with the firm. This important definition will be revisited and refined at several points in this volume.

17 It has even resisted the public provision of health care. Friedman and Friedman (1980, p. 145) thus wrote that 'there is no case whatsoever for socialized medicine'.

18 Notably, this fact is admitted by a prominent member of the Austrian school. As Steele (1992, p. 22) puts it in his energetic – and otherwise largely uncritical – exposition of Austrian school principles: 'Contrary to what Mises and some of his followers have occasionally seemed to imply, it is perfectly reasonable for a welfare-statist or interventionist to accept the economic calculation argument in its entirety. No inconsistency is entailed in this.'

19 This quotation is from the translation of Sombart found in Mises (1960, p. 138). The accuracy of the translation has been checked from the original German.

20 Similar views, long held by economists of the German historical school, were an important influence on Walter Eucken, Wilhem Röpke and other architects

of the concept of the 'social market economy' that emerged in the politics of post-war Germany (Tribe, 1995; Nicholls, 1994).

21 For this reason, the concept of the 'socialized market' advanced by Elson (1988) – see below – could be slightly misleading. It may suggest the possibility of a market that is not socially embedded. It has to be emphasised that *all* markets are constituted by social institutions and rooted in a social context. Elson was clearly using the term 'socialized' to mean more than this, while rightly recognising a potential variety of market institutions. In contrast, in her critique of neo-liberalism, Wainwright (1994) seemed more interested in taming 'the market' by use of exogenous, non-market regulatory agencies than a full recognition of the potential for internal institutional variation within markets would suggest. Furthermore, she regarded 'the market' as solely concerned with '*ex post* co-ordination' (p. 273), overlooking the fact that all costs in markets involve (socially constructed) calculations concerning the future. In particular, futures markets are specialist institutions concerned largely with *ex ante* adjustments. Wainwright has rightly rejected the possibility of completely centralised planning, but her overall treatment of the market exhibited some degree of doctrinal equivocation. She seemed to accept markets in one instance and reject them in another. To add to the confusion she offered support for the socialistic proposals of *both* Elson (1988) and Devine (1988), and failed to see that they were based on quite different presuppositions and led to quite different conclusions. Some of these differences were admitted by Adaman and Devine (1997) themselves.

22 The neoclassical economist Wicksteed (1933) defined 'an economic transaction' is one in which the each person in the trade does not consider the other 'except as a link in the chain' (p. 174). An unfortunate consequence of this overly restrictive definition would be that much trading activity in many societies, including the employment contract in most or all capitalist economies, would on close inspection turn out not to be 'economic' in character. However, while Wicksteed's definition of economics is unacceptable, his conceptual analysis is enlightening, because it makes explicit the possibility of exchange involving personal relationships that are based on more than narrowly instrumental features.

23 Kozul-Wright and Rayment (1997), and Grabher and Stark (1997), indicated that this issue has been of enormous policy significance since 1989 in the former Eastern Bloc countries. The idea that economies are made up of densely layered and entangled social institutions was neglected in the misconceived policies of 'shock therapy'. Policy initiatives in transitional economies are obliged to build steadily upon existing institutions and routines, even if the eventual aim is to build new institutions and to dismantle some old ones. Markets, for instance, do not arise spontaneously without a number of previously established institutions, customs and rules.

24 For discussions of the basic income proposal see Atkinson (1995), Parker (1989), Purdy (1988), Van Parijs (1992).

25 With a population of 100 wage earners, this would be the ratio between the wage incomes of the 90th and the 10th earners. By this measure, the higher the figure then the higher the degree of inequality.

26 For further data on income distribution in developed and transforming economies see Bishop *et al.* (1991) and Atkinson and Micklewright (1992).

4 THE UNIVERSALITY OF MAINSTREAM ECONOMICS

1 As noted above, this definition may exclude some recent developments in mainstream economic theory, such as in game theory. Nevertheless, the assumption of rational economic man and the predilection for equilibrium theorising is still typical of the neoclassical tradition, for example, as exemplified in mainstream textbooks. Although some birds are flightless, the ability to fly is still characteristic of the genus as a whole.

2 A similar universalising tendency has been advanced by many sociologists. For example, 'exchange theory' (Homans, 1961) proposes that a wide range of activities – including gift-giving and interpersonal communications – are 'exchanges'. This universal concept of exchange obscures its specific form in a market society: in particular the exchange of *property rights* within a system of *private property relations* (Commons, 1924, 1934). By contrast to the universalising sociologists, Weber (1949) recognised the problem of historical specificity and developed his methodology of 'ideal types' to deal with it.

3 Prominent practitioners include Becker (1976b) and Hirshleifer (1977, 1985). See also Radnitzky and Bernholz (1987) and Radnitzky (1992) and the critiques in Nicolaides (1988) and Udéhn (1992).

4 Note also the challengeable statements and *non sequiturs* in this passage. Contrary to Hayek, there is no good reason in principle why regularities should not be observed in complex systems (Cohen and Stewart, 1994). As a result, empirical observation of complex phenomena does not necessarily fail to reveal regularities, or necessarily lead to the false methodological claim that the sole task of economic science is description. Furthermore, modern students of complexity are aware that such regularities do not necessarily have to emanate from any presumed 'permanent nature of the constituting elements'. Finally, if there were any such enduring elements, then arguably these too would be 'the product of social or legal institutions'. Like other Austrian school theorists, Hayek is all too keen to throw out the historical school baby with its bathwater.

5 Ioannides (1992, p. 38) rightly pointed out that: 'The price mechanism is not the only knowledge-dispersion system … the rules of conduct and the social institutions which have evolved through centuries … themselves constitute a knowledge disseminating system.'

6 For similar and related points see Commons (1934, p. 713), Dosi (1988a) and Hodgson (1988, Chapter 8).

7 A similar problem arises in an earlier work by North (1978, p. 970) where he suggested that the United States has adopted political regulation of economic transactions rather than pure markets because of the relative price of these two options. He does not describe the structural context in which such selection between (say) market and non-market orders takes place. In response, Mirowski (1981, p. 609) pointed out that this leaves unresolved the issue of 'what structures organize this "meta-market" to allow us to buy more or less market organization'.

8 See, for example, Allee (1951), Augros and Stanciu (1987), Benedict (1934), Lewontin (1978), Mead (1937), Montagu (1952), Wheeler (1930), Whitehead (1926).

9 Sahlins was a pupil of the institutionalist Karl Polanyi.

10 Polanyi, Sahlins and others have been criticised by Granovetter (1985) for denying the universal application of such 'economic' principles as the

work–leisure trade-off, or the influence of supply and demand on price. In their place, Polanyi and his followers assert the universality of human relations such as reciprocity. Part of the problem here is the definition of the nature of the 'economic' and the boundaries of the 'economy'. It should not be assumed that the 'economy' is necessarily defined as a domain in which the principles of neoclassical economics apply. Such a presumption would wrongly imply that neoclassical economics supplies an adequate and acceptable picture of capitalism, markets, exchange, and so on. I have criticised this idea elsewhere (Hodgson, 1992a). In the present work it is accepted that some universal principles of socio-economic analysis are necessary and indeed unavoidable, but it should not be taken for granted that these are the principles of neoclassical economics. Much of the debate about the 'embeddedness' of the economy suffers from such a presumption, or from taking for granted what is meant by the 'economic' domain.

11 For a survey of neoclassical and other approaches to the analysis of institutions see Hodgson (1993a).

12 For a discussion of the treatment of women in economic theory from Smith to Pigou see Pujol (1992).

13 It is notable that Becker's bold and frequent attempts to extend 'economic' analysis to specific institutions have typically employed parametric variations in an universal theoretical structure. Hence Becker (1991, Chapter 8) discussed such factors as the higher degree of 'altruism' found in the family, compared with the open market, but attributed this difference to universal variables such as the degree of familiarity in relationships, driven by universal considerations such as 'efficiency'.

14 In erecting a conceptual opposition between 'markets' and 'hierarchies' the work of Coase (1937) and Williamson (1975, 1985) is a partial exception here. However, by focusing on 'transaction costs', even in non-market situations, a market-oriented and contractarian bias remains. Furthermore, Williamson – in contrast to North (1990) – has consistently argued that market competition selects the more efficient organisational forms, thus denying path dependence and a major source of variety within capitalism.

15 See Shackle (1972, p. 122), Loasby (1976, p. 5) and Hodgson et al. (1994, vol. 1, pp. 134–8) for examples and discussions of these arguments.

16 Becker (1996) is an apparent exception. In this work specific 'cultural' variables enter in as additional arguments in the utility function. However, an immanently conceived preference function for each individual is still assumed at the outset; it is an unexplored 'black box' that still remains to be explained. Becker thus neglects the *formative* influences of culture and institutions on the preference function itself.

17 It should be noted, however, that Hayek did begin to discuss the formation of preferences and habits of thought in his works of the 1970s and 1980s. The individual appeared less as an atom, and explanations involve groups and cultures, as well as subjective individuals. Accordingly, his verbal allegiance to 'methodological individualism' and the idea that socio-economic phenomena should be explained exclusively in terms of given individuals became increasingly ceremonial rather than substantive (Böhm, 1989; Vanberg, 1986).

18 Related or similar positions have been developed by structuration theorists such as Giddens (1984) and by critical realists such as Bhaskar (1979, 1989) and M. Archer (1995).

5 KARL MARX AND THE TRIUMPH OF CAPITALISM

1 Although Marx had long adopted the analytical approach of moving from the key characteristics of a historically specific mode of production, it was not until the publication of the *Contribution to the Critique of Political Economy* in 1859 that the concept of the commodity was located as the starting point in the analysis of capitalism. Note the famous transitional passage in the *Grundrisse* (Marx, 1973b, pp. 100–8) which was probably written in 1857, and the important comments by Nicolaus in his foreword (Marx, 1973b, pp. 36–41). Starting from the commodity, the Aristotelian distinction between use value and exchange value became a Hegelian 'unity of opposites'. It was out of the warp and weft of the 'dialectical' concept of the commodity that Marx wove the entire theoretical structure in *Capital*.

2 Marx does not explicitly use this three-word definition of capitalism and some have expressed a distaste for it, for various reasons. In its defence, these three words do connote the key issues of property rights, markets, employment relations and thereby class divisions within capitalism. As long as the word 'generalised' is not taken to mean 'universalised', then the existence of 'impurities' and non-commodity forms within capitalism can be accommodated. Furthermore, it must be recognised that some commodities, notably labour and land, are not *deliberately* produced for sale, although they may be typically *destined* for sale under the capitalist system.

3 The term 'work' is preferable to 'labour' because the latter often connotes manual rather than mental work. Notably, Marx always included both mental and manual labour in concepts such as 'labour power'.

4 Several authors, from Cliff (1955) to Screpanti (1997) have argued that private ownership is an unnecessary criterion and the most basic feature of capitalism is control by a minority of the labour process. It is argued that ownership and control have become *de facto* separated within modern capitalism and that the issue of ownership is thus relatively unimportant. Unimpeded by any definitional reference to private ownership of the means of production or the existence of capital markets, Cliff and others argued that the former Soviet Union was 'capitalist'.

Briefly, the argument against this exclusive definitional focus on 'control' is as follows. First, the separation of ownership from control is indeed an important phenomenon, but it is wrong to conclude from this that ownership is unimportant or does not carry with it significant powers. In particular, owners have significant legal and real powers over the managers, even if these powers are not exercised daily. Second, and in particular, ownership of the means of production is a means of obtaining property income *even if* direct control of the labour process is not exercised. Third, the employment contract itself always involves some form of (public or private) *ownership* of the means of production and in particular the *private ownership* of labour power itself. Fourth, the employment contract does not involve *absolute* control and typically is accompanied by a significant zone of autonomy and discretion for the worker (Littler and Salaman, 1982; Nelson, 1981).

As well as recognising that significant power does emanate from ownership, one of the advantages of retaining *both* private ownership of the means of production *and* the existence of an employment relationship in the definition of capitalism is that such a denotation differentiates the former Eastern Bloc countries from capitalism. This conceptual differentiation underlines the major structural, behavioural and ideological contrasts between East and West that dominated the world scene from 1917 to 1989. Arguably, even today, the question of ownership still retains much of its importance. Capitalism is still reasonably defined in terms of private ownership of the means of production *and* the ubiquity of the employment relationship.

5 An impressive attempt to defend Marx's theory of history from its critics is by Cohen (1978).

6 It is thus no accident that Marxist sympathisers have often defended models of socialism using neoclassical theoretical tools, the case discussed in a preceding chapter being the work of Lange and Taylor (1938) which is built explicitly on Walrasian foundations. Note also the modern school of neoclassical or 'rational choice Marxists' (Carling, 1986), such as Elster (1985) and Roemer (1988) who attempt to develop Marxism using 'standard tools of microeconomic analysis' (Roemer, 1988, p. 172).

7 As Zelizer (1993, p. 193) has suggested, modern sociology as a whole has been obsessed 'with the vision of an ever-expanding market inevitably dissolving all social relations and corrupting culture and personal values.' Arguably, the pervasive influence of Marx upon sociology has been crucial here.

8 Of course, slavery has existed alongside capitalism, such as in the south of the United States before the Civil War. This involved a combination of slave and capitalist modes of production and the denial of citizenship and other legal rights to blacks. Slavery was incompatible with an universal 'free' labour market and the further development of the capitalist system required the emancipation of the slaves.

9 With the rise of modern feminism in the 1970s, some Marxian theorists attempted to analyse the family as a distinctive entity. Yet their dominant theoretical approach was to subsume this institution within the parameters of the 'labour theory of value' and the guiding prerogatives of the capitalist order, just as neoclassical economists treat the family simply as another contract-based institution within capitalism. For an overview, see the comparative readings in Amsden (1980).

10 This argument is made in Hodgson (1984, pp. 104–6). In the same work there is a brief discussion of the erroneous theoretical foundation upon which Luxemburg (1951) reached the valid conclusion that non-capitalist structures played a necessary role within capitalism (Hodgson, 1984, pp. 85–6). See also the introduction by Robinson to Luxemburg (1951).

11 Towards the end of his life, inspired by debates about the possibility of a quite different path of capitalist development in Russia, Marx showed a clearer recognition of path dependence and historical contingency. He wrote in 1877:

> events strikingly analogous but taking place in different historical surroundings led to totally different results. By studying each of these forms of evolution separately and then comparing them one can easily find the clue to this phenomenon, but one will never arrive there by using as one's master key a general historico-philosophical theory, the supreme virtue of which consists in being super-historical.
>
> (Marx, 1977, p. 572)

An institutionalist would readily agree with this limited but valid statement.

12 A similar criticism can be made of the work of Schumpeter. He defined economic development as involving 'only such changes in economic life as are not forced upon it from without but arise by its own initiative, from within' (Schumpeter, 1934, p. 63). Schumpeter never made a secret of the fact that his theory of capitalist development – with its emphasis on the role of endogenous change – was highly influenced by Marx. Nevertheless, the importance of the endogenous factors specifically emphasised by Schumpeter, such as entrepreneurial activity and technological innovation, should not be denied. The point is that Schumpeter should have given due stress to exogenous factors as well. Arguably, in this omission he was misled by Marx.

13 This interpretation differs notably from attempts at the opposite extreme, by Elster and others, to recast Marx's thought in the framework of methodological individualism: where social structures are explained in terms of individuals, not the other way round. The analysis of Kontopoulos (1993, p. 198) of Marx's texts is apposite here:

> Contrary to Elster's attempt at recasting it, these examples make it clear that Marx's view favors an understanding of the social process based on macrostructural considerations. ... it is obvious to a systematic reader of his work that he placed emphasis on the structural mode of analysis.

14 This picture of human beings pursuing their own material self-interests was one of the reasons for Parsons's (1937, p. 110) observation: 'Marx's historical materialism ... is ... fundamentally, a version of utilitarian individualism'. Mills (1963, p. 113) concurred: 'Marx's view of class consciousness is ... as utilitarian and rationalist as anything out of Jeremy Bentham.'

15 See also Lockwood (1981).

16 It should be emphasised that this paragraph does not necessarily imply a philosophical relativism, where the possibility of objective truth is denied. A single, objective reality can still be assumed and also the possibility of a true account of its essential elements. Although science is never culture-free, some versions of science are more adequate in the search for truth, and for effective practice, than others.

6 INSTITUTIONALISM AND VARIETIES OF CAPITALISM

1 Note that Hayek also recognised the concept of habit, especially in his later works. For a comparison of Hayek and Veblen on this and related issues see Leathers (1990).

2 The interpretation of Marx's theory of history as 'teleological' remains controversial. Writers such as Elster (1985) have argued this view and others such as Sanderson (1990) and Sayer (1989) have qualified or opposed it. Resolution of this issue in part involves a clarification of the meaning of 'teleology'. The sense it which it is used here is in terms of a conception of immanent tendencies of capitalist development. For Marx, these tendencies pointed inexorably towards a more harmonious and rational future.

3 Lawson (1997, p. 317 n.) has identified in the writings of Veblen and subsequent institutionalists 'a failure to elaborate the notion of social structure, i.e., of a level of social reality which, though dependent upon, is irreducible to human thought and practice'. This is partly true, in the sense that the concept

of structure is insufficiently elaborated in institutionalism. But it is also treated very inadequately in other schools of economics, from the Austrian to the Post Keynesian. In fact, institutionalism understands more than most the structural burden of the past. The Veblenian emphasis on institutions, from the beginning, involved a recognition that social reality was not reducible to the thought and practice of living human beings. Hence Veblen (1914, pp. 6–7) wrote:

> The apparatus of ways and means available for the pursuit of whatever may be worth seeking is, substantially all, a matter of tradition out of the past, a legacy of habits of thought accumulated through the experience of past generations.

Similar remarks about the role of the past are found elsewhere in his works, implying that there is much more to institutions or structures than the thoughts and practices of the living. The dependence of social structure on the legacy of 'past generations' is a key part of the excellent overview and elaboration of the concept by M. Archer (1995).

4 Although Veblen did not see class position as determining ideology, he did suggest that the 'machine process' of modern industrial society would help to inculcate mechanical 'habits of life and thought'. Nevertheless, this proposition was generally qualified. For instance, Veblen (1904, pp. 309–10) wrote:

> Of course, in no case and with no class does the discipline of the machine process mould the habits of life and thought fully into its own image. There is present in the human nature of all classes too large a residue of the propensities and aptitudes carried over from the past and working to a different result. The machine's régime has been of too short duration, strict as its discipline may be, and the body of inherited traits and traditions is too comprehensive and consistent to admit of anything more than a remote approach to such a consummation.

Hence Veblen saw technology as a 'remote' promoter of change but he never embraced an unmitigated 'technological determinism'.

5 For a critique of the epistemological assumptions of the rational expectation hypothesis see Wible (1984–85). The general argument here on the limits of rational reflection is also an implicit rebuttal of the kind of faith in reasoned persuasion found in the writings of John Maynard Keynes (Hodgson, 1985).

6 Friedman's theoretical argument was heavily criticised by Winter (1964). See also Hodgson (1994).

7 In David (1997) the term 'path dependence' is clarified enormously, and several misconceptions are corrected.

8 Similar ideas have been stressed in biological evolution by Gould (1980, 1989) and others. Their relevance to social science was discussed in Hodgson (1993b).

9 In this respect, institutionalism follows both Marxism and the German historical school. For example, as a leading member of the latter group, Schmoller (1898, p. 229) wrote: 'Scientific method depends on the nature of the subject matter under enquiry.' Contrary to a modern caricature of the historical school as 'purely descriptive', Schmoller went on to insist that: 'Observation and description, definition and classification are preparatory work only. ...

there must remain before our eyes, as the ideal of all knowledge, the explanation of all facts in terms of causation' (p. 277).

10 Arguments similar to this were developed by leaders of the German historical school. Accordingly, Sombart (1930, p. 247) distinguished between:

> three different kinds of economic concepts: 1. The universal-economic primary concepts ... which are valid for all economic systems; 2. the historical-economic primary concepts ... which ... are valid only for a definite economic system: and 3. the subsidiary concepts ... which are constructed with regard to a definite working idea.

Von Mises (1960, p. 138) rebutted Sombart's arguments, but only by criticising Sombart's exaggerated and weaker formulations, such as the assertion that price formations in two very different types of market are 'two *altogether incomparable* occurrences' and price and price 'are *completely different* things from market to market' (Sombart, 1930, p. 305, emphasis added; all translations taken from von Mises, 1960, p. 138). Sombart over-eggs the pudding. But von Mises refuses to taste even the hors d'œuvre. Sombart's argument can survive if the exaggerations are removed. But his substantive point is entirely missed, and the entire German historical school is consigned by the Austrian school to the garbage can of rejected economic theory.

11 In addition, Veblen suggested that the specifically Darwinian mechanism of 'natural selection' could be applied to institutions (Veblen, 1899, p. 188), although he was insufficiently clear about the precise mechanisms and criteria of such selection. Other writers have favoured a Lamarckian analogy rather than an appeal to Darwin (Hayek, 1988; Nelson and Winter, 1982). These differences are important, but secondary to the two ontological principles of novelty and persistence discussed above, and there is no doctrinal requirement by institutional economists in favour of one particular type of evolutionary mechanism.

12 See Tool (1991) for a review of institutionalist theories of corporate pricing.

13 This is widely recognised in philosophy but barely understood even by leading economists. The frequent invocation that the main problem with modern economics is simply to enrich it with adequate data is a classic illustration of such misunderstandings.

14 For readings by many authors on institutional economics see Hodgson (1993c) and Hodgson *et al.* (1994).

15 However, despite its spectacular overall success in the post-war period, the protracted slowdown in Japanese growth in the 1990s must also be taken into account. There is a case to be made that the Japanese capitalist system is more vulnerable to macroeconomic shocks than its Western counterparts. Furthermore, while it excels in what have been called 'incremental innovations', and in innovations in management organisation, its relatively conformist and collectivist culture does not seem to encourage an equivalent success in more 'radical innovations' requiring a degree of eccentricity and nonconformist entrepreneurship. (For a discussion of these categories of innovation see Freeman and Perez, 1988.) The illuminating case studies of Japanese innovation in Nonaka and Takeuchi (1995) are largely confined to incremental innovations.

16 When these East Asian economies have problems – as in the crash of 1997–98 – then the conventional verdict is suddenly reversed. It is then proclaimed

that there is substantial and 'excessive' state intervention in these economies, and the remedial policy becomes the greater market liberalisation and free competition. In neither boom nor slump are the complexities of the situation – and the possible benefits of constructive state intervention – acknowledged. Those requiring an antidote to any over-confidence in the deregulated system in the USA should read Albert (1993) and Mishel and Schmitt (1995).

17 In their speculative and important study of complex systems, Cohen and Stewart (1994) come to related conclusions. They show the phenomenon of path dependence, and tendencies towards (incomplete) convergence, can be combined into a unified overall perspective on systemic development.

7 CONTRACT AND CAPITALISM

1 For an exception see Hayek (1944). The thrust of Hayek's argument was that the growth of monopoly power, if it had happened at all, had been the result of government policy rather than of technological change. However, while governments have often promoted monopoly power in business, it would be reckless to exclude the possibility that there are also tendencies for some firms to grow larger without government aid.

2 See, for example, Prais (1976) and Steele (1992, pp. 276–9).

3 Even in the economies in transition to capitalism in the former Eastern Bloc, the state has retained a significant proportion of its former economic power (Ellman, 1995, p. 222).

4 For example, Schneider (1977), Ekholm and Friedman (1982) and Rowlands et al. (1987). While these studies show the importance of markets in earlier societies, the kinds of market discovered are quite different from, and economically more peripheral than, the markets found in modern capitalist economies. Compare the earlier work on ancient markets by K. Polanyi et al. (1957).

5 In contrast, Commons (1924) defined capitalism in somewhat broader terms, loosely involving the existence of markets and the dominance of exchange-values. Accordingly, he saw capitalism as having been well established in England as early as the sixteenth and seventeenth centuries, and thereby placed less emphasis on the later development of wage-labour and employment contracts.

6 After Marx's Capital, and derivative work by other Marxists, there is not much else of significance on this topic, other than by Commons (1924). Arguably, Marx's analysis of economic structures is much stronger than his rudimentary theoretical analysis of the category of social class (Hodgson, 1991).

7 These figures exclude the self-employed. On the alleged decline of the working class see Pierson (1995, pp. 7–17).

8 The common conceptual division of the workers into 'manual' and 'non-manual' categories ignores the fact that – short of manual disablement – all work involves the simultaneous application of both hand and brain.

9 Payment by output produced, or 'piece work', has traditionally been quite common in the history of capitalism. It is less common today because of the growing complexity of output and the existence of more sophisticated systems of employee motivation. Piece work is best regarded as employment rather than self-employment, as long as the employer retains the power to exercise detailed control of the work process. In many piece work systems the

employer also retained liability for normal costs incurred and, rather than the worker, was the original owner of the product.

10 Even in Britain – the first industrial capitalist country – the explicit legal definition of the employment contract, in terms involving an exchange between consenting parties, is a relatively recent phenomenon. Wedderburn (1971, p. 76) quoted a legal authority who observed that 'ideas which had come down from the days of serfdom and villeinage lingered on, so that a master was regarded as having a proprietary right in his servant'. As late as the early twentieth century, 'master–servant' relations entailing waged labour were often framed and understood in terms of legal service, established status and traditional obligation. These terms are more reminiscent of the distant feudal past than the consensual transactions of modern contract law (Kahn-Freund, 1977). The conception of an employment contract, involving voluntary agreement akin to trade, did not become firmly established until well into the twentieth century. It took the National Insurance Act of 1946 to consolidate the general position, and belatedly to extend the terminology of employment law to professional workers such as doctors, lecturers and administrators (Deakin, 1997). Yet the key feature of employer control over the manner and pattern of work is common to both the phraseology of 'legal service' and to the modern contractual formulation. The persistence of the notions of duty and service in this context is probably no accident. Schumpeter (1976) argued persuasively that, to some degree, employment always and necessarily involves hierarchy and duty, as well as contract and agreement. Such notions of status and obligation survived in part for functional reasons and partly as a result of relatively undisturbed and long-ingrained tradition. For a long while the enduring notion of legal service dominated the contractarian features of the employment relationship. The modern formulation of the employment contract was very much a result of trade union pressure and the development of the modern welfare state and taxation law (Deakin, 1997).

11 Analyses of the vital distinction between an employment relationship and a contract for services are relatively rare, with most economists avoiding such technicalities. The works of Simon (1951) and Screpanti (1997) are exceptions. However, Screpanti (1997, p. 119) argued that with self-employed workers selling their services to the factory and machine owners – rather than entering into an employment contract – the factor incomes deriving from ownership of those means of production would be driven by competition down to zero. He thus argued that in an employment contract 'surplus value' or profit is extracted largely as a result of capitalist 'control and management of the labour process' and without such control the profit would disappear. However, there is no reason why the factor incomes of the machine owners should be driven down to zero, even if the workers are self-employed, and even in a competitive equilibrium. With relations of self-employment, as well as employment, the owners of the means of production are likely to receive a positive factor income, even in a competitive equilibrium.

12 In a criticism of Coase (1937), Fourie (1989) argued that all production must take place in firms, markets themselves do not produce, and therefore markets and firms are not alternative configurations of production. Unfortunately, this was a misreading of Coase's argument. Coase did not argue that the market is itself productive, but that the market is a possible way of co-ordinating the work of individual, self-employed producers. Furthermore, by a 'firm', Coase and Fourie meant different things. For Coase, the firm always involved the organisation and co-ordination of multiple

agents. With independent, self-employed producers, production is not organised under the rubric of the firm, because the unit of production involves one individual only. While the management of production is central to the firm, production does not always involve firms in Coase's sense. Fourie, in contrast to Coase, saw anything productive, including the self-employed producer, as a 'firm', and as a result their argument is at cross-purposes. Essentially, Fourie's 'criticism' stems from a different – and less conventional – definition of 'the firm'. What is involved is a clash of terminology rather than a serious criticism of Coase's position.

13 However, if the notion of a firm is – quite reasonably – defined broadly to include non-capitalist institutions as well (such as producer co-operatives), then the employment contract is *not* central to the generic definition. Coase's (1937, 1988) equivocation and confusion on this point is discussed in Hodgson (1998a). However, Coase (1996) has clarified matters somewhat, saying that in 1937: 'The firm I was talking about was undoubtedly what you [Hodgson] call "the capitalist firm".'

14 Sanford Jacoby (1990, p. 334) suggested why employee non-cooperation and opportunism are often not usefully alleviated by such measures:

> as industrial studies have repeatedly shown, the presumption of innate opportunism is fatal to trust. … It leads to a proliferation of control structures – supervision, rules, and deferred rewards – intended to inhibit opportunism. These create resentment and distrust among employees, who correctly perceive the controls as expressions of their employer's distrust.

15 For discussions of contested exchange theory see Baker and Weisbrot (1994) and Rebitzer (1993).

16 An important critique of Braverman's work is by Littler and Salaman (1982). Notably, some followers of Braverman went too far in stressing the distinction between labour and labour power. For example, Edwards (1979, p. 12) wrote: 'Workers must provide labor power in order to receive their wages, that is, they must show up for work; but they need not necessarily provide *labor*.' However, if a worker did not work then he or she would clearly be in breach of contract, and the employment relationship would be ended.

17 The concepts of voice and exit were originally developed in the classic work of Hirschman (1970).

18 This erroneous view was also advanced by Commons (1924, p. 285) who wrote: 'The labor contract is not a contract, it is a continuing renewal of a contract at every successive moment, implied simply from the fact that the laborer keeps at work and the employer accepts his product.' However, the latter does not imply the former. If it were true, it would suggest also that slavery was a 'continuing renewal of a contract' between master and slave, because the slave 'keeps at work' and the slaveowner 'accepts his product'. Furthermore, despite Commons's detailed use of case law and legal theory, in this instance he failed to note that the law in most Western countries has traditionally regarded the employment relation as a binding contract. Contrary to Commons, it is not renegotiated continuously and it is not normally terminated at will without mutual agreement or due notice.

19 The dangers in the reckless attribution of 'implicit contracts' to a multitude of social relations are illustrated by the case of a Civil War defender of American slavery, the Reverend Samuel Seabury (1861), who argued that there was an implicit and acceptable legal contract between slave owner and slave. The

fact that many slaves took the first opportunity to escape their enslavement did not shake Seabury's conviction in the 'voluntary' nature of their bondage. In history, examples of voluntary enslavement do exist but they do not provide a basis for the suggestion that all slavery is based on an implicit contract between master and slave.

20 In an earlier work this proposition formed a part of a theory of worker exploitation, but not involving the labour theory of value (Hodgson, 1982).

8 KNOWLEDGE AND EMPLOYMENT

1 Two good introductions to the philosophy and practice of scenario planning are Loasby (1990) and Van der Heijden (1996). For another example of the application of scenario techniques to socio-economic systems rather than corporations see Central Planning Bureau (1992).

2 The concept of complexity has proved notoriously difficult to define. Stent (1985, pp. 215–16) made a useful stab at the problem, arguing that 'the complexity of a phenomenon is not to be measured by the number of component events of which it is constituted, but rather by the diversity of the interactions among its component events'. See Lloyd (1990) for a review of definitions of complexity and Saviotti (1996) for an analytical discussion of complexity and variety in socio-economic systems.

3 Relevant general discussions of the evolution of complex systems include: Cohen and Stewart (1994), Kauffman (1993, 1995), Laszlo (1987) and Prigogine and Stengers (1984).

4 Those giving some succour to a general principle of increasing complexity in evolving systems include Morgan (1927), Stebbins (1969) and – most forcibly in recent years – Saunders and Ho (1976, 1981, 1984). Those against any general evolutionary law of increasing complexity include Williams (1966), McCoy (1977), Levins and Lewontin (1985), and Hull (1988).

5 It has been argued persuasively that the increasing complexity of technology and production was a major factor in the stagnation and eventual downfall of Soviet-type economies (Bergson, 1978; Haddad, 1995). Centralised planning systems based on aggregate targets were unable to cope with increasing variety and complexity, as well as the increasing consumer knowledge of the ever more sophisticated consumer goods available in the West (Nove, 1983, 1991; Stiglitz, 1994, pp. 200–5). If these arguments are correct, and the thesis in the following chapters is valid, then it shows that the forward march of complexity in modern socio-economic systems has undermined both Soviet-type and capitalist economies.

6 R. E. Lane (1966) was one of the first authors to use the term 'knowledgeable society'. Early analyses of an the growing importance of the knowledge sector are in Machlup (1962) and Bell (1973). Machlup's data for the US are updated in Rubin and Huber (1986). Works in the 1990s that stress the economic role of knowledge include Senge (1990), Toffler (1990), Reich (1991), Rose (1991), Quinn (1992), Drucker (1993) and Webster (1995). Nonaka and Takeuchi (1995) explored the conceptual underpinnings of learning in more depth and detail than most of the works in this area.

7 Following the insight of W. James (1890), it could reasonably be assumed that the relative use of habit and tacit knowledge will increase as human intelligence attempts to cope with the increasing levels of economic complexity and knowledge-intensity. In contrast to Darwin in *The Descent of Man*, James saw

human behaviour to be more flexible and intelligent than other animals because it relied on more instincts, not fewer. Modern research seems to support James on this point (Cosmides and Tooby, 1994). Accordingly, there is no reason to presume that as human work becomes more complex, less mental activity will have to be consigned to the tacit realm of habit and routine. Habits and routines are necessary to free up the higher levels of awareness, mental deliberation and decision-making for the more complex decisions. With the advance of information technology and artificial intelligence, some of the more routinised and well-specified problems could be taken over by computers. For useful discussions of the relationship and shifting boundaries between tacit and explicit knowledge see Hedlund (1994) and Nonaka and Takeuchi (1995).

8 It has been noted above that Marx's lack of recognition of the importance of tacit knowledge and the inevitability of specialist skills was betrayed by his idea that the division of labour could and should be abolished (Marx, 1977, pp. 169, 569).

9 In developed countries in recent years, unemployment has increased substantially among unskilled workers. This is partly because of increasing penetration of imports from developing countries produced by unskilled workers on much lower wages. A detailed study of this phenomenon by A. Wood (1994, 1995) reinforces the Veblenian point that the most crucial question is not the lack of availability of capital goods to support employment, but the lack of availability of employable skills. The consequence of global trade where skills are increasingly at a premium, is to widen further, in any single country, the gap in remuneration and work prospects between the skilled and the unskilled workers.

10 Gorz (1985) saw the amount of human labour time required for production as diminishing rapidly due to technological changes. Several years later, there has been no significant reduction in the hours worked by employed workers in developed capitalist economies. Neither is such a reduction inevitable, as the complexity of the production system increases and more enhanced, intuitive and cognitive skills are required.

11 Is this alternative scenario too much like science fiction? Alas no. Unemployment in many developed capitalist countries has increased from less than 5 per cent to well over 10 per cent of the workforce in the last three decades of the twentieth century. In the same period, employment in manufacturing has diminished by a huge proportion and computer technology has developed by leaps and bounds. As Rifkin (1995) has elaborated, a scenario based on automation and unemployment is by no means implausible for the coming decades.

12 Compare also with Webster and Robins (1986).

13 Some of these problems have now been recognised by mainstream economic theorists (Stiglitz, 1987, 1994).

14 As Drucker (1993, p. 27) has pointed out, tacit knowledge involves an extra dimension of *mystery*, well acknowledged in the pre-industrial use of that term to describe production skills:

> As late as 1700, or even later, the English did not speak of 'crafts.' They spoke of 'mysteries' ... because a craft by definition was inaccessible to

anyone who had not been apprenticed to a master and thus learned by example.

15 Implicitly, this was Knight's answer to the important theoretical question: 'why do firms exist?' Giving a different answer, Coase (1937, pp. 400–1) attempted to rebut Knight's argument, writing: 'We can imagine a system where all advice or knowledge was bought as required.' Coase thus missed the point. Compared with goods and other services, knowledge cannot be so readily 'bought as required' (Foss, 1996a). As Knight (1921, p. 268) argued, uncertainty and ignorance create the 'necessity of acting upon opinion rather than knowledge'. For Knight, what was involved with managerial and entrepreneurial skills was not mere information or knowledge but sophisticated but essentially idiosyncratic judgements and conjectures in the context of uncertainty.

16 It must be noted that Taylorism is frequently caricatured. The Taylor movement in America had radical rather than conservative aims and was supported by progressive thinkers such as Veblen (1921). It believed that workers should be invested with responsibility and that enhanced productivity was a major instrument in the elimination of poverty. Its 'scientific' and 'pro-planning' credentials aligned it with American progressives and trade unionists until the 1950s (Nyland, 1996; Wrege and Greenwood, 1991). It is only since the 1970s, and with the post-Braverman Marxist literature, that Taylorism has been readily and exclusively associated with the destiny, prerogatives and greed of the capitalist corporation. Although Veblen was an enthusiast, Commons opposed 'scientific management' because – alongside his support for collective bargaining – he believed that workers should be given no responsibility for matters concerning production. The early criticisms of Taylorism by Hobson were of greater substance. Hobson (1914, p. 219) noted that even routine work 'still contains a margin for the display of skill, initiative and judgement' and that the elimination of this margin 'would mean the conversion of large bodies of skilled, intelligent workers into automatic drudges'. Furthermore, 'it is doubtful whether a somewhat shortened work-day and somewhat higher wages would compensate such damage'. And 'some detailed liberty and flexibility should be left to the worker'.

17 However, an exhaustive review of precedents is not possible. However, it must be noted that some of the ideas raised above were prefigured – in flawed terms – in the literature on the so-called 'managerial revolution' and 'new class' (Burnham, 1941; Djilas, 1957). Stabile (1984, p. 8) claimed that the 'new class' of managers and specialists with some degree of control over their own production process increased from 9.5 per cent of the US workforce in 1920 to 25.3 per cent in 1978. Undoubtedly the percentage is now significantly greater. Stabile further noted that 'their human capital-knowledge replaces private property as the primary currency of power and status'.

18 A partial exception is Marshall (1949, p. 115) who gave distinctive emphasis in at least one passage to knowledge and organisation: 'Knowledge is our most powerful engine of production. ... Organization aids knowledge; it has many forms ... it seems best sometimes to reckon organization apart as a distinct agent of production'.

19 For a critique see Hodgson (1991).

20 These 'physicalist' views of production derived substantially from the prevailing mechanistic notions of nineteenth-century physics (Mirowski, 1989). Marshall was relatively more inspired by Spencerian biology. By

contrast, Veblen's rejection of these conceptions of production was based on a radical attempt to incorporate into his economics the metaphors, philosophy and methods of Darwinism (Hodgson, 1993b).

21 It must be emphasised that, despite his consistent emphasis of the importance of technological knowledge, Veblen remained critical of the market mechanism and did not put forward any argument for its future retention, such as one based on the importance of innovation and the impossibility of collective access to all knowledge. In this respect, Veblen was reflecting the inadequate views of the majority of socialists of his time.

22 After wholesale industrial devastation in the Second World War, the subsequent experiences of reconstruction and dynamic recovery in Germany and Japan give strong support to Veblen's argument.

23 Schumpeter (1954, pp. 323) put his finger on the issue when he explained that the word

> capital ... came to denote the sums of money or their equivalents brought by partners into a partnership or company, the sum total of a firm's assets, and the like. Thus the concept was essentially monetary, meaning either actual money, or claims to money, or some goods evaluated in money. ... What a mass of confused, futile, and downright silly controversies it would have saved us, if economists had had the sense to stick to those monetary and accounting meanings of the term instead of trying to 'deepen' them!

His remarks are appropriate in regard to the confusing plethora of modern terms, such as 'human capital', 'social capital', 'personal capital', 'cultural capital', 'organizational capital' and even 'self-command capital'. These are all abuses of the word 'capital' which is properly confined to the notion of the money value of an owned stock of assets that exist in, or are readily convertible into, a monetary form. Outside slavery, therefore, there is no 'human capital' or 'social capital', as these are not stocks of assets that can be bought for money. At the most, outside slavery, human beings can be hired but not bought, but capital goods can be both. It is not until one owns – rather than merely rents – the stock of assets that one becomes the owner of capital.

24 Note also that deficiencies of the mainstream approach have more recently led Scott (1989) to question the standard definition of investment in terms of tangible assets. He contends that investment should include research and development, the creation of new production-related institutional structures, and the formation of new management teams. Scott argued that economic growth is predominately a cognitive, learning process in which the scope for learning is progressively extended by gross investment.

25 Income inequality has widened in many capitalist countries since the 1970s, most markedly in Britain and the United States. While institutional, political and other changes have clearly affected the distribution of income (Fortin and Lemieux, 1997; Nickell and Bell, 1996), there is strong evidence that rising skill differentials, and rising relative wages for skilled and experienced workers, are a major force behind the change (Gottschalk, 1997; Johnson, 1997; Topel, 1997; A. Wood, 1994, 1995).

26 Apparently, Sveiby and Risling (1986) and Sveiby and Lloyd (1987) were some of the first authors to establish the concept of the knowledge-intensive firm, and to argue that the increasing role and intensity of knowledge challenge conventional forms of ownership based on the dominance of physical

capital. The analysis of knowledge-intensive firms has been extended by Starbuck (1992) and others.

27 As Lawson (1997, p. 176) explains: 'an entity or aspect is said to be *emergent* if there is a sense in which it has arisen out of some 'lower' level, being conditioned by and dependent upon, but not predictable from, the properties found at the lower level.' For further discussions of the concept of emergence see M. Archer (1995), Hodgson (1998d, 1998e), Kontopoulos (1993) and D. A. Lane (1993).

9 THE END OF CAPITALISM?

1 One of the best analyses of this process is still found in Anderson's (1974a, 1974b) two classic volumes. But see also Mann (1986, 1993), which in some respects takes a different perspective.

2 There is a vast literature here. For theoretical arguments for the superiority of the participatory, codetermined, or labour managed firm see: Aoki (1988, 1990b), Bonin (1981, 1984), Bonin *et al.* (1993), Bonin and Putterman (1987), Bowles and Gintis (1993a), Brewer and Browning (1982), Doucouliagos (1990), Horvat (1982, 1986), Kahana and Nitzan (1993), Pagano and Rowthorn (1996), Putterman (1984), Sertel (1991), S. C. Smith (1991). Empirical studies on the comparative efficiency of participatory or labour managed firms include: Bartlett *et al.* (1992), Blumberg (1968), Bradley and Gelb (1986), Buchele and Christiansen (1992), Espinosa and Zimbalist (1978), Estrin *et al.* (1987), Jackall and Levin (1984), D. C. Jones (1985), Jones and Svejnar (1982, 1985), Kissler (1994), Mygind (1987), Pagano and Rowthorn (1996), S. K. Smith (1995), Stephen (1982).

3 Note that this undermines Ellerman's (1992) absolutist moral rejection of all employment contracts. Overall, a key problem with his argument is the existence of a grey area between employment and self-employment. Ellerman may reasonably attempt to draw the line, in the belief that there is, in essence, a distinction between the two. However, the distinction can only be maintained on the basis of historically specific principles. The distinction is sustained on the basis of the Enlightenment principles which, while real in modern capitalism, are historically transient, rather than 'natural' and everlasting. In contrast, Ellerman (1992, pp. 7, 240) explicitly took the contractarian and Enlightenment framework of thought as 'natural' and for granted, and argued entirely within its terms. He did not consider the possibility of an analysis that transcends Enlightenment presuppositions. He did not perceive the historical limits of his own Enlightenment assumptions, and he ended up – in the manner of classic Enlightenment utopians – proposing a socio-economic system drawn in absolutist terms, with little internal structural variation, or capacity for further evolution. On the contrary, I raise here the question of the limits of the reigning framework of contractarian and Enlightenment thought, as a basis for future legal systems.

4 Pagano (1985) has argued that the efficiency of a socio-economic system cannot be assessed independently of the preferences of the workers, including the utility of work itself. Typically, in welfare analysis, the latter is ignored, while the utility gained from leisure or consumption is included. The erosion of the work–leisure distinction adds further weight to Pagano's argument.

5 The modern 'workaholic' defies the neoclassical and Marxian notion of work as a disutility, and the idea that, other things being equal, any worker will attempt to minimise the number of hours worked. In Japan, often seen as a pointer to a possible future, the phenomenon of long hours leading to *karoshi* – meaning death by overwork – is quite widespread among knowledge-intensive and other workers, and has prompted political campaigns to deal with the problem (National Defense Council for the Victims of Karoshi, 1990).

6 See G. F. Thompson (1993, p. 825) for data on share ownership and growth of ESOPs in the 1980s in the UK. D. C. Jones (1987) reviewed data on, and public policy measures for promoting, employee-owned enterprises in the USA. Research suggests that employee ownership *per se* may have no more than slight positive effects on corporate profitability and productivity (Conte, 1989; General Accounting Office, 1987; Rooney, 1988; Rosen and Quarrey, 1987). However, these studies have also found that when employee owner-ship and a programme of employee participation are combined, marked increases in profitability and productivity can be attained.

7 Some normative issues are raised in the final chapter of this book. The concept of exploitation was discussed and redefined in Hodgson (1982) and it was admitted than exploitation was possible in a post-capitalist system.

8 For expositions and summaries of the theoretical issues from the perspective of neoclassical economics see, for example, Bonin and Putterman (1987), Estrin (1983) and Ireland and Law (1982). Note also the criticisms and elabo-rations of Horvat (1982, 1986) and Meade (1986, 1988, 1989).

9 In his intelligent and generally thoughtful book, Steele (1992) makes this assertion. However, despite claiming to be of 'Austrian' rather than neoclas-sical persuasion, he seems to accept the validity of the neoclassical analysis of worker co-operatives wholesale (pp. 346–9, 423). Yet, when it comes to central planning, the neoclassical approach is rejected (pp. 152–72). A more balanced critical discussion of the mainstream theory behind worker co-operatives is found in Pierson (1995).

10 See, for example, Bonin *et al.* (1993), Bonin and Putterman (1987), Bowles and Gintis (1993a), Horvat (1986), Jarsulic (1980), Kahana and Nitzan (1993), Miyazaki and Neary (1983), Pagano and Rowthorn (1996), Pfouts and Rosefielde (1986).

11 Williamson (1975, 1985) argued that because worker co-operatives are not very numerous, compared to the number of capitalist firms, then this means that they are being forced out by competition, and must be relatively ineffi-cient. Hodgson (1996) contests this, by showing that even in a competitive system (non)existence does not imply (in)efficiency. One reason is that competitive selection depends on the economic context, and while the institu-tional context of a capitalist system may be more conducive for the capitalist firm, a different context may favour the co-operative firm. There is evidence that this may be happening in Mondragon in Spain, where the co-operative firms are assisted by co-operative banks and other institutions (Thomas and Logan, 1982).

12 This general failure of the market system to invest adequately to meet the 'overhead costs' of the workforce – that is the costs of nurture, health and education – was examined at length by the institutional economist J. M. Clark (1923). See also Stabile (1996).

13 At least at the outset, exponents of the fashionable theory of endogenous growth seemed remarkably ignorant of precursors of their ideas such as by Young (1928) and Kaldor (1967, 1972, 1978, 1985).

14 The assumption of homogeneous labour is clearly unacceptable in anything else but an internal critique of mainstream theory, as in this case. The unrealistic assumption that capital goods are also homogeneous is also widespread in mainstream economics. On the general consequences of dropping this assumption see Harcourt (1972), and in regard to the theory of the labour managed firm, see Jarsulic (1980).

10 THE LEARNING FRONTIER

1 Charles Babbage (1846) criticised Adam Smith for assuming that differences in basic ability could be ignored and, with appropriate education or training, everyone could acquire specific skills. For Babbage, in contrast to Smith, much variation in skill pre-existed specific training. For Babbage the division of labour was *founded* on different types and degrees of skill; such variety is its origin not its result. Smith considered differences in skills to be a consequence rather than a cause of the division of labour, whereas for Babbage it was the other way round. Notably, Babbage's ontological stress on prior variety was inspirational for Charles Darwin. For discussions of these issues see Pagano (1991) and Hodgson (1993b).

2 There are a number of technical problems remaining here. For instance, the 'optimal' distribution will depend upon the distribution of income, and the measure of 'net output' would depend on a price vector, also dependent on income distribution. However, problems of this kind are common to all aggregative measures in economics. If we were dissuaded by such technical problems, then few, if any, measures of economic performance, output, income or productivity would be viable. It is not being suggested that these technical problems should be ignored: further theoretical refinement is required. The aim here is simply to sketch out a possible approach to the pressing problem of skill measurement.

3 One hundred years ago this position was not obvious, nor widely accepted. Many people believed that human evolution progressed along Lamarckian lines, that the inheritance of acquired characteristics was possible, and that the relatively rapid development of human civilisation could also be explained in terms of changes in human biology and innate potential. The British biologist Morgan (1896) argued against this Lamarckian position from a Darwinian standpoint. His argument was influential for Veblen (1899, p. 108; 1914, p. 18) and crucial for the foundation of institutional economics (Hodgson, 1998d).

4 Marshall (1949, p. 237) saw such external economies as being caused, for example, by the growing spread of 'all matters of Trade-knowledge' via 'newspapers, and trade and technical publications of all kinds'. However, he stressed the importance of the general spread of technical knowledge for the employer and underemphasised its relevance and importance for the worker.

5 Slightly different results can be obtained, here and elsewhere, depending on whether the earlier or the later date is taken as the base-point for comparison. These differences also affect price index calculations, but need not concern us at this stage, where the focus is on general principles rather than details.

6 This also contests the neoclassical theory of distribution, based on the aggregate production function. Previously criticised by Hobson (1914) and Veblen (1919), the logical foundations of this position were undermined in the famous 'Cambridge capital controversies' (Harcourt, 1972).

NOTES

11 SOME NORMATIVE AND POLICY ISSUES

1 There is another problem with the rhetoric of flexible labour markets: the process of *competition between firms* may be *endangered* by excessive labour mobility from firm to firm. If competition is to weed out the more efficient firms then this requires stability of the firm as a unit. Movements of individuals from firm to firm confound the competitive selection of firms with higher levels of skill and competence. This is true *a fortiori* if the processes of group and individual learning take a substantial amount of time, or depend on the stability of employment of the personnel in the work groups. The policy conclusion is diametrically opposed to the proposal that labour markets should have to be made more free to improve labour mobility. Instead, the emphasis is on the stability and longevity of the employment relationship, the enhancement of trust and learning, and the promotion of organisational integration to facilitate dynamic growth. This important but neglected argument was put forward by Campbell (1994).

2 This is similar to the idea of 'instrumental valuation' adopted by the Ayresian wing of institutional economics (Ayres, 1944; Tool, 1995). However, where the argument here differs is that institutions are seen as necessary repositories of knowledge, rather than the – one-sided and untenable – Ayresian depiction of them as solely archaic and negative constraints.

3 Within its own utilitarian assumptions, mainstream economics has frequently considered versions of 'cooperation' or 'altruism' (Axelrod, 1984; Collard, 1978). However, these still emerge from the interactions of those who are exclusively maximising their own individual utility. At best, the utility of 'altruistic' individual A is enhanced by the higher utility of individual B. But if an individual increases his or own utility by helping or co-operating with others then he or she is still self-serving, rather than being genuinely altruistic in a wider and more adequate sense. Accordingly, neoclassical treatments attempt to reduce such transcendent and intersubjective phenomena as trust and culture to characteristics of utility maximising, individual agents. In these terms, 'cooperation' and 'altruism' are still self-seeking in that sense and therefore do not capture fuller and more adequate meanings of those two words (Khalil, 1994).

4 Some investigations have suggested that university courses in mainstream economics have the real effect of discouraging cooperative and considerate behaviour in the students. Frank *et al.* (1993) found evidence consistent with the view that differences in cooperation between economics students and others 'are caused in part by training in economics' (p. 170). Somewhat different evidence was presented by Yezer *et al.* (1996) but Frank *et al.* (1996, p. 192) re-emphasised the conclusion shared by both groups of authors that 'economics training encourages the view that people are motivated primarily by self-interest'. As Frank *et al.* suggested, this raises a serious question of whether economists should be taught exclusively such a narrow view of human motivation. An exclusive education in mainstream economics may not be in the interests of society, or of the students themselves.

290

BIBLIOGRAPHY

Adaman, Fikret and Devine, Patrick (1994) 'Socialist Renewal: Lessons from the "Calculation Debate"', *Studies in Political Economy*, no. 43, Spring, pp. 63–77.
—— (1996a) 'A Response to Professor Foss', *Studies in Political Economy*, no. 49, Spring, pp. 163–8.
—— (1996b) 'The Economic Calculation Debate: Lessons for Socialists', *Cambridge Journal of Economics*, **20**(5), September, pp. 523–37.
—— (1997) 'On the Economic Theory of Socialism', *New Left Review*, no. 221, January–February, pp. 54–80.
Aganbegyan, Abel (1988) *The Challenge: Economics of Perestroika* (London: Hutchinson).
Albert, Michael and Hahnel, Robert (1990) *The Political Economy of Participatory Economics* (Princeton, NJ: Princeton University Press).
Albert, Michel (1993) *Capitalism Against Capitalism*, translated by Paul Haviland from the French edition of 1991 (London: Whurr Publishers).
Alchian, Armen A. and Demsetz, Harold (1972) 'Production, Information Costs, and Economic Organization', *American Economic Review*, **62**(4), December, pp. 777–95. Reprinted in Buckley and Michie (1996).
Allee, Warder C. (1951) *Cooperation Among Animals: With Human Implications* (New York: Henry Schuman).
Amin, Ash (1996) 'Beyond Associative Democracy', *New Political Economy*, **1**(3), pp. 309–33.
Amin, Ash and Thrift, Nigel (eds) (1994) *Globalization, Institutions, and Regional Development in Europe* (Oxford: Oxford University Press).
Amsden, Alice H. (ed.) (1980) *The Economics of Women and Work* (Harmondsworth: Penguin).
—— (1989) *Asia's Next Giant: South Korea and Late Industrialization*(Oxford and New York: Oxford University Press).
Anderson, Perry (1974a) *Passages from Antiquity to Feudalism* (London: NLB).
—— (1974b) *Lineages of the Absolutist State* (London: NLB).
—— (1992) *A Zone of Engagement* (London: Verso).
Aoki, Masahiko (1988) *Information, Incentives and Bargaining in the Japanese Economy* (Cambridge: Cambridge University Press).
—— (1990a) 'Towards an Economic Model of the Japanese Firm', *Journal of Economic Literature*, **26**(1), March, pp. 1–27.
—— (1990b) 'The Participatory Generation of Information Rents and the Theory of the Firm', in Aoki, Masahiko, Gustafsson, Bo and Williamson, Oliver E. (eds) (1990) *The Firm as a Nexus of Treaties* (London: Sage), pp. 26–51.

Appelbaum, Eileen and Schettkat, Ronald (eds) (1990) *Labor Market Adjustments to Structural Change and Technological Progress* (New York: Praeger).

Archer, Margaret S. (1995) *Realist Social Theory: The Morphogenetic Approach* (Cambridge: Cambridge University Press).

Archer, Robin (1995) *Economic Democracy: The Politics of Feasible Socialism* (Clarendon Press: Oxford).

Archibugi, Daniele and Michie, Jonathan (1995) 'The Globalisation of Technology: A New Taxonomy', *Cambridge Journal of Economics*, **19**(1), February, pp. 121–140.

Arendt, Hannah (1958) 'What Was Authority?', in Friedrich, Carl J. (ed.) *Authority* (Cambridge, MA: Harvard University Press), pp. 81–112.

Argyris, Chris and Schön, Donald (1978) *Organizational Learning: A Theory of Action Perspective* (Reading, MA: Addison-Wesley).

Arrighetti, Alessandro, Bachman, Reinhard and Deakin, Simon (1997) 'Contract Law, Social Norms and Inter-Firm Cooperation', *Cambridge Journal of Economics*, **21**(2), March, pp. 171–95.

Arrow, Kenneth J. (1962a) 'Economic Welfare and the Allocation of Resources to Invention', in Nelson, Richard R. (ed.) *The Rate and Direction of Inventive Activity: Economic and Social Factors* (Princeton, NJ: Princeton University Press), pp. 609–25. Reprinted in Kenneth J. Arrow (1972) *Essays in the Theory of Risk-Bearing* (Amsterdam: North Holland).

—— (1962b) 'The Economic Implications of Learning by Doing', *Review of Economic Studies*, **29**(2), June, pp. 155–73.

—— (1974) *The Limits of Organization* (New York: Norton).

—— (1986) 'Rationality of Self and Others in an Economic System', *Journal of Business*, **59** (October), pp. S385–99. Reprinted in Robin M. Hogarth and Melvin W. Reder, (eds) (1987) *Rational Choice: The Contrast Between Economics and Psychology* (Chicago, University of Chicago Press).

Arthur, W. Brian (1989) 'Competing Technologies, Increasing Returns, and Lock-in by Historical Events', *Economic Journal*, **99**(1), March, pp. 116–31.

—— (1990) 'Positive Feedbacks in the Economy', *Scientific American*, **262**(2), February, pp. 80–5.

Ashby, W. Ross (1952) *Design for a Brain* (New York: Wiley).

—— (1956) *An Introduction to Cybernetics* (New York: Wiley).

Ashton, Basil, Hill, K., Piazza, A. and Zeitz, R. (1984) 'Famine in China, 1958–61', *Population and Development Review*, **10**(4), December, pp. 613–45.

Ashton, David and Green, Francis (1996) *Education, Training and the Global Economy* (Cheltenham: Edward Elgar).

Åslund, Anders (ed.) (1992) *Market Socialism or the Restoration of Capitalism* (Cambridge: Cambridge University Press).

Atiyah, Patrick S. (1979) *The Rise and Fall of Freedom of Contract* (Oxford: Clarendon Press).

Atkinson, Anthony B. (1995) *Public Economics in Action: The Basic Income/Flat Tax Proposal* (Oxford: Clarendon Press).

Atkinson, Anthony B. and Micklewright, John (1992) *Economic Transformation in Eastern Europe and the Distribution of Income* (Cambridge: Cambridge University Press).

Attewell, Paul (1992) 'Skill and Occupational Changes in U.S. Manufacturing', in Adler, Paul (ed.) (1992) *Technology and the Future of Work* (Oxford and New York: Oxford University Press), pp. 46–88.

Attlee, Clement R. (1937) *The Labour Party in Perspective* (London: Gollancz).

Augros, Robert and Stanciu, George (1987) *The New Biology: Discovering the Wisdom in Nature* (Boston: Shambhala).

Axelrod, Robert M. (1984) *The Evolution of Cooperation* (New York: Basic Books).

Ayres, Clarence E. (1944) *The Theory of Economic Progress*, 1st edn (Chapel Hill, North Carolina: University of North Carolina Press).

Babbage, Charles (1846) *On the Economy of Machinery and Manufactures*, 4th edn (1st edn 1832), (London: John Murray).

Baisch, Helmut (1979) 'A Critique of Labour Values for Planning', *World Development*, **7**(10), pp. 965–72.

Baker, Dean and Weisbrot, Mark (1994) 'The Logic of Contested Exchange', *Journal of Economic Issues*, **28**(4), December, pp. 1091–114.

Barber, Bernard (1977) 'The Absolutization of the Market: Some Notes on How We Got from There to Here', in Dworkin, G., Bermant, G. and Brown, P. (eds) (1977) *Markets and Morals* (Washington, DC: Hemisphere), pp. 15–31.

—— (1983) *The Logic and Limits of Trust* (New Brunswick, NJ: Rutgers University Press).

Bardhan, Pranab K. and Roemer, John E. (1992) 'Market Socialism: A Case for Rejuvenation', *Journal of Economic Perspectives*, **6**(3), Summer, pp. 101–16.

—— (eds) (1993) *Market Socialism: The Current Debate* (Oxford and New York: Oxford University Press).

—— (1994) 'On the Workability of Market Socialism', *Journal of Economic Perspectives*, **8**(2), Spring, pp. 177–81.

Barnard, Chester J. (1938) *The Function of the Executive* (Cambridge, MA: Harvard University Press).

Bartlett, W., Cable, John, Estrin, Saul, Jones, Derek C. and Smith, Stephen C. (1992) 'Labor-Managed Cooperatives and Private Firms in North Central Italy: An Empirical Comparison', *Industrial and Labor Relations Review*, **46**(1), pp. 103–18.

Bateson, Gregory (1972) *Steps to an Ecology of Mind* (New York: Ballantine Books).

Batt, Francis R. (1929) *The Law of Master and Servant* (New York: Pitman Publishing).

Bauman, Zygmunt (1976) *Socialism: The Active Utopia* (London: George Allen and Unwin).

Baumol, William J. and Oates, Wallace E. (1988) *The Theory of Environmental Policy*, 2nd edn (Cambridge and New York: Cambridge University Press).

Beal, H. and Dugdale, T. (1975) 'Contracts Between Businessmen: Planning and the Use of Contractual Remedies', *British Journal of Law and Society*, **2**, pp. 45–60.

Beck, Ulrich (1992) *The Risk Society* (London: Sage).

Becker, Gary S. (1976a) *The Economic Approach to Human Behavior* (Chicago: University of Chicago Press).

—— (1976b) 'Altruism, Egoism, and Genetic Fitness: Economics and Sociobiology', *Journal of Economic Literature*, **14**(2), December, pp. 817–26.

—— (1991) *A Treatise on the Family*, 2nd edn (Cambridge, MA: Harvard University Press).

—— (1996) *Accounting for Tastes* (Cambridge, MA: Harvard University Press).

Beer, Max (1940) *A History of British Socialism*, 2 vols (London: Allen and Unwin).

Beer, Stafford (1972) *Brain of the Firm* (London: Allen Lane).

Bell, Daniel (1973) *The Coming of Post-Industrial Society: A Venture in Social Forecasting* (New York: Basic Books).

Bellamy, Edward (1888) *Looking Backward, 2000–1887* (Boston).

Benedict, Ruth (1934) *Patterns of Culture* (New York: New American Library).

Bentham, Jeremy (1823) *An Introduction to the Principles of Morality and Legislation* (London: Froude).

Berg, Maxine (1991) 'On the Origins of Capitalist Hierarchy', in Gustafsson, Bo (ed.) (1991) *Power and Economic Institutions: Reinterpretations in Economic History* (Aldershot: Edward Elgar), pp. 173–94.

Berger, Hans, Noorderhaven, Niels G. and Nooteboom, Bart (1995) 'Determinants of Supplier Dependence: An Empirical Study', in Groenewegen, John, Pitelis, Christos and Sjöstrand, Sven-Erik (eds) (1995) *On Economic Institutions: Theory and Applications* (Aldershot: Edward Elgar), pp. 195–212.

Berger, Suzanne and Dore, Ronald (eds) (1996) *National Diversity and Global Capitalism* (Ithaca, NY: Cornell University Press).

Bergson, Abram (1948) 'Socialist Economies', in Ellis, Howard (ed.) *Survey of Contemporary Economies* (Philadelphia, PA : Blakiston), pp. 430-58.

——(1978) 'The Soviet Economic Slowdown', *Challenge*, **20**(6).

Berkson, William and Wettersten, John (1984) *Learning from Error: Karl Popper's Psychology of Learning* (La Salle: Open Court).

Bernard, Andrew B. and Jones, Charles I. (1996) 'Comparing Apples to Oranges: Productivity Convergence and Measurement Across Industries and Countries', *American Economic Review*, **86**(5), December, pp. 1216–38.

Bertalanffy, Ludwig von (1971) *General Systems Theory: Foundation Development Applications* (London: Allen Lane).

Best, Michael H. (1990) *The New Competition: Institutions of Industrial Restructuring* (Cambridge: Polity Press).

Bestor Jr, Arthur E. (1948) 'The Evolution of the Socialist Vocabulary', *Journal of the History of Ideas*, **9**(3), June, pp. 259–302.

Bhaskar, Roy (1979) *The Possibility of Naturalism: A Philosophic Critique of the Contemporary Human Sciences* (Brighton: Harvester).

—— (1989) *Reclaiming Reality: A Critical Introduction to Contemporary Philosophy* (London: Verso).

Binger, Brian R. and Hoffman, Elizabeth (1989) 'Institutional Persistence and Change: The Question of Efficiency', *Journal of Institutional and Theoretical Economics*, **145**(1), March, pp. 67–84. Reprinted in Hodgson (1993c).

Bishop, John A., Formby, John P. and Smith, W. James (1991) 'International Comparisons of Income Inequality: Tests for Lorenz Dominance Across Nine Countries', *Economica*, **58**(4), November, pp. 461–77.

Blackburn, Robin (1991) 'Fin de Siècle: Socialism After the Crash', *New Left Review*, no. 185, January/February, pp. 5–66.

Blair, Margaret M. (1995) *Ownership and Control: Rethinking Corporate Governance for the Twenty-First Century* (Washington DC: The Brookings Institution).

Blanchflower, D. and Freeman, Richard B. (1992) 'Unionism in the United States and Other Advanced OECD Countries', *Industrial Relations*, **31**(1), Winter, pp. 56–79.

Blaug, Mark (1993) Review of D. R. Steele *From Marx to Mises*, *Economic Journal*, **103**(6), November, pp. 1570–1.

Block, Walter (ed.) (1989) *Economics and the Environment: A Reconciliation* (Vancouver, BC: Fraser Institute).

Blumberg, Paul (1968) *Industrial Democracy: The Sociology of Participation* (London: Constable).

Boguslaw, Robert (1965) *The New Utopians: A Study of System Design and Social Change* (Englewood Cliffs, NJ: Prentice-Hall).

Böhm, Stephan (1989) 'Hayek on Knowledge, Equilibrium and Prices: Context and Impact', *Wirtschaftspolitische Blätter*, **36**(2), pp. 201–13.

Böhme, Gernot and Stehr, Nico (eds) (1986) *The Knowledge Society: The Growing Impact of Scientific Knowledge on Social Relations* (Dordrecht: Reidel).

Boisot, Max H. (1995) *Information Space: A Framework for Learning in Organizations, Institutions and Culture* (London: Routledge).

Bonin, John P. (1981) 'The Theory of the Labor-Managed Firm from the Membership's Perspective with Implications for Marshallian Industry Supply', *Journal of Comparative Economics*, 5, pp. 337–51.

—— (1984) 'Membership and Employment in an Egalitarian Cooperative', *Economica*, 51, pp. 295–305.

Bonin, John P. and Putterman, Louis (1987) *The Economics of Cooperation and the Labor-Managed Economy* (London: Harwood Academic Publishers).

Bonin, John P., Jones, Derek C., and Putterman, Louis (1993) 'Theoretical and Empirical Studies of Producer Cooperatives: Will Ever the Twain Meet?', *Journal of Economic Literature*, 31(3), September, pp. 1290–320.

Boswell, Jonathan (1990) *Community and the Economy: The Theory of Public Co-operation* (London: Routledge).

Boudon, Raymond (1981) *The Logic of Social Action* (New York: Routledge and Kegan Paul).

Boulding, Kenneth E. (1966) 'The Economics of Knowledge and the Knowledge of Economics', *American Ecoonomic Review (Papers and Proceedings)*, 56, pp. 1–13.

Bowie, Norman E. (1988) 'The Paradox of Profit', in N. Dale Wright (ed.) (1988) *Papers on the Ethics of Administration* (Provo, UT: Brigham Young University Press).

Bowles, Samuel and Gintis, Herbert (1988) 'Contested Exchange: Political Economy and Modern Economic Theory', *American Economic Review*, 78(2), May, pp. 145–50.

—— (1993a) 'A Political and Economic Case for the Democratic Enterprise', *Economics and Philosophy*, 9(1), March, pp. 75–100.

—— (1993b) 'The Revenge of Homo Economicus: Contested Exchange and the Revival of Political Economy', *Journal of Economic Perspectives*, 7(1), Winter, pp. 83–102.

Bowles, Samuel, Gintis, Herbert and Gustafsson, Bo (eds) (1993) *Markets and Democracy: Participation, Accountability and Efficiency* (Cambridge: Cambridge University Press).

Boyer, Robert and Drache, Daniel (eds) (1996) *States Against Markets: The Limits of Globalization* (London: Routledge).

Bradley, Keith and Gelb, Alan (1986) 'Cooperative Labour Relations: Mondragon's Response to Recession', *Industrial Relations Journal*, 17, pp. 177–97.

Braverman, Harry (1974) *Labor and Monopoly Capital: The Degradation of Work in the Twentieth Century* (New York: Monthly Review Press).

Bresser Pereira, Luiz Carlos, Maraval, José Maria, Przeworski, Adam (1993) *Economic Reforms in New Democracies: A Social-Democratic Approach* (Cambridge: Cambridge University Press).

Brewer, Anthony A. and Browning, Martin J. (1982) 'On the "Employment" Decision of a Labour-Managed Firm', *Economica*, 49, pp. 141–6.

Brown, James A. C. (1954) *The Social Psychology of Industry* (Harmondsworth: Penguin).

Bruner, Jerome S. (1973) *Beyond the Information Given* (London: George Allen and Unwin).

Brus, Wlodzimierz and Laski, Kazimierz (1989) *From Marx to the Market: Socialism in the Search of an Economic System* (Oxford: Clarendon).

Brusco, Sebastiano (1982) 'The Emilian Model', *Cambridge Journal of Economics*, **6**(2), June, pp. 167–84.

Brutzkus, Boris D. (1923) *Sotsialisticheskoe khozyaistvo [The Socialist Economy]* (Paris: Poiski).

Buchanan, James M. and Vanberg, Viktor J. (1991) 'The Market as a Creative Process', *Economics and Philosophy*, **7**(2), October, pp. 167–86.

Buchele, Robert and Christiansen, Jens (1992) 'Industrial Relations and Productivity Growth: A Comparative Perspective', *International Contributions to Labour Studies*, **2**, pp. 77–97.

Buckley, Peter J. and Michie, Jonathan (eds) (1996) *Firms, Organizations and Contracts: A Reader in Industrial Organization* (Oxford: Oxford University Press).

Burawoy, Michael (1979) *Manufacturing Consent* (Chicago: University of Chicago Press).

Burchell, Brendan and Wilkinson, Frank (1997) 'Trust, Business Relationships and the Contractual Environment', *Cambridge Journal of Economics*, **21**(2), March, pp. 217–37.

Burnham, James (1941) *The Managerial Revolution* (New York).

Caldwell, Bruce J. (1988) 'Hayek's Transformation', *History of Political Economy*, **20**(4), Winter, pp. 513–41.

—— (1997) 'Hayek and Socialism', *Journal of Economic Literature*, **35**(4), December, pp. 1856–90.

Callon, Michel (1994) 'Is Science a Public Good?', *Science, Technology and Human Values*, **19**(4), Autumn, pp. 395–424.

Campbell, David and Harris, Donald (1993) 'Flexibility in Long-Term Contractual Relationships: The Role of Cooperation', *Journal of Law and Society*, **20**, pp. 166–91.

Campbell, Donald T. (1974) 'Evolutionary Epistemology', in P. A. Schilpp (ed.) (1974) *The Philosophy of Karl Popper* (Vol. 14, I & II). *The Library of Living Philosophers* (La Salle, IL: Open Court), pp. 413–63.

—— (1994) 'How Individual and Face-to-Face-Group Selection Undermine Firm Selection in Organizational Evolution', in Baum, Joel A. and Singh, Jitendra V. (eds) (1994) *Evolutionary Dynamics of Organizations* (Oxford: Oxford University Press), pp. 23–38.

Carling, Alan (1986) 'Rational Choice Marxism', *New Left Review*, no. 160, November/December, pp. 24–62.

Carlyle, Thomas (1847) *Past and Present* (London: Chapman and Hall).

Carneiro, Robert L. (1972) 'The Devolution of Evolution', *Social Biology*, **19**, pp. 248–58.

—— (1973) 'The Four Faces of Evolution', in John J. Honigmann (ed.) (1973) *Handbook of Social and Cultural Anthropology* (Chicago: Rand McNally).

Cartier, Kate (1994) 'The Transaction Costs and Benefits of the Incomplete Contract of Employment', *Cambridge Journal of Economics*, **18**(2), April, pp. 181–96.

Central Planning Bureau (1992) *Scanning the Future: A Long-Term Scenario Study of the World Economy 1990–2015* (The Hague: Sdu Publishers).

Chan, Anita (1995) 'Chinese Enterprise Reforms: Convergence with the Japanese Model?', *Industrial and Corporate Change*, **4**(2), pp. 449–70.

Chang, Ha-Joon and Rowthorn, Robert E. (eds) (1995) *The Role of the State in Economic Change* (Oxford: Clarendon Press).

Chavance, Bernard (1985) 'The Utopian Dialectic of Capitalism and Communism in Marx', *Economic Analysis and Workers' Management*, **19**(3), pp. 249–62.

—— (1995) 'Hierarchical Forms and Coordination Problems in Socialist Systems', *Industrial and Corporate Change*, **4**(1), pp. 271–91.

Chavance, Bernard and Magnin, Eric (1995) 'The Emergence of Various Path-Dependent Mixed Economies in Post-Socialist Central Europe', *Emergo*, **2**(4), Autumn, pp. 55–75.

—— (1997) 'The Emergence of Path-Dependent Mixed Economies in Central Europe', in Amin, Ash and Hausner, Jerzy (eds) (1997) *Beyond Market and Hierarchy: Interactive Governance and Social Complexity* (Cheltenham: Edward Elgar), pp. 196–232.

Choo, C. W. (1998) *Knowing Organization: How Organizations Use Information* (Oxford: Oxford University Press).

Clark, Andy (1997) *Being There: Putting the Brain, Body and World Together Again* (Cambridge, MA: MIT Press).

Clark, John Maurice (1923) *Studies in the Economics of Overhead Costs* (Chicago: University of Chicago Press).

Clegg, Stuart R. and Redding, S. Gordon (1990) *Capitalism in Contrasting Cultures* (New York: de Gruyter).

Cliff, Tony (1955) *Stalinist Russia: A Marxist Analysis* (London: Michael Kidron). Later reprinted and enlarged as *Russia: A Marxist Analysis* (London: International Socialism, no date).

Coase, Ronald H. (1937) 'The Nature of the Firm', *Economica*, **4**, November, pp. 386–405. Reprinted in Buckley and Michie (1996) and Williamson and Winter (1991).

—— (1960) 'The problem of social cost', *Journal of Law and Economics*, **3**, October, pp. 1–44.

—— (1988) 'The Nature of the Firm: Origin, Meaning, Influence', *Journal of Law, Economics, and Organization*, **4**(1), Spring, pp. 3–47. Reprinted in Williamson and Winter (1991).

—— (1996) Personal communication to G. Hodgson, dated 15 February.

Cockshott, W. Paul and Cottrell, Allin F. (1993) *Towards a New Socialism* (Nottingham: Spokesman).

Cohen, Gerald A. (1978) *Karl Marx's Theory of History: A Defence* (Oxford: Oxford University Press).

—— (1989) *History, Labour and Freedom: Themes from Marx* (Oxford: Oxford University Press).

—— (1996) *Self-Ownership, Freedom, and Equality* (Cambridge: Cambridge University Press).

Cohen, Ira J. (1989) *Structuration Theory: Anthony Giddens and the Constitution of Social Life* (London: Macmillan).

Cohen, Jack and Stewart, Ian (1994) *The Collapse of Chaos: Discovering Simplicity in a Complex World* (London and New York: Viking).

Cohen, Michael D. and Sproull, Lee S. (eds) (1996) *Organizational Learning* (London: Sage).

Cohen, Wesley M. and Levinthal, Daniel A. (1990) 'Absorptive Capacity: A New Perspective on Learning and Innovation', *Administrative Science Quarterly*, **35**, pp. 128–52.

Cole, George D. H. (1917) *Self-Government in Industry* (London: G. Bell). Reprinted 1972 with an introduction by John Corina (London: Hutchinson).

—— (1932) *The Intelligent Man's Guide Through World Chaos* (London: Gollancz).

Collard, David (1978) *Altruism and Economy: A Study in Non-Selfish Economics* (Oxford: Martin Robertson).

Commons, John R. (1893) *The Distribution of Wealth*, reprinted 1963 (New York: Augustus Kelley).
—— (1924) *Legal Foundations of Capitalism* (New York: Macmillan). Reprinted 1995 with a new introduction by Jeff E. Biddle and Warren J. Samuels (New Brunswick, NJ: Transaction).
—— (1934) *Institutional Economics – Its Place in Political Economy* (New York: Macmillan). Reprinted 1990 with a new introduction by Malcolm Rutherford (New Brunswick, NJ: Transaction).
—— (1950) *The Economics of Collective Action*, edited by Kenneth H. Parsons (New York: Macmillan).
—— (1965) *A Sociological View of Sovereignty*, reprinted from the *American Journal of Sociology* (1899–1900) and edited with an introduction by Joseph Dorfman (New York: Augustus Kelley).
Conte, Michael (1989) 'Employee Stock Ownership Plans in Public Companies', *The Journal of Employee Ownership Law and Finance*, **1**(1), pp. 89–138.
Coriat, Benjamin (1995) 'Incentives, Bargaining and Trust: Alternative Scenarios for the Future of Work', *International Contributions to Labour Studies*, **5**, pp. 131–51.
Cornuelle, Richard (1976) *De-Managing America* (New York: Vintage).
Cosmides, Leda and Tooby, John (1994) 'Beyond Intuition and Instinct Blindness: Towards an Evolutionary Rigorous Cognitive Science', *Cognition*, **50**(1–3), April–June, pp. 41–77.
Cottrell, Allin F. and W. Paul Cockshott (1993) 'Calculation, Complexity and Planning: The Socialist Calculation Debate Once Again', *Review of Political Economy*, **5**(1), January, 73–112.
Cowling, Keith and Sugden, Roger (1993) 'Control, Markets and Firms', in Pitelis, Christos (ed.) (1993) *Transaction Costs, Markets and Hierarchies* (Oxford: Basil Blackwell), pp. 66–76.
——(1994) *Beyond Capitalism: Towards a New World Economic Order* (London: Pinter).
Crosland, C. Anthony R. (1956) *The Future of Socialism* (London: Jonathan Cape).
Crowley, Brian L. (1987) *The Self, The Individual, and the Community: Liberalism in the Political Thought of F. A. Hayek and Sidney and Beatrice Webb* (Oxford: Clarendon Press).
Cunningham, William (1892) 'The Perversion of Economic History', *Economic Journal*, **2**, pp. 491–506.
Cutler, Anthony (1978) 'The Romance of "Labour"', *Economy and Society*, **7**(1), February, pp. 74–95.
Cyert, Richard M. and March, James G. (1963) *A Behavioral Theory of the Firm* (Engelwood Cliffs, NJ: Prentice-Hall).
Czepiel, John A. (1975) 'Patterns of Interorganizational Communications and the Diffusion of a Major Technological Innovation in a Competitive Industrial Community', *Academy of Management Journal*, **18**, pp. 6–24.
Dahrendorf, Ralf (1990) *Reflections on the Revolution in Europe* (London: Chatto and Windus).
Dallago, Bruno, Brezinski, Horst and Andreff, Wladimir (eds) (1992) *Convergence and System Change: The Convergence Hypothesis in the Light of the Transition in Eastern Europe* (Aldershot: Dartmouth).
Daly, Herman E. and Cobb Jr, John B. (1990) *For the Common Good: Redirecting the Economy Towards Community, the Environment and a Sustainable Future* (London: Green Print).
Danzinger, Sheldon and Gottschalk, Peter (1995) *America Unequal* (Cambridge, MA: Harvard University Press).

Darwin, Charles (1859) *On the Origin of Species by Means of Natural Selection, or the Preservation of Favoured Races in the Struggle for Life*, first edn (London: Murray). Facsimile reprint 1964 with an introduction by Ernst Mayr (Cambridge, MA: Harvard University Press).

—— (1904) *The Descent of Man*, 2nd edn (New York: Hill).

Davenport, Thomas H. (1993) *Process Innovation: Re-engineering Through Information Technology* (Boston, MA: Harvard Business School Press).

David, Paul A. (1975) *Technological Choice, Innovation and Economic Growth* (Cambridge: Cambridge University Press).

—— (1997) 'Path Dependence and the Quest for Historical Economics: One More Chorus of the Ballad of QWERTY', paper presented at the November 1997 conference of the European Association for Evolutionary Political Economy in Athens.

Deakin, Simon (1997) 'The Origins of the Contract of Employment: Economic Evolution and Legal Form', unpublished.

Deakin, Simon and Morris, G. (1995) *Labour Law* (London: Butterworth).

Dei Ottati, Gabi (1991) 'The Economic Bases of Diffuse Industrialization', *International Studies of Management and Organization*, **21**, pp. 53–74.

De Jong, Henk W. (1995) 'European Capitalism: Between Freedom and Social Justice', *Review of Industrial Organization*, **10**(4), August, pp. 397–419.

Demsetz, Harold (1967) 'Toward a theory of property rights', *American Economic Review (Papers and Proceedings)*, **57**(2), May, pp. 347–59.

Denzau, Arthur T. and North, Douglass, C. (1994) 'Shared Mental Models: Ideologies and Institutions', *Kyklos*, **47**, Fasc. 1, pp. 3–31.

Devine, Patrick (1988) *Democracy and Economic Planning: The Political Economy of a Self-Governing Society* (Cambridge: Polity Press).

Dewey, John (1935) *Liberalism and Social Action* (New York: G. P. Putnam's Sons).

Dickenson, Henry D. (1933) 'Price Formation in a Socialist Community', *Economic Journal*, **43**, pp. 237–50.

——: (1939) *Economics of Socialism* (Oxford: Oxford University Press).

Dietrich, Michael (1993) 'Total Quality Control, Just-in-Time Management, and the Economics of the Firm', *Journal of Economic Studies*, **20**(6), pp. 17–31.

—— (1994) *Transaction Cost Economics and Beyond: Towards a New Economics of the Firm* (London: Routledge).

Djilas, Milovan (1957) *The New Class: An Analysis of the Communist System* (New York: Praeger).

Dobb, Maurice (1937) *Political Economy and Capitalism*, 1st edn (London: Routledge and Kegan Paul).

—— (1969) *Welfare Economics and the Economics of Socialism: Towards a Commonsense Critique* (Cambridge: Cambridge University Press).

Doeringer, Peter B. and Piore, Michael J. (1971) *Internal Labor Markets and Manpower Analysis* (Lexington, MA: Heath).

Dore, Ronald (1973) *British Factory-Japanese Factory: The Origins of National Diversity in Industrial Relations* (London: George Allen and Unwin).

—— (1983) 'Goodwill and the Spirit of Market Capitalism', *British Journal of Sociology*, **34**(4), pp. 459–82. Reprinted in Buckley and Michie (1996) and Granovetter and Swedberg (1992).

—— (1993) 'What Makes the Japanese Different?', in Crouch, Colin and Marquand, David (eds) *Ethics and Markets* (Cambridge: Polity Press).

Dosi, Giovanni (1988a) 'Institutions and Markets in a Dynamic World', *The Manchester School*, **56**(2), June, pp. 119–46.

—— (1988b) 'The Sources, Procedures, and Microeconomic Effects of Innovation', *Journal of Economic Literature*, **26**(3), September, pp. 1120–71.

Dosi, Giovanni and Marengo, Luigi (1994) 'Some Elements of an Evolutionary Theory of Organizational Competences', in England (1994, pp. 157–78).

Dosi, Giovanni, Freeman, Christopher, Nelson, Richard, Silverberg, Gerald and Soete, Luc (eds) (1988) *Technical Change and Economic Theory* (London: Pinter).

Doucouliagos, Chris (1990) 'Why Capitalist Firms Outnumber Labor-Managed Firms', *Review of Radical Political Economics*, **22**(4), pp. 44–66.

Douglas, Mary (1987) *How Institutions Think* (London and Syracuse: Routledge and Kegan Paul and Syracuse University Press).

Dow, Gregory K. (1991) Review of G. Hodgson *Economics and Institutions*, *Journal of Economic Behavior and Organization*, **15**, pp. 159–69.

Downie, Jack (1955) *The Competitive Process* (London: Duckworth).

Doyal, Leonard and Gough, Ian (1991) *A Theory of Human Need* (London: Macmillan).

Dreyfus, Hubert L. and Dreyfus, Stuart E. (1986) *Mind Over Machine: The Power of Human Intutition and Expertise in the Era of the Computer* (New York: Free Press).

Drucker, Peter F. (1993) *Post-Capitalist Society* (Oxford: Butterworth-Heinemann).

Dunning, John H. (1993) *The Globalization of Business: The Challenge of the 1990s* (London and New York: Routledge).

Durbin, Evan F. M. (1936) 'Economic Calculus in a Planned Economy', *Economic Journal*, **46**(4), December, pp. 676–90.

Durkheim, Emile (1982) *The Rules of Sociological Method*, translated from the French edition of 1901 by W. D. Halls with an introduction by Steven Lukes (London: Macmillan).

—— (1984) *The Division of Labour in Society*, translated from the French edition of 1893 by W. D. Halls with an introduction by Lewis Coser (London: Macmillan).

Dyer, Alan W. (1986) 'Veblen on Scientific Creativity', *Journal of Economic Issues*, **20**(1), March, pp. 21–41. Reprinted in Mark Blaug (ed.) (1992) *Thorstein Veblen (1857–1929)* (Aldershot: Edward Elgar).

Edgell, Stephen and Townshend, Jules (1993) 'Marx and Veblen on Human Nature, History, and Capitalism: Vive la Différence!', *Journal of Economic Issues*, **27**(3), September, pp. 721–39.

Edquist, Charles (ed.) (1997) *Systems of Innovation: Technologies, Institutions and Organizations* (London: Pinter).

Edwards, Richard (1979) *Contested Terrain: The Transformation of the Workplace in the Twentieth Century* (New York: Basic Books).

Egidi, Massimo (1992) 'Organizational Learning, Problem Solving and the Division of Labour', in Simon, Herbert A., with Egidi, Massimo, Marris, Robin and Viale, Riccardo (1992) *Economics, Bounded Rationality and the Cognitive Revolution* (Aldershot: Edward Elgar), pp. 148–73.

Ekholm, Kajso and Friedman, Jonathan (1982) '"Capital" Imperialism and Exploitation in Ancient World-Systems', *Review*, **4**, pp. 87–109.

Eliasson, Gunnar (1991) 'Deregulation, Innovative Entry and Structural Diversity as a Source of Stable and Rapid Economic Growth', *Journal of Evolutionary Economics*, **1**(1), January, pp. 49–63.

Ellerman, David P. (1973) 'Capitalism and Workers' Self-Management', in Hunnius, G., Garson, G. D. and Case, J. (eds), *Workers' Control: A Reader in Labor and Social Change* (New York: Random House). Reprinted in Vanek (1975).

—— (1992) *Property and Contract in Economics: The Case for Economic Democracy* (Oxford: Blackwell).

Ellis, Richard J. (1993) 'The Case for Cultural Theory: Reply to Friedman', *Critical Review*, 7(1), Winter, pp. 81–128.

Ellman, Michael (1989) *Socialist Planning*, 2nd edn (Cambridge: Cambridge University Press).

—— (1995) 'The State under State Socialism and Post-Socialism', in Chang and Rowthorn (1995, pp. 215–36).

Elson, Diane (1988) 'Market Socialism or Socialization of the Market?' *New Left Review*, no. 172, November/December, pp. 3–44.

Elster, Jon (1982) 'Marxism, Functionalism and Game Theory', *Theory and Society*, 11(4), pp. 453–82. Reprinted in Roemer, John E. (ed.) (1986) *Analytical Marxism* (Cambridge: Cambridge University Press).

—— (1985) *Making Sense of Marx* (Cambridge: Cambridge University Press).

Elster, Jon and Moene, Karl Ove (eds) (1989) *Alternatives to Capitalism* (Cambridge: Cambridge University Press).

Emery, Fred E. (ed.) (1981) *Systems Thinking*, 2 vols (Harmondsworth: Penguin).

Engels, Frederick (1962) *Anti-Dühring: Herr Eugen Dühring's Revolution in Science*, translated from the 3rd German edition of 1894 (London: Lawrence and Wishart).

England, Richard W. (ed.) (1994) *Evolutionary Concepts in Contemporary Economics* (Ann Arbor: University of Michigan Press).

Espinosa, Juan G. and Zimbalist, Andrew S. (1978) *Economic Democracy: Workers' Participation in Chilean Industry, 1970–1973* (New York: Academic Press).

Estrin, Saul (1983) *Self-Management: Economic Theory and Yugoslav Practice* (Cambridge: Cambridge University Press).

Estrin, Saul, Jones, Derek C. and Svejnar, Jan (1987) 'The Productivity Effects of Worker Participation: Producer Cooperatives in Western Economies', *Journal of Comparative Economics*, 11(1), pp. 40–61.

Etzioni, Amitai (1988) *The Moral Dimension: Toward a New Economics* (New York: Free Press).

Fleetwood, Steven (1995) *Hayek's Political Economy: The Socio-Economics of Order* (London: Routledge).

Fligstein, Niel (1990) *The Transformation of Corporate Control* (Cambridge, MA: Harvard University Press).

Ford, David (1990) *Understanding Business Markets: Interaction, Relationships, Networks* (London: Academic Press).

Forsyth, Murray (1988) 'Hayek's Bizarre Liberalism: A Critique', *Political Studies*, 36(2), June, pp. 235–50.

Fortin, Nicole M. and Lemieux, Thomas (1997) 'Institutional Changes and Rising Wage Inequality: Is There a Linkage?', *Journal of Economic Perspectives*, 11(2), Spring, pp. 75–96.

Foss, Nicolai Juul (1993) 'Theories of the Firm: Contractual and Competence Perspectives', *Journal of Evolutionary Economics*, 3(2), May, pp. 127–44.

—— (1994) 'Realism and Evolutionary Economics', *Journal of Social and Evolutionary Systems*, 17(1), pp. 21–40.

—— (1996a) 'The "Alternative" Theories of Knight and Coase, and the Modern Theory of the Firm', *Journal of the History of Economic Thought*, 18(1), Spring, pp. 76–95.

—— (1996b) 'The Coordination of Investments in a Market Economy: Comments on a Revitalized Marxian Theme', *Studies in Political Economy*, no. 49, Spring, pp. 149–61.

Foss, Nicolai Juul and Knudsen, Christian (eds) (1996) *Towards a Competence Theory of the Firm* (London: Routledge).

Fourie, Frederick C. v. N. (1989) 'The Nature of Firms and Markets: Do Transactions Approaches Help?', *South African Journal of Economics*, **57**(2), pp. 142–60.

Fox, Alan (1974) *Beyond Contract: Work, Power and Trust Relations* (London: Faber and Faber).

Frank, Robert H. (1988) *Passions Within Reason: The Strategic Role of the Emotions* (New York: Norton).

—— (1993) 'The Strategic Role of the Emotions: Reconciling Over- and Undersocialized Accounts of Behavior', *Rationality and Society*, **5**(2), April, pp. 160–84.

Frank, Robert H., Gilovich, Thomas D. and Regan, Dennis T. (1993) 'Does Studying Economics Inhibit Cooperation', *Journal of Economic Perspectives*, **7**(2), Spring, pp. 159–71.

—— (1996) 'Do Economists Make Bad Citizens?', *Journal of Economic Perspectives*, **10**(1), Winter, pp. 187–92.

Frankel, S. Herbert (1977) *Money: Two Philosophies; The Conflict of Trust and Authority* (Oxford: Blackwell).

Fransman, Martin (1994) 'Information, Knowledge, Vision and Theories of the Firm', *Industrial and Corporate Change*, **3**(3), pp. 713–57.

—— (1995) 'Is National Technology Policy Obsolete in a Globalised World? The Japanese Response', *Cambridge Journal of Economics*, **19**(1), February, pp. 95–119.

Freeman, Christopher (1982) *The Economics of Industrial Innovation*, 2nd edn (London: Pinter).

—— (1987) *Technology Policy and Economic Performance: Lessons from Japan* (London: Pinter).

Freeman, Christopher and Perez, Carlota (1988) 'Structural Crises of Adjustment, Business Cycles and Investment Behaviour', in Dosi *et al.* (1988, pp. 38–66).

Freeman, Richard B. (1995) 'The Limits of Wage Flexibility to Curing Unemployment', *Oxford Review of Economic Policy*, Spring, **11**(1), pp. 63–72.

Friedman, Milton (1953) 'The Methodology of Positive Economics', in M. Friedman, *Essays in Positive Economics* (Chicago: University of Chicago Press), pp. 3–43.

—— (1962) *Capitalism and Freedom* (Chicago: University of Chicago Press).

Friedman, Milton and Friedman, Rose (1980) *Free to Choose: A Personal Statement* (Harmondsworth: Penguin).

Fukuyama, Francis (1989) 'The End of History', *The National Interest*, Summer, pp. 3–18.

—— (1990) 'Are We at the End of History?', *Fortune*, **121**(2), January, pp. 75–8.

—— (1992) *The End of History and the Last Man* (New York: Free Press).

—— (1995) *Trust: The Social Virtues and the Creation of Prosperity* (London and New York: Hamish Hamilton).

Gambetta, Diego (ed.) (1988) *Trust: Making and Breaking Cooperative Relations* (Oxford: Basil Blackwell).

Gamble, Andrew (1996) *Hayek: The Iron Cage of Liberty* (Cambridge: Polity Press).

General Accounting Office, United States Government (1987) *Employee Stock Ownership Plans: Little Evidence of Effects on Corporate Performance* (Washington, DC: GAO).

Geoghegan, Vincent (1987) *Utopianism and Marxism* (London: Methuen).

Georgescu-Roegen, Nicholas (1966) *Analytical Economics* (Cambridge, MA: Harvard University Press).

—— (1971) *The Entropy Law and the Economic Process* (Cambridge, MA: Harvard University Press).

Gerlach, Michael L. (1992) *Alliance Capitalism: The Social Organization of Japanese Business* (Berkeley, CA: University of California Press).

Geroski, Paul A. and Jacquemin, Alexis (1984) 'Dominant Firms and Their Alleged Decline', *International Journal of Industrial Organization*, **2**, March, pp. 1–27.

Gibson-Graham, J. K. (1996) *The End of Capitalism (As We Know It): A Feminist Critique of Political Economy* (Oxford: Blackwell).

Giddens, Anthony (1984) *The Constitution of Society: Outline of the Theory of Structuration* (Cambridge: Polity Press).

—— (1990) *The Consequences of Modernity* (Cambridge: Polity Press).

—— (1994) *Beyond Left and Right: The Future of Radical Politics* (Cambridge: Polity Press).

Gide, Charles and Rist, Charles (1915) *A History of Economic Doctrines From the Time of the Physiocrats to the Present Day*, translated from the French edition of 1913 by William Smart and R. Richards (London: George Harrap).

Gintis, Herbert (1972) 'A Radical Analysis of Welfare Economics and Individual Development', *Quarterly Journal of Economics*, **86**(4), November, pp. 572–99.

—— (1974) 'Welfare Criteria With Endogenous Preferences: The Economics of Education' *International Economic Review*, **15**(2), June, pp. 415–30.

—— (1976) 'The Nature of Labor Exchange and the Theory of Capitalist Production', *Review of Radical Political Economics*, **8**, Summer, pp. 36–54.

Gintis, Herbert and Bowles, Samuel (1981) 'Structure and Practice in the Labor Theory of Value', *Review of Radical Political Economics*, **12**(4), Winter, pp. 1–26.

Goldberg, Victor P. (1980a) 'Bridges Over Contested Terrain: Exploring the Radical Account of the Employment Relationship', *Journal of Economic Behavior and Organization*, **1**, pp. 249–74.

—— (1980b) 'Relational Exchange: Economics and Complex Contracts', *American Behavioral Scientist*, **23**(3), pp. 337–52.

Goldin, Claudia and Katz, Lawrence F. (1996) 'Technology, Skill, and the Wage Structure: Insights from the Past', *American Economic Review (Papers and Proceedings)*, **86**(2), May, pp. 252–7.

Goodman, Edward and Bamford, Julia (eds) (1989) *Small Firms and Industrial Districts in Italy* (London: Routledge).

Goodwin, Barbara (1978) *Social Science and Utopia: Nineteenth-Century Models of Social Harmony* (Hassocks and Atlantic Highlands: Harvester and Humanities Press).

Gorz, André (1985) *Paths to Paradise: On the Liberation from Work* (London: Pluto).

Gottschalk, Peter (1997) 'Inequality, Income Growth, and Mobility: The Basic Facts', *Journal of Economic Perspectives*, **11**(2), Spring, pp. 21–40.

Gough, Ian (1994a) 'Economic Institutions and the Satisfaction of Human Needs', *Journal of Economic Issues*, **28**(1), March, pp. 25–66.

—— (1994b) 'Need, concept of', in Hodgson *et al.* (1994, vol. 2, pp. 118–26).

Gould, Stephen Jay (1980) *The Panda's Thumb: More Refelections in Natural History* (New York: Norton).

—— (1989) *Wonderful Life: The Burgess Shale and the Nature of History* (London: Hutchinson Radius).

Grabher, Gernot (ed.) (1993) *The Embedded Firm: On the Socioeconomics of Industrial Networks* (London: Routledge).

Grabher, Gernot and Stark, David (eds) (1997) *Restructuring Networks in Post-Socialism: Legacies, Linkages and Localities* (Oxford: Oxford University Press).

Granovetter, Mark (1985) 'Economic Action and Social Structure: The Problem of Embeddedness', *American Journal of Sociology*, **91**(3), November, pp. 481–510. Reprinted in Granovetter and Swedberg (1992).

—— (1993) 'The Nature of Economic Relationships', in Swedberg (1993, pp. 3–41).

Granovetter, Mark and Swedberg, Richard (eds) (1992) *The Sociology of Economic Life* (Boulder, CO: Westview Press).

Gray, John (1980) 'F. A. Hayek on Liberty and Tradition', *Journal of Libertarian Studies*, **4**, pp. 119–37.

—— (1984) *Hayek on Liberty* (Oxford: Basil Blackwell).

—— (1995) *Enlightenment's Wake: Politics and Culture at the Close of the Modern Age* (London: Routledge).

Green, Thomas H. (1888) *Philosophical Works*, vol. 3 (London: Longmans).

Gregg, Lee W. (ed.) (1974) *Knowledge and Cognition* (New York: Wiley).

Groenewegen, John (1997) 'Institutions of Capitalisms: American, European, and Japanese Systems Compared', *Journal of Economic Issues*, **31**(2), June, pp. 333–47.

Groenewegen, Peter and McFarlane, Bruce (eds) (1995) *Socialist Thought in the Post Cold War Era* (Manila, Philippines: Journal of Contemporary Asia Publishers).

Haddad, Louis (1995) 'The Disjunction Between Decision-Making and Information Flows: The Case of the Former Planned Economies', in Groenewegen and McFarlane (1995, pp. 69–88).

Hagstrom, Warren O. (1965) *The Scientific Community* (New York: Basic Books).

Hahn, Frank H. (1988) 'On Monetary Theory', *Economic Journal*, **98**(4), December, pp. 957–73.

Hain, Peter (1995) *Ayes to the Left: A Future for Socialism* (London: Lawrence and Wishart).

Halm, Georg (1935) 'Further Considerations on the Possibility of Adequate Calculation in a Socialist Economy', in Hayek (1935, pp. 131–200).

Hamilton, Gary G. and Feenstra, Robert C. (1995) 'Varieties of Hierarchies and Markets: An Introduction', *Industrial and Corporate Change*, **4**(1), pp. 51–87.

Hamilton, Walton H. (1932) 'Institution', in E. R. A. Seligman and A. Johnson (eds) *Encyclopaedia of the Social Sciences*, vol. 8, pp. 84–89. Reprinted in Hodgson (1993c).

Hammer, Michael and Champy, James (1993) *Reengineering the Corporation* (New York: Harper).

Hampden-Turner, Charles and Trompenaars, Alfons (1993) *The Seven Cultures of Capitalism: Value Systems for Creating Wealth in the United States, Japan, Germany, France, Britain, Sweden, and the Netherlands* (New York: Currency Doubleday).

Handy, Charles B. (1984) *The Future of Work: A Guide to a Changing Society* (Oxford: Basil Blackwell).

Harcourt, Geoffrey C. (1972) *Some Cambridge Controversies in the Theory of Capital* (Cambridge, Cambridge University Press).

Harris, Abram L. (1932) 'Types of Institutionalism', *Journal of Political Economy*, **40**(4), December, pp. 721–49.

Hartz, Louis (1955) *The Liberal Tradition in America: An Interpretation of American Political Thought Since the Revolution* (New York: Harcourt, Brace, World).

Hausner, Jerzy, Jessop, Bob and Nielsen, Klaus (1993) *Institutional Frameworks of Market Economies: Scandinavian and Eastern European Perspectives* (Aldershot: Avebury).

Hayek, Friedrich A. (1933) 'The Trend of Economic Thinking', *Economica*, **1**(2), May, pp. 121–37. Reprinted in F. A. Hayek (1991) *The Trend of Economic*

Thinking: Essays on Political Economists and Economic History, Collected Works of F. A. Hayek, vol. III (London: Routledge).

—— (ed.) (1935) *Collectivist Economic Planning* (London: George Routledge). Reprinted 1975 by Augustus Kelley.

—— (ed.) (1944) *The Road to Serfdom* (London: George Routledge).

—— (1948) *Individualism and Economic Order* (London and Chicago: George Routledge and University of Chicago Press).

——. (1960) *The Constitution of Liberty* (London: Routledge and Kegan Paul).

—— (1978) *New Studies in Philosophy, Politics, Economics and the History of Ideas* (London: Routledge and Kegan Paul).

—— (1982) *Law, Legislation and Liberty*, 3-volume combined edn (London: Routledge and Kegan Paul).

—— (1988) *The Fatal Conceit: The Errors of Socialism, the Collected Works of Friedrich August Hayek*, vol. I, ed. W. W. Bartley III (London: Routledge).

Hedlund, Gunnar (1994) 'A Model of Knowledge Management and the N-form Corporation', *Strategic Management Journal*, **15**, pp. 73–90.

Heimann, Eduard (1922) *Mehrwert und Gemeinwirtschaft* (Berlin: H. R. Hengelmann).

Helm, Dieter and Pearce, David W. (1991) 'Economic policy towards the environment: An overview', in Helm, Dieter (ed.) (1991) *Economic Policy Towards the Environment* (Oxford: Basil Blackwell), pp. 1–24.

Hicks, John R. (1965) *Capital and Growth* (Oxford: Oxford University Press).

Hill, Forest G. (1958) 'Veblen and Marx', in Dowd, D. F. (ed.) (1958) *Thorstein Veblen: A Critical Appraisal* (Ithaca, NY: Cornell University Press), pp. 129–49.

Hippel, Eric von (1987) 'Cooperation Between Rivals: Informal Know-How Trading', *Research Policy*, **16**, pp. 291–302.

—— (1988) *The Sources of Innovation* (Oxford: Oxford University Press).

Hirsch, Fred (1977) *Social Limits to Growth* (London: Routledge).

Hirschman, Albert O. (1970) *Exit, Voice, and Loyalty: Responses to Decline in Firms, Organizations, and States* (Cambridge, MA: Harvard University Press).

—— (1982) 'Rival Interpretations of Market Society: Civilizing, Destructive, or Feeble?', *Journal of Economic Literature*, **20**(4), December, pp. 1463–84. Reprinted in Albert O. Hirschman (1986) *Rival Views of Market Society and Other Essays* (New York: Viking).

—— (1985) 'Against Parsimony: Three Ways of Complicating Some Categories of Economic Discourse', *Economics and Philosophy*, **1**(1), March, pp. 7–21.

Hirshleifer, Jack (1977), 'Economics from a Biological Viewpoint', *Journal of Law and Economics*, **20**(1), April, pp. 1–52.

—— (1985) 'The Expanding Domain of Economics', *American Economic Review*, **75**(6), December, pp. 53–68.

Hirst, Paul Q. (1994) *Associative Democracy: New Forms of Economic and Social Governance* (Cambridge: Polity Press).

Hirst, Paul Q. and Thompson, Grahame F. (1996) *Globalization in Question: The International Economy and the Possibilities of Governance* (Cambridge: Polity Press).

Hobson, John A. (1902) *The Social Problem: Life and Work* (London: James Nisbet). Reprinted 1995 with an introduction by James Meadowcroft (Bristol: Thoemmes Press).

—— (1914) *Work and Wealth: A Human Valuation* (London: Macmillan).

—— (1936) *Veblen* (London: Chapman and Hall). Reprinted 1991 by Augustus Kelley.

Hodgson, Geoffrey M. (1974a) 'The Theory of the Falling Rate of Profit', *New Left Review*, no. 84, March-April, pp. 55–82. Reprinted in Hodgson (1991).

—— (1974b) 'Marxian Epistemology and the Transformation Problem', *Economy and Society*, **3**(4), November, pp. 357–92.

—— (1977) 'Papering Over the Cracks: Comments on Fine and Harris' Survey of the Current Controversy Within Marxist Economics', *Socialist Register, 1977*, pp. 88–105.

—— (1982) *Capitalism, Value and Exploitation: A Radical Theory* (Oxford: Martin Robertson).

—— (1984) *The Democratic Economy: A New Look at Planning, Markets and Power* (Harmondsworth: Penguin).

—— (1985) 'Persuasion, Expectations and the Limits to Keynes', in Lawson, Antony and Pesaran, Hashem (eds), *Keynes's Economics: Methodological Issues* (London: Croom Helm), pp. 10–45.

—— (1988) *Economics and Institutions: A Manifesto for a Modern Institutional Economics* (Cambridge and Philadelphia: Polity Press and University of Pennsylvania Press).

—— (1991) *After Marx and Sraffa: Essays in Political Economy* (London: Macmillan).

—— (1992a) 'The Reconstruction of Economics: Is There Still a Place for Neoclassical Theory?', *Journal of Economic Issues*, **26**(3), September, pp. 749–67. Reprinted and revised in Hodgson (1998e).

—— (1992b) 'Thorstein Veblen and Post-Darwinian Economics', *Cambridge Journal of Economics*, **16**(3), September, pp. 285–301.

—— (1993a) 'Institutional Economics: Surveying the "Old" and the "New"', *Metroeconomica*, **44**(1), February, pp. 1–28. Reprinted in Hodgson (1993c).

—— (1993b) *Economics and Evolution: Bringing Life Back Into Economics* (Cambridge, UK and Ann Arbor, MI: Polity Press and University of Michigan Press).

—— (ed.) (1993c) *The Economics of Institutions* (Aldershot: Edward Elgar).

—— (1994) 'Optimisation and Evolution: Winter's Critique of Friedman Revisited', *Cambridge Journal of Economics*, **18**(4), August, pp. 413–30. Reprinted in Hodgson (1998e).

—— (1996) 'Organizational Form and Economic Evolution: A Critique of the Williamsonian Hypothesis', in Pagano, U. and Rowthorn, R.E. (eds), *Democracy and Efficiency in Economic Enterprises* (London: Routledge), pp. 98–115.

—— (1997) 'The Ubiquity of Habits and Rules', *Cambridge Journal of Economics*, **21**(6), November, 663–84.

—— (1998a) 'The Coasean Tangle: The Nature of the Firm and the Problem of Historical Specificity', in Medema, S.G. (ed.) (1998), *Coasean Economics: Law and Economics and the New Institutional Economics* (Boston: Kluwer), pp. 23–49. Reprinted in Hodgson (1998e).

—— (1998b) 'Evolutionary and Competence-Based Theories of the Firm', *Journal of Economic Studies*, **25**(1), pp. 25–56. Reprinted in Hodgson (1998e).

—— (1998c) 'Competence and Contract in the Theory of the Firm', *Journal of Economic Behavior and Organization*, **35**(2), April, pp. 179–201.

—— (1998d) 'On the Evolution of Thorstein Veblen's Evolutionary Economics', *Cambridge Journal of Economics*, **22**(3), July, pp. 415–31.

—— (1998e) *Evolution and Institutions: On Evolutionary Economics and the Evolution of Economics* (Cheltenham: Edward Elgar) forthcoming.

—— (1998f) 'Socialism Against Markets? A Critique of two Recent Proposals', *Economy and Society* (forthcoming).

Hodgson, Geoffrey M. and Screpanti, Ernesto (eds) (1991) *Rethinking Economics: Markets, Technology and Economic Evolution* (Aldershot: Edward Elgar).

Hodgson, Geoffrey M., Samuels, Warren J. and Tool, Marc R. (eds) (1994) *The Elgar Companion to Institutional and Evolutionary Economics* (Aldershot: Edward Elgar).

Hoff, Trygve J. B. (1949) *Economic Calculation in the Socialist Society*, translated from the Norwegian edition of 1938 by M. A. Michael (London: William Hodge). Republished 1981 (Indianapolis: Liberty Press).

Homans, George C. (1961) *Social Behaviour: Its Elementary Form* (London: Routledge and Kegan Paul).

Horvat, Branko (1982) *The Political Economy of Socialism: A Marxist Social Theory* (Oxford and Armonk, NY: Martin Robertson and M. E. Sharpe).

—— (1986) 'The Theory of the Worker-Managed Firm Revisited', *Journal of Comparative Economics*, **10**, pp. 9–25.

Hoyle, Fred (1966) *October the First is Too Late* (London: Heinemann).

Hull, David L. (1988) *Science as Progress: An Evolutionary Account of the Social and Conceptual Development of Science* (Chicago: University of Chicago Press).

Hutchinson, Frances and Burkitt, Brian (1997) *The Political Economy of Social Credit and Guild Socialism* (London: Routledge).

Hutton, Will (1995) *The State We're In* (London: Jonathan Cape).

—— (1997) *The State To Come* (London: Vintage).

Imai, Ken-ichi and Itami, Hiroyuki (1984) 'Interpenetration of Organization and Market: Japan's Firm and Market in Comparison with the US', *International Journal of Industrial Organisation*, **6**(4), pp. 285–310. Reprinted in Buckley and Michie (1996).

Ingram, John K. (1915) *A History of Political Economy*, 2nd edn (1st edn 1888: New York). Reprinted 1967 (New York: Augustus Kelley).

Ioannides, Stavros (1992) *The Market, Competition and Democracy: A Critique of Neo-Austrian Economics* (Aldershot: Edward Elgar).

Ireland, Norman J. and Law, Peter J. (1982) *The Economics of Labour-Managed Enterprises* (London: Croom Helm).

Itoh, Makoto (1995) *Political Economy for Socialism* (London: Macmillan).

Jackall, Robert and Levin, Henry M. (eds) (1984) *Worker Cooperatives in America* (Berkeley, CA: University of California Press).

Jacobs, Michael (1991) *The Green Economy: Environment, Sustainable Development and the Politics of the Future* (London: Pluto Press).

Jacoby, Sanford M. (1990) 'The New Institutionalism: What Can it Learn from the Old?', *Industrial Relations*, **29**(2), Spring, pp. 316–59.

James, Philip S. (1966) *Introduction to English Law*, 6th edn (London: Butterworths).

James, William (1890) *The Principles of Psychology*, 1st edn (New York: Holt).

Jarsulic, Marc (1980) 'Worker-Management and the Choice of Technique', *Cambridge Journal of Economics*, **4**(3), September, pp. 259–63.

Johnson, Chalmers (1982) *MITI and the Japanese Miracle: The Growth of Industrial Policy, 1925–1975* (Stanford: Stanford University Press).

Johnson, George E. (1997) 'Changes in Earnings Inequality: The Role of Demand Shifts', *Journal of Economic Perspectives*, **11**(2), Spring, pp. 41–54.

Jones, Derek C. (1985) 'The Economic Performance of Producer Cooperatives Within Command Economies: Evidence for the Case of Poland', *Cambridge Journal of Economics*, **9**(2), June, pp. 111–26.

—— (1987) 'Alternative Sharing Arrangements: A Review of the Evidence of their Effects and some Policy Implications for the U.S.', *Economic and Industrial Democracy*, **8**, pp. 489–516.

Jones, Derek C. and Svejnar, Jan (eds) (1982) *Participatory and Self-Managed Firms* (Lexington, MA: Heath).

—— (1985) 'Participation, Profit Sharing, Worker Ownership and Efficiency in Italian Producer Cooperatives', *Economica*, **52**, pp. 449–65.

Jones, R. J. Barry (1995) *Globalization and Interdependence in the International Political Economy* (London: Pinter).

Kagel, John H., Battalio, Raymond C., and Green, Leonard (1995) *Economic Choice Theory: An Experimental Analysis of Animal Behaviour* (Cambridge and New York: Cambridge University Press).

Kagel, John H., Battalio, Raymond C., Rachlin, Howard and Green, Leonard (1981) 'Demand Curves for Animal Consumers', *Quarterly Journal of Economics*, **96**(1), pp. 1–16.

Kahana, Nava and Nitzan, Shmuel (1993) 'The Theory of the Labour-Managed Firm Revisited: The Voluntary Interactive Approach', *Economic Journal*, **103**(4), July, pp. 937–45.

Kahn-Freund, O. (1977) 'Blackstone's Neglected Child: The Contract of Employment Law', *Law Quarterly Review*, **93**, pp. 508–28.

——(1983) *Labour and the Law*, 3rd edn, ed. P. Davies and M. Freedland (London: Stevens).

Kaldor, Nicholas (1967) *Strategic Factors in Economic Development* (New York: Cornell University Press).

—— (1972) 'The Irrelevance of Equilibrium Economics', *Economic Journal*, **82**(4), December, pp. 1237–55. Reprinted in Kaldor (1978).

—— (1978) *Further Essays on Economic Theory: (Collected Economic Essays Vol. 5)* (London: Duckworth).

—— (1985) *Economics Without Equilibrium* (Cardiff: University College Cardiff Press).

Kapp, K. William (1976) 'The Nature and Significance of Institutional Economics', *Kyklos*, **29**, Fasc. 2, pp. 209–32. Reprinted in Warren J. Samuels (ed.) (1988) *Institutional Economics* (Aldershot: Edward Elgar), vol. 1.

—— (1978) *The Social Costs of Business Enterprise*, 3rd edn (1st edn 1950) (Nottingham: Spokesman).

Kauffman, Stuart A. (1993) *The Origins of Order: Self-Organization and Selection in Evolution* (Oxford and New York: Oxford University Press).

—— (1995) *At Home in the Universe: The Search for Laws of Self-Organization and Complexity* (Oxford and New York: Oxford University Press).

Kautsky, Karl (1902) *The Social Revolution* (Chicago: Charles Kerr).

—— (1925) *The Labour Revolution* (London: George Allen and Unwin).

Kay, Neil M. (1984) *The Emergent Firm: Knowledge, Ignorance and Surprise in Economic Organization* (London: Macmillan).

—— (1997) *Pattern in Corporate Evolution* (Oxford: Oxford University Press).

Kelly, Gavin, Kelly, Dominic and Gamble, Andrew (eds) (1997) *Stakeholder Capitalism* (Basingstoke: Macmillan).

Kenworthy, Lane (1995) *In Search of National Economic Success: Balancing Competition and Cooperation* (Thousand Oaks, CA and London: Sage).

Keynes, John Maynard (1936) *The General Theory of Employment, Interest and Money* (London: Macmillan).

—— (1972) *Essays in Biography*, 1st edn 1933 (London: Macmillan).

—— (1980) *The Collected Writings of John Maynard Keynes, Vol. XXVII, 'Activities 1940–1946: Shaping the Post-War World: Employment and Commodities'* (London: Macmillan).

Khalil, Elias L. (1990) 'Rationality and Social Labor in Marx', *Critical Review*, **4**(1–2), Winter-Spring, pp. 239–65.

—— (1992) 'Nature and Abstract Labor in Marx', *Social Concept*, **6**(2), June, pp. 91–117.

—— (1994) 'Trust', in Hodgson *et al.* (1994, vol. 2, pp. 339–46).

Kirzner, Israel M. (1991) *The Meaning of the Market Process: Essays in the Development of Modern Austrian Economics* (London: Routledge).

Kissler, Leo (1994) 'Industrial Modernization by Workers' Participation', *Economic and Industrial Democracy*, **15**(2), May, pp. 179–210.

Klein, Lawrence R. (1947) 'Theories of Effective Demand and Employment', *Journal of Political Economy*, **55**, April.

Kley, Roland (1994) *Hayek's Social and Political Thought* (Oxford: Clarendon Press).

Knight, Frank H. (1921) *Risk, Uncertainty and Profit* (New York: Houghton Mifflin).

Kolakowski, Leszek (1993) 'On the Practicability of Liberalism: What About the Children?', *Critical Review*, **7**(1), Winter, pp. 1–13.

Kontopoulos, Kyriakos M. (1993) *The Logics of Social Structure* (Cambridge: Cambridge University Press).

Kornai, Janos (1971) *Anti-Equilibrium: On Economic Systems Theory and the Tasks of Research* (Amsterdam: North-Holland). Reprinted 1991 (New York: Augustus Kelley).

Kozul-Wright, Richard (1995) 'The Myth of Anglo-Saxon Capitalism: Reconstructing the History of the American State', in Chang and Rowthorn (1995, pp. 81–113).

Kozul-Wright, Richard and Rayment, Paul (1997) 'The Institutional Hiatus in Economics in Transition and its Policy Consequences', *Cambridge Journal of Economics*, **21**(5), September, pp. 641–61.

Kramer, Roderick M. and Tyler, Tom R. (eds) (1996) *Trust in Organizations* (London: Sage).

Kropotkin, Petr A. (1972) *Mutual Aid: A Factor of Evolution*, (1st edn published 1902,) (London: Allen Lane).

Krugman, Paul R. (1990) *Rethinking International Trade* (Cambridge, MA: MIT Press).

—— (1994) *Peddling Prosperity: Economic Sense and Nonsense in the Age of Diminished Expectations* (New York and London: Norton).

Kukathas, Chandran (1989) *Hayek and Modern Liberalism* (Oxford: Clarendon Press).

Kumar, Krishan (1987) *Utopia and Anti-Utopia in Modern Times* (Oxford: Blackwell).

Lachmann, Ludwig M. (1969) 'Methodological Individualism and the Market Economy', in Streissler, Erich W. (ed.) (1969) *Roads to Freedom: Essays in Honour of Friedrich A. von Hayek* (London: Routledge and Kegan Paul), pp. 89–103. Reprinted in Lachmann, Ludwig M. (1977) *Capital, Expectations and the Market Process*, edited with an introduction by W. E. Grinder (Kansas City: Sheed Andrews and McMeel).

Landauer, Carl A. (1959) *European Socialism: A History of Ideas and Movements from the Industrial Revolution to Hitler's Seizure of Power*, 2 vols (Berkeley, CA: University of California Press).

Lane, Christel (1997) 'The Social Regulation of Inter-Firm Relations in Britain and Germany: Market Rules, Legal Norms and Technical Standards', *Cambridge Journal of Economics*, **21**(2), March, pp. 197–215.

Lane, David A. (1993) 'Artificial Worlds and Economics' parts I and II, *Journal of Evolutionary Economics*, **3**(2), May, pp. 89–107 and 3(3), August, pp. 177–97.

Lane, Robert E. (1966) 'The Decline of Politics and Ideology in a Knowledgeable Society', *American Sociological Review*, **31**(6), pp. 649–62.

Lange, Oskar R. (1967) 'The Computer and the Market', in Feinstein, C. (ed.) (1967) *Capitalism, Socialism and Economic Growth: Essays Presented to Maurice Dobb* (Cambridge: Cambridge University Press), pp. 158–61.

—— (1987) 'The Economic Operation of a Socialist Society', 2 lectures delivered in 1942, *Contributions to Political Economy*, **6**, pp. 3–24.

Lange, Oskar R. and Taylor, Frederick M. (1938) *On the Economic Theory of Socialism*, ed. Benjamin E. Lippincot (Minneapolis: University of Minnesota Press).

Langlois, Richard N. (1988) 'Economic Change and the Boundaries of the Firm', *Journal of Institutional and Theoretical Economics*, **144**(3), September, pp. 635–57. Reprinted in Hodgson (1993c).

Laszlo, Ervin (1972) *Introduction to Systems Philosophy: Toward a New Paradigm of Contemporary Thought* (New York: Harper and Row).

—— (1987) *Evolution: The Grand Synthesis* (Boston, MA: New Science Library – Shambhala).

Lavoie, Donald (1985a) *Rivalry and Central Planning: The Socialist Calculation Debate Reconsidered* (Cambridge: Cambridge University Press).

—— (1985b) *National Economic Planning: What is Left?* (Cambridge, MA: Ballinger).

Lawson, Antony (1994) 'Hayek and Realism: A Case of Continuous Transformation', in Colonna, Marina, Hagemann, Harald and Hamouda, Omar F. (eds) (1994) *Capitalism, Socialism and Knowledge: The Economics of F. A. Hayek, Volume 2* (Aldershot: Edward Elgar).

—— (1996) 'Developments in Hayek's Social Theorising', in Stephen F. Frowen (ed.) (1996) *Hayek, the Economist and Social Philosopher: A Critical Retrospect* (London: Macmillan).

—— (1997) *Economics and Reality* (London: Routledge).

Lazonick, William (1991) *Business Organization and the Myth of the Market Economy* (Cambridge: Cambridge University Press).

Lea, Stephen E. G., Tarpy, Roger M. and Webley, Paul (1987) *The Individual in the Economy: A Survey of Economic Psychology* (Cambridge and New York: Cambridge University Press).

Leathers, Charles G. (1990) 'Veblen and Hayek on Instincts and Evolution', *Journal of the History of Economic Thought*, **12**(2), June, pp. 162–78.

Le Grand, Julian and Estrin, Saul (eds) (1989) *Market Socialism* (Oxford: Clarendon Press).

Lenin, Vladimir Ilich (1967) *Selected Works in Three Volumes* (London: Lawrence and Wishart).

Leontief, Wassily (1966) *Input-Output Economics* (Oxford: Oxford University Press).

Lepenies, Wolf (1991) 'Hopes Derailed on Way from Utopia', *Times Higher Education Supplement*, 27 December, p. 8.

Lerner, Abba P. (1934) 'Economic Theory and Socialist Economy', *Review of Economic Studies*, **2**, pp. 157–75.

—— (1944) *The Economics of Control* (New York: Macmillan).

Leslie, Thomas E. Cliffe (1888) *Essays in Political Economy*, 2nd edn (1st edn 1879) (London: Longmans, Green). Reprinted 1969 (New York: Augustus Kelley).

Levins, Richard and Lewontin, Richard C. (1985) *The Dialectical Biologist* (Cambridge, MA: Harvard University Press).

Levitt, Barbara and March, James G. (1988) 'Organizational Learning', *Annual Review of Sociology*, **14**, pp. 319–40.

Levy, Frank and Murnane, Richard J. (1996) 'With What Skills are Computers a Complement?', *American Economic Review (Papers and Proceedings)*, **86**(2), May, pp. 258–62.

Lewontin, Richard C. (1978) 'Adaptation', *Scientific American*, no. 239, pp. 212–30.

Lim, Linda (1983) 'Singapore's Success: The Myth of the Market', *Asian Survey*, **18**, pp. 73–94.

Lipietz, Alain (1992) *Towards a New Economic Order: Postfordism, Ecology and Democracy* (Cambridge: Polity Press).

Lippi, Marco (1979) *Value and Naturalism in Marx* (London: NLB).

Littler, Craig R. and Salaman, Graeme (1982) 'Bravermania and Beyond: Recent Theories of the Labour Process', *Sociology*, **16**(2), May, pp. 251–69.

Lloyd, Barbara B. (1972) *Perception and Cognition: A Cross-Cultural Perspective* (Harmondsworth: Penguin).

Lloyd, Seth (1990), 'The Calculus of Intricacy', *The Sciences*, pp. 38–44.

Loasby, Brian J. (1976) *Choice, Complexity and Ignorance: An Enquiry into Economic Theory and the Practice of Decision Making* (Cambridge: Cambridge University Press).

—— (1990) 'The Use of Scenarios in Business Planning', in Stephen F. Frowen (ed.) (1990) *Unknowledge and Choice in Economics* (London: Macmillan), pp. 46–63.

Lockwood, David (1981) 'The Weakest Link in the Chain?: Some Comments on the Marxist Theory of Action', in Simpson, S. and Simpson, I. (eds) (1981) *Research in the Sociology of Work*, **1** (Greenford, Connecticut: JAI Press).

Luhmann, Niklas (1982) *The Differentiation of Society* (New York: Columbia University Press).

—— (1995) *Social Systems*, translated from the German edition of 1984 by John Bednarz with a foreword by Eva M. Knodt (Stanford: Stanford University Press).

Lukes, Steven (1973) *Individualism* (Oxford: Basil Blackwell).

—— (1974) *Power: A Radical View* (London: Macmillan).

—— (1985) *Marxism and Morality* (Oxford: Oxford University Press).

—— (1995) *The Curious Enlightenment of Professor Cariat* (London: Verso).

Lundvall, Bengt-Åke (ed.) (1992) *National Systems of Innovation: Towards a Theory of Innovation and Interactive Learning* (London: Pinter).

Lundvall, Bengt-Åke and Johnson, Björn (1994) 'The Learning Economy', *Journal of Industrial Studies*, **1**(2), 23–42.

Luxemburg, Rosa (1951) *The Accumulation of Capital* (London: Routledge and Kegan Paul).

Lyons, Bruce and Mehta, Judith (1997) 'Contracts, Opportunism and Trust: Self-Interest and Social Orientation', *Cambridge Journal of Economics*, **21**(2), March, pp. 239–57.

McCarney, Joseph (1993) 'Shaping Ends: Reflections on Fukuyama', *New Left Review*, no. 202, November/December, pp. 37–53.

Macaulay, Stewart (1963) 'Non-Contractual Relations in Business: A Preliminary Survey', *American Sociological Review*, **28**(1), pp. 55–67. Reprinted in Buckley and Michie (1996).

311

McCoy, J. Wynne (1977) 'Complexity in Organic Evolution', *Journal of Theoretical Biology*, **68**, pp. 457–8.

MacFarquhar, Roderick and John K. Fairbank (eds) (1987, 1991) *The Cambridge History of China, Vols 14–15* (Cambridge University Press: Cambridge).

McGregor, Douglas (1960) *The Human Side of Enterprise* (New York: McGraw-Hill).

Machlup, Fritz (1962) *The Production and Distribution of Knowledge in the United States* (Princeton, NJ: Princeton University Press).

——(1967) 'Theories of the Firm: Marginalist, Behavioral, Managerial', *American Economic Review*, **57**(1), March, pp. 1–33.

MacIntyre, Alasdair (1985) *After Virtue: A Study in Moral Theory*, 2nd edn (1st edn 1981) (London: Duckworth).

McIntyre, Richard (1992) 'Consumption in Contemporary Capitalism: Beyond Marx and Veblen', *Review of Social Economy*, **50**(1), Spring, pp. 40–60.

McKelvey, Maureen (1993) 'Japanese Institutions Supporting Innovation', in Sjöstrand (1993, pp. 199–225).

McLeod, Jack M. and Chaffee, Steven H. (1972) 'The Construction of Social Reality', in J.T. Tedeschi, *The Social Influence Processes* (Chicago: Aldine-Atherton), pp. 50–99.

Macmillan, Harold (1938) *The Middle Way: A Study of the Problem of Economic and Social Progress in a Free and Democratic Society* (London: Macmillan).

McNally, David (1993) *Against the Market: Political Economy, Market Socialism and the Marxist Critique* (London: Verso).

Macpherson, Crawford B. (1962) *The Political Theory of Possessive Individualism: Hobbes to Locke* (Oxford: Oxford University Press).

Magill, Michael and Quinzii, Martine (1996) *Theory of Incomplete Markets*, 2 vols (Cambridge, MA: MIT Press).

Malthus, Thomas Robert (1798) *An Essay on the Principle of Population, as it Affects the Future Improvement of Society, with Remarks on the Speculations of Mr. Godwin, M. Condorcet, and other Writers* (London: Johnson).

—— (1836) *Principles of Political Economy*, 2nd edn (London: Pickering). Reprinted 1986 (New York: Augustus Kelley).

Mandel, Ernest (1983) 'Economics', in McLellan, David (ed.) (1983) *Marx: The First Hundred Years* (London: Collins), pp. 189–238.

Mann, Michael (1986) *The Sources of Social Power, Volume 1: A History of Power from the Beginning to A.D. 1760* (Cambridge: Cambridge University Press).

—— (1993) *The Sources of Social Power, Volume 2: The Rise of Classes and Nation-States, 1760–1914* (Cambridge: Cambridge University Press).

Manuel, Frank E. (ed.) (1973) *Utopias and Utopian Thought* (London: Souvenir Press).

Manuel, Frank E. and Manuel, Fritzie P. (1979) *Utopian Thought in the Western World* (Oxford: Basil Blackwell).

Margolis, Howard (1994) *Paradigms and Barriers: How Habits of Mind Govern Scientific Beliefs* (Chicago: University of Chicago Press).

Marquand, David (1993) 'After Socialism', *Political Studies*, **41**, special issue, pp. 43–56.

Marquand, Judith (1989) *Autonomy and Change: The Sources of Economic Growth* (Hemel Hempstead: Harvester Wheatsheaf).

Marsden, David (1986) *The End of Economic Man? Custom and Competition in Labour Markets* (Brighton: Wheatsheaf Books).

Marshall, Alfred (1949) *The Principles of Economics*, 8th (reset) edn (1st edn 1890) (London: Macmillan).

Martilla, J. A. (1971) 'Word-of-Mouth Communication in the Industrial Adoption Process', *Journal of Marketing Research*, **8**, pp. 173–8.

Marx, Karl (1971) *A Contribution to the Critique of Political Economy*, translated from the German edition of 1859 by S. W. Ryazanskaya and edited with an introduction by Maurice Dobb (London: Lawrence and Wishart).

—— (1973a) *The Revolutions of 1848: Political Writings – Volume 1*, edited and introduced by David Fernbach (Harmondsworth: Penguin).

—— (1973b) *Grundrisse: Foundations of the Critique of Political Economy*, translated by Martin Nicolaus (Harmondsworth: Penguin).

—— (1974) *The First International and After: Political Writings – Volume 3*, edited and introduced by David Fernbach (Harmondsworth: Penguin).

—— (1976a) *Capital*, vol. 1, translated by Ben Fowkes from the fourth German edition of 1890 (Harmondsworth: Pelican).

—— (1976b) 'Marginal Notes on Wagner', in Albert Dragstedt (ed.) (1976) *Value: Studies by Marx*(London: New Park), pp. 195–229.

—— (1977) *Karl Marx: Selected Writings*, ed. David McLellan (Oxford: Oxford University Press).

—— (1978) *Capital*, vol. 2, translated by David Fernbach from the German edition of 1893 (Harmondsworth: Pelican).

—— (1981) *Capital*, vol. 3, translated by David Fernbach from the German edition of 1894 (Harmondsworth: Pelican).

Marx, Karl and Engels, Frederick (1982) *Karl Marx and Frederick Engels, Collected Works, Vol. 38, Letters 1844–51* (London: Lawrence and Wishart).

Matsushita, Konosuke (1988) 'The Secret is Shared', *Manufacturing Engineering*, **100**(2), February, p. 15.

Mead, Margaret (1937) *Cooperation and Competition Among Primitive Peoples* (New York: McGraw-Hill).

Meade, James E. (1986) *Different Forms of Share Economy* (London: Public Policy Centre).

Meade, James E. (1988) *The Collected Economic Papers of James Meade. Volume II: Value, Distribution and Growth*, edited by Susan Howson (London: Unwin Hyman).

—— (1989) *Agathotopia: The Economics of Partnership* (Aberdeen: Aberdeen University Press).

—— (1993) *Liberty, Equality and Efficiency: Apologia pro Agathotopia Mea* (London: Macmillan).

Meadows, Donella H., Meadows, Dennis L. and Randers, Jorgen (1992) *Beyond the Limits: Global Collapse or a Sustainable Future* (London: Earthscan Publications).

Meadows, Donella H., Meadows, Dennis L., Randers, Jorgen and Behrens, W. W., III (1974) *The Limits to Growth* (London: Pan).

Medvedev, Roy A. (1989) *Let History Judge: The Origins and Consequences of Stalinism*, revised and expanded edn (Columbia University Press: New York).

Ménard, Claude (1996) 'On Clusters, Hybrids, and Other Strange Firms: The Case of the French Poultry Industry', *Journal of Institutional and Theoretical Economics*, **152**(1), March, pp. 154–83.

Menger, Carl (1981) *Principles of Economics*, edited by J. Dingwall and translated by B. F. Hoselitz from the German edition of 1871 (New York: New York University Press).

Metcalfe, J. Stanley (1988) 'Evolution and Economic Change', in Silberston, Aubrey (ed.) (1988) *Technology and Economic Progress* (Basingstoke: Macmillan), pp. 54–85. Reprinted in Witt, Ulrich (ed.) (1993) *Evolutionary Economics* (Aldershot: Edward Elgar).

Miliband, David (ed.) (1994) *Reinventing the Left* (Cambridge: Polity Press).

Miliband, Ralph (1995) *Socialism for a Sceptical Age* (Cambridge: Polity Press).

Mill, John Stuart (1844) *Essays on Some Unsettled Questions of Political Economy* (London: Longman, Green, Reader and Dyer). Reprinted 1948 by the London School of Economics.

—— (1871) *Principles of Political Economy with Some of Their Applications to Social Philosophy*, 7th edn (London: Longman).

—— (1964) *Utilitarianism, Liberty and Representative Government* (London: Dent).

Miller, David (1989) *Market, State and Community: Theoretical Foundations of Market Socialism* (Oxford: Clarendon Press).

Miller, Gary J. (1992) *Managerial Dilemmas: The Political Economy of Hierarchy* (Cambridge: Cambridge University Press).

Miller, James G. (1978) *Living Systems* (New York: McGraw-Hill).

Mills, C. Wright (1953) *White Collar* (Oxford and New York: Oxford University Press).

—— (1963) *The Marxists* (Harmondsworth: Penguin).

Mirowski, Philip (1981) 'Is There a Mathematical Neoinstitutional Economics?', *Journal of Economic Issues*, **15**(3), pp. 593–613.

—— (1987) 'The Philosophical Bases of Institutional Economics', *Journal of Economic Issues*, **21**(3), September, pp. 1001–38. Reprinted in Philip Mirowski (1988) *Against Mechanism: Protecting Economics from Science* (Totowa, NJ: Rowman and Littlefield).

—— (1989) *More Heat Than Light: Economics as Social Physics, Physics as Nature's Economics* (Cambridge: Cambridge University Press).

Mises, Ludwig von (1935) 'Economic Calculation in the Socialist Commonwealth', in Hayek (1935, pp. 87–130). A translation by S. Adler of Ludwig von Mises (1920) 'Die Wirtshaftsrechnung im sozialistischen Gemeinwesen', *Archiv für Sozialwissenschaften und Sozialpolitik*, **47**(1), April.

—— (1949) *Human Action: A Treatise on Economics* (London: William Hodge).

—— (1960) *Epistemological Problems of Economics* (Van Nostrand: New York).

—— (1981) *Socialism: An Economic and Sociological Analysis*, translated by J. Kahane from the second German edition of 1932 (1st edn 1922) (Indianapolis: Liberty Classics).

Mishel, Lawrence and Schmitt, John (eds) (1995) *Beware the U.S. Model: Jobs and Wages in a Deregulated Economy* (Washington, DC: Economic Policy Institute).

Misztal, Barbara A. (1996) *Trust in Modern Societies: The Search for the Bases of Social Order* (Cambridge: Polity).

Mitchell, Wesley C. (1937) *The Backward Art of Spending Money and Other Essays* (New York: McGraw-Hill).

Miyazaki, Hajime and Neary, Hugh M. (1983) 'The Illyrian Firm Revisted', *Bell Journal of Economics*, **14**(1), pp. 2259–70.

Montagu, M. F. Ashley (1952) *Darwin, Competition and Cooperation* (New York: Henry Schuman).

Moore, Stanley (1980) *Marx on the Choice Between Socialism and Communism* (Cambridge, MA: Harvard University Press).

Morgan, C. Lloyd (1896) *Habit and Instinct* (London and New York: Edward Arnold).

—— (1927) *Emergent Evolution*, 2nd edn (1st edn 1923) (London: Williams and Norgate).

Morishima, Michio (1982) *Why Has Japan 'Succeeded'?: Western Technology and the Japanese Ethos* (Cambridge: Cambridge University Press).

Morris, William (1973) *Political Writings of William Morris*, edited with an introduction by A. L. Morton (London: Lawrence and Wishart).

Morris-Suzuki, Tessa (1989) *A History of Japanese Economic Thought* (London: Routledge).

Mueller, Dennis C. (1986) *Profits in the Long Run* (Cambridge: Cambridge University Press).

Murrell, Peter (1983) 'Did the Theory of Market Socialism Answer the Challenge of Ludwig von Mises? A Reinterpretation of the Socialist Controversy?', *History of Political Economy*, **15**(1), Spring, pp. 92–105.

—— (1991) 'Can Neoclassical Economics Underpin the Reform of Centrally Planned Economies?', *Journal of Economic Perspectives*, **5**(4), Fall, pp. 59–76.

Mygind, Neils (1987) 'Are Self-Managed Firms Efficient? The Experience of Danish Fully and Partly Self-Managed Firms', *Advances in the Economic Analysis of Participatory and Labor-Managed Firms*, **2**, pp. 243–323.

Myrdal, Gunnar (1957) *Economic Theory and Underdeveloped Regions* (London: Duckworth).

—— (1958) *Value in Social Theory* (New York: Harper).

—— (1978) *Political and Institutional Economics*, the Eleventh Geary Lecture (Dublin: Economic and Social Research Institute).

National Defense Council for the Victims of Karoshi (1990) *Karoshi: When the 'Corporate Warrior' Dies* (Tokyo: Mado-Sha).

Neisser, Ulrich (1983) 'Toward a Skillful Psychology', in Rogers, D. and Sloboda, J. A. (eds) (1983) *The Acquisition of Symbolic Skills* (New York: Plenum Publishing), pp. 1–17.

Nelson, Richard R. (1959) 'The Simple Economics of Basic Scientific Research', *Journal of Political Economy*, **67**(3), June, pp. 297–306.

—— (1981) 'Research on Productivity Growth and Productivity Differences: Dead Ends and New Departures', *Journal of Economic Literature*, **29**, September, pp. 1029–64.

—— (1991) 'Why Do Firms Differ, and How Does it Matter?', *Strategic Management Journal*, **12**, Special Issue, Winter, pp. 61–74.

—— (ed.) (1993) *National Innovation Systems: A Comparative Analysis* (Oxford: Oxford University Press).

—— (1994) 'The Coevolution of Technologies and Institutions', in England (1994, pp. 139–56).

Nelson, Richard R. and Winter, Sidney G. (1982) *An Evolutionary Theory of Economic Change* (Cambridge, MA: Harvard University Press).

Nicholls, Anthony J. (1994) *Freedom with Responsibility: The Social Market Economy in Germany, 1918–1963* (Oxford and New York: Clarendon Press).

Nickell, Stephen and Bell, Brian (1996) 'Changes in the Distribution of Wages and Unemployment in OECD Countries', *American Economic Review (Papers and Proceedings)*, **86**(2), May, pp. 302–8.

Nicolaides, Phedon (1988) 'Limits to the Expansion of Neoclassical Economics', *Cambridge Journal of Economics*, **12**(3), September, pp. 313–28.

Nonaka, Ikujiro and Takeuchi, Hirotaka (1995) *The Knowledge-Creating Company: How Japanese Companies Create the Dynamics of Innovation* (Oxford and New York: Oxford University Press).

Nooteboom, Bart (1992) 'Towards a Dynamic Theory of Transactions', *Journal of Evolutionary Economics*, **2**(4), December, pp. 281–99.

Nooteboom, Bart, Berger, Hans and Noorderhaven, Niels G. (1997) 'Effects of Trust and Governance on Relational Risk', *Academy of Management Journal*, **40**(2), pp. 308–38.

North, Douglass C. (1978) 'Structure and Performance: The Task of Economic History', *Journal of Economic Literature*, **16**(3), September, pp. 963–78.

—— (1990) *Institutions, Institutional Change and Economic Performance* (Cambridge: Cambridge University Press).

Nove, Alexander (1980) 'The Soviet Economy: Problems and Prospects', *New Left Review*, no. 119, January-February, pp. 3–19.

—— (1983) *The Economics of Feasible Socialism* (London: George Allen and Unwin).

—— (1991) *The Economics of Feasible Socialism Revisited*, 2nd edn (London: George Allen and Unwin).

Nove, Alexander and Thatcher, Ian D. (eds) (1994) *Markets and Socialism* (Aldershot: Edward Elgar).

Nozick, Robert (1974) *Anarchy, State, and Utopia* (New York: Basic Books).

Nuti, Domenico Mario (1992) 'Market Socialism: The Model that Might have Been but Never Was', in Åslund (1992, pp. 17–31).

Nyland, Christopher (1996) 'Taylorism, John R. Commons, and the Hoxie Report', *Journal of Economic Issues*, **30**(4), December, pp. 985–1016.

Oakeshott, Michael (1962) *Rationalism in Politics and Other Essays* (London: Methuen).

OECD (1993) *Employment Outlook* (Paris: Organization for Economic Cooperation and Development).

Ollman, Bertell (1977) 'Marx's Vision of Communism: A Reconstruction', *Critique*, no. 8, Summer, pp. 4–41.

O'Neill, John (1989) 'Markets, Socialism, and Information: A Reformulation of a Marxian Objection to the Market', *Social Philosophy and Policy*, **6**, pp. 200–10.

—— (1993) *Ecology, Policy and Politics* (London: Routledge).

Orrù, Marco (1993) 'Institutional Cooperation in Japanese and German Capitalism', in Sjöstrand (1993, pp. 171–98).

Owen, Robert (1991) *A New View of Society and Other Writings*, edited with an introduction by Gregory Clays (Harmondsworth: Penguin).

Pagano, Ugo (1985) *Work and Welfare in Economic Theory* (Oxford: Basil Blackwell).

——(1991) 'Property Rights, Asset Specificity, and the Division of Labour Under Alternative Capitalist Relations', *Cambridge Journal of Economics*, **15**(3), September, pp. 315–42. Reprinted in Hodgson (1993c).

Pagano, Ugo and Rowthorn, Robert E. (eds) (1996) *Democracy and Efficiency in the Economic Enterprise* (London: Routledge).

Pareto, Vilfredo (1971) *Manual of Political Economy*, translated from the French edition of 1927 by A. S. Schwier, and edited by A. S. Schwier and A. N. Page (New York: Augustus Kelley).

Parker, Hermione (1989) *Instead of the Dole: An Enquiry into Integration of the Tax and Benefit Systems* (London: Routledge).

Parsons, Talcott (1937) *The Structure of Social Action*, 2 vols (New York: McGraw-Hill).

Patnaik, Prabhat (1991) *Economics and Egalitarianism* (Oxford: Oxford University Press).

Paul, Ellen Frankel (1988) 'Liberalism, Unintended Orders and Evolutionism', *Political Studies*, **36**(2), June, pp. 251–72.

Pavitt, Keith and Patel, Pari (1988) 'The International Distribution and Determinants of Technological Activities', *Oxford Review of Economic Policy*, **4**(4), pp. 35–55.

Pearce, David W. and Turner, R. Kerry (1990) *Economics of Natural Resources and the Environment* (New York and London: Harvester Wheatsheaf).

Peirce, Charles Sanders (1893) 'Evolutionary love', reprinted in Charles Sanders Peirce (1923) *Chance, Love, and Logic*, ed. M. R. Cohen (New York: Harcourt, Brace), pp. 272–5.

—— (1934) *Collected Papers of Charles Sanders Peirce, Volume V, Pragmatism and Pragmaticism*, edited by C. Hartshorne and P. Weiss (Cambridge, MA: Harvard University Press).

Pelikan, Pavel (1989) 'Evolution, Economic Competence, and Corporate Control', *Journal of Economic Behavior and Organization*, **12**, pp. 279–303.

Penrose, Edith T. (1959) *The Theory of the Growth of the Firm* (Oxford: Basil Blackwell). Reprinted 1995 (Oxford: Oxford University Press).

Perrow, Charles (1986) *Complex Organizations* (New York: Random House).

—— (1990) 'Economic Theories of Organization', in S. Zukin and Paul DiMaggio (eds), *Structures of Capital: The Social Organization of the Economy* (Cambridge: Cambridge University Press), pp. 121–52.

Pfouts, Ralph W. and Rosefielde, Steven (1986) 'The Firm in Illyria: Market Syndicalism Revisited', *Journal of Comparative Economics*, **10**, pp. 160–70.

Pierson, Christopher (1995) *Socialism After Communism: The New Market Socialism* (Cambridge and Philadelphia: Polity Press and University of Pennsylvania Press).

Pigou, Arthur C. (1920) *The Economics of Welfare* (London: Macmillan).

Piore, Michael J. (1995) *Beyond Individualism* (Cambridge, MA: Harvard University Press).

Piore, Michael J. and Sabel, Charles F. (1984) *The Second Industrial Divide* (New York: Basic Books).

Polanyi, Karl (1944) *The Great Transformation* (New York: Rinehart).

—— (1947) 'Our Obsolete Market Mentality: Civilization Must Find a New Thought Pattern', *Commentary*, **3**, pp. 109–17.

Polanyi, Karl, Arensberg, Conrad M. and Pearson, Harry W. (eds) (1957) *Trade and Market in the Early Empires* (Chicago: Henry Regnery).

Polanyi, Michael (1958) *Personal Knowledge: Towards a Post-Critical Philosophy* (London: Routledge and Kegan Paul).

—— (1967) *The Tacit Dimension* (London: Routledge and Kegan Paul).

Popper, Sir Karl R. (1972) *Objective Knowledge: An Evolutionary Approach* (Oxford: Oxford University Press).

Porpora, Douglas V. (1989) 'Four Concepts of Social Structure', *Journal for the Theory of Social Behaviour*, **19**(2), pp. 195–211.

Porter, Michael E. (1990) 'The Competitive Advantage of Nations', *Harvard Business Review*, **68**, pp. 73–93.

Porter, Michael E. and Linde, Claas van der (1995) 'Towards a New Conception of the Environment-Competitiveness Relationship', *Journal of Economic Perspectives*, **9**(4), Fall, pp. 97–118.

Posner, Richard A. (1994) *Sex and Reason* (Cambridge, MA: Harvard University Press).

Powell, Walter W. and DiMaggio, Paul J. (eds) (1991) *The New Institutionalism in Organizational Analysis* (Chicago and London: University of Chicago Press).

Prais, Sigbert J. (1976) *The Evolution of Giant Firms in Britain* (Cambridge: Cambridge University Press).

—— (1981) *Productivity and Industrial Structure: A Statistical Study of Manufacturing Industry in Britain, Germany and the United States* (Cambridge: Cambridge University Press).

Pratten, Clifford F. (1976) *Labour Productivity Differences in International Companies* (Cambridge: Cambridge University Press).

Prigogine, Ilya and Stengers, Isabelle (1984) *Order Out of Chaos: Man's New Dialogue With Nature* (London: Heinemann).

Proudhon, Pierre Joseph (1969) *Selected Works*, translated and edited by S. Edwards (New York: Doubleday).

Prychitko, David L. (1991) *Marxism and Workers' Self-Management: The Essential Tensions* (New York: Greenwood Press).

Przeworski, Adam (1991) *Democracy and the Market: Political and Economic Reforms in Eastern Europe and Latin America* (Cambridge: Cambridge University Press).

Pujol, Michèle A. (1992) *Feminism and Anti-Feminism in Early Economic Thought* (Aldershot: Edward Elgar).

Purdy, David L. (1988) *Social Power and the Labour Market: A Radical Approach to Labour Economics* (London: Macmillan).

Putterman, Louis (1984) 'On Some Recent Explanations of Why Capital Hires Labor', *Economic Inquiry*, **22**, pp. 171–87.

Pyke, Frank, Becattini, Giacomo and Sengenberger, Werner (eds) (1990) *Industrial Districts and Inter-Firm Co-operation in Italy* (Geneva: Italian Institute for Labour Studies).

Quarta, Cosimo (1996) 'Homo Utopicus: On the Need for Utopia', *Utopian Studies*, **7**(2), pp. 153–65.

Quinn, James B. (1992) *Intelligent Enterprise: A Knowledge and Service Based Paradigm for Industry* (New York: Free Press).

Radice, Hugo (forthcoming) ' "Globalization" and National Differences', *Economy and Society*, forthcoming.

Radin, Margaret Jane (1996) *Contested Commodities* (Cambridge, MA: Harvard University Press).

Radner, Roy (1968) 'Competitive Equilibrium Under Uncertainty', *Econometrica*, **36**(1), January, pp. 31–58.

Radnitzky, Gerard (ed.) (1992) *Universal Economics: Assessing the Achievements of the Economic Approach* (New York: Paragon House).

Radnitzky, Gerard and Bernholz, Peter (eds) (1987) *Economic Imperialism* (New York: Paragon House).

Rebitzer, James B. (1993) 'Radical Political Economy and the Economics of Labor Markets', *Journal of Economic Literature*, **31**(3), September, pp. 1394–434.

Reibel, R. (1975) 'The Workingman's Production Association, or the Republic in the Workshop', in Vanek (1975), pp. 39–46.

Reich, Robert B. (1991) *The Work of Nations* (New York: Alfred Knopf).

Reinheimer, Herman (1913) *Evolution by Co-operation: A Study in Bioeconomics* (London: Kegan, Paul, Trench, Trubner).

Richardson, George B. (1972) 'The Organisation of Industry', *Economic Journal*, **82**, pp. 883–96. Reprinted in Buckley and Michie (1996).

Rifkin, Jeremy (1995) *The End of Work: The Decline of the Global Labor Force* (New York: G. P. Putnam's Sons).

Robbins, Lionel (1932) *An Essay on the Nature and Significance of Economic Science*, 1st edn (London: Macmillan).

Roemer, John E. (1988) *Free to Lose: An Introduction to Marxist Economic Philosophy* (Cambridge, MA: Harvard University Press).

—— (1994) *A Future for Socialism* (Cambridge, MA: Harvard University Press).

Roland, Gérard (1990) 'Gorbachev and the Common European Home: The Convergence Debate Revisited?', *Kyklos*, **43**, Fasc. 3, pp. 385–409.

Romer, Paul M. (1986) 'Increasing Returns and Long-Run Growth', *Journal of Political Economy*, **94**(5), October, pp. 1002–37.

—— (1990) 'Endogenous Technological Change', *Journal of Political Economy*, **98**, pp. 71–102.

—— (1994) 'The Origins of Endogenous Growth', *Journal of Economic Perspectives*, **8**(1), Winter, pp. 3–22.

Rooney, Patrick (1988) 'New Research Suggests Employee Ownership Firms More Participative', *Journal of Economic Issues*, **22**(2), June, pp. 451–58.

Rose, Margaret A. (1991) *The Post-Modern and the Post-Industrial* (Cambridge: Cambridge University Press).

Rosen, Corey and Quarrey, Michael (1987) 'How Well is Employee Ownership Working?', *Harvard Business Review*, **65**(5), pp. 126–32.

Ross, Dorothy (1991) *The Origins of American Social Science* (Cambridge: Cambridge University Press).

Rothwell, Roy (1992) 'Successful Industrial Innovation: Critical Factors in the 1990s', *R & D Management*, **22**(3), pp. 221–39.

Rowland, Barbara M. (1988) 'Beyond Hayek's Pessimism: Reason, Tradition and Bounded Constructivist Rationalism', *British Journal of Political Science*, **18**, pp. 221–41,

Rowlands, Michael, Larsen, Mogens, and Kristiansen, Kristian (eds) (1987) *Centre and Periphery in the Ancient World* (Cambridge: Cambridge University Press).

Rowthorn, Robert E. and Wells, John R. (1987) *De-Industrialization and Foreign Trade* (Cambridge: Cambridge University Press).

Rubery, Jill and Wilkinson, Frank (eds) (1994) *Employer Strategy and the Labour Market* (Oxford: Oxford University Press).

Rubin, Michael R. and Huber, Mary T. (1986) *The Knowledge Industry in the United States, 1960–1980* (Princeton, NJ: Princeton University Press).

Ruigrok, Winfried and van Tulder, Rob (1995) *The Logic of International Restructuring* (London: Routledge).

Ruskin, John (1866) *Unto This Last: Four Essays on the First Principles of Political Economy* (London: John Wiley).

—— (1898) *Munera Pulveris*, 3rd edn (London: George Allen).

Rustin, Mike (1992) 'No Exit from Capitalism?', *New Left Review*, no. 193, May/June, pp. 96–107.

Rutherford, Malcolm C. (1988) 'Learning and Decision-Making in Economics and Psychology: A Methodological Perspective', in P. E. Earl (ed.) (1988) *Psychological Economics: Development, Tensions, Prospects* (Boston: Kluwer), pp. 35–54.

Sabel, Charles F. and Zeitlin, Jonathan (1985) 'Historical Alternatives to Mass Production: Politics, Markets and Technology in Nineteenth Century Industrialization', *Past and Present*, no. 108, August, pp. 132–76. Reprinted in Swedberg (1996).

Sah, Raaj (1991) 'Fallibility in Human Organizations and Political Systems', *Journal of Economic Perspectives*, **5**(1), Winter, pp. 67–88.

Sahlins, Marshall D. (1972) *Stone Age Economics* (London: Tavistock).

Sako, Mari (1992) *Prices, Quality and Trust: Inter-Firm Relations in Britain and Japan* (Cambridge: Cambridge University Press).

Salanti, Andrea and Screpanti, Ernesto (eds) (1997) *Pluralism in Economics: New Perspectives in History and Methodology* (Aldershot: Edward Elgar).

Salter, Wilfred E. G. (1966) *Productivity and Technical Change*, 2nd edn (Cambridge: Cambridge University Press).

Samuelson, Paul A. (1948) *Economics*, 1st edn (New York: McGraw-Hill).

Sanderson, Stephen K. (1990) *Social Evolutionism: A Critical History* (Oxford: Blackwell).

Saunders, Peter T. and Ho, Mae-Wan (1976) 'On the Increase in Complexity in Evolution', *Journal of Theoretical Biology*, **63**, pp. 375–84.

—— (1981) 'On the Increase in Complexity in Evolution II: The Relativity of Complexity and the Principle of Minimum Increase', *Journal of Theoretical Biology*, **90**, pp. 515–30.

—— (1984) 'The Complexity of Organisms', in J. W. Pollard (ed.) (1984) *Evolutionary Theory: Paths into the Future* (London and New York: Wiley).

Saviotti, Pier Paolo (1996) *Technological Evolution, Variety and the Economy* (Aldershot: Edward Elgar).

Sayer, Andrew (1989) *The Violence of Abstraction: The Analytical Foundations of Historical Materialism* (Oxford: Basil Blackwell).

Scharpf, Fritz W. (1991) *Crisis and Choice in European Social Democracy* (Ithaca: Cornell University Press).

Schelling, Thomas C. (1984) *Choice and Consequence* (Cambridge, MA: Harvard University Press).

Schmoller, Gustav (1898) *Über einige Grundfragen der Socialpolitik und der Volkswirtschaftslehre* (Leipzig: Duncker and Humblot).

Schneider, Jane (1977) 'Was There a Precapitalist World System?', *Peasant Studies*, **6**, pp. 20–9.

Schumpeter, Joseph A. (1909) 'On the Concept of Social Value', *Quarterly Journal of Economics*, **23**, February, pp. 213–32. Reprinted in Richard V. Clemence (ed.) (1951) *Essays of Joseph Schumpeter* (Cambridge, MA: Addison-Wesley), pp. 1–20.

—— (1934) *The Theory of Economic Development: An Inquiry into Profits, Capital, Credit, Interest and the Business Cycle* translated by Redvers Opie from the second German edition of 1926, first edition 1911 (Cambridge, MA: Harvard University Press). Reprinted 1989 with a new introduction by John E. Elliott (New Brunswick, NJ: Transaction).

——(1954) *History of Economic Analysis* (New York: Oxford University Press).

—— *Capitalism, Socialism and Democracy*, 5th edn (1st edn 1942) (London: George Allen and Unwin).

Schutz, Alfred (1967) *The Phenomenology of the Social World* (Evanston: Northwestern University Press).

Schweickart, David (1993) *Against Capitalism: Studies in Marxism and Social Theory* (Cambridge and New York: Cambridge University Press).

Scott, Maurice Fitzgerald (1989) *A New View of Economic Growth* (Oxford: Clarendon Press).

Screpanti, Ernesto (1992) 'The Advent of the Capitalist Utopia: Transition and Convergence', in Bruno Dallago, Horst Brezinski and Wladimir Andreff (eds) (1992) *Convergence and System Change: The Convergence Hypothesis in the Light of the Transition in Eastern Europe* (Aldershot: Dartmouth), pp. 87–120.

—— (1997) 'Towards a General Theory of Capitalism: Suggestions from Chapters 23 and 27', in Ricccardo Bellofiore (ed.) *Marxian Economics Revisited*, vol. 1 (London: Macmillan), pp. 110–24.

Seabury, Samuel (1861) *American Slavery Justified by the Law of Nature* (New York: Mason).

Sekine, Thomas T. (1975) '*Uno-Riron*: A Japanese Contribution to Marxian Political Economy', *Journal of Economic Literature*, **8**, pp. 847–77.

Sen, Amartya K. (1987) *On Ethics and Economics* (Oxford and New York: Basil Blackwell).

Senge, Peter M. (1990) *The Fifth Discipline: The Art and Practice of the Learning Organization* (New York: Doubleday).

Sertel, Murat R. (1991) 'Workers' Enterprises in Imperfect Competition', *Journal of Comparative Economics*, **15**, pp. 698–710.

Shackle, George L. S. (1972) *Epistemics and Economics: A Critique of Economic Doctrines* (Cambridge: Cambridge University Press).

Sheridan, Kyoko (1993) *Governing the Japanese Economy* (Cambridge: Polity Press).

Shleifer, Andrei and Vishny, Robert W. (1994) 'The Politics of Market Socialism', *Journal of Economic Perspectives*, **8**(2), Spring, pp. 165–76.

Shubik, Martin (1982) *Game Theory in the Social Sciences: Concepts and Solutions* (Cambridge, MA: MIT Press).

Sik, Ota (ed.) (1991) *Socialism Today? The Changing Meaning of Socialism* (London: Macmillan).

Simon, Herbert A. (1951) 'A Formal Theory of the Employment Relationship', *Econometrica*, **19**, July, pp. 293–305. Reprinted in Simon (1957).

—— (1957) *Models of Man: Social and Rational* (New York: Wiley).

—— (1991) 'Organizations and Markets', *Journal of Economic Perspectives*, **5**(2), Spring, pp. 25–44.

Sjöstrand, Sven-Erik (ed.) (1993) *Institutional Change: Theory and Empirical Findings* (Armonk, NY: Sharpe).

Skidelsky, Robert (1995) *The World After Communism: A Polemic for Our Times* (London: Macmillan).

Slawson, W. David (1996) *Binding Promises: The Late 20th-Century Reformation of Contract Law* (Princeton, NJ: Princeton University Press).

Slichter, Sumner H. (1924) 'The Organization and Control of Economic Activity', in Rexford G. Tugwell (ed.) *The Trend of Economics* (New York: Alfred Knopf), pp. 301–56.

Smith, Adam (1976) *An Inquiry into the Nature and Causes of the Wealth of Nations*, 2 vols, originally published 1776, edited by R. H. Campbell and A. S. Skinner (London: Methuen).

Smith, Stephen C. (1991) 'On the Economic Rationale for Codetermination Law', *Journal of Economic Behavior and Organization*, **16**(3), December, pp. 261–81.

Smith, Suzanne Konzelmann (1995) 'Internal Cooperation and Competitive Success: The Case of the US Steel Minimill Sector', *Cambridge Journal of Economics*, **19**(2), April, pp. 277–304.

Sombart, Werner (1930) *Die drei Nationalökonomien: Geschichte und System der Lehre von der Wirtschaft* (Munich: Dunker and Humbolt).

Spencer, Herbert (1862) *First Principles*, 1st edn (London: Williams and Norgate).

Sraffa, Piero (1960) *Production of Commodities by Means of Commodities: Prelude to a Critique of Economic Theory* (Cambridge: Cambridge University Press).

Stabile, Donald R. (1984) *Prophets of Order: The Rise of the New Class, Technocracy and Socialism in America* (Boston: South End Press).

—— (1996) *Work and Welfare: The Social Cost of Labor in the History of Economic Thought* (Westport, CO: Greenwood Press).

Starbuck, William H. (1992) 'Learning by Knowledge-Intensive Firms', *Journal of Management Studies*, **29**(6), pp. 713–40.

Stata, Ray (1989) 'Organizational Learning: The Key to Management Innovation', *Sloan Management Review*, **32**, pp. 63–74.

Stebbins, G. Ledyard (1969) *The Biological Basis of Progressive Evolution* (Chapel Hill, NC: University of North Carolina Press).

Steedman, Ian (1980) 'Economic Theory and Intrinsically Non-Autonomous Preferences and Beliefs', *Quaderni Fondazione Feltrinelli*, no. 7/8, pp. 57–73.

Reprinted in Ian Steedman (1989) *From Exploitation to Altruism* (Cambridge: Polity Press).

Steele, David Ramsay (1992) *From Marx to Mises: Post-Capitalist Society and the Challenge of Economic Calculation* (La Salle, IL: Open Court).

Steindl, Joseph (1952) *Maturity and Stagnation in American Capitalism* (Oxford: Blackwell).

Stent, Gunther S. (1985) 'Hermeneutics and the Analysis of Complex Biological Systems', in David Depew and Bruce H. Weber (eds) , *Evolution at a Crossroads: The New Biology and the New Philosophy of Science* (Cambridge, MA: MIT Press), pp. 209–25.

Stephen, Frank H. (ed.) (1982) *The Performance of Labour-Managed Firms* (London: Macmillan).

Stigler, George J. (1961) 'The Economics of Information', *Journal of Political Economy*, **69**(2), June, pp. 213–25.

Stigler, George J. and Becker, Gary S. (1977) 'De Gustibus Non Est Disputandum', *American Economic Review*, **76**(1), March, pp. 76–90.

Stiglitz, Joseph E. (1987) 'The Causes and Consequences of the Dependence of Quality on Price', *Journal of Economic Literature*, **25**(1), March, pp. 1–48.

—— (1994) *Whither Socialism?* (Cambridge, MA: MIT Press).

Storper, Michael and Salais, Robert (1997) *Worlds of Production: The Action Frameworks of the Economy* (Cambridge, MA: Harvard University Press).

Streeck, Wolfgang (1989) 'Skills and the Limits of Neo-Liberalism: The Enterprise of the Future as a Place of Learning', *Work, Employment and Society*, **3**(1), March, pp. 89–104.

—— (1992) *Social Institutions and Economic Efficiency* (London: Sage).

Sveiby, Karl E. and Lloyd, Tom (1987) *Managing Knowhow: Add Value – By Valuing Creativity* (London: Bloomsbury).

Sveiby, Karl E. and Risling, A. (1986) *Kunskapsforetaget – Seklets vikligzaste ledarutmaning?* (Malmo: Liber AB).

Swedberg, Richard (1993) *Explorations in Economic Sociology* (New York: Russell Sage).

—— (ed.) (1996) *Economic Sociology* (Aldershot: Edward Elgar).

Swift, Graham (1983) *Waterland* (London: Heinemann)

Tabb, William K. (1995) *The Postwar Japanese System: Cultural Economy and Economic Transformation* (Oxford and New York: Oxford University Press).

Taylor, Barbara (1983) *Eve and the New Jerusalem: Socialism and Feminism in the Nineteenth Century* (London: Virago).

Taylor, Frederick Winslow (1911) *The Principles of Scientific Management* (New York: Harper).

Teece, David J. (1988) 'Technological Change and the Nature of the Firm', in Dosi *et al.* (1988), pp. 256–81.

Teece, David J. and Pisano, Gary (1994) 'The Dynamic Capabilities of Firms: An Introduction', *Industrial and Corporate Change*, **3**(3), pp. 537–56.

Thomas, Henk T. and Logan, Christopher (1982) *Mondragon: An Economic Analysis* (London: George Allen and Unwin).

Thompson, Edward P. (1955) *William Morris: Romantic to Revolutionary* (London: Merlin).

Thompson, Grahame F. (1993) *The Economic Emergence of a New Europe? The Political Economy of Cooperation and Competition in the 1990s* (Aldershot: Edward Elgar).

Thompson, Grahame F., Frances, J., Levacic, R. and Mitchell, J. (eds) (1991) *Markets, Hierarchies and Networks: The Coordination of Social Life* (London: Sage).

Thompson, Noel (1988) *The Market and its Critics: Socialist Political Economy in Nineteenth Century Britain* (London: Routledge).

Thurow, Lester C. (1992) *Head to Head: The Coming Economic Battle Among Japan, Europe and America* (New York: Morrow).

—— (1996) *The Future of Capitalism: How Today's Economic Forces Shape Tomorrow's World* (New York: Morrow).

Toffler, Alvin (1990) *Powershift: Knowledge, Wealth and Violence at the Edge of the 21st Century* (New York: Bantam Books).

Tomer, John F. (1987) *Organizational Capital: The Path to Higher Productivity and Well-Being* (New York: Praeger).

Tomlinson, James (1982) *The Unequal Struggle? British Socialism and the Capitalist Enterprise* (London: Methuen).

—— (1990) *Hayek and the Market* (London: Pluto Press).

Tool, Marc R. (1979) *The Discretionary Economy* (Santa Monica, CA: Goodyear).

—— (1991) 'Contributions to an Institutionalist Theory of Price Determination', in Hodgson and Screpanti (1991, pp. 19–39). Reprinted in Tool (1995).

—— (1995) *Pricing, Valuation and Systems: Essays in Neoinstitutional Economics* (Aldershot: Edward Elgar).

Topel, Robert H. (1997) 'Factor Proportions and Relative Wages: The Supply-Side Determinants of Wage Inequality', *Journal of Economic Perspectives*, **11**(2), Spring, pp. 55–74.

Traxler, Franz and Unger, Brigitte (1994) 'Governance, Economic Restructuring, and International Competitiveness', *Journal of Economic Issues*, **28**(1), March, pp. 1–23.

Tribe, Keith (1995) *Strategies of Economic Order: German Economic Discourse, 1750–1950* (Cambridge: Cambridge University Press).

Tullock, Gordon (1994) *The Economics of Non-Human Societies* (Tuscon, Arizona: Pallas Press).

Udéhn, Lars (1992) 'The Limits of Economic Imperialism', in Ulf Himmelstrand (ed.), *Interfaces in Economic and Social Analysis* (London: Routledge), pp. 239–80.

Uno, Kozo (1980) *Principles of Political Economy: Theory of a Purely Capitalist Society*, translated from the Japanese edition of 1964 by Thomas T. Sekine (Brighton: Harvester).

Van der Heijden, Kees (1996) *Scenarios: The Art of Strategic Conversation* (Chichester: Wiley).

Van Parijs, Philippe (ed.) (1992) *Arguing for Basic Income:Ethical Foundations for a Radical Reform* (London and New York: Verso).

——(1995) *Real Freedom for All: What (If Anything) Can Justify Capitalism?* (Oxford: Clarendon Press).

Vanberg, Viktor J. (1986) 'Spontaneous Market Order and Social Rules: A Critique of F. A. Hayek's Theory of Cultural Evolution', *Economics and Philosophy*, **2**, June, pp. 75–100.

Vanek, Jaroslav (1970) *The General Theory of Labor-Managed Market Economies* (Ithaca, NY: Cornell University Press).

—— (ed.) (1975) *Self-Management: The Economic Liberation of Man* (Harmondsworth: Penguin).

Vaughn, Karen I. (1980) 'Economic Calculation Under Socialism: The Austrian Contribution', *Economic Inquiry*, **18**, pp. 535–54.

Veblen, Thorstein B. (1899) *The Theory of the Leisure Class: An Economic Study of the Evolution of Institutions* (New York: Macmillan).

—— (1904) *The Theory of Business Enterprise* (New York: Charles Scrbners). Reprinted 1975 by Augustus Kelley.

—— (1914) *The Instinct of Workmanship, and the State of the Industrial Arts* (New York: Macmillan). Reprinted 1990 with a new introduction by Murray G. Murphey and a 1964 introductory note by Joseph Dorfman (New Brunswick: Transaction Books).

—— (1915) *Imperial Germany and the Industrial Revolution* (New York: Macmillan). Reprinted 1964 by Augustus Kelley.

—— (1919) *The Place of Science in Modern Civilization and Other Essays* (New York: Huebsch). Reprinted 1990 with a new introduction by Warren J. Samuels (New Brunswick: Transaction).

—— (1921) *The Engineers and the Price System* (New York: Harcourt Brace and World).

—— (1934) *Essays on Our Changing Order*, ed. L. Ardzrooni (New York: The Viking Press).

Vickers, Douglas (1995) *The Tyranny of the Market: A Critique of Theoretical Foundations* (Ann Arbor: University of Michigan Press).

Vincenti, Walter (1990) *What Engineers Know and How They Know It: Analytical Studies from Aeronautical History* (Baltimore: Johns Hopkins University Press).

Vroom, Victor H. and Deci, E. L. (eds) (1970) *Management and Motivation* (Harmondsworth: Penguin).

Wade, Robert (1990) *Governing the Market: Economic Theory and the Role of Government in East Asian Industrialization* (Princeton, NJ: Princeton University Press).

Wainwright, Hilary (1994) *Arguments for a New Left: Answering the Free-Market Right* (Oxford: Basil Blackwell).

Walras, Léon (1936) *Études d'économie politique appliquée: Théorie de la production de la richesse sociale*, 2nd edn (Paris: Pichon et R. Durand-Auzias).

Walras, Léon (1954) *Elements of Pure Economics, or The Theory of Social Wealth*, translated from the French edition of 1926 by W. Jaffé (1st edn 1874), (New York: Augustus Kelley).

Ward, Benjamin (1958) 'The Firm in Illyria: Market Syndicalism', *American Economic Review*, **48**, pp. 566–89.

—— (1967) *The Socialist Economy: A Study of Organizational Alternatives* (New York: Random House).

Weber, Max (1949) *Max Weber on the Methodology of the Social Sciences*, translated and edited by Edward A. Shils and Henry A. Finch (Glencoe, ILL: Free Press).

—— (1968) *Economy and Society*, 2 vols (Berkeley, CA: University of California Press).

Webster, Frank (1995) *Theories of the Information Society* (London: Routledge).

Webster, Frank and Robins, Kevin (1986) *Information Technology: A Luddite Analysis* (Norwood, NJ: Ablex).

Wedderburn, Kenneth W. (1971) *The Worker and the Law*, 2nd edn (Harmondsworth: Penguin).

—— (1993) *Labour Law and Freedom: Further Essays in Labour Law* (London: Lawrence and Wishart).

Westergaard, John and Resler, Henrietta (1976) *Class in a Capitalist Society: A Study of Contemporary Britain* (Harmondsworth: Penguin).

Westphal, Larry (1990) 'Industrial Policy in an Export-Propelled Economy: Lessons from South Korea's Experience', *Journal of Economic Perspectives*, **5**(1), Winter, pp. 41–59.

Wheeler, William M. (1930) *Social Life Among the Insects* (New York: Harcourt).

White, Gordon (1988) *Development States in East Asia* (London: Macmillan).

White, Harrison C. (1988) 'Varieties of Markets', in Barry Wellman and S. D. Berkowitz (eds) *Social Structure: A Network Approach* (Cambridge, MA: Harvard University Press).

Whitehead, Alfred N. (1926) *Science and the Modern World* (Cambridge: Cambridge University Press).

Whitley, Richard (1992) *Business Systems in East Asia: Firms, Markets and Societies* (London: Sage).

—— (1994) 'Dominant Forms of Economic Organization in Market Economies', *Organization Studies*, **15**(2), pp. 153–82.

Whittington, Richard C. (1989) *Corporate Strategies in Recession and Recovery: Social Structure and Strategic Choice* (London: Unwin Hyman).

Wible, James R. (1984–85) 'An Epistemic Critique of Rational Expectations and the Neoclassical Macroeconomics Research Program', *Journal of Post Keynesian Economics*, **7**(2), Winter, pp. 269–81.

—— (1995) 'The Economic Organization of Science, the Firm, and the Marketplace', *Philosophy of the Social Sciences*, **25**(1), March, pp. 35–68.

Wicksteed, Philip H. (1933) *The Commonsense of Political Economy*, ed. by Lionel Robbins, 1st edn 1910 (London: George Routledge).

Wikström, Solveig and Norman, Richard (1994) *Knowledge and Value* (London: Routledge).

Wilde, Oscar (1963) *The Works of Oscar Wilde* (London: Spring Books).

Williams, David (1994) *Japan: Beyond the End of History* (London: Routledge).

Williams, George C. (1966) *Adaptation and Natural Selection* (Princeton, NJ; Princeton University Press).

Williamson, Oliver E. (1975) *Markets and Hierarchies: Analysis and Anti-Trust Implications: A Study in the Economics of Internal Organization* (New York: Free Press).

—— (1985) *The Economic Institutions of Capitalism: Firms, Markets, Relational Contracting* (London: Macmillan).

Williamson, Oliver E. and Winter, Sidney G. (eds) (1991) *The Nature of the Firm: Origins, Evolution, and Development* (Oxford and New York: Oxford University Press).

Winter Jr, Sidney G. (1964) 'Economic 'Natural Selection' and the Theory of the Firm', *Yale Economic Essays*, **4**(1), pp. 225–72.

—— (1982) 'An Essay on the Theory of Production', in S. H. Hymans (ed.) *Economics and the World Around It* (Ann Arbor, MI: University of Michigan Press), pp. 55–91.

—— (1988) 'On Coase, Competence, and the Corporation', *Journal of Law, Economics, and Organization*, **4**(1), Spring, pp. 163–80. Reprinted in Williamson and Winter (1991).

Wittgenstein, Ludwig (1972) *Philosophical Investigations*, 1st edn 1953 (Oxford: Basil Blackwell).

Wood, Adrian (1994) *North-South Trade, Employment and Inequality: Changing Fortunes in a Skill-Driven World* (Oxford: Clarendon Press).

—— (1995) 'How Trade Hurt Unskilled Workers', *Journal of Economic Perspectives*, **9**(3), Summer, pp. 57–80.

Wood, Stephen (ed.) (1982) *The Degradation of Work? Skill, Deskilling and the Labour Process* (London: Hutchinson).

—— (ed.) (1989) *The Transformation of Work? Skill, Flexibility and the Labour Process* (London: Unwin Hyman).

Wrege, Charles D. and Greenwood, Ronald J. (1991) *Frederick W. Taylor, The Father of Scientific Management: Myth and Reality* (Homewood, IL: Irwin).

Yezer, Anthony M., Goldfarb, Robert S. and Poppen, Paul J. (1996) 'Does Studying Economics Discourage Cooperation? Watch What We Do, Not What We Say or How We Play', *Journal of Economic Perspectives*, **10**(1), Winter, pp. 177–86.

Young, Allyn A. (1928) 'Increasing Returns and Economic Progress', *Economic Journal*, **38**(4), December, pp. 527–42.

Yunker, James A.(1992) *Socialism Revised and Modernized: The Case for Pragmatic Market Socialism* (New York: Praeger).

—— (1995) 'Post-Lange Market Socialism: An Evaluation of Profit-Oriented Proposals', *Journal of Economic Issues*, **29**(3), September, pp. 683–717.

Zadek, Simon (1993) *An Economics of Utopia: Democratising Scarcity* (Aldershot: Avebury).

Zelizer, Viviana A. (1993) 'Making Multiple Monies', in Swedberg (1993, pp. 193–212).

Zolo, Danilo (1992) *Democracy and Complexity: A Realist Approach* (Cambridge: Polity Press).

Zon, Hans van (1995) 'Reflection on Variety of Path Dependence in Central and Eastern Europe', *Emergo*, **2**(3), Summer, pp. 4–15.

Zuboff, Shoshana (1988) *In the Age of the Smart Machine: The Future of Work and Power* (Oxford: Heinemann).

Zucker, Lynne G. (1986) 'Production of Trust: Institutional Sources of Economic Structure 1840–1920', *Research in Organisational Behaviour*, **8**, pp. 53–111.

INDEX